The Orphan Brigade

Bob

from

mother

Books by William C. Davis

THE ORPHAN BRIGADE
BATTLE AT BULL RUN
DUEL BETWEEN THE FIRST IRONCLADS
THE BATTLE OF NEW MARKET
BRECKINRIDGE: STATESMAN, SOLDIER, SYMBOL

WILLIAM C. DAVIS

The Orphan Brigade

The Kentucky Confederates Who Couldn't Go Home

LOUISIANA STATE UNIVERSITY PRESS
BATON ROUGE AND LONDON

LIBRARY OF CONGRESS CATALOGING IN PUBLICATION DATA

Davis, William C., 1946–
  The Orphan Brigade.

  Bibliography: p.
  Includes index.
  1. Confederate States of America. Army. Kentucky
Brigade, First. 2. United States—History—Civil War,
1861–1865—Regimental histories. I. Title.
E564.5 1st.D38   1983   973.7'469   82-18700
ISBN 0-8071-1077-9 (pbk.)

This work is offered in loving dedication to my grandparents, Colonel Joseph and Melissa Shanks, themselves the products of a Kentucky heritage. They always encouraged a young boy's interest in history.

Contents

Illustrations

Acknowledgments

A NUMBER OF INDIVIDUALS have contributed of their time and resources to the preparation of this book. Their mention here is a small but happy measure of recompense for the debt owed. No historian is entirely a free agent. The craft naturally accumulates obligations to those who almost always cheerfully assist in the task of giving the past to the present.

Several private individuals have graciously lent of their private family papers, among them Mrs. J. C. Breckinridge of Summit Point, West Virginia; Mr. and Mrs. Thomas D. Winstead of Elizabethtown, Kentucky; Helene Lewis Gildred of San Diego, California; Mrs. Howard Jones of Glasgow, Kentucky; and W. Maury Darst of Galveston, Texas. All gave materials of substantial value to this current work. Also helpful were items gleaned by several kind Kentucky ladies, among them Sadie M. Wade, Grace E. Reed, and Ruby T. Rabey.

Professional archivists, of course, are the mainstay of any historian's research, and many contributed to this work. Chief among these have been Michael Musick of the Old Army and Navy Branch, National Archives, Washington, D.C. His is a special patience with the questions and posings of the Civil Warrior. Mrs. Thomas Winstead of the Hardin County Historical Society in Elizabethtown, Kentucky, went far beyond hospitality in making Orphan Brigade documents available to the author. And Pat Hodges of the Kentucky Library, Western Kentucky University at Bowling Green, likewise gave service. Robert

Kinnaird and James C. Klotter of the Kentucky Historical Society at
Frankfort did all they could to be helpful.

Old and good friends lent their aid whenever asked. Robert J.
Younger of Dayton, Ohio, gave unsparingly of his collection of rare
Confederate histories and journals, as he has on each of my previous
books. Here is a special friend to all who search for the past. Charles
Cooney of Alexandria, Virginia; Dennis Byrne of Fairfax, Virginia;
and John E. Stanchak of Harrisburg, Pennsylvania, each contributed
of their time as well in the search for sources.

To everyone the author offers all he can, his thanks.

Introduction

CAPTAIN ED PORTER THOMPSON had an idea. Indeed, for some time in this fall of 1864, there was little else to do. After the incessant months of fighting in Georgia that spring and summer, autumn brought a lull. For the better part of September and October, Thompson and his compatriots had only picket duty and an occasional scout south of Atlanta.

And for Thompson there was even less. He took a bullet in the great charge at Stones River twenty months before, the charge that killed so many of his comrades. It left him unfit for front-line duty. Now he spent his time as brigade quartermaster and commissary—less hazardous and demanding to be sure, but still no simple task for a man whose wound continued to discharge fluid, a man frequently on crutches. The work of filing reports and inspecting and requisitioning stores hardly challenged his bookish, inquiring mind.

He found much on which to reflect this autumn. To most mature minds the outcome of the war was self-evident, as predictable as it was immutable. The Confederacy would not survive the next twelvemonth. The Federals controlled the entire length of the Mississippi, splitting the South in two. Sherman and his "bummers" had wrenched the citadel of Atlanta from its defenders. Robert E. Lee and the once invincible Army of Northern Virginia now huddled in trenches around Petersburg, facing the besieging hordes of a man who lost battles, but never a campaign—Grant. Foreign recognition of the Confederate

States of America—and concomitant military intervention and assistance—still lay an unrealized dream, now more distant than ever. To
face the overwhelming might of the North, the Confederacy on every
front could offer only too few with too little. Thus the winter ahead
would be for many like Captain Thompson, the worst of the war, a
cruel pause in which he and others must pass the time in agonizing anticipation of the inevitable denouement. The New Year would bring
more hopeless fighting, more losses. For the slaves in the South, after
two centuries in bonds, it would be the year of "jubilo." For their
masters, it would be the day of judgment.

Thompson had studied history before the war. He knew the exploits
of the Roman 10th Legion, of Bonaparte's Old Guard, of many of the
immortal military units of antiquity. And he knew even better the record achieved by his own command in this war. For, though sometimes
detached in hospital thanks to his wound, and once held captive in an
enemy prison, the captain was always attached in spirit to the 1st Kentucky Brigade. In his kindly eye this brigade's performance looked
every bit as bright as that of the legions of old.

Why not, he thought, prepare a history of the command, a memo-
rial to the men and their service? Should the South through some mir-
acle achieve its independence, then such a history would present to the
victorious people an example of the heroic deeds that helped gain their
freedom. In the more probable event of defeat, this same book might
offer solace, a sense of pride, to the veterans as they faced the dark and
uncertain days ahead. And on the most personal level, the work on
such a history would help Captain Thompson to pass the lonely hours
of the winter. Nothing could dispel the gloomy sense of impending disaster, but at least it would give him something to do.

In his mind he laid the boundaries of his story. Not only would he
tell the story of the brigade as a unit, but also that of its component
regiments individually. The work must be exhaustive, including even
biographies of general and field officers, and of the men in the ranks
themselves. He would, he believed, do "more for the private soldier
than was ever before the case in military annals." Fortunately,
Thompson knew well all of the officers of the brigade. He prepared an
outline or statement of purpose for the contemplated history and cir-
culated it among them. The response was universally affirmative. Thus
encouraged, the captain determined to proceed.

By November 1864, as the days grew shorter and the nights more cold, he was ready to commence in earnest. In order to interest the men and officers of the brigade in the project, he put his intent in writing, printed several hundred copies, and distributed it. With the pardonable pride of youth, he declared in the circular, "However this war may terminate, if a man can truthfully claim to have been a worthy member of the Kentucky Brigade he will have a kind of title of nobility."

Thus launched, the work began, though in a desultory fashion. The brigade staff, chiefly the assistant adjutant general, Fayette Hewitt, offered the use of the organization's official papers and reports. From the individual companies comprising the several regiments, Thompson gathered muster rolls and a smattering of personal recollections. Slowly the story came together. But of course it was a tale already familiar to the captain. Perhaps because of this, as well as a certain diehard hope that the Confederacy might yet prevail, the Kentuckian did not press the work as he might. Then later in November the brigade resumed active operations. Sherman was moving toward the sea, and the 1st Kentucky Brigade joined in the futile attempt to stop him.

Still, from time to time, Thompson gathered his information. Out of the gleanings came a host of old names, old memories. Men living and dead appeared in the pages of the reports and diaries—names like Hanson, Helm, Trabue, and Breckinridge. Places that once had been only sluggish streams or farmers' fields, or peaceful churches, came back to him with visions of terrible battle and imperishable glory. Shiloh, Vicksburg, Baton Rouge, Stones River, Chickamauga, Missionary Ridge, Resaca, Kennesaw Mountain, Atlanta—all leaped from the stiff, formal script of the handwritten accounts. These men, these places, the memories of both, haunted Captain Ed Porter Thompson. Perhaps he was right. Perhaps these men, this brigade—a unit unique in all the Confederate Army—perhaps they did have "a kind of title of nobility." If so, they earned it with their blood. In this last war winter, Thompson might well shudder not only from the icy north wind blowing across the South but from the inner chill of recollection as well.[1]

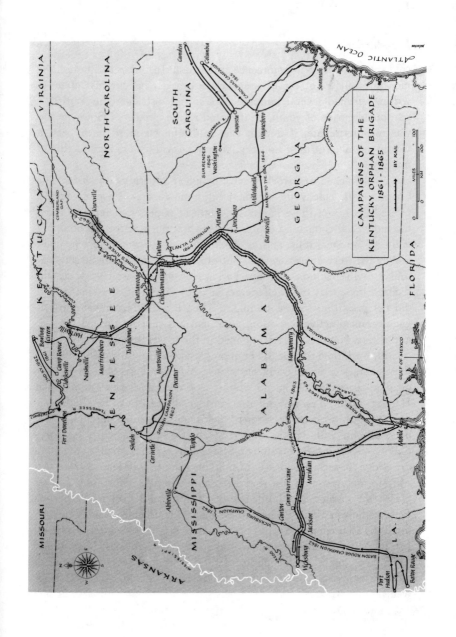

CAMPAIGNS OF THE
KENTUCKY ORPHAN BRIGADE
1861 - 1865

The Orphan Brigade

ONE

"God Save
the Commonwealth"

PHILIP LIGHTFOOT LEE of Bullitt County said it best when he declared in 1860 why he supported the Union. Should it be dissolved, then he was for Kentucky. If Kentucky fell apart, he would stand by Bullitt County. Bullitt dissolved, his sympathies lay with his hometown of Shepherdsville. And if the unthinkable should happen, and Shepherdsville be torn asunder, then he was for his side of the street.[1]

In no other state of the Union in 1860 were the choices so hard, the loyalties so strained and divided, as in the dark and bloody ground of Kentucky. Every act of civil and military strife of that decade played in microcosm on this troubled stage. It traced in large part from the geographical location of the state, but far more from the very nature of its people. Kentuckians *were* different from other Americans. No one knew so better than they did themselves.

They were born of the Revolution, the stepchild of the Scotch-Irish by their natural mother, Virginia. In infancy they teethed on Indian wars and came to adulthood in the War of 1812 when, left to their own devices by a preoccupied war administration in Washington, they independently managed the defense of the trans-Allegheny West against the British. More anxious to belong to the Union than to Virginia, Kentucky strove for years to achieve statehood. The goal attained, the struggle did not end. Already the eastern states assumed a condescending attitude toward Westerners. For years to come Kentuckians fought for the respect and equality in national counsels that their statehood should have insured. The ascendancy of Jefferson and the performance of Kentucky in the second war against the British finally won them their deserved respect. One proper Bostonian was moved to declare that Kentuckians "are the most patriotic people I have ever seen or heard of," and a New York editor asserted that "there are no people on the globe who have evinced more national feeling, more disinterested patriotism, or displayed a more noble enthusiasm to defend the honor and rights of their common country." By 1815 Kentuckians arrived on the national scene as first-class Americans.[2]

Or almost. For in making that trip these sons of the Bluegrass traveled at different speeds. Some overshot their destination, becoming more ardent Unionists than their compatriots in the East. Others never made the full journey at all, since it came at a price. Those years of being seemingly ignored by the Washington government and looked down upon by the establishment in the seaboard states took a toll. Faced with the fact that they, and only they, had their interests and future in mind, Kentuckians developed in those early years a powerful individuality and an iron self-reliance. This melded naturally with the temperament of the state's people, since the majority of the population came from the southern states, where local interests and prerogatives generally held greater claim on loyalties than things national. It is hardly surprising that quite a few Kentuckians' first priority was their "side of the street."

In the first decades of the nineteenth century the Bluegrass managed to function with this dual personality—intense Unionism and ardent localism—without great difficulty. Indeed, the state made major contributions to both causes. In the Nullification crisis of 1833, Kentucky stood squarely with the Union against John C. Calhoun and South Carolina in their attempt to threaten secession. Kentucky would not consent, said her governor, "that her sister state shall give to our children waters of bitterness to drink." Yet ironically, one of the cornerstones of Calhoun's nullification policy was in large part the spawn of Kentucky. In 1798 and 1799 the Frankfort legislature passed the so-called Kentucky Resolutions, a declaration that Congress, as the creation of the compact of individual states, was subject to the judgment and approval of those states in its acts. Should the federal body ignore the will of the states and attempt to impose unjust legislation, then it was their right to nullify such acts and prevent their imposition, even to the point of force. The Kentucky Resolutions, chiefly the product of Jefferson's pen, also bore the stamp of a Kentuckian, Jefferson's confidant and the man who presented them to the legislature, John Breckinridge of Lexington. As President, Jefferson would later make Breckinridge his Attorney General.[3]

What kept Kentuckians together with this dichotomy in their nature was largely their common heritage of struggle against adversity. They were cemented as well by an intense pride in the progress of the state. Thanks to her position, with vital waterways like the Ohio River, her northern boundary, the Mississippi on the west, and the Cumberland Gap, the nation's chief gateway to westward movement, at her southeastern corner, Kentucky was a vital link for trade North and South, East and West. Economically, the Bluegrass identified more with the Union as a whole than with any section. Then, too, a remarkable society burgeoned in the rolling grasslands of the state's central region. Newly wealthy sons of Virginia's first families built magnificent homes, started universities, bred arguably the best blood horses in the nation, and unquestionably distilled the finest whisky in the hemisphere. Indeed, some regarded Kentucky as a "de luxe edition" of Virginia.[4]

Above all, however, the force that bound Kentucky and Kentuckians together in the first half of this century was a man, the incomparable Henry Clay. Born of Virginia, like Kentucky herself, he moved early to Lexington, and thereafter made the fortunes of the state his own. Not for nothing did he become known throughout the nation as the "Great Pacificator." The craft of persuasion and compromise that he exercised so deftly on the national scene was merely an outgrowth of the same diplomacy and tact by which he single-handedly melded the disparate elements within his own state. He kept men of all stripes together, nationalists, state righters, protariff, antitariff, Whigs, Democrats. Along with Lincoln, he stands as the most remarkable American of his century. It is no accident that, in her own way, Kentucky produced them both.

As the state approached midcentury, affairs local and national became ever more complex, and so did the strains and pulls on the affection and loyalties of the people of the Bluegrass. Following the nullification controversy, state rights became an increasingly volatile issue. Lurking in its shadow was its motive force, southern nationalism. The chosen battleground in the whole controversy was the issue of slavery, and here Kentucky stood particularly divided. Clay and a substantial portion of the state's people in principle and practice opposed slavery. Yet with the exception of Virginia, Kentucky held more small slave-owners than any other state. Probably a majority of abolitionists movements had their origin in the Bluegrass. Kentuckians like Cassius Clay and James G. Birney stood among the foremost emancipationists in the Union. More moderate solutions to slavery such as gradual emancipation and African colonization enjoyed wide popularity in the state's ruling families, the Clays, Crittendens, and Breckinridges. Yet every attempt to abolish slavery within Kentucky's borders met failure. It was an outgrowth of that fierce independence nurtured in infancy. Slavery was a right guaranteed in the federal and state constitutions. No matter that many Kentuckians disapproved of the institution. It was a right, and no one would take that right away, regardless of whether or not they chose to exercise it.

Despite this preoccupation with constitutional prerogatives, Kentuckians in no way saw state rights as being incompatible with a fervent love for the Union. Indeed, the two naturally went together in their minds and were to be defended with equal fervor. To Clay the latter took precedence over the former. "If Kentucky tomorrow unfurls the banner of resistance," said he during the crisis leading to the Compromise of 1850, "I will never fight under that banner. I owe a paramount allegiance to the whole Union; a subordinate one to my own state." When a convention met in Nashville, Tennessee, that year to discuss secession, Kentucky declined participation, and instead made her position known by sending a block of native stone to be built into the Washington Monument, then under construction. "Under the auspices of Heaven and the precepts of Washington," they chiseled into the stone, "Kentucky will be the last to give up the Union."[5]

Henry Clay could not live forever. In 1852 he went to rest beneath Lexington's sod, and the erosion of Kentucky's unity dates from his passing. Indeed, it had already begun before his death, marked by the rise of the Democratic Party in the state. Clay made Kentucky a Whig bastion for decades, but in 1851 Clay's old congressional district fell to a charismatic young Democrat, John C. Breckinridge, grandson of Jefferson's Attorney General. The rise of a Democrat in Clay's home district signaled a slow explosion all over the state. Within a few years the governor's mansion, the state house in Frankfort, and the congressional delegation all lay in Democratic hands. To be sure, the Democrats of Kentucky were just as much attached to the Union as

Clay and his Whigs. Relations between Clay and young Breckinridge were such that most in the state believed the elder statesman, before his death, spiritually adopted him as his successor. Yet there was a more strident attachment to state rights in these new men than in their Whig predecessors, a closer identification with their neighbors to the south. As crisis followed crisis in this troubled decade, Kentuckians became increasingly polarized, increasingly divided. By 1860, as a friend of Senator John J. Crittenden saw it, there were three Kentuckys. Along her southern border—and sprinkled throughout the state—were those who now avowed secession, those who would see Kentucky out of the Union. At her northern border, along the Ohio, were their opposites, men like Clay whose allegiance would always be first to the Union. The third Kentucky, "the great, sound, conservative, central heart of the Commonwealth, who are for the Union the Constitution—the whole flag, every stripe & star in its place," could be found everywhere. They would support the Union so long as compromise without forfeiture of their rights could be achieved. But should the Union be sundered, warned Crittenden's friend, then "this party goes South."[6]

Sad to say, numbered among these last was Henry Clay's own son, James B. Clay. So did the solidarity Henry Clay had built for the Union crumble in his passing.

In the election year of 1860 the crumbling pieces plummeted away from each other. Kentucky had basically two functioning party organizations: the Democrats, powerful, largely prosouthern, but falling from grace with those Kentuckians of firm Union attachments; and a Constitutional Union Party whose chief platform was the naïve hope that if everyone ignored the sectional crisis and stopped talking about it, maybe it would go away. John Brown's electrifying raid on Harpers Ferry the previous October, and his hanging two months later, drove the proslave state rights element farther toward their southern brethren, while the boastful posturing of South Carolina's fire-eaters only made the Union element in Kentucky more determined. Therefore, to both extremes, the middle road, the do-nothing Constitutional Union approach, seemed the only safe solution. In November 1860, with two native sons in the presidential race—Republican Abraham Lincoln, and John C. Breckinridge, reluctantly the nominee of the state rights Democrats—the state gave her vote to John Bell, the Constitutional Union candidate. Surrounded by extremists North and South, Kentucky declared for peace and Union, and seemingly buried her head in the Bluegrass.

Of course, it could not last. Immediately after the election of Lincoln, South Carolina declared the Union dissolved, and seceded. Other states followed in rapid succession. Once again Kentucky found herself caught squarely in the middle. Those in the North expected the state of Clay to stand with them. Meanwhile, hard on the secession of South Carolina, commissioners from southern states arrived in Frankfort to persuade Governor Beriah Magoffin to join with them. Here was a dilemma. Most Kentuckians did not favor secession, yet most did not favor forceful coercion to keep states in the Union either. Barring compromise, a confrontation, perhaps even armed conflict, seemed inevitable. Already thousands of volunteers formed companies in the South. Should a war come, Kentucky would have to pick a side, or else take her stand in the middle, and probably defend herself against both North and South. The state provided too natural a pathway for invasion, too vital a territory for southern defense, too indispensable to any Union strategy, for her to sit out the war that might come. Kentucky needed an army of her own.

In fact, Magoffin began his "army" sometime before the election of 1860. Kentucky's militia had been moribund for some years after the Mexican War. But then came Brown's Harpers Ferry raid, and with it the resurrection of old paranoid fears of slave insurrections, now multiplied by the aggressively antislavery pronouncements of the Republicans. "The Harper's Ferry affair warns us that we know not at what moment we may have need of an active, ardent, reliable, patriotic, well-disciplined, and thoroughly organized militia in Kentucky," the governor warned the legislature. The lawmakers responded with unaccustomed speed. On March 5, 1860, they enacted a measure that revamped the state's militia system entirely. Every man of sound mind and body between the ages of eighteen and forty-five would be henceforward a member of the "enrolled militia." And from their number were to come the volunteers to form the strong arm of the state's military forces, the Kentucky State Guard. An inspector general would supervise the enrollment and training and equipping of the Guard. He would muster them into service, see to the election of their officers, drill them, and oversee the state's arsenals. It was an ambitious undertaking, creating a small army out of nothing. As a result, the post of inspector general called for an ambitious man, a man of talent and enterprise. Not surprisingly, the post of inspector went to the chief architect of the new legislation, and the man who conceived the idea for the position he was now to fill, Simon Bolivar Buckner.[7]

Here was a man to stir martial ardor. A young man, just one month short of thirty-seven, tall, handsome, broad forehead, wide mustache, with the graceful demeanor and almost exaggerated courtesy that had come to be associated with Kentucky "gentlemen," Buckner came from Hart County. He won appointment to the U. S. Military Academy at West Point, and graduated eleventh in his class in 1844. With a commission in the 2d United States Infantry he went back to West Point as an assistant professor of ethics before the Mexican War called him into the field. Buckner fought at Cerro Gordo, Churubusco, Molino del Rey, and Chapultepec, winning promotion, taking a wound, and standing among those who first entered the capital of the Montezumas. With the war behind him, now Captain Buckner remained on post and garrison duty until 1855, when he resigned. Promotion was too slow in the peacetime Army. He had a family to support. For two years he practiced law in Chicago, then moved back to Kentucky, to Louisville. Still, Buckner gravitated toward things military, and in 1858 he organized a local militia company, the Citizens' Guard. Thus, he was a natural choice for Magoffin's inspector general of the new State Guard.[8]

Buckner jumped into his new assignment with will and enthusiasm, but little else. There was almost no money available to arm and equip a standing militia, no uniforms, and a scattering of weapons of all descriptions. Undaunted, Buckner started his task with those various militia companies, like his own Citizens' Guard, that were already armed and equipped. These would be the nucleus of the new State Guard, and from their number he hoped to train enough men of promise to act as officers in the much larger organization he envisaged. In August of 1860 he brought the dozen or more companies together in an encampment on the state fairgrounds at Louisville for training. Most of these units had their origins in informal, even ignominious, beginnings, frequently with the expectation of the formation of the new State Army. The company from Henderson organized the month after John Brown's raid, in the counting office of a commercial firm, conducting its first drill in the front room of the Hord House hotel thanks to the good offices of the company's captain, the hotel's manager. Other com-

panies like John Hunt Morgan's Lexington Rifles had been in existence since 1857.

A festive air swirled about the encampment. An ice-cream and re-
freshment salon served the men beside the parade ground. A local
photographer persuaded the various companies to pose for his camera.
He caught the Lexington Rifles in a casual camp pose, several of the
men apparently taking a cool drink, others reading and writing letters
home, some talking or lounging on the grass. No matter that every
man posed in full-dress uniform as if on parade. The Citizens' Guard
and National Blues and other companies with sobriquets equally
expressive of their ardor and patriotism, all postured in like manner.
The camera even caught the entire assemblage drawn up on the parade, their uniforms a potpourri of cockades and kepis, tricorns,
stripes, buttons, and brass. Some companies appeared outfitted more
for an eighteenth-century war than for any modern conflict. They
were all in varying degrees motivated by what one of their number
called the "inflated military ardour and love for brass buttons and gold
lace, which so attracts the variety of young men." Spurred largely by
this encampment, that "ardour and love," he said, "broke out with the
violence of a prairie fire in many places of the State."

The encampment even attracted some national notice. One of the
photographs taken turned up in *Harper's Weekly*, the country's leading illustrated newspaper. The success of the affair prompted many
citizens in the commonwealth to make donations for the training and
equipping of the companies now to be formed. And Buckner's hopes of
identifying suitable officers from among those at the encampment were
admirably realized. His own staff already included Thomas L. Crittenden, son of the senator, and President-elect Abraham Lincoln's
brother-in-law Ben Hardin Helm. Now more than a score of "alumni"
of the Louisville encampment went home to raise new companies of
their own. Thomas Hunt, who came to Louisville commanding a company, showed so much promise that Buckner promoted him to colonel
in the Guard and gave him charge of one of the two regiments to be
formed. A few months later he would send Hunt to organize a camp
of instruction for new recruits. Joseph Nuckols of Glasgow went forth
and with his own purse equipped a company in beautiful gray uniforms, providing them with the finest arms. Martin Cofer whipped
into shape a company in Elizabethtown. By the end of the year
Buckner's State Guard numbered more than 4,000 men in 61 com-

panies. Sufficient arms had been acquired—with the men in the ranks often providing their own—so that there were, in fact, nearly five rifles or muskets for every man. Magoffin was understandably proud. There was not a state in the Union, he declared, that had "a more gallant corps than our 'State Guard,' composed as it is, of the very best material in the State, and embracing men of all parties. The soldiers are gentlemen, and the officers men of the highest tone and character."[9]

But hard times lay ahead for the Guard, as for Kentucky and the Union. Following the adjournment of the festive Louisville encampment came Lincoln's election and the secession of South Carolina. With the once-unthinkable prospect of civil war now a real threat, Union men in Kentucky took a stern look at the Guard. What they saw had a distinctly prosouthern flavor. Since these companies were in part an outgrowth of the unrest in slave states following the Harpers Ferry raid, it was natural that they would be filled chiefly by those who felt common cause with the other slave states. "It is not surprising," wrote a young Kentuckian, Basil W. Duke, "that the State Guard . . . should have conceived a feeling of antagonism for the Northern, and an instinctive sympathy for the Southern, people." Indeed, the younger men of the state were generally southern sympathizers and, with few exceptions, these were the men now composing the rank and file of the Guard. Duke even admitted that the officers of the various companies frequently won their posts in part because of their attachment to the southern viewpoint.[10]

This hardly disquieted Union men. Here, in their midst, sat an armed and organized "army" that, in a crisis, would almost surely side with the South and against the Union. Soon they accused Magoffin and Buckner of deliberately organizing a corps of secessionists. The Union men retaliated in the legislature. Buckner estimated that he would need $3.5 million in 1861 to continue the organization and arming of the full quota of the Guard. The legislature gave him less than $20,000.

There was worse to come. The firing on Fort Sumter in April 1861 set the nation ablaze. Kentucky's parent state, Virginia, finally, and reluctantly, joined her southern sisters in secession. President Lincoln issued a call for 75,000 volunteers to quell the rebellion, and informed Governor Magoffin that Kentucky's quota would be four regiments. The Kentuckian responded tersely. "Kentucky will furnish no troops for the wicked purpose of subduing her sister Southern States," he

notified Washington. Instead, just as the state refused to take a stand
in the election the year before, Magoffin and Buckner sought to avoid
one now. Kentucky would remain neutral in the coming conflict. On
May 16 the legislature approved that course and endorsed the governor's refusal to send troops to Lincoln, but Magoffin was deluded if he
thought their action implied unqualified support. For at the same time
the Union men in Frankfort began eroding the governor's control over
the state's military affairs. Appropriations for the Guard became so
minuscule that Magoffin sent agents out to neighboring states to try to
acquire more arms. Buckner himself went to the North, while
Magoffin actually began dealing with the Secretary of War of the
newly formed Confederate States of America, trying to cajole arms
and supplies from him. With hostile armies glaring at each other from
Ohio and Tennessee, the no-man's-land of Kentucky in between could
not hope to enforce her neutrality without a powerful State Guard.[11]

The effect of these events on the companies of the Guard was hardly
unmixed. The threat of imminent warfare impelled many hotspurs to
volunteer while, at the same time, the more ardent Union men in the
Guard rethought their decision to enlist. Very few companies retained
their 1860 rolls, and several actually fell apart entirely. Men refused to
march or parade under certain banners that expressed unpalatable sectional sentiments. Internal struggles developed over who would control
the unit colors and arms, often resulting in minor violence. Many
Guardsmen simply took their rifles home with them and failed to report for further muster. And at least one company, Nuckols' Glasgow
men of Barren County, actually unfurled the Confederate colors and
marched under them that spring. Some Guardsmen joined informal
companies that left the state in May, bound for Virginia and the service of the Confederacy. Clearly, neutrality or no, the day rapidly
approached when Kentucky, and the men comprising her State Guard,
could no longer avoid taking a stand North or South.[12]

That same month the legislature hastened the time for decision.
Reflecting the divided counsels of the state, its lawmakers now provided for a second militia "army," these to be called Home Guard. A
clear move to raise a force that could counter the prosouthern State
Guard, the call brought forth Union men with fervor equal to that of
Buckner's enlistments the year before. Soon rival companies paraded in
the same towns, one to the tune of "The Star-Spangled Banner," and
the other to "Dixie" and the "Bonnie Blue Flag." Ed Thompson, then

still a civilian, saw that "blue coats and gray coats rubbed against each other in public places with a smothered energy that told too plainly the conviction of the wearers of each that the other would furnish a most desirable and beautiful target for practice at musket range." Thanks only to the preoccupation with recruiting, and the mad scramble for arms, was violence between the rivals averted. Few saw promise in the future. "If it requires all these men and all this money, to keep up an armed neutrality," moaned one editor, "God save the Commonwealth from active war."[13]

Both factions in the state now abandoned restraint in the race to arm and prepare for confrontation. Union sympathizers began smuggling guns into the state to arm the Home Guard. Indeed, the federal government covertly assisted in equipping the loyal men of the state, sending thousands of "Lincoln guns" by a variety of routes. It was an ill-kept secret that only spurred the southern sympathizers in their own mobilization, and considerably enhanced the already hot feud between State Guard and Home Guard. Magoffin was quickly losing control of the state's military forces, and of the course of state affairs. In mid-July the Union press in the state declared that the State Guard must be disbanded, or at least strangled by withholding appropriations and equipment. "Our State has supported a camp of instruction for the Southern Confederacy quite long enough," shouted a Frankfort editor. Soon the legislature required renewed oaths of allegiance to the Union from State Guardsmen. As the summer progressed, all funds stopped, and an attempt was made to call into the arsenals the arms in the hands of the Guard.[14]

During all this, poor Buckner, true to the spirit of neutrality, struggled to arm the Guard as best he could to counteract the Home Guard, and at the same time worked with Magoffin to try to forge a band of neutral states, including Ohio. Such a bloc could confront both hostile parties and prevent violation of their neutrality. Tennessee's Confederate governor, Isham G. Harris, agreed, as did Major General George B. McClellan, commanding Ohio's volunteer forces. This protected all of Kentucky's southern border, and most of its northern line. Buckner sent Colonel Lloyd Tilghman with several State Guard companies to Columbus, overlooking the Mississippi, to guard the western approaches to the Bluegrass. It made a peace of sorts, but all too fragile. It could not last.

In mid-June came a special congressional election. The Union party

in the state won the polls overwhelmingly. By July, recruiting camps
for loyal Kentuckians went up just across the border in Ohio and Indiana. As the northern sympathizers in the state became more powerful,
so they became more strident as well. Soon they spoke in open derision
of neutrality. Then General William Nelson formed an active Union
recruiting camp within the state's borders. Some of McClellan's troops
—for whom he lamely declined responsibility—crossed the river and
briefly invaded Columbus to take down a Confederate flag. Clearly
neutrality was hopeless. Sooner or later Kentucky would cast her lot
with the Union.

By comparison, the new Confederacy rather strictly honored Kentucky's stance. On May 24, 1861, after the declaration of neutrality,
Confederate Inspector General Samuel Cooper directed that no attempts be made to recruit in the state and withdrew his recruiting
agents from Louisville. Attempting to enlist men openly in Kentucky
would only have inflamed the Union sentiment and speeded the
official abandonment of neutrality. The embarrassing reverse to federal
arms in the Battle of Bull Run near Manassas, Virginia, more than
offset any benefits from Confederate restraint, however. The humiliation in the face of a now insolent—and, worse, victorious—foe, impelled the loyal men of Kentucky forward. More guns came into the
state, more federal companies were recruited, and finally, in September, there were enough votes in the legislature to declare neutrality at
an end. All Confederate forces were ordered out of the state in the
middle of the month, and on September 18 the legislature officially
ended neutrality and aligned itself with the Union. By this time increasing numbers of men from both contending armies were operating
within her borders, and on this same date a small army of Confederates marched north from Tennessee toward Bowling Green. For
many in this new army, it was a homecoming, for they had been training in Tennessee for several months in the absence of recruiting camps
within their own state. Now they were back, organized regiments of
Kentucky infantry, in the Confederate service, and invading their
homeland. At their head rode General Simon Bolivar Buckner.[15]

TWO

"Men of Kentucky!"

THREE KENTUCKIANS selected a lovely spot in Montgomery County, Tennessee. It was just seven miles from the county seat, Clarksville, two miles west of the Louisville & Nashville tracks, and James Hewitt, Robert Johnson, and William T. "Temp" Withers liked what they saw. Here was a place with wide, flat fields suitable for drilling military companies. An abundance of water flowed nearby, and ample forests promised firewood. Best of all, it sat just a few miles south of the Kentucky border, within easy reach of Kentuckians who wanted to join the Confederacy without violating the state's neutrality. The gentlemen already held authorization from the Confederate authorities to establish a recruiting and training camp to raise companies for the Confederacy. As well, prominent citizens within the Bluegrass gave them pledges of financial support for arming and equipping and transporting the expected volunteers. Now, in early July 1861, they had the ideal spot for their enterprise. Ever mindful of their past as Kentuckians, the gentlemen named the place Camp Boone.[1]

At once commenced the task of clearing the underbrush from the parade grounds. They plotted a camp large enough to handle several hundred men, and not before time. Within days the young hotbloods of Kentucky began pouring into Camp Boone, intent upon joining the Confederacy even if their native state would not. Withers, nominally in command with the temporary rank of general, was overwhelmed. The Confederate Secretary of War authorized him only to raise one regiment, to be designated the 2d Kentucky Infantry. Yet Withers found that "our movements have thoroughly aroused a military spirit in Kentucky." Several applications arrived each day from men wishing to form companies. By July 12 he already had twenty of the twenty-six companies his orders allowed. He suggested that now a third regiment should be formed as well. "I would advise by all means to receive all Kentucky troops that offer," he wrote the War Office, "as we not only get good men, but ultimately secure Kentucky to the South." By July 25, fifty companies had applied for the service, and Withers believed that within forty to sixty days he could have ten thousand men enlisted. "It seems to me," he advised, "that it would be good policy to take the Kentuckians while we can get them."[2]

Indeed, anxious Kentuckians flocked to Camp Boone in July and August. Philip Lightfoot Lee brought 106 men from Shepherdsville, having decided that he could best protect his side of the street by defending the South. James W. Moss brought 90 men from Columbus. Lloyd Tilghman arrived with some followers. On July 4 Tilghman, Moss, Lee, and young Captain Robert J. Breckinridge, cousin of the unsuccessful presidential candidate, helped Withers and the others lay out the camp, and Moss and his company claimed the honor of being the first to pitch their tents. These unofficial captains paid from their own pockets the costs of transporting their men to Tennessee, promptly filing expense vouchers to be reimbursed by the Confederate Government.[3]

Soon the exodus to Camp Boone caused concern to both northern and southern sympathizers in Kentucky. Union men complained that "so many of our giddy young men have gone into the Southern army, that almost every man who goes into our army, knows that he has to fight a neighbor, a relative, a brother, son or father." The Frankfort press lamented that "thousands . . . have been ruined by the fatal delusion" of "going South." Meanwhile, those of the opposite persuasion were equally curious about the large number of men leaving the state for Camp Boone, and just what was taking place there in Montgomery County. They wanted to know how many young Confederates were training there, how they were armed and fed, and what they intended to do once organized.

"The general concensus of opinion was to the effect that it was an army several thousand strong of veteran soldiers," wrote one Kentuckian, though "how they had become veterans no one stopped to

15

consider." They were believed to be well armed, and the talk was that "in due time [they] would over-run Kentucky, capture Cincinnati and then make a 'flank movement' on Washington." In the face of this, clearly someone from the state had to visit Camp Boone and see for himself what was happening there, particularly if southern sympathizers in the state hoped to be of assistance in any attempt to occupy Kentucky. The people of Hopkinsville held a meeting and elected a man named Scott to visit Camp Boone. He was intelligent, though quite ignorant of the practices of the military. His sole experience with armed men was witnessing the Clarksville Guards, sixty-five strong, parading on the Fourth of July.

Scott went to Camp Boone and met with Tilghman, nominally in charge. The colonel received him cordially, showed him all about the camp, and allowed him to watch the recruits in training. By this time there were about 700 of them in camp, and Scott was impressed. "Scott thought that the beneficent heavens had been fairly raining Confederate soldiers," recalled a friend, "and the fact that nearly three-fourths of them were unarmed was a little matter which he totally overlooked." Impressed beyond words, Scott could hardly contain his desire to tell the folks in Hopkinsville of the grand military spectacle at Camp Boone. But then Tilghman told him that "More wars have been lost, Mr. Scott, by loose and indiscreet talk than by all other causes combined." How Scott's heart sank when the colonel enjoined, "I must request you to disclose nothing that you learn here to any one."

Scott promised to keep confidence and went home to Hopkinsville to face the eager townsfolk. Even with tears they begged him to tell about his trip. Many had sons and fathers at Camp Boone from whom they heard nothing. But Scott remained silent. "No, gentlemen," he said, "I can't tell you. Colonel Tighlman [*sic*] and I agreed that it wouldn't be safe to let any one else know what he and I know." In exasperation, Scott's frustrated would-be hearers sent for his longtime friend and former business partner John Fisher. If anyone could make Scott talk, surely Fisher was the man. A telegram found him in Louisville and he rushed to Hopkinsville to start his work. But Scott would not talk. After Fisher's repeated pleadings, Scott agreed that if Fisher would meet him at 6 P.M. at a specified place a mile from town on the Cadiz road, he might tell him "something."

Fisher got there an hour ahead of time. When Scott arrived, full-blown with the self-importance of a man who knows something that everyone else wants to learn, he took his friend one hundred yards off the road into the woods, away from all possible auditors. Backing Fisher against a tree, the great Scott finally spoke with proper solemnity.

"John J. Fisher," he said, "I've known you for more than forty years, and I'd tell you things that I wouldn't tell any other livin' man; but there are some things I can't even tell you. But I'll say this much to you: If old Abe Lincoln had seen what I saw down at Camp Boone he'd 'a' thought he had a mighty heavy contract on his hands."[4]

It is doubtful that Mr. Fisher was much satisfied with the "something" he finally learned, but certainly Mr. Scott was delighted. The episode symbolized considerably more than Scott's brief moment in the limelight. It showed that, even to an untrained eye, something unusual, something impressive, characterized this ill-armed band of Kentuckians at Camp Boone, something to inspire pride. And as well, the plight of the people of Hopkinsville proved a harbinger of the years ahead for all of Kentucky. Almost from the day those young men left the state for Camp Boone they were cut off from home, and home from them. They were children orphaned from their mother, and for four long years news of them was as sparse in the Bluegrass as Scott's confidence to Fisher.

Within days the regiments began organizing officially. Since the Kentuckians who went to Virginia late that spring had been designated the 1st Kentucky Infantry, the first regiment to be formed here at Camp Boone was the 2d Kentucky. The regiment organized on July 13 and Withers mustered it into the Confederate service three days later. Its colonel took his commission three weeks earlier in anticipation of forming the regiment. James M. Hawes, a thirty-seven-year-old native of Lexington, a West Pointer and a combat veteran of the war with Mexico, seemed a man who knew how to form raw volunteers into an effective unit. He worked with good material. His lieutenant colonel, Robert A. Johnson of Louisville, showed a peculiar intelligence and a ready ability to learn the military way of things. Among the captains of the various companies—there were ten of them—Hawes had good men with experience, some of them from the State Guard. James Moss, a stern, exacting man, gruff and taciturn, captained Company A. Yet behind his blunt façade lurked a warm and generous heart. Relieving those in distress, said a friend of Moss's, "was the greatest pleasure of his life."

Company B went to Captain Breckinridge who, like most of that family, had political ambitions. An eighteen-year-old private in his company was the tall, handsome son of John C. Breckinridge, Joseph C. He left home and entered the Confederacy against the wishes of his father, who was trying mightily to remain loyal to the Union. The ever-cheerful Captain Philip Lightfoot Lee took Company C. He regarded neutrality as a "foolish and impractical thing," and was entirely delighted to be here in rebellion. Among other things, the maintenance of company morale afforded him ample opportunity for impromptu stump speaking. He loved repeating his philosophy about his side of the street. In Company G there was young Charles C. Ivey, now a drillmaster, but the year before secretary to then Vice President of the United States, John C. Breckinridge. And so it went.[5]

A few days later another regiment formed, this the 3d Kentucky Infantry. Lloyd Tilghman would be its colonel. A striking, erect, thoroughly soldierly figure, his connection with his regiment would end in a few months. He would not survive the coming war, like so many here at Camp Boone in this last summer of American innocence.[6]

With these two regiments organized, a problem arose. There were still a number of men in camp, but not quite enough for another regiment. Indeed, many of the bodies of men who came across the line did not number enough to organize companies. Thomas W. Thompson brought several men from his old State Guard command South with him. Yet his, like other groups, did not make up a whole company, even though it had a full complement of officers. Unable to organize officially, they could only drill and parade and bide their time until some solution to their problem appeared.

Robert P. Trabue worked on just such a solution. With regiments starting to form at Camp Boone, he and an associate went to Louisville in August, where Trabue arranged with Ben Monroe to recruit quietly in and around Frankfort. Trabue oversaw transporting the enlistees to Tennessee. After making arrangements to funnel recruits by way of Louisville, Trabue and his staff repaired to Camp Boone to await the fruits of Monroe's labors. They were not long in coming, but their journeys hardly passed without incident.[7]

There is the case of John L. Marshall of northeastern Kentucky. The Union men so controlled his area that a virtual blockade existed on pistols and knives, and a man of southern leanings caught so armed could expect detention at least. He had to take a midnight coach for Lexington, his little Navy boarding pistol secreted in his valise. In Louisville he nervously passed the blockade, thanks in part to the concealment provided by the other contents of his bag. In it were several pairs of woolen socks, lovingly knitted by an old woman who was dying of tuberculosis. In her pain, she still double-knitted the heels and toes of every sock and then, in giving them to Marshall, enjoined: "Never let me hear of the heels of those socks being turned to the faces of your country's enemies."

Better yet is the peculiar story of Joseph P. Nuckols. He managed to hold together his State Guard company, even enhancing its ranks until it numbered eighty-three young men, not one of them married. All were anxious to leave for Camp Boone that July, but there was a political contest in the offing in Barren County, and Nuckols and his band of celibates stayed long enough to cast their votes for the southern rights candidate. The irony of their act apparently escaped them, delaying their departure for the Confederacy in order to cast a vote when, by joining in the rebellion, they were in effect abandoning the democratic process. And this was not the only irony. Nuckols, a stickler for law and order, had armed his State Guard company with weapons furnished by the state of Kentucky. Since the state still remained officially neutral, and since the guns belonged to the state, he boxed them and turned them over to the county judge, knowing full well that they would soon be in the hands of the Home Guard, his enemies. It did not matter that most other members of the State Guard took their weapons with them to the Confederacy. Nuckols would take nothing that did not belong to him. These Kentuckians were a contradictory lot. Even their hopes and ambitions of southern independence could not make them compromise their principles. If they had forgotten what Henry Clay taught them about compromise, still they would not forget his code of honor. He had said he would rather be "right" than be President. When given a choice, these sons of the Bluegrass, too, would always prefer to be "right."

Nuckols and his company reached Camp Boone on August 9, even as other companies arrived, one of them armed with bowie knives and following a banner declaring "Southern rights, or Northern blood." Trabue awaited them. Recognizing that the organization of a regiment from these several companies and demicompanies would be more difficult than the task faced by Hawes and Tilghman, he arranged a separate training place two miles from Camp Boone. Here, called Camp Burnett, he directed the recruits who arrived through July and August. His main problem was too many officers. Every group that came South, even if only half a company in size, had enough elected officers for a full company. The men naturally wished to serve under their own chosen leaders, yet to form companies some of these groups would have to combine. That meant that many officers would have to relinquish their posts. Most of them led their men out of Kentucky at no little expense to themselves, both for recruiting and transportation, and at some danger. Many made promises to families at home that they would look after the men entrusted to their care. Obviously, few of these men relished relinquishing their position in the cause of proper organization. They talked among themselves, both rank and file, of going to Virginia instead, or of joining with new cavalry companies, or even of returning to Kentucky rather than be consolidated with other companies. They reckoned without Robert P. Trabue.

Born on New Year's Day in 1824 in Columbia, Kentucky, Trabue came of one of the oldest families in the Bluegrass. He went to Mexico in a regiment of Kentucky volunteers and returned in 1848 a captain. He was a lawyer by profession, and in the decade before the outbreak of the Civil War he settled in Mississippi. Yet, when sectional war became a certainty in the dark early days of 1861, he quickly obtained authorization to return to his native state and raise a regiment. Having formed that resolve, he would not be thwarted now by the conflicting loyalties and ambitions of a lot of excess officers. "Colonel Trabue was entirely too shrewd a man to allow these objections to disturb him," recalled a man of the regiment-to-be. "Once get enough men into camp and he would very soon organize his regiment." A master of tact, Trabue ignored the problem for a time. Then he moved quietly among the officers, speaking soothingly of the manner in which the cause might best be served, reminding them that there would certainly be opportunities for advancement as the war progressed. He found other places for those most disappointed. The policy worked. Trabue combined the demicompanies smoothly, with as few ruffled military plumes as possible. Indeed, some managed their consolidation even without "Old Trib," so completely did his diplomatic spirit of compromise capture Camp Burnett. When William Blanchard led his minicompany into camp, Thomas Thompson, languishing in his own understrength, learned of it, and the two "captains" got together. Between themselves they agreed that Thompson would take the captaincy of their combined companies, dividing the remainder of the new company positions equally between the officers of their two squads. On August 30, 1861, the men of these companies of Trabue's, many of them still forming, mustered into the Confederate service. Two days later they organized officially the 4th Kentucky Infantry.[8]

While the foot soldiers slowly learned the routine of Army life, another branch of the service appeared. Edward P. Byrne, a native of Kentucky, lived in Mississippi when South Carolina seceded. At once he decided to raise and equip a battery of artillery for the Confederate service. Going to Memphis, Tennessee, he contracted with the foundry firm of Quinby & Robinson to produce for him four bronze six-pounder field pieces, which he paid for from his own pocket. He bought the finest horses and harness, and every other piece of equipment for the contemplated battery was of the best to be had. While awaiting the manufacture of the cannon, he went on to Louisville early in April and met with Withers and Bob Johnson, then recruiting the 2d Kentucky. Byrne hoped to take his battery to Charleston but now, learning of the surrender of Fort Sumter, he proposed that he attach his command-to-be with the Kentucky troops. The proposition accepted, Byrne began recruiting quietly. After the others left to plot Camp Boone, he stayed in Louisville for a time, assisting in sending recruits and supplies South. It was no simple task, for federal agents carefully watched the depot of the Louisville & Nashville for any sign of war material being sent to the Confederacy. The agents had armed men at their command, but were prevented from actually stopping recruits and their baggage by the crowds of relatives and southern sympathizers who thronged about the departing trains. Any attempt to interfere with their leaving would have resulted in violence.

This work done, Byrne himself returned to Mississippi early in July and recruited for his battery. By the beginning of August three of his six-pounders arrived and enough Mississippians to handle them so that he could move to Camp Boone to complete the formation of the battery. Here, near the state line, he filled his numbers with Kentuckians and began training.[9]

Turning these raw boys and men into soldiers was a task to match the best efforts of the men in command. Supply was the most immediate and long-continuing problem, despite the constant smuggling of clothing and equipment across the line from friends in Kentucky. When Byrne reached Camp Boone he came well equipped with tents, wagons, blankets, and everything else required for his men. But he found many of those already in camp nearly destitute of things, among them blankets. He sent word of the situation to the ladies of his hometown in Greenville, Mississippi, and they promptly forwarded five hundred pairs of woolen blankets, many of them taken from their own beds, enough to provide for most of the men of the 2d Kentucky alone.[10]

Clothing and food presented less of a problem than medical supplies, but the Kentuckians brought good doctors with them. Dr. B. M. Wible came from Nelson County to be surgeon for the 2d Kentucky. He organized the hospital at Camp Boone on August 1. Within a week the infirmary tents filled with twenty-nine cases of measles and one of typhoid. The latter would occur from time to time thanks to foul water, but the measles remained an ever-present scourge in this Army. In training camp men were, often for the first time, exposed to large numbers of others. Relatively few Americans of the time contracted measles in childhood, thereby building immunity. Now as adults they made fair game for the far more virulent strains that could kill hundreds, if not thousands. On August 10 Dr. Wible recorded seventeen new cases of rubeola during the past week. The next day fourteen new cases came into the hospital from the 2d Kentucky alone. At any one time during the latter part of the month he had at least thirty-two cases. From the 2d Kentucky, during the final three weeks of August, Wible admitted 127 patients. Of that number, 113 were for measles. Among them was young Rice E. Graves of the 2d, regimental adjutant, a particular favorite with the regiment. Unlike many others, he would recover, to be heard from in the days ahead.

Other dangers besides measles threatened. In at least one case a Kentuckian apparently fell susceptible to his own weakness. For all the blue blood in the 2d Kentucky, there was a little red-blooded male in them all as well. It must have been too much for poor Private Henry Self of Company K. Perhaps he brought it from Kentucky, or maybe he found it with one of the ladies who must inevitably have done business near Camp Boone. On August 12 Dr. Wible entered poor Self into the hospital and diagnosed his case as syphilis. Here for the next month Henry suffered treatment, the regiment's first casualty to the battle of the sexes.[11]

Wible did not last long here, leaving in September after a disagreement with the colonel of the 2d Kentucky, but he left behind an efficient, well-organized, and well-fed hospital. Not so, alas, the Camp Boone armory. From the very day the camp began, arms supply ran short. Of course, many of the Kentuckians brought their own rifles with them, particularly former members of the State Guard—excepting the honorable Captain Nuckols. But still there existed a great shortage of long arms. When Mr. Scott of Hopkinsville visited the camp in July, there were about 700 men, only one fourth of them armed. By the first week of August it was far worse. With 2,500 men in camp, Colonel Bob Johnson believed there were not more than 120 muskets available. The lack of guns was not for want of trying.

Kentucky's position of neutrality caused the major problem. Just as Nuckols regarded Guard arms as state property that he was not free to take into the Confederacy, so did Governor Magoffin share that opinion. Consequently, the governor repeatedly tried to recover state arms taken to Camp Boone. As early as July 19, learning that three boxes of rifles had been misdirected to Camp Boone, Magoffin's Secretary of State, Thomas B. Monroe, told Withers to send them back. Aware of the tense situation with the state still neutral, Monroe cautioned to "have them returned quietly, so as to avoid any unnecessary excitement about the matter." Withers inaugurated a practice of returning state-owned arms brought South by his recruits, and continued to do so. On July 20 a number of Kentuckians brought out of the state to Union City, Tennessee, a lot of muskets and a full field battery of artillery. Withers declined to receive the arms, a policy seconded by the Confederate Secretary of War. Hoping eventually to lure Kentucky into joining the Confederacy, they could ill afford to antagonize the state while neutral. A wise course diplomatically, perhaps, but one not calculated to aid in arming the Kentuckians at Camp Boone.

Even while authorizing Withers to raise another regiment of infantry, the Confederate War Department told him to return any arms belonging to the state of Kentucky. To Withers this seemed incongruous, to say the least. Writing a few days after the Confederate victory at Bull Run, he affirmed his hope that "it will be in your power to arm them." He could provide everything needed except guns. Several companies now formed would not be received into the Confederate Army if not armed, and they would "be greatly disappointed." Governor Isham Harris of Tennessee took Withers' case, declaring it was "a matter of importance, if not of absolute necessity, that the Kentucky regiments, under command of General Withers, at Camp Boone, on the Kentucky line, should be armed at the earliest moment practicable." He needed the regiments to guard the border of the two states, particularly because of the strong Union sentiment in much of Tennessee, "but without arms of course they are useless." "If you can arm the brigade at Camp Boone," wrote Harris in mid-August, "I can take care of Middle Tennessee."[12]

By this time only Byrne's battery was fully armed, with three of his bronze cannon in hand, and a requisition in for two twelve-pounder howitzers. Yet even Byrne found trouble, for Quinby & Robinson delayed in delivering the fourth six-pounder. They finished the gun, but refused to send it, complaining that they needed it instead to complete an order from the Confederate Government. Bob Johnson had to write to Major General Leonidas Polk, commanding in Memphis, to try to get Byrne's cannon sent, and eventually it was.

Johnson also lent a hand to arm the men of his regiment, the 2d Kentucky. Probably without Withers' knowledge—for surely he would have disapproved the action—Johnson ordered Phil Lee to select one hundred men and cross the line into Kentucky, going as far as possible. There Lee was to disarm any of the Union Home Guard that could be found and take their rifles back to Camp Boone. Lee left on August 20 with his command, among them Rice Graves, now out of the hospital.

The raid began auspiciously. Lee captured a train and boarded his men. They steamed toward Bowling Green, sixty miles northeast of Camp Boone. There several companies of Home Guard camped along the railroad, and these Lee hoped to capture. Unfortunately, word of his coming preceded him, and the Union men abandoned their posts. By the time he approached Bowling Green, Lee had not seen one Home Guardsman. He could not afford to leave his captured train and pursue them. Consequently, rather dejected, Lee retraced his course to Camp Boone, empty-handed. He found small consolation in having had the honor of leading the first Confederate raid into Kentucky.[13]

Another such raid proved more successful, though at some cost spiritually. When Trabue organized his regiment, he argued that it must have a chaplain, and shortly produced a parson. "As he was up to Col. Trabue's idea of tastefulness in manner and dress," wrote one of the Kentuckians, "he was quickly installed as the spiritual advisor of the jolly Fourth." The new chaplain performed his duties in a brick church at Camp Burnett, then filled with measles cases.

It was a trying place, the 4th at the time being a "gasted measely old regiment," and the parson did double duty as a nurse. "I suppose he got along creditably enough," wrote John Weller, "consoling the poor homesick boys with their flushed and speckled faces, with now and then a case of typhoid pneumonia thrown in to keep the congregation down to a proper regard for the trying situation." If the parson encountered Henry Self and his syphilis, poor Henry probably got more sermon than sympathy.

Thus engaged, some time passed before the chaplain arranged for his first sermon. With the Sunday's approach, he made great preparations for an impressive ceremony. The church being occupied, he selected a spot under a stately oak near the officers' tents. There, at 2 P.M. on the appointed day, the 4th Kentucky gathered around the tree, minus a detachment from Company C. The chaplain took his place under the oak and commenced preaching. The audience stayed respectively attentive until a great shout arose some distance away on the road leading toward Kentucky. "The congregation rose as one man, and fled toward the joyful sound," recalled one of the boys.

The shout came from the detachment of Company C. A few days earlier they stole into Kentucky to capture a field piece known to be nearby. Sure enough they got it, and now in triumph they brought the gun into Camp Burnett. "The capturing party were nearly idolized," said Weller, "and were heroes grand in our estimation." After a time, in ones and twos the men started back toward the oak, the Sabbath exercises forgotten with the excitement of the cannon. "Nothing but the oak stood to greet us." The parson was gone, silently taking his leave from an uncouth lot that preferred cannon to canon. "Though he may have packed his clothes and tendered and had accepted his formal resignation," said Weller, "I am satisfied none of the Fourth ever heard of him again." It was a long time before the regiment got another parson.[14]

Right now guns were more important than preachers. By mid-September, after months of pleading and cajoling and thieving, a respectable number of the Kentuckians held arms, though a motley variety of calibers, rifles, muskets, and shotguns. It was not before time, either. Events in Kentucky progressed quickly while her sons trained and organized at Camps Boone and Burnett. While Magoffin continued to try to maintain neutrality, Confederate sympathizers violated it covertly, and the Union men did so in the open. When Magoffin asked Lincoln to have a federal recruiting camp removed to Ohio, the President declined. Thanks to the heavy Union majority in the legislature, Confederate men in the state held ever more tenaciously to neutrality, seeing in it the only alternative to Kentucky joining hand-in-hand with the Federals. Any possibility of secession was out of the question.

It could not last. Violations increased, as did the tension in the state. Finally it was a Confederate who precipitated the crisis. Both sides recognized the strategic necessity of controlling the western part of the state where it commanded transportation on three rivers, the Mississippi, Cumberland, and Tennessee. On September 3, 1861, acting on orders from General Polk, Brigadier General Gideon J. Pillow moved from Tennessee and occupied Columbus, Kentucky, on the Mississippi. The excuse was that the Federals had been recruiting for some time in the state, and were then marshaling troops across the river in Missouri, intent on taking Columbus themselves. Three days later Brigadier General U. S. Grant occupied Paducah at the mouth of the Tennessee with federal troops. Neutrality was now a shambles. On September 11 the legislature passed its resolution ordering Confederate troops out of the state.

For Simon Bolivar Buckner, this was the turning point. Both governments courted Buckner. As part of his attempt to arrange and maintain neutrality, the Kentuckian visited Washington in July, and met with Lincoln, who tacitly assured that he would honor the state's position. On August 17, in an obvious attempt to lure Buckner's support to the Union, Lincoln sent him an unsolicited commission as brigadier general. The Confederates, while less obvious, still made it clear that he could expect a good position if he "went South." Buckner consistently declined both. "I have alike refused office from the North and the South," he declared on September 12, "because the position of my state was respected." With the increasing violations by Union men and with Lincoln's assurances of support apparently hollow, it remained only for the legislature to abandon neutrality, for Buckner to choose his side. In Nashville, Tennessee, on the day that Confederates were ordered out of Kentucky, he advised the Confederate War Department that "No political necessity now exists for withholding a commission, if one is intended for me." The next day

he issued a call for Kentuckians to defend their homeland against the
northern invasion.[15]

On September 14 the new commanding general of the Confederate
Army west of the Alleghenies, Albert Sidney Johnston, appointed
Buckner a brigadier general. At the same time, regarding it as imperative that more Confederate troops occupy Kentucky to protect southern interests, Johnston decided to seize Bowling Green. Positioned
on the Louisville & Nashville Railroad where the line from Memphis
joined, it was the most important transportation junction in the southern part of the state. The task of organizing and commanding the
movement Johnston gave to Buckner.

He moved quickly. The day after being commissioned, he sent to
Mississippi for one thousand arms to equip the Kentuckians at Camp
Boone. He would take fifteen hundred men and Byrne's battery, still
with only its three six-pounders. The soldiers were to have fifty rounds
of ammunition and rations for a week. It would be a quick movement,
by rail up the Louisville & Nashville in only a couple of hours. To
achieve as much surprise as possible, Buckner did not advise the men
and officers of the time of departure until just before leaving. He
would take with him as well spare track and road tools should Federals try to cut the line, and several hundred spades, picks, and axes.
Buckner planned on staying in Bowling Green for some time.[16]

In advance of the movement, Buckner had sympathizers in Ken-
tucky ready to assist, many of them still in the State Guard. Thomas
H. Hays captained the Salt River Battalion, which every Sunday
drilled alongside the Louisville & Nashville line thirty miles south of
Louisville, near Colesburg. One of the engineers of that line, Andy
Clarke, delighted in watching the drill. If Hays and his men "went
South," Andy declared, he would join them with his locomotive.
"Whinever ye want Andy and No. 27, jist tip me the wink an' I'll be
with ye," he told Hays. On September 17 came advance word from
Buckner that now was the time to move; Hays should capture trains at
nearby Elizabethtown and Lebanon Junction, destroy a bridge over the
Rolling Fork River, then move toward Bowling Green. Word went to
Andy Clarke, who was found on his engine with the steam up, but he
refused rather loudly to go with them. The engine belonged to the railroad and he would not steal it. "Moind ye," shouted the Irishman,
"I'll never desert and stale their property." However, he whispered to
one of the startled Kentuckians, should he be ordered to accompany

them at gunpoint, he would have no choice but to obey. The pistol pointed, Clarke threw up his hands and cried out—presumably for any L&N people thereabouts to hear—"Don't shoot; I surrender to Gineral Buckner and the Confederacy. Let me run over and kiss my wife and darling babies and I'll go with ye." And go he did, proving invaluable to Hays in successfully carrying out his orders.[17]

On the morning of September 18, 1861, Buckner boarded the 2d Kentucky, and those armed portions of the 3d and 4th regiments. Flatcars carried Byrne's field pieces. The remaining unarmed Kentuckians he sent to Nashville, where they would soon be provided weapons. When the light was full, they blew the engine's whistles and bade farewell to Camp Boone. They were going to Kentucky.

Buckner arrived first, reaching Bowling Green at 10 A.M. Half an hour later Colonel Hawes brought the remainder of the command, and later in the day some regiments of Tennessee troops arrived from Nashville. The whole movement took place without opposition. Now was the time for the formalities. Buckner sent a telegram to Governor Magoffin informing him of his action, and declaring that it was only a "defensive measure." Then Buckner printed for circulation a broadside dated the day before. Addressed "To the People of Kentucky," it reaffirmed that the Confederates were acting only on the defensive, and launched into the history of federal crimes against the state. "Men of Kentucky!" he said, "are we indeed slaves, that we are thus to be dragged in chains at the feet of despotic power?" Of course not. "Let us rise, freemen of Kentucky, and show that we are worthy of our sires." He was entering the lists for freedom, he said. Now he called upon them to "Join with me in expelling from our firesides the armies which an insane despotism sends amongst us to subjugate us to the iron rule of Puritanical New England." On the very day of occupying Kentucky, the renewed recruiting of her sons began.[18]

THREE

"They Are All Gentlemen"

JOHN S. JACKMAN walked to the Bardstown depot to get the daily Louisville newspaper. He chanced to meet there an old friend who, without prior discussion on the subject, said, "Let us go to Bloomfield to-night and join the party going through to Dixie." "I had scarcely thought of such a thing before," Jackman recalled, but instantly his mind was decided. "All right," he said, and so cast his fortunes with the Confederacy. Since Buckner's entry into the state, hundreds of young Kentucky men formed this same resolve, though presumably upon a little more reflection. All of them made their way toward Bowling Green eventually, though not without mishap and adventure on the way.

Jackman went home and changed clothes, trying to slip out of the house without his parents noticing. Failing in that, he lied, telling them he would be back in a few days. With no baggage but a shawl, he mounted his horse, joined his friend and four others, and rode into the night. "Not one in the party was able to support a whisker, nor a visible mustache; neither was there a well-defined political idea in the crowd." They were simply off for adventure. One of their number, standing six feet, seven inches tall, they elected their "captain," and then they followed him into the moonlight. As they approached Bloomfield the challenge "Who comes there?" rang out. The "captain" replied that they were "Recruits for the Rebel army." The voice commanded them to halt, and soon a soldier came into view brandishing a rifle and a bayonet. Satisfied of the strangers' intentions, the Confederate sent them to the main camp, where they were challenged yet again, this time with cocked gun. "I thought this extreme vigilence," wrote Jackman. Soon Captain John C. Wickliffe brought them into camp where a fire burned and the boys exchanged excited stories with other friends who preceded them. Weary from the ride, however, they soon retired, John Jackman rolling himself in his shawl and pillowing his head on the gnarled root of an old beech tree. "I lay a moment watching the 'lamps of heaven' as they twinkled through the foliage of the old tree, my thoughts busy contemplating the *sublimeness* of soldiering." Then it was off to sleep.

He awoke the next morning with rain spattering his face. After a breakfast of cornbread and fat bacon broiled at the end of a stick, he explored this new place, called Camp Charity. The men enjoyed good clothing and shelter, and excellent food by later standards. He found about three hundred men in camp, among them the Lexington Rifles of Captain John H. Morgan, who was in overall charge of the recruits here assembled. Soon it was time to exchange his civilian clothing for a jacket of Confederate gray, Jackman noting with perverse pleasure that the largest trousers available extended little below the knees of his outsized "captain" of the day before, while his arms from the elbows down protruded beyond the jacket sleeves.

With the uniform came a rifle with a gleaming bayonet, and that night Jackman went on guard in a dense wood behind the camp. "How proud I felt as I paced to and fro on my beat," he wrote, longing for an opportunity to issue the same stentorian challenge that he encountered just the night before. After midnight he heard two men approaching and crouched in hiding, hoping they would wander across the line of his beat. They did, and at once came Jackman's prideful "Halt." The men begged to be passed into the camp but, not to be done out of his grand moment, the guard refused, bawling into the night, "Corporal of the guard, post No. 8." "Even the owls stopped hooting," Jackman discovered, "either through respect, or being terror-stricken." When the swearing corporal arrived, the strangers were brought into camp, and Johnny Jackman returned to his solitary beat, entirely satisfied with the glorious life of a soldier.

On the afternoon of September 28, the party, now 400 strong, left to join Buckner. The infantry took the lead, the cavalry acting as rear guard, while Morgan rode at the front of the column. The very first day out Jackman was rudely disenchanted. Almost the entire party turned into a panicked, disorganized mob when it was thought there were armed Federals or Home Guard in their front. Briefly he toyed with taking "French leave," abandoning the column, but thought better of it after a night's rest. Still, the novelty and romance faded fast. The next night they were so tired that one man fell asleep on a pile of rails that some time before had been a campfire. He awoke in the morning to find his coat singed to cinders. The next day brought them to the L&N's Green River crossing near Munfordville, and here they found Hawes's 2d Kentucky, which Buckner had sent forward to guard the bridge. The veterans welcomed the recruits with band music and the salute of cannon—Byrne's six-pounders. Amid the huzzas and the strains of "Dixie," Jackman and his compatriots marched into camp and collapsed. They had walked nearly one hundred miles in the preceding thirty-six hours.

The next two days in camp took much of the remainder of romance out of soldiering. The "veterans" of the 2d Kentucky looked to Jackman "very ragged and dirty." He was surprised at how quickly bright, gay uniforms became tattered and dingy. The men of the 2d guyed and teased the "tenderfeet," but still Jackman and the 400 decided to enter the service formally. Morgan took his Lexington Rifles toward Bowling Green to enlist as cavalry, while the others were sworn into service by Major James Hewitt, their term three years. The veterans looked on, jeering "sold to the Dutch, sold to the Dutch" as Jackman took his oath. Finally, on the evening of October 5, the new companies entrained for Bowling Green. It was past dark when they arrived, seeing before them hundreds of campfires in the suburbs of the town. Jackman thought "the world was there encamped." Now, at last, he was ready for war in an army that would whip the Yankees.[1]

Johnny Jackman's was only one of hundreds of stories told by the men flocking to Bowling Green. Buckner's call to arms was not ignored in the first weeks after his march into the state. The very day they took Bowling Green, he sent Hawes and the 2d Kentucky, with Byrne's battery, forward to the Green River, both to cover the bridge as well as to "rally around your command as strong a force of Kentuckians as possible." He empowered Hawes to muster armed companies into the service for three years, and further to communicate with sympathizers in the interior of the state to aid in their recruiting. Buckner authorized special recruiting agents to go to Lexington and elsewhere in the Bluegrass to raise companies, placing Major Alexander Cassady in charge of enlisting men to the banner. They came in large numbers: 400 on September 19, 500 more six days later. Enlistment stations burgeoned at places like Cave City and Russellville, and the young "Southrons" flocked to them singly and in informal companies.[2]

They presented a motley aspect, these ardent Kentuckians, but most of the townspeople loved them. At Russellville the entire town, all southern in sympathy, turned out as the recruits entered, the townspeople bringing the best delicacies their larders could offer. Yet some were less than overwhelmed. "What a sad, beaten-down sight awaited our eyes," wrote a lady passing through town. "They, in their tatters, partly barefooted, gave more the effect of a robber band than the corps of trained soldiers." In the public square the town's society ladies mixed with those of lesser reputation in preparing meals for the volunteers and mending their clothes. Amid blazing campfires and the comings and goings of couriers, officers mingled with civilians, standing aside as wagons bearing the sick passed by, stepping out to greet those who straggled in the last miles. A band played "Dixie," and everyone in the square stopped to join in singing. It was a joyful yet sober occasion, and symbolic. These men were leaving everything behind. Their state did not support them, and in many cases neither did their families. They looked hungry. Many were ailing, already homesick. "Their whole outward appearance was sad, self-sufficient and serious," recalled a witness. It was of these men that Buckner hoped to build his regiments. And in time a brigade.[3]

Morgan's Lexington Rifles took active service first, though they would not be mustered officially into the service until November 7. The dashing young captain had quite an adventure just reaching Bowling Green. Indeed, he nearly precipitated an armed confrontation as far back as August 20, when he and his men determined to capture a shipment of "Lincoln guns" coming to Lexington for federal recruits. Only the intervention of John C. Breckinridge, still trying to preserve the neutral peace, prevented Morgan from fighting for the guns.

One month later to the day Morgan confided to his most trusted and reliable men that he would take them and their state-owned arms to the Confederates. They loaded their weapons in two wagons and, with seventeen men behind him, Morgan rode South. Behind him he had several of his men making a great noise in the Lexington Rifles' armory to fool Union men into thinking the entire command was there. The next morning, the weapons safely out of town, Morgan returned to Lexington and gathered the rest of his men. That day the Union men decided to disarm the Lexington Rifles' armory and were not a little surprised to find it empty. The ensuing debate eventually resulted in shooting, and by nightfall Morgan and his followers were on their way to the rendezvous near Bloomfield. From there, with Jackman and several hundred others in tow, he made his way to the camps at Green River. Immediately upon arrival, Morgan was attached to the regiment then forming under his uncle, Thomas Hunt, and began at once to operate mounted patrols. For months he and his small band of mounted scouts forayed deep into the state's interior, sometimes even in the guise of federal soldiers. Four and five times a week he went on his missions, sometimes riding over sixty miles in twenty hours or less. It was exciting duty, and hazardous in its way, suiting exactly the temperament of this romantic on horseback. A fellow Kentuckian at this time described Morgan as being of "a mild and unassuming demeanor, gentle and affable in his manners, handsome in person, and possessed of all that polish of address which is supposed to best qualify men for the drawing-room and parlor." Yet "no enterprise, however dangerous, no reconnoissance, however tiresome and wearying, could daunt his spirits or deter him from his purpose." Here was the *beau sabreur* ideal.[4]

As for his men, they were of the same stripe as all Kentucky soldiers —hard-fighting, independent, and a bit wild. His men were known to "requisition" blankets and other odd items from the local citizens regardless of political persuasion, sometimes even taking things of no real consequence. One local complained to Morgan that his men stole his thermometer. Embarrassed, Morgan began consigning offenders to the guardhouse, which quelled the problem until the case of the "coffee boiler." One "mess," or group of about a dozen men who cooked and ate together, had plenty of coffee but nothing but an open kettle in which to boil it. This allowed most of the flavor to escape in the steam. Tinware was so scarce that a good pot or "boiler" could not be purchased. Worse, perverse Fate had set a fine brightly polished coffee boiler on a farmer's workbench next to his smokehouse, and within sight of camp. "No doubt the demon of temptation was urged on by the ease with which the covetted article might be captured," lamented one of the mess. It was easy enough to purloin the treasure, but how to keep the farmer from thinking the soldiers had done the deed? "The fear of being caught deterred us for several days," he recalled, but Kentuckians were nothing if not innovative. They had dug several holes in the clay near their tents to act as water retainers. Unused now, they were filled with leaves. The boiler, someone suggested, could be hidden in one of these until the inevitable camp search was completed.

On the appointed night, one of them, made a "coffee-boiler scout," successfully captured the prize in the dark, and immediately buried it in a hole. Then for over a week the men kept quiet, awaiting the search. It never came. Eventually the mess brought forth their treasure from the hole and examined it for the first time in the light. The bottom was burned out. It was absolutely useless. Now the men had another problem. Not only did they have to keep the theft a secret from their superiors, but also from their fellow soldiers, who would jeer them mercilessly. It was not to be. Even while they tried hastily to reinter the utensil, the word spread through camp. Soon and thereafter they were known as the "Coffee-boiler Rangers."[5]

Morgan was not the only cavalry forming in and about Bowling Green. While he patrolled to the north, a genuine mounted regiment, to be designated the 1st Kentucky Cavalry, was aborning. Theirs was a rigid discipline. Company drill in the morning, regimental drill in the afternoon, brigade drill on Friday, inspection on Saturday, and leisure hours occupied with saber drill and fatigue and guard duty. To any onlooker it was obvious that this regiment was in the hands of a professional. Those hands happened to belong to the brother-in-law of the President of the *United* States, Colonel Benjamin Hardin Helm.

He was just barely thirty years old, the son of Governor John Helm of Kentucky, and connected with one of the oldest and most prominent families of the Bluegrass. A cadet at Kentucky Military Institute, he obtained an appointment to the U. S. Military Academy at West Point and graduated ninth in his class in 1851. He served only a year in the cavalry before resigning due to ill health, and thereafter practiced law in partnership with Martin H. Cofer, served a term in the legislature, and then took his place with Buckner in organizing the State Guard. In April 1861 President Lincoln offered Helm a position as paymaster in the United States Army with the rank of major. It was a hard decision for Helm. Five years before he had married Emily Todd, sister of Mary Todd Lincoln. Helm and Lincoln were close, dear friends. Through the maze of conflicting loyalties, however, he saw the way he must take. To his brother-in-law he said no. Then, with an endorsement from Magoffin that claimed "some of the best blood of Ky. flows in his veins," Helm offered his services to the Confederacy. On October 19, 1861, he received his commission as colonel and orders to organize the 1st Kentucky Cavalry.[6]

While these horsemen trained at Bowling Green, the infantry regiments continued forming. With the 2d, 3d, and 4th regiments organized, the next in line was the 5th Kentucky, or so it would seem. In fact, without planning to, the Confederacy shortly found itself blessed with two 5th Kentucky infantries.

On October 1 Thomas Hunt surveyed the unorganized companies in and around Bowling Green, and six days later, with a colonel's commission in his pocket, he started forming his regiment. There were four companies in camp, among them the newly arrived Bloomfield contingent and the still-weary John Jackman. With them, Hunt established Camp Warren, created a camp guard, acquired a kettle drum and a Professor François Gevers to play it, and began the drill. The men stayed in wall tents with good wooden floors, seven men to the tent and one blanket among them. "The boards at first seemed pretty hard sleeping," wrote Johnny Green, "but it was not long before we looked back upon these comforts as princely luxuries." One luxury none of them recalled fondly, however, was Hunt's order to pull up all the ragweed within the camp limits. "Actual soldiering is so vastly different from ideal soldiering," lamented Jackman.

Hunt shortly relocated his camp to Russellville, where another three companies joined, as well as several more drums. At reveille each morning the field band marched through the streets of town. "The noise was sufficient to wake the Seven Sleepers," thought Jackman, but the men drilled the better for it. Better drilled, perhaps, but not entirely happy. For now they slept on the ground, and it was wet. The "Citizen Guards" of Louisville, Johnny Green's company, had enjoyed quite some distinction at Bowling Green for the luxury of their habitations. A jealous Johnny Jackman recalled, "They had wall tents scalloped and fringed and . . . they even had up lace curtains." There had been rugs on the wooden floors, and even a dresser or two. But when the move to Russellville came, Hunt emphatically denied transportation to carry all the boards for the tent floors. "Then the 'cussing' began," wrote Jackman. It "volleyed and thundered" all through the company. One of the "ringleaders" in the profanity was young Johnny

Green. He, too, was beginning to find soldiering a bit less fun than he expected.[7]

By late November Hunt returned his men to Bowling Green. It was said that he knew every man in his command by name, and as well an estimate of each man's pluck and stamina. It is not surprising, for this colonel took unusual care to look after his men. The last day's march into Bowling Green was in mud and pouring rain. Drenched, the men foraged for straw to spread beneath their tents. When Johnny Green returned to his tent he sank down on the ground and could not rise the next morning. He had measles. Hunt sent him to the hospital in town, and personally accompanied him to assure the very best accommodation and treatment.

Hunt's regiment did not muster regulation strength yet, but he still entered them formally into service. From the War Department in Richmond, Virginia, came orders designating his command the 5th Kentucky Infantry temporarily, pending enlistment of the remainder needed to fill the regiment. But then arose a problem. Some days before, on November 14, another regiment of Kentuckians reached regulation size and formally organized. Since the War Department's designation for Hunt's command was only an interim measure, awaiting completion of his regiment, it was now deemed proper that this new regiment should have the permanent appellation of 5th Kentucky. By the time Hunt was up to strength the next available number was 9th Kentucky but, for unknown reasons, Hunt did not receive that order for a full year. Thus, until October 1862, there were two Confederate regiments of infantry called the 5th Kentucky.[8]

This new 5th Kentucky was cut of the same cloth as the other regiments at Bowling Green. Its colonel was John S. Williams, called "Cerro Gordo" thanks to his Mexican War service, a balding, mutton-chopped, overweight fellow marvelously adept at lauding his own achievements. His regiment was formed largely of companies from the eastern part of the state, the men furnishing their own guns. Some were hardly men. Jimmie South of Company D stood tall for his age, lied, and enlisted at fourteen. So did Johnny Foster of Company B. He was thirteen.

Like many other companies in these regiments, the men of the 5th Kentucky often had quite a time leaving home, and quite a time afterward. Hiram Hawkins provided a good example. "I was among the first to raise the standard of rebellion in eastern Ky," he boasted proudly. Gathering several men along the way, he led his own former State Guardsmen to Prestonburg and there established the first recruiting camp in the area. He took command, and soon filled and armed several companies, many of them with fine Enfield rifles. But then Williams appeared on the scene with authority from Richmond to muster Hawkins' men into service as a regiment, and Hawkins began to perceive that there was no place in the regiment for him, after all he had done. He resigned as camp commander and tried to raise a mounted company to act as cavalry, but Williams would hear none of it. Frustrated again, Hawkins finally entered himself and his men as private soldiers. He did not stay down for long. Three days later his men elected him captain of their company, and on November 14, when the 5th Kentucky formally organized, the regiment voted almost unanimously to elect him major. Thus was patience, and ambition, rewarded.[9]

Still Kentucky could offer enough of her sons for one more regiment. When Buckner entered Kentucky he ordered Joseph H. Lewis to establish a camp at Cave City in Barren County, thirty miles northeast of Bowling Green. At the same time Buckner authorized Martin Cofer to recruit, hoping that both men would raise enough men to form two additional regiments. They proved energetic. On September 20 Lewis established his camp and three days later issued the obligatory broadside addressed "To the Public," in which he set forth the wrongs done to southern men in Kentucky. Lincoln was as corrupt and despotic as the Austrian or Russian monarchs, he declared. "Where is the honor of Kentucky" that her people should stand idle in their subjugation? Their only hope was to unite and show that they would defend themselves. "Then let every man come to the camp," he concluded. "Come at once. Delay is sure destruction."

This Lewis was a handsome fellow, blue-eyed, fair-complected, nearly six feet tall. He was a native of Barren County, and would turn thirty-seven while enlisting his men in October. He practiced law professionally until 1857, when he made an unsuccessful bid for Congress, then ran again in 1861, not expecting to win, but hoping to raise southern sympathies by publicizing his view of the issues. It worked. Defeated for office, he still won enough support to start the enlistment of several hundred men for his regiment. It was a support that his temperament alone might not have earned for him, for Lewis was not the friendliest of men. Ed Thompson said he was "as far removed from obsequiousness as any man living." Outwardly he displayed a scornful nature, irascible, begrudging, sometimes offensive. Once having made an enemy, he rarely did anything to heal the breach. Yet within lurked a compassionate, caring man, ever solicitous of the welfare of his men, one of those natures that, in spite of themselves, win the undying loyalty of those who follow.

Through late September and into October the recruits appeared. In some cases Lewis even sent agents to lead them out of Louisville. Cofer worked at his enlistments as well, but neither, by mid-November, produced enough men to organize regiments. Another compromise seemed in order. Lewis and Cofer agreed to consolidate their commands, just as Trabue did with some companies of his 4th Infantry, and on November 19 they formally organized the 6th Kentucky. Eight days earlier Lewis was commissioned its colonel, and Cofer lieutenant colonel. On November 27 Cofer consolidated the last two companies, defeating "the expectations of one or two men who had expected office." Still, as in almost every case in the formation of these Kentucky regiments, the idea of compromise for the good of the command took precedence over personal ambitions. Certainly the spirit of Henry Clay did not entirely go to dust with him.[10]

Meanwhile the artillery expanded. Byrne added a field piece captured at Bowling Green to his battery, and with it joined the 2d Kentucky at Green River. At the same time H. B. Lyon and Robert Cobb recruited a battery, with Lyon as captain and Cobb his first lieutenant. The Confederate Government furnished them with their complement of field pieces, but for some time they suffered with horses unfit for the arduous duty required. The battery was, at least, well supplied with ammunition, 1,032 rounds by mid-November.[11]

Just as Lyon's battery completed, yet another formed. On November 7 Buckner learned of an understrength battery available that might be attached to his Kentuckians, and that the 2d Kentucky was willing to provide the necessary men to fill it. Buckner got the guns, and on November 16 sixty-six men detailed from among the 2d, 3d, 4th, 5th (Hunt's), and 6th regiments. Early in December more men were provided, the entire Company B of the 4th Kentucky while, at the same time, the 2d Kentucky added twenty of its number to Byrne's battery. To captain the new battery Rice E. Graves was selected, an enormously popular young man, just twenty-three, who left West Point at the outbreak of war, leaving behind an almost spotless scholastic and deportment record.[12]

With Graves's battery, the recruiting of Buckner's Kentucky units was done. Even before some of the regiments were organized, they had been loosely combined into a brigade, for the time being commanded by Colonel Roger W. Hanson. Hawes resigned his commission on September 3, thus giving Hanson command of the 2d Kentucky and Hanson, as senior colonel, thereby naturally took over the informal brigade then forming. Here was a peculiar man in many ways, yet distinctly a Kentuckian.

He stood medium high, five feet, nine inches, a bit heavy, and frankly of rather a sinister aspect. Just thirty-four, he packed a good deal of living into his years. When barely twenty he went to Mexico in a company led by "Cerro Gordo" Williams, and conducted himself with a wild recklessness that quickly attracted notice. Yet there was sparkle to him as well. Campmates found that he had a sense of humor that "turned discomfort, difficulty, danger, absence from home and friends—everything—into sources of laughter and amusement."

There was a serious side to this Hanson, dead serious.

Just returned from the war, he apparently fell in love with a young lady who soon thereafter announced her engagement to Mr. William Duke. An embittered Hanson called on her and rather intemperately denounced Duke as a coward entirely unworthy of her. Naturally Duke asked for redress, and in January 1848 the two met in a secluded spot just across the Ohio River from Kentucky, near Vevay, Indiana. Hanson practiced with the pistols daily, as did Duke, both being pronounced excellent marksmen. Yet in their meeting they went three rounds of firing before blood flowed, a graze on Duke's knuckles. This satisfied neither, and a fourth round was called. Hanson missed his mark, but Duke's bullet shattered his opponent's right thighbone, causing Hanson to walk with a peculiar gait for the rest of his life. Duke married the young lady and Hanson immersed himself in the practice of law, with time out to go to California briefly during the Gold Rush.

Returning to Kentucky, Hanson ran for the legislature against his old captain, Williams. Here was a race, and here Hanson once again displayed his singular ability for denunciations. Williams campaigned on his Mexican War record, boasting proudly of the captured cannon he brought back to the state and of his being the first to plant the Stars and Stripes on the heights at Cerro Gordo. Well, Hanson had been there too, and he told a different story. The cannon had been spiked and abandoned to the Americans, not won from them in hand-to-hand combat, as Williams attested. And as for the heroism at Cerro Gordo, Williams' company broke and ran for cover at the first fire from a masked Mexican battery. Hanson told how he broke ranks and ran as fast as his legs would carry him when the enemy opened on them. He was six feet, three inches at the start of that run, he said, but in trying to keep up with Williams he lost six inches! He was certain he would be the first of the command to reach cover at the bottom of a hill, "but, by God, when I got there I found that Capt. Williams had preceded me and had the rest of the company already drawn up on dress parade." Meanwhile, other troops took Cerro Gordo. Relating this on the stump, Hanson would turn on his opponent and "with the utmost contemptuous gesture and insulting sneer designate him as 'Cerro Gordo Williams.'" Hanson lost the election by six votes, the irony of it being that Williams carried the derisive sobriquet Hanson gave him for the rest of his life, using it proudly and advantageously in furthering his political career.

Hanson finally won a seat in the legislature, and in 1860 vigorously supported the Union against the state's "fire eaters." Increasingly, however, his fears of federal encroachments persuaded him in another direction, first for neutrality, and finally toward the Confederacy. On August 19, 1861, he was commissioned a colonel and shortly thereafter took command of the 2d Kentucky. "He had, almost to perfection," wrote Ed Thompson, "that rare power of individualizing." Hanson called it "horse sense."

With his wit and perception and intelligence, there was also a measure of forgiveness. When his fellow officers from Kentucky raised money to buy him a fine horse and saddle, his old enemy William Duke—now riding with Morgan—contributed substantially, and the two became fast friends. It was appropriate that Duke should assist in having Hanson ride in comfort, since he had done so much to make it hard for him to walk.[13]

Hanson was in the saddle when General A. S. Johnston formally organized his Army of Central Kentucky on October 28. He brigaded the Kentuckians together, informally attaching the cavalry commands of Morgan and Helm to them. Buckner hoped to have the command of the outfit, now officially designated the 1st Kentucky Brigade. Johnston assigned him instead to command of a division, even though

Buckner "indicated my preference to be limited to the command of the Kentucky troops with whom I felt peculiarly identified." The decision saddened him, but he acquiesced. The loss was made less hurtful, as well, by the news that the man who would get command of the brigade was a good friend, perhaps the most popular Kentuckian of his day, and a person who just eight months before had been Vice President of the United States, John C. Breckinridge.[14]

Surely here was the most magnificent Kentuckian of them all and, as well, a man who represented within himself all of the turmoil that his state and her sons suffered in this year of the beginning, 1861. He was of the most distinguished blood in the Bluegrass. Grandfather was Jefferson's Attorney General. Father was Secretary of State of the Commonwealth before an untimely death ended his political rise. The son, John Cabell, was born January 16, 1821, in Lexington. Orphaned at an early age, he grew to manhood largely under the guidance of his uncle, Robert J. Breckinridge, a nationally known Presbyterian divine and an ardent friend of emancipation. John took to the law, as did all the Breckinridge men, and moved West for a time, toying once with the idea of settling in Jacksonville, Illinois. The irony is that two other members of the bar in that county were Stephen A. Douglas and Abraham Lincoln, both his opponents in the presidential election of 1860.

Back in Kentucky, Breckinridge identified officially with the Democratic Party, breaking with the family's Whig antecedents. When war came with Mexico, he did not immediately enlist, biding his time for a good position, which came in 1847, when he was made major of the 3d Kentucky Volunteers. Significantly, his appointment was the only one given to a Democrat by Kentucky's then Whig governor. It foretold things to come, for when Breckinridge returned from the war and entered politics, he displayed from the first a remarkable ability to win the votes even of those in the opposition.

The young major saw no action in Mexico, but he met many influential and later important officers—Robert E. Lee, U. S. Grant, John S. Williams, Roger Hanson, and perhaps Braxton Bragg. Once home in Lexington, he found his law practice too enervating to hold his interest. Politics seemed more his fare. In 1849 he won a seat in the legislature even though his district was predominantly Whig. Two years later he electrified the nation by winning the congressional seat in Henry Clay's old Ashland district. Many even believed that Clay himself privately supported the young Democrat. Once in Congress, Breckinridge quickly attracted attention for his oratorical abilities. Tall, over six feet, muscular, handsome to a fault, with deep-set blue eyes and gestures of infinite grace, he spellbound audiences. Breckinridge won re-election in 1853, and was offered various appointments, an ambassadorship, a territorial governorship, before he "retired" in 1855 at the age of thirty-four. Politics had almost ruined his personal finances, and he had to look to his family.

In 1856 he went to the Democratic convention as a delegate, and came home the vice-presidential nominee. No one expected it less than he. He was only five months past the constitutionally required minimum age. With his running mate, James Buchanan of Pennsylvania, Breckinridge won election in November, setting a precedent in the process by being the first executive candidate to campaign actively. He set another precedent when he took the oath of office in March 1857. He became, and remains, the youngest Vice President in his nation's history.

It was a troubled administration, little helped by Buchanan's being the oldest and weakest President in his country's career. The two did not get along. Breckinridge was not consulted at all during the critical days leading up to secession. Frequently spoken of himself as a probable President, Breckinridge had no wish to be involved in the election of 1860. He saw that, whoever got the vote, no one could really win in the current climate. When the Democrats met in convention, he gave strict orders not to place his name in nomination. Yet when the party split and a northern faction nominated Douglas, the Southerners—with large northern backing—selected Breckinridge. Determined to decline, he changed his mind when friends—among them Jefferson Davis—persuaded him that, by accepting, he would force Douglas and Constitutional Union candidate John Bell to withdraw. Then Breckinridge himself might withdraw, and the party reunite on a single candidate who could defeat Breckinridge's old friend Lincoln. The strategy did not work. Realizing from the outset that he was leading a "forlorn hope," Breckinridge accepted defeat in November. He polled second to Lincoln in the electoral college, and was the only candidate whose popular vote came almost equally from both sections of the country.

The Kentuckian was widely attacked as a secessionist and a friend of slavery. Both charges were false, yet he was strict in his construction of the Constitution. Elected to the Senate when his vice-presidential term expired, he spoke repeatedly for calm, for compromise, for federal recognition of the individual rights of the states. He espoused neutrality wholeheartedly, and worked and spoke widely to encourage the state to maintain its position. When his own son went to Camp Boone to enlist in the 2d Kentucky, it was against his father's wishes. In Lexington, he was chiefly responsible for preventing violence when Morgan wished to take "Lincoln guns" meant for the Home Guard. Breckinridge planned a series of "peace picnics" at which he would speak for neutrality and moderation. By the end of August, however, events got out of control. Though Breckinridge was no secessionist, many of the more powerful Union men were convinced that he was. And even if not, they wanted Kentucky for the Union, and someone of Breckinridge's force and popularity stood in the way. Consequently, they determined to arrest him early in September. The attempt failed and was not renewed, probably for want of charges that would hold. But Breckinridge was now on the defensive. He went to Frankfort to consult with friends, many of them good Union men. The Confederacy could not succeed, he told them. He knew as well that if he spoke out in favor of the Lincoln administration and its policy, he could expect to be rewarded amply with at least an important command in the United States Army, and probably with the presidency three years hence. But of course he could not do this. He must continue to stand for neutrality to the end. Friends pleaded with him to change his mind, but he could not. He was, he said, "already over the dam."

For the next ten days Breckinridge went unmolested, but the abandonment of neutrality on September 18 untied the hands of federal military men. The next day they issued orders for Breckinridge's arrest. The senator was warned in time to plan his escape. Forced out of the Union he loved since birth, he saw no other home for him but the Confederacy. Even now, he hoped secretly that somehow the two antagonists might compromise and reunite. His influence in Kentucky might help achieve the balance of power necessary to get the two sides talking as equals. But if compromise could not be met, he had no illusions. "I go where my duty calls me," he said in making his farewell. "It is a hopeless cause."

Accounts conflict on how Breckinridge eluded his would-be captors. Apparently he and a friend who accompanied him could find nothing better than a broken-down gray mare, which the two of them had to share. Breckinridge, one of the finest horsemen in a state of excellent riders, and his friend, a noted horse breeder, thus presented rather an ironic aspect bouncing along the road north of Lexington. Soon Breckinridge and his friend, Keene Richards, changed to a buggy and, accompanied by a slave boy, turned the horse toward the mountains to the east. At several points they were seen. "One of the figures was closely muffled," wrote one who believed Breckinridge was in the buggy, "and, whenever they were about meeting anyone, the negro boy raised himself so as to cover the muffled figure." Several members of the State Guard followed the buggy to act as bodyguard for Breckinridge, and when they reached Prestonburg enlisted with Hiram Hawkins. Behind him Breckinridge's enemies gloated over the fact that they had seemingly been right all along. By his flight, the senator confirmed the belief that he was a secessionist. None seemed to care that they had, in fact, forced him to flee. "John C. Breckinridge escaped from Lexington," blasted one editorial, "by skulking in a buggy behind a small nigger."

Now for the cause, Breckinridge spoke to raise recruits for the Kentucky regiments, went into Virginia, then to Knoxville, Tennessee, and on to Bowling Green to meet with Buckner. Approaching Buckner's camps, the senator met with an Alabama regiment sent to escort him into town. One soldier, obviously drunk, referred to the Kentuckian's flight from the Union and quipped, "As they wouldn't give you what you wanted over there, you can come now to us." Breckinridge only smiled. He had come back to Kentucky, to the Kentuckians forming under Buckner. Now, if he could, he would join them. On October 8 he issued his last public address, resigning his position in the United States Senate. He had committed no crimes, he said, yet he would be arrested. He had tried only to represent Kentucky's neutrality by resisting Lincoln's war measures. "I resign," he said, "because there is no place left where a Southern Senator may sit in council with the Senators of the North." The Federals daily violated the Constitution and the laws. Indeed, suspected secessionists languished in prison indefinitely without habeas corpus. Otherwise he would have allowed himself to be taken so that he might have his day in court. But now he urged Kentucky not to stand for it any longer. He wanted peace, but had to defend his birthright. He had no other choice but imprisonment or exile. "I intend to resist," he declared. He would defend his birthright, and to that end he now exchanged "with proud satisfaction, a term of six years in the Senate of the United States for the musket of a soldier." [15]

Of course, no one supposed that Breckinridge would be allowed to enter the lists as a private soldier. After meeting with him, Buckner wrote to Richmond on his behalf. "He will enter the army, if necessary, as a private soldier," said Buckner. However, Breckinridge "will accept any position that may be tendered him." The writer took it a step further by suggesting that Breckinridge be made a brigadier and be given command of the 1st Kentucky Brigade—since Buckner could not have it—or a similar command. No one need to be reminded that, as the best-known and -loved Kentuckian of his time, Breckinridge might be instrumental in rallying the men of the state to southern arms, and hopefully of bringing Kentucky into the Confederacy. The Richmond press expressed this view to the public later in October, even as Breckinridge arrived in the capital, having left Bowling Green to confer with President Jefferson Davis. "Kentucky cannot be rallied by Confederate generals or anything else. It can only be rallied by its own native citizens to whom they have a habit of looking up," they said. "Breckinridge . . . and others can bring Kentucky into line with the South."

There were actually some in Richmond who distrusted Breckinridge because he took so long to "go South." Had they known his views of the futility of the Confederate effort for independence, they would have been even less enchanted with him. But Davis was no fool. A Kentuckian himself, he wanted Kentucky. If anyone could give it to him, Breckinridge was the man. Despite apparently considering the former Vice President for the post of Secretary of War in the Cabinet, Davis chose the immediately wiser course of appointing him a general. On November 2, 1861, Breckinridge received the appointment and accepted it the next day. "No one doubts that he is now with us," wrote a clerk in his diary, "and will do good service." The Kentuckian left three days later to take command of the 1st Kentucky Brigade at Bowling Green.[16]

Ordered to assume command of the brigade on November 16, Breckinridge arrived in Bowling Green a few days early, and spent the interim speaking there and in surrounding communities, advocating secession. He helped organize a rump convention that was to meet in Russellville on November 18 to take Kentucky out of the Union. Yet, until Kentucky actually seceded, he could not bring his legalistic mind to countenance flying the Confederate flag in the state. He might do nothing about it at Bowling Green in Buckner's camps, but out on the hustings he could. After a speech at Hopkinsville, he rode in a buggy to Fairview for another talk. Before getting in the buggy, however, Breckinridge walked to the horse's head and removed a small Confederate flag from its headstall. "First I will take this flag down," he told the fifteen-year-old driver. "Wait, my boy, 'til Kentucky adopts that flag and then we'll do our best to keep it flying." For thirty miles the general and the teen-ager talked. Finally the boy, in wonder, said he thought it "took smart men to be Vice President's and Senators." Breckinridge winked to the others in the buggy and replied, "It does."[17]

It also took smart men to command an ill-supplied, undertrained, inexperienced brigade composed almost entirely of Kentuckians, perhaps the most independent Americans of them all. Certainly they tested his capacity in ways that politics never did though, as well, it required something of the politician to keep them in hand. Hanson temporarily held command until Breckinridge formally took over on November 16. He found an organization that on paper should have numbered 5,000 but that, in fact, totaled 3,400 infantry, 120 artillerymen in Byrne's battery, and 160 cavalrymen under Morgan. Even this was deceptive, for at any time at least 500 men lay ill, under arrest, or absent. Of the remainder, many still had no arms. For a man like Breckinridge, with no real military experience, such a command might have been a nightmare. Yet he brought to it advantages that no other could. Most of the men in the brigade voted for him in 1856 and 1860. Scattered throughout the regiments were relatives, from his son in the 2d Kentucky to cousins in the others. The colonels of the regiments were old friends, even those like Hanson who had been political foes. Indeed, in appointing his own staff, the general more often than not chose men who had opposed him on the stump, but their personal loyalty to him was unquestioned. And these Kentuckians were mostly young men. Breckinridge always felt a special fondness for youth, perhaps because of his own achievements when so young himself. Young men gravitated to him as well, and strong bonds of friendship grew with men like the youthful Rice E. Graves. In time he came to be their father, and they his 4,000 sons. The loss of each one of them was to him a pain, and for both separation from one another was unthinkable. Their story would be his, and the ever-increasing attachment and affection between them would stand unexcelled in the Confederate service.[18]

Now he must care for his children and ready them for battle. There must be a commissary to feed them. That would be Major Alfred Boyd. There must be a quartermaster to clothe them. That would be Major Clint McClarty, who had done his best to aid Breckinridge in 1860. Thomas T. Hawkins would be his aide-de-camp, a general assistant and errand runner, and George B. Hodge became Breckinridge's adjutant. Hodge graduated from the United States Naval Academy at Annapolis and had enlisted as a private in the summer. Now he ran Breckinridge's headquarters.

The men needed clothing. Winter approached. The men of the 2d Kentucky, 940 of them, shivered without overcoats. Even before Breckinridge effected something for them, their own Lieutenant Colonel James Hewitt provided coats for them from his own purse at an estimated cost of over $10,000. Items obtained from the government came more slowly. Requisitioning enough clothing for an entire company, the quartermaster might only receive complete uniforms for a half dozen. Ed Porter Thompson, first sergeant for Company E of the 6th Kentucky, received in one shipment 38 military jackets, but only 16 shirts, 7 caps, and 12 pairs of trousers. Worse yet, the government sent only four pairs of "draws," underwear. When Trabue ordered 250 pairs of shoes for the 4th Kentucky, what he received were all too large. He returned them for a smaller size. It took so long that, in the dead of winter, many of his men went barefooted. And much was too small. There were a number of large men in the brigade, above average height and weight. Hunt had several in his regiment. When specially ordered clothing for them finally arrived, it did not fit. Hunt returned it and requested a proper size, but feared that "with the same kind of delay about it the Winter will have entirely passed by." The poor Kentuckians even had to guard what they did obtain. Lloyd Tilghman, perhaps feeling that his early connection with the Kentuckians gave him the right, adopted the unfortunate habit of seizing materials from the Kentuckians' quartermaster stores. In one foray alone he liberated 1,722¼ yards of "jeans" that belonged to the 5th Kentucky. Only earnest protests from Hodge and Breckinridge put an end to Tilghman's depredations.[19]

The situation with the brigade's arms, even after the efforts of the previous summer, was equally unsatisfactory. The story of the 2d Kentucky alone told the tale. On October 29 Bob Johnson reported that, of 832 men in the ranks on that date, 131 had no guns at all, 63 had unreliable weapons, 94 others carried flintlocks, 270 men had guns that were "totally useless," and a few even carried shotguns made of scrap iron. Only 250 men had good muskets. Many of the guns in the regiment had no locks, or firing mechanisms. Others had split barrels, their hardware falling off for want of screws, and some with springs so weak they would not drive the hammers with force sufficient to fire the gun. "Most of them were manufactured between 1803 & 1815," Johnson complained. Others believed some of the weapons dated back at least to Miles Standish. "The men are afraid to discharge many of the guns," lamented Johnson, "and have no confidence in their use."

"There were squirrel rifles of every age, style, and bore," Ed Thompson said, "shot-guns, single-barreled, double-barreled, old and new, flintlock, percussion, or no lock at all; carbines of every character, pistols of every patent, and huge knives that were looked upon as too little to be useful if they weighed less than two pounds avoirdupois."[20]

Even before Breckinridge arrived, Johnson got 250 good rifles for the 2d Kentucky. When the new brigade commander took over, he worked immediately on lack of arms. From his old political friend, Governor John Letcher of Virginia, he got 1,000 percussion muskets less than two weeks after assuming command. He apportioned them among the five regiments according to need, meanwhile thanking Letcher for the gift "to my ill-armed brigade." This still left a variety of weapons—Harpers Ferry rifles, Belgian rifles, Allen rifles, smoothbore muskets, Mississippi rifles, and a few shotguns—that required a seemingly exasperating variety of ammunition. Yet, by mid-December Breckinridge had nearly 100,000 rounds of varying kinds of cartridges in hand for the brigade. The New Year found Hunt's 5th Kentucky—soon to be the 9th Kentucky—the only regiment still not well armed. Hunt had only 246 rifled muskets, and no proper ammunition. "The Regiment may be said to be now in almost an unarmed condition." he complained. To keep as many able men armed as possible, he redistributed the guns from the sick to the healthy. Still, if he could not be better armed, he felt he was useless. Breckinridge complained as well that if the government could not provide guns for the 5th, then he might as well send the men home. Eventually Hunt, too, would have sufficient weapons, but only after months of struggle.[21]

Unfortunately, there were plenty of sick men whose guns were available for redistribution. "Thare is a good many of hour Rigement Sick with the mezals," H. E. Ferguson wrote from the 6th Kentucky. They seemed to fill the "horse pittle," he said. At any day in November the surgeons in Bowling Green reported between 300 and 500 Kentuckians in their hospitals. In December it escalated to as high as 840 on a single day. "The most common and alarming sickness," wrote Ed Thompson, "was a singular type of measles, that, in many instances, baffled the skill of the medical department, and carried off scores of men." Doctors established excellent hospital facilities in and around Bowling Green, but they could not combat the spread of infectious disease with much success. On some days nearly 15 per cent of the brigade was in the hospital. On December 5, one fourth of the 1st Kentucky Brigade reported sick. In the 4th Kentucky one half the regiment was down at one time. Many died, and when one did, his fellow soldiers lamented, "He has gone before getting a fire at the Yanks."

Breckinridge did what he could to combat disease. He placed guards at the head of the stream providing the camp to keep men and animals from polluting the water. When smallpox or fevers appeared in the private homes near camp, he placed guards around the houses to keep the men from coming in contact with their occupants. In mid-December 1861, the crisis passed abruptly, immunities built up, and the sick list stabilized. The men learned a little of sanitation and proper preparation of food, and became accustomed to camp life. After a time the surgeons reported more cases of "nostalgia" than measles. This nostalgia could kill, though. When asked what it was, one of the brigade's surgeons replied, "Home-sickness, that's the plain English of it." Yet some men would die. All the surgeons could do for nostalgia, "malaise," and similar psychological "diseases" was to prescribe placebos, which became standard practice.

As for the ever-present malingerer who did anything to escape duty, the Kentucky surgeons proved more than a match. One morning at sick call, a Kentuckian claimed he was ill, marched to the surgeon's tent, and stuck out his tongue. Alas, it seemed in perfect order. Undaunted, he next determined to starve himself in hopes of appearing deathly ill and obtaining a discharge. He was too sick to eat, he would say. But starve though he did, the hard-hearted surgeons would not give in. Faced with sure death from hunger, he finally opted instead for the less certain lottery of the battlefield. In later years he delighted in telling around the campfire the tale of his defeat at the hands of the doctors.[22]

Of course, the would-be malingerer wanted to escape the grinding routine of drill and fatigue duty. Almost from the first, Breckinridge set his men digging trenches, performing engineering chores, carpentry, even bricklaying in the Bowling Green camps. And the drill seemed incessant. Breckinridge detailed his old clerk from the vice-presidential days, Charlie Ivey, to brigade headquarters in spite of Hanson's loud protests at losing his drillmaster. But before leaving, Ivey sat several nights with Hanson in his tent and instructed him in the latest company and regimental drill, using grains of corn to represent the men as he acted out the procedure on a tabletop. Breckinridge ordered battalion drill every day, and skirmish drill as well. Regiments were to report daily before noon to headquarters, and Sundays before divine services. Men who knew bayonet drill were assigned to instruct officers so they could in turn teach the men.[23]

It was not without mishap. Thanks to Major Thomas B. Monroe, the 4th Kentucky was perhaps the best drilled at the time. He started a school for officers, gave them daily lessons, with recitations, and then drilled them in the field, with mixed results. Lieutenant Nat Clayton of Company A had more than a bit of difficulty with military terminology. When Monroe asked him in class what maneuver he would perform if an enemy appeared on his right front, Nat replied with some hesitation, "I would move the reegi*ment* stauchendiciler to the front." Another captain of the 4th Kentucky proved equally inept in the argot of close-order drill, but made his point. Monroe asked him what he would do to meet an approaching enemy, and Captain John Trice replied, "Well, Major, I can't answer that according to the books, but I would risk myself with the Trigg County boys, and go in on main strength and awkwardness."

The language of an Army proved baffling to the mountain boys in the ranks. One private of the 6th Kentucky returned from the commissary with a pot full of potatoes not listed on his requisition. "I went to the conersary to draw some visions," was his explanation, "and seein' these taters I consecated them."

Guard duty at night was a particularly onerous task for these citizen soldiers, especially as they had to prevent their campmates from passing out of the lines and into Bowling Green for liquor and women. "It makes a man feel very serious to Stand way of[f] in the dark by him-

Self when exspecting the enemy," complained Ferguson, "and when bed time seems near I miss my soft bed on the frozen ground." A password was assigned each night, without which no one could leave camp, and generally it was chosen from military history or jargon. The night Corporal Leander Washington Applegate of Company H, 9th Kentucky, stood guard, the word was "Borodino." His beat brought him near the sentinel at the back of some tents of one company. To prevent would-be revelers from hearing the password, he cupped his hand to his mouth and whispered the sign.

"What is it?" said the sentinel rather loudly.

"Borodino," whispered Applegate again.

"What is it?" the sentinel said again, in a lower tone.

"Borodino," said Applegate, a little louder.

The scene repeated several times, the sentinel growing ever more quiet, and Applegate ever louder. Finally, exasperated, the corporal fairly shouted into the other man's ear.

"B-o-r-o-d-i-n-o, by God! Now do you understand it?"

Yes, the sentinel did understand it now, and so did most of the men in the nearby tents. "Thus armed with the mystic word," wrote one of them, they "passed the lines that night and had a 'huge' time in town."[24]

Besides drilling the men, Breckinridge and his officers had to impose discipline, no easy task with these independent Kentuckians. Some of the backwoods boys simply did not understand rules. One, chided for leaving his guard post to light his pipe, thought he adequately excused himself when he explained that it was only "a little cob pipe." Breckinridge repeatedly issued orders prohibiting firing guns in camp. To the men this simply seemed the most logical way of changing loads. There were the little matters of pilfering and petty thievery always attendant to a volunteer army. One man caught filling his haversack from a hogshead at the supply depot was turned over to Colonel Hunt, who read the charge against him. "I did get the sugar," replied the soldier, "and was caught in the act; but I do not think you ought to punish me, Colonel, as I always give you part of every thing I *find.*" Hunt tumbled to the joke and dropped the charges. Indeed, some officers tacitly approved the pilfering. One captain of the 4th Kentucky lectured his men on not breaking ranks on the march to raid orchards and barns. The men seemed to listen, but the next time they passed a field of apple trees they dispersed without a word to fill their pockets. "Boys," the captain called after them, "if you *will* go, bring your captain a few."[25]

One of the best watchdogs on camp discipline was Hanson. "Old Flintlock," the men called him or, in reference to his stiff limb, "Bench-leg." His methods were, to say the least, unorthodox. Believing that there were too many malingerers on the sick list trying to avoid duty, he published an order that henceforward there would be only two sick men at a time in each company. Just how well he was able to enforce the order is conjecture, but he tried in his way. Almost every day he visited the 2d Kentucky's hospital. "His insight into character was extraordinary," wrote a Kentuckian at Bowling Green. Hanson despised dissimulation and sham. It aroused in him an ire that had bizarre consquences upon his features. The individual parts of his face seemed to work without concert, his head moving in quick, jerking contrast to his otherwise heavy, "inactive manner." He had, said a friend, "a German face with all the Irish expressions."

"Sick! sick!" he exploded to a malingerer. "Why, I was twelve months with the Army in Mexico, and wasn't sick a day." He used the same tactic on those begging furloughs. "What, sir! Furlough? Now, I was twelve months in Mexico, and never had a furlough." And so it went. Perhaps the men took him seriously on these issues. For sure, it did not work when it came to drinking.

A Kentuckian was, almost by definition, a man with a powerful interest in Bourbon, the more so in the boring routine of camp life at Bowling Green. With the ingenuity of soldiers, many of them found liquor where their superiors thought there was none. Finally, Basil Duke of Morgan's company confiscated the entire stock of the "article" from a nearby store that had been selling it to the men. He put it under guard inside the camp, but of course could not keep its presence long a secret. Soon one of the guards exhibited signs of having had commerce with the prisoner, and before long others were drunk as well. Duke reluctantly took the whisky back to the store owner, feeling it was safer there, but of course the merchant immediately began selling it again, and Duke narrowly escaped arrest for the unauthorized confiscation.

"Bench-leg" Hanson's remedy proved no more effective. His own fondness for whisky was well known. Consequently, when one day he found a drunken soldier in camp, a number of men gathered round for the inevitable reminiscence of the days in Mexico. Sure enough it came.

"Drunk here, eh? Drunk!" said Hanson. "I was twelve months in Mexico, and in all that time . . ." He paused for a moment, reflecting, and then the men laughed. Without another word he turned abruptly and walked away.[26]

Not all breaches of discipline by these Kentuckians could be laughed away, and there were many. "Give them officers that they love, respect, and rely on," Duke said of Kentucky soldiers, "and any thing can be accomplished with them." But they were "almost irrepressibly fond of whisky," incorrigible about straggling and escaping camp when not on active campaign, and "always behaving badly" when there was time to fill. Many of their transgressions were in the name of good fun, like the time that men of the 4th Kentucky stole a valuable piece of camp cookery from the 9th, and the latter retaliated by purloining every camp utensil belonging to the other regiment in one masterful night raid.

Other pranks were not so easily overlooked. Men of Morgan's command broke into a church, apparently seeking shelter, and Breckinridge ordered them arrested and punished. To protect the citizens of Bowling Green—whose feelings toward all these soldiers in their midst were mixed—Breckinridge canceled all leaves on December 1 and restricted the entire command to the camps. Yet there were still a few, men who learned the magical passwords, who got into the town. There they drank and whored. Not a few of them, like poor George Allen of Hanson's Company G, came back to camp with gonorrhea.

On November 8 alone, thirty-eight men of the brigade sat under arrest. For that month there was a daily average of nineteen men in the guardhouse, and it went higher in December. Interestingly, the 2d Kentucky, eldest of the regiments, acted the part of unruly older child by providing the majority of offenders. Indeed, on some days the guardhouse was in fact little more than a bivouac for the 2d Kentucky. In the last two months of 1861, 75 per cent of the men arrested came from Hanson's command. It is small wonder that "Old Flintlock" made a habit of visiting the guardhouse every day to lecture its inmates on their sins. The Kentucky men took their punishment cheerfully, so long as they did not feel it degrading.

There were those, of course, who would not stay long enough to be punished. The number reported as absent without leave took a sharp jump in early December, many of them, too, from the 2d Kentucky. Fortunately, most returned, but not all. There were desertions, two in December from the ranks of "Bench-leg," and another just after the New Year. The 5th Kentucky lost six at least from Bowling Green. Guards apprehended many, but fortunately the war was too young yet to warrant making them examples by execution. The time would come, however.[27]

The officers, too, had much to learn, including discipline. Some just could not count, or did not think to. Hodge had to be instructed by Colonel Hunt to keep better track of the details he ordered for police and camp duty, having ordered more in details than the 5th Regiment had in men. Officers lagged in forwarding their reports to brigade headquarters, often embarrassing Breckinridge with his superiors.

"I think I am under one of the Best Captains in the world," said a recruit in Lewis' regiment of his company officer. Yet occasionally they abused the men, and here lay real danger when dealing with Kentuckians. Major John R. Throckmorton, cantankerous at any time, gave one man a terrible time when the offender merely remarked on the size of his horse's lower lip. "What in the hades is that to you?" shouted Throckmorton. "What have you got to do with it? Am I responsible for his lip? Did I make it? Every blamed fool I meet has something to say about this horse's lip. I believe there are more blamed fools in this army around Bowling Green—especially among the Kentucky troops—than anywhere else in the world." In response to apologies Throckmorton added, "You've got too much lip yourself." A few minutes later he turned and shouted, "See here, I've thought this thing over, and have come to the conclusion that I ought to shoot the next man who alludes to this horse's lip."

Jealous of the dignity of his Kentuckians, Breckinridge would not allow officers to degrade them. When Lieutenant Thomas Steele of Company E, 4th Kentucky, did "wantonly maltreat abuse and oppress" Private Ed Bishop of the 6th Infantry, Breckinridge ordered the officer publicly reprimanded in a general order, and furthermore directed him to apologize to Bishop's colonel. Even more pointed was the episode of an officer who told a private to sweep his tent for him. The private promptly responded that the captain might "go to hell."

The officer arrested the soldier immediately and sent him to the guardhouse, thinking nothing more of it. Breckinridge learned of the incident, mounted at once, and rode to the captain's tent, whipping his horse with his hat in his haste.

"Sir," said the breathless general, "I understand you have ordered a private to sweep about your tent, and he has refused, and you sent him to the guardhouse."

"I did, sir."

"I want you to understand that when a private refuses to voluntarily sweep out my tent I will do it myself. They are not menials in [this] brigade. They are all gentlemen, and you have no right to command one of them to do a menial service. Now you go to the guardhouse and apologize to the soldier you have insulted and sweep about your own tent, or you will take his place."

It is small wonder that the men of the 1st Kentucky Brigade came to form such an unusual attachment for this general. Not only would he protect them from harm without, but also from bullying within.[28]

The advancing winter only added to the boredom of garrison life in and around Bowling Green. "The severity of the winter," wrote a Mississippian, "exceeded anything I had ever known." The snow lay on the ground for weeks, freezing everything. Icy winds raged through the camps. Orders from brigade headquarters prohibited using farmers' fence rails for firewood but, as Johnny Green said, "we were actually freezing & had no axes to cut fire wood." Colonel Hunt, realizing the plight of his men, gave them a way around the prohibition by telling them they must only refrain from burning "whole rails." Soon there were roaring fires made from pieces of rails. "The truth is," wrote Green, "it was but little time before every rail in that fence had been converted into pieces."

The men built rude fireplaces of sod in their tents, used more "pieces" of rails and other lumber to floor them, and found straw to soften their beds. "It is wonderful how comfortable we made ourselves," Green recalled. There were a few camp entertainments. The 4th Kentucky had the beginnings of a regimental band, and in the 2d, Private Bob Chapman, a Pennsylvanian by birth, entertained the men with his violin. "Shoot-the-cat," they called him. There were political diversions here, as well. The Provisional Government of Kentucky having formed at Russellville on November 20, the camps at Bowling Green swarmed with minor politicians. Many of them enlisted in the brigade immediately after signing their so-called ordinance of secession. Their new "governor," Breckinridge's cousin by marriage,

George W. Johnson, established himself in the town both to conduct state affairs with Richmond and to help look after the interests of the 1st Kentucky Brigade. Here and there a wife, like Mrs. Phil Lee, made her way to Bowling Green to look after a husband. Company B of the 2d Kentucky did not have wives to entertain them, but they did have a mascot dog, Frank. And there was always discussion of events in the North, particularly federal debate on raising Negro soldiers. Should that happen, decided men of the 6th Kentucky, then they were "in favor of the South hoisting the black flag," neither asking nor giving quarter, and shooting anyone found advocating the use of black troops.

On celebratory occasions a little whisky was permitted, though it was always more plentiful in the camps of regiments from other states. Reuben Davis of Mississippi kept a full barrel of "Kentucky shuck," obtained chiefly as a medicinal for his men with measles. Yet every few days Breckinridge himself stopped by Davis' tent for a taste. "He was a goodly sight," wrote Davis, "sitting on stool or table, with a glass of old shuck in his hand, and that grand voice of his vibrating through the tent like a deep-toned bell." The Kentuckian asked how Davis came by such a luxury, and Davis said it was because General Johnston, commanding the Army, favored his Mississippians and relied on their antiquated shotguns to save his Army when danger came. Breckinridge laughed and said Johnston surely was right. "Men armed with those guns *ought* to have everything possible to support their spirits, even genuine old Kentucky shuck." Whenever Breckinridge left Davis he usually produced a small demijohn "artfully concealed somewhere," and as the Kentuckian put it, "loaded up for emergencies." Davis always remembered those good days. "I fancy I can see him laughing and merry," he wrote of the Kentuckian. "He was not only a most elegant gentleman, but genial and full of spirit, and ready to meet the worst of days with a sort of gay courage that sat well upon his stalwart manhood."[29]

Finally Christmas came. Breckinridge had challenged the commander of the 1st Missouri Infantry to drill against the 2d Kentucky on Christmas Eve but, learning how good the Missourians were, he wisely backed out. It was just as well. This was the first Christmas of the war, the first away from home. The men of the brigade needed the time to themselves. It was a cold Christmas, but they ate well. Johnny Green's mess bought a turkey and he made biscuits. "We thought we had a sumptuous dinner for soldiers," he wrote. Others made eggnog and cakes and bought pies. Shipments of chickens, eggs, apples, butter, bread, cakes, hams, and turkeys arrived from back home to enliven the holiday.

That evening an anonymous soldier of the 4th Kentucky wrote in the clothing account book of Company C his verdict on the day, and the war: "Dec 25th 1861, The birth day of Christ our redeemer finds our country Struggling in the holy cause of liberty with the vile horde of Robbers & assasins sent to burn and destroy by their master Abraham Lincoln who occupies the chair at Washington." The 1st Kentucky Brigade was trained now, armed in a fashion, and ably led. The coming New Year would show them the test. The writer and all his fellow Kentuckians would have their chance to fight in "the holy cause of liberty." How they would stand in battle, and where they would be on Christmas next, none had the prescience to foretell.[30]

FOUR

"The War Is About Over for Us"

COLONEL JOSEPH H. LEWIS of the 6th Kentucky Infantry already knew that his men would stand and fight. At least, fourteen of them would. As far back as October 10, 1861, his men shed first blood in Kentucky when the stalwart fourteen, guarding the home of a southern sympathizer in Barren County, fired on a party of Federals, killing one and wounding several more. Thereafter nearly two months passed before another Kentuckian fired his rifle in anger. Breckinridge's brigade divided its time between training in Bowling Green and occupying Russellville, the Green River crossing, and parts in between.

While "Old Joe" Lewis inflicted the first casualties, it was "Uncle Tom" Hunt's 5th Kentucky that felt the first pain of battle, modest though it was. Hunt occupied Russellville early in November, and on December 1 retired to Bowling Green, leaving a detail of thirteen behind to guard the crossing of the Louisville & Memphis Railroad at Whippoorwill Bridge. On December 5 a body of about ninety Home Guards approached, intent upon destroying the bridge. Its defenders made a gallant stand until surrounded, when they surrendered, but not before George Campbell and Hatch Jupin were killed, and Joe Wilson severely wounded. Ironically, theirs was the only blood that the Kentucky Brigade would ever shed on its native soil. The remaining Kentuckians were taken as prisoners, not to be released for nearly a year.[1]

Since the episode at Whippoorwill Creek, the only action seen by the Kentuckians was an occasional march to meet reported enemies

who did not materialize. Nothing could be more debilitating to their
martial ardor, particularly when this winter marching was so exhaust-
ing and cold. On December 21 Breckinridge received a report that an
enemy column was actually moving toward Bowling Green. He was ordered to move the next day to meet it. Early on December 22 the regiments formed to march twenty-five miles east toward Skeggs Creek.
The men hoped this was to be the start of a campaign to move on
Louisville and liberate the state, and cheer after cheer rang from their
icy breath. They struck their tents and started the march, soon realizing that they were not on their way to Louisville. The mood turned
more gloomy when the muddy road started clinging to their feet and
the ice-cold rain that fell all day soaked their uniforms. By afternoon
the rain froze as it fell, and a north wind drove the sleet into their
faces. Hunt, riding at the head of the 5th Kentucky, looked back constantly to see his men shivering in the cold, often wading through
swollen creeks only to have their soaked trousers freeze stiff around
their legs. Finally he dismounted from Old Pomp, threw the bridle
over his arm, and henceforward marched on foot through the mud
and streams with his men. They made only ten miles that day,
bivouacking at a place called Merry Oaks. There was little merriment.
"We pitched our tents that night over the grass which was covered
with sleet," wrote Gervis Grainger of the 6th Kentucky. The next
morning they awoke to find the ground frozen and a layer of snow
over their camp. Then came word that the enemy was not approaching after all. There was nothing to do but return whence they came.
Along the way they passed the debris of their march of the day before.
Some men, for whom this had been the first real trek of the war, burdened themselves with up to fifty pounds and more of food and clothing, extra shoes, even slippers. "We also carried knives from eighteen
to twenty inches long," said Grainger, "with which we expected to
hack the Yankees up on sight." Now they left much of this excess by
the roadside in lightening their heavy loads. "A Soldier has a hard
road to travel," complained Private Ferguson. Ever after the Kentuckians spoke with sobriety of the "Merry Oaks march." It was one of
the "hard times" they would as soon forget. [2]

If the Kentuckians themselves enjoyed relative inactivity, however,
other events taking place in Kentucky and Tennessee soon changed
that. General Albert S. Johnston had established a defensive line that
ran from Cumberland Gap at the southeast corner of the state,

through Bowling Green, to Columbus on the Mississippi. On January 19, 1862, at Logan's Cross Roads eighty miles east of Bowling Green, a small federal army defeated Confederate defenders led by Brigadier General George B. Crittenden—son of the senator—and thus pierced the right of Johnston's line. A few days later a Union army led by U. S. Grant joined with gunboats in moving against Fort Henry on the Tennessee River just a few miles south of the Kentucky line. Midway between Columbus and Bowling Green, this fort and neighboring Fort Donelson on the Cumberland River blocked two waterways that provided a virtual highway into the heart of Confederate Tennessee. Lloyd Tilghman commanded at Fort Henry. Surrounded, he had no choice but to surrender the fort on February 6. The very next day Grant moved on Fort Donelson. Should that bastion fall, then Johnston's center at Bowling Green would be dangerously exposed and he would have no choice but to abandon it, and Kentucky.

On January 20 Johnston ordered 8,000 men from Bowling Green to be sent under Brigadier General John B. Floyd to Clarksville, Tennessee, within supporting distance of Donelson. Floyd took his own brigade and, to fill out the required strength, Buckner added to it the 2d Kentucky and Rice Grave's battery. Floyd left the Kentuckians at Russellville until February 8 when, with Fort Henry gone, he had to bring every available man to Donelson. That day Buckner put Hanson and Graves on trains and sent them south to Clarksville, while in Bowling Green those left behind grumbled. "Buckner's pets," the other Kentuckians called Hanson's men. "Our regiment envied the Second," wrote a man of the 4th Kentucky, "and thought General Buckner displayed a great deal of partiality in selecting it." Buckner himself accompanied the trains to Clarksville. There the men boarded a steamer for Dover, Tennessee, remained there until February 10, and then marched into their places in line at Donelson. It would be a long time before their comrades in Bowling Green heard from them again.[3]

But they were busy that day themselves. Three days before, Johnston decided that Fort Donelson could not hold for long, and that he would have to give up his Kentucky line and abandon Bowling Green. On the evening of February 11 orders went to Breckinridge to be ready to evacuate the next morning. Without actually knowing what was happening, the Kentuckians felt a great uneasiness. Some whispered that Kentucky was to be abandoned. Yet others still held to the hope that they were actually to advance farther into the state. At 9 A.M., February 12, the birthday of another Kentuckian now waging war against them, the men of the brigade lined up on the road awaiting instructions. "The Kentucky Brigade experienced nothing but gloom and apprehension on that morning," wrote Ed Thompson. Johnny Green found the men "altogether in doubts as to our movements." The men awaited the order that would tell them to face north and march to liberate their homes and families, or else turn south and abandon all. They were a few miles north of Bowling Green this morning, and "it was with sinking, sickened hearts that their faces were turned toward Bowling Green." They were going south. Kentucky was left to its fate.

Breckinridge issued strict rules for the march, and was mortified to see them ignored all the way by his dispirited regiments. In fact, in their gloom many of his officers failed even to read the orders to the men. The column straggled badly on the road into Bowling Green. Here, settled for the night in huts left by Hanson, the men briefly revived hope that they would face north again the next morning. But it was not to be so. The next morning's marching orders set them on the road south toward Nashville, ordering all the sick of the brigade to precede them on trains. Breckinridge's command would be the rear guard of the retreating army. He left a company of Trabue's 4th Kentucky as brigade rear guard, sent Morgan's cavalry in his front, and marched south, 2,478 strong. Behind him the advancing Federals, knowing the evacuation was afoot, closed in on Bowling Green and shelled the city even before all the Confederates had gone.[4]

That night Breckinridge bivouacked a few miles north of Franklin, Kentucky. The weather, mild for the past few days, now turned bitterly cold. On the morning of February 14, St. Valentine's Day, snow carpeted the ground. The command arose early, but got no farther than Franklin, when they were halted. Standing in the cold, with an icy north wind seemingly trying to push them out of Kentucky, they straggled in large numbers and went into town, stealing food and whisky. The march resumed, only to stop again, with more plundering of private property. Hundreds of yards of rail fence along the road quickly became a string of fires to warm their frostbitten hands and feet. Then came the march again.

At last they reached the state line. Hodge caught the mood of the moment. "For the Kentuckians all was apparently lost. Behind their retiring regiments were the graves of their fathers, and the hearthstones about which clustered every happy memory of their childhood. . . . Everything which could contribute to crush the spirits and weaken the nerves of men, seemed to have combined." In a symbolic act done perhaps unconsciously, or perhaps to give heart to the men, Breckinridge, his staff, and the field officers dismounted in what Hodge termed a "common impulse," and took their places on foot at the head of the column. "With sad and solemn countenances, but with erect and soldierly bearing," wrote Hodge, they led the brigade across the line and into Tennessee. Breckinridge was the first to cross. He could not know or suspect that, with the irony so beloved of history, he would be the last of them ever to return to Kentucky."[5]

That night they camped in the rain and sleet, then marched on through the snow the next day. They had stayed the night inside old huts with ventilation so poor that the fires burned for warmth made many of the men ill from inhaling the smoke. Yet this day, February 15, they marched twenty-seven miles, some of it at double time to meet a supposed threat to their route of retreat. The alarm proved false, but the men found that the excitement warmed their blood and girded them to continue the march. The next day they crossed the Cumberland River bridge and entered Nashville, to find much of the city ablaze. Some thought the fires were to honor their arrival. In fact, panicked by the collapse of Johnston's defense line, many citizens fled their city, and others burned anything that might be valuable to the enemy. Yet the Kentuckians marched on. "Where are we going?" John Marshall of the 4th Kentucky asks. The question courses through the column, but none can answer. Remembering the old lady's injunction never to turn the backs of his new socks to the enemy, Marshall began to fear "the heels of my socks are like 'the wicked, who flee when no man pursueth.' "[6]

They did not stop in Nashville, but marched five miles beyond on the road to Murfreesboro. As they passed through the Tennessee capital, Breckinridge, who had been quiet and reflective since crossing the state line, confided in Captain John Cripps Wickliffe of Hunt's regiment. "He told me that there was no hope for the Confederacy, unless there was an uprising of the Northern Democrats to stay the coercive arm of the Federal Government, and that, as he had no expectation of that, there was nothing before us but to do our duty to the end, and make any sacrifice for our convictions which honor and manhood demanded."

And here it was, perhaps—none can say for sure—that Breckinridge minted a name for his command. To be sure, they were the 1st Kentucky Brigade, a designation they guarded jealously in the months to come. But there was more to them than that. They were Kentucky's sons, his sons. Yet they were forcibly taken from their mother state, and he, their father, might lose them at any time, as he had already lost Hanson and the 2d Kentucky. Unable, like Tennessee or Mississippi or Alabama soldiers, to see their homeland and, with fortune, visit their firesides, the Kentuckians were now outcasts, fighting for a cause their state denied. They were orphans of the storm, and Breckinridge regarded them as such. He did not call them so in public, it would be too demoralizing, but one day in agony he would give to them a name they bore with fierce pride to death and posterity. Now, perhaps, already he regarded them as the "Orphan Brigade."[7]

Orphans they were, and none more so than Roger W. Hanson and his rowdy regiment. Even as Breckinridge rode through Nashville, "Old Flintlock" and his men marched on their way to a place farther from home than ever they imagined.

When Hanson reached Clarksville, he met with General Gideon J. Pillow, a Mexican War veteran now directing the marshaling of troops for Fort Donelson. "The redoubtable Gen Pillow," as Hanson called him, ordered the Kentucky regiment and battery to proceed immediately to Donelson, which they did by steamboat. When he arrived, Hanson found a distressing situation. Fort Donelson consisted of a large earthwork erected on high ground on the south side of the Cumberland River, three quarters of a mile west of Dover, Tennessee. General Floyd, now in overall command, had just fifteen thousand men to defend over two miles of entrenchments that Pillow had begun building after the fall of Fort Henry. Grant, whose numbers were unknown but certain to be larger, was advancing overland while a gunboat fleet steamed up the river to attack Floyd from his rear. When Hanson marched into the entrenchments, Pillow sent him to the extreme right of the line, closest to Fort Donelson itself, with Hanson's own right resting near the river. On February 11, immediately upon taking his place, Hanson began constructing more trenches and rifle pits in his front. "We had a great deal of work to do," he wrote his wife, and precious little time to do it. By relays, the Kentuckians worked all through the night and the next day until they relinquished their tools so that other regiments might do the same. Meanwhile,

Graves's battery emplaced itself at the center of the line commanded now by Buckner. The other half of the line belonged to Pillow.

On Wednesday, February 12, Grant first appeared in their front but showed no great anxiety to attack. He awaited his gunboats. That night Hanson put four of his companies in their intrenchments, expecting an attack the next day, and in the morning sent the remaining six in advance to the rifle pits. Few slept the night of February 12. Indeed, for Hanson at least there was almost no sleep at any time. "I had seen some hard times as a soldier in the Mexican War," he wrote a month later, "but the hardest time I have ever experienced was during the siege of Donaldson." Most of the time his men had no tents, and the rest of their stay they had no blankets. "From the exposed position we had we were unable to sleep for several nights." Hanson slept not at all, and when he did lie down it was only to awake with both ears frostbitten.[8]

The morning of February 13 Grant finally opened fire. Just past light the federal artillery began, and shortly afterward the Kentuckians saw a line of bluecoated soldiers moving toward them through the woods in their front. They advanced in unbroken ranks to within a hundred yards of Hanson's rifle pits before the Confederates fired. Undeterred, the Federals came another forty yards until Hanson's fire disrupted their line and forced them back. Twice more this day they charged, and twice were repulsed.

It unsettled the "Orphans." For almost all of them these were the first hostile shots ever fired their way, an uncomfortable feeling. The men in reserve in the trenches, unable to fire at the enemy with six companies of their comrades out front in the pits, sat and bore the enemy bullets in silence. They dodged and ducked at every buzzing missile they heard, but Hanson walked among them calmly and told them not to bother. By the time a bullet was heard, he said, it was already past. Then one came dangerously close to "Bench-leg" and, as it whistled past, he involuntarily ducked his head, much to the delight of the men. With his usual good humor, he finally relented. "Boys, you may dodge a little if they come too close."

The dodge worked only for a few. Those who did not duck in time were hit, and here for the first time death found the Orphans in a real battle. At the first enemy volley, Sergeant Neil Hendricks of Company B took a bullet in the chest. He recovered, but H. B. Nelson of Company G did not. A federal bullet must have hit an artery for, even though his captain tried to stanch the flow with a handkerchief, Nelson bled to death in a few minutes. That night, the fighting done, several of his friends stole back to Dover and found boards to make a rude coffin. They buried Private Nelson in the Tennessee sod, a long way from home, the first of hundreds to die as Orphans.[9]

Reinforcements arrived for Hanson that night, and again the following day. Now the enemy boats started their bombardment, which would be incessant for almost two days. This alone, despite the cold, prevented sleep for the already weary Kentuckians. They stood under arms all day, expecting an attack that did not come, though constant sharpshooting kept them alert. At about 3 A.M., Saturday, February 15, Buckner appeared at Hanson's bivouack and ordered his men to follow him to Graves's position, where they were to act as a reserve. Pillow would attack in the morning and the Orphans might be needed.

Graves opened the attack by firing on a federal battery, which coolly replied for some time, Buckner all the while pacing calmly back and forth in front of Hanson's men. At 9 A.M. Buckner sent two regiments forward to take the enemy battery. They made a valiant attempt, but fell back and Buckner, after replacing them in their intrenchments, went to Hanson. "The Second Kentucky will have to do that work!" he shouted. At the same moment a mounted man appeared in rear of the regiment, "purporting to be an officer," said Hanson. Some thought it was Graves himself. Whoever it was, he cried out, "Where is the Second Kentucky? Come to the aid of my battery." The captains of Companies B and G on Hanson's left took this as an order and moved out, past Graves's position, and forward against the battery that was giving him so much trouble. They got within fifty yards of the Federals, and there traded bullets for almost fifteen minutes. Then they started falling back, as the enemy pressed forward.

Hanson was in a quandary. He sent for Buckner, but he could not be found. "There was no time for delay," he decided. "I examined the state of the contest." He saw cavalry led by Colonel Nathan B. Forrest make two unsuccessful charges on his left. "My men were eager for the fight," he believed. Now "Bench-leg" decided not to await authority, but to advance on his own responsibility, believing he could stop the enemy advance and drive them back. At almost this same instant he received a request from Forrest to assist in another attempt to take the federal battery.

Hanson marched his regiment forward, across their line of defenses, and down the slope to a ravine where Forrest awaited. Here his two detached companies rejoined him, and here Hanson told the men, "Hold your fire until at close quarters!" He would depend upon the bayonet if possible. Ahead of them lay 200 yards of open ground to cross before they reached the wood in which the enemy battery and its infantry supports sheltered. Forrest would charge the battery, Hanson the infantry.

Steady, as if on parade, the Kentuckians moved forward. They took casualties. Lieutenant William Hill of Company F saw a cannon ball strike the ground in front of him and "come bounding along like a rabbit." It hit him in the knee. Though removed to the field hospital, he died that night. Lieutenant Ed Keene took a mortal wound and was sent back. Hanson lost by his count fifty men in crossing that open space, yet not a man fired his rifle until they reached the woods. Then the Orphans poured forth a volley, while Forrest engaged hand-to-hand for the battery. When the Kentuckians got within forty yards of the Federals, the bluecoats abandoned their position and their artillery. Now Hanson saw Graves bring his battery forward to their support. The young artillerist took over the splendid captured cannon, and "Old Flintlock" led his regiment forward again several hundred yards. The enemy had retired completely, opening to them a road that led to the federal flanks and rear, and both Hanson and Forrest saw the worth of what they had taken. While they prepared to hold what they felt might be a pivotal position, orders came from Pillow directing them to return to their trenches on the right of the line. Grant, too, had been busy.[10]

While Buckner attacked the federal center, Grant sent part of his own Army against the right of the Confederate line, the very area Hanson had left. Now, as "Bench-leg" and his rowdy Orphans returned to the right, they found the enemy advancing. He sent six companies running for the advance rifle pits, hoping to slow the Federals long enough for him to reoccupy the trenches with his remaining companies. A few of the men actually got into their rifle pits before the enemy, but they were too few. After a brief but hot firefight, the Confederates retreated. The casualties, by now, about 4 P.M., were substantial. Company B lost its captain, Ed Keene, early in the fight. Now it was led by the captain of Company G, Ed Spears, even though he was hit and carrying his arm in a sling. Yet Spears, like the rest of the Kentuckians, abandoned the rifle pits to the enemy.

Hanson re-formed the regiment somewhat, and then three times assaulted the trenches. Spears, wound and all, "seemed ready, indeed anxious," as one man of his company put it, "to lead us in a bayonet charge to drive the enemy out of the works which they had taken from us." The best that the Kentuckians could accomplish was to drive the Federals out of the trenches briefly, but the bluecoats only stopped on the other side of the earth rampart thrown up in front of the trenches, where they turned and used the rampart as a breastwork. Finally Hanson and another regiment, the 18th Tennessee, withdrew in some confusion. They rallied on the rear crest of the hill, though much intermingled, when Buckner arrived and ordered them into line, ignoring company or regimental organization. Indeed, one who was there said Buckner "stood where men were falling around him as calm as on review." Hanson, too, steadied the men by his example. Despite their situation, darkness approaching, the enemy in possession of his trenches, and the men exhausted, he had time to be pleased with his regiment. "The entire regiment did all I expected of them," he would tell his wife in a few weeks, "and that you know was a great deal."

Hanson himself narrowly escaped injury. The lower left leg of his trousers was shot away without hurt to him. A bullet came close enough to pass through the nightshirt that he kept stuffed in the pocket of his uniform jacket. And when he started to mount his horse during one of the charges, a cannon ball struck and killed the animal. Graves, who brought two pieces from his battery to assist in stabilizing Hanson's new line atop the hill, also had narrow misses. After the firing died in the fading light, he walked forward over the contested field and found a young federal soldier, severely wounded and in great suffering. Graves brought him behind the lines to a rifle pit occupied by Company B of the 4th Kentucky, the company assigned to Graves. One of the gunners in the company, Oliver Steele of Henderson County, recognized the young federal soldier as his own brother. Here for the first time, though certainly not the last in this war, the Orphans discovered the horror of what was, for Kentucky, truly a "brothers' war." How much more an Orphan Ollie Steele felt when his brother died in the pit that night.

With the safety of nightfall, Buckner pulled Hanson farther up the hill he occupied, and there attempted to build a new defense. "This position was a stronger one than the one lost, and every effort was made that night to construct defenses," Hanson reported, "but the

men were so exhausted from labor and loss of sleep that it was utterly
impossible." Buckner continued moving among the Orphans calming
them, but he knew that another battle the next day would certainly be
the end of them. That night in a conference with Pillow and Floyd he
declared that the 2d Kentucky was "as good a regiment as there was in
the service." Yet in attempting to retake the trenches this afternoon,
he had been actually forced to grasp as many as twenty men to turn
them to forward against the enemy. Many of the Orphans were so
exhausted from loss of sleep and exposure that they could not think,
much less fight. "It was not your fault, my brave boys," Buckner said
to them as they futilely worked at new defenses, "it was not your
fault." Those sensible enough to realize what had happened that day
felt downcast that in their first battle they lost their position to the
enemy. Buckner's words were a little reassuring. Then he left to discuss
the gravity of the situation with the other generals, and the Orphans
were alone.

The cold, perhaps forgotten in the fight, returned with renewed bitterness. The men started pitiful little fires atop the hill and huddled
around them for warmth, sulking moodily over the failure of the day,
or else looking with equal gloom toward the bloody work that dawn
must surely bring. A few managed sleep, only to be aroused at 3 A.M.,
February 16. Hanson formed them in line and led them to the left
again, in the direction of the road along which they attacked so successfully the day before. Yes, certainly, they would go into action here
again. Most believed they knew why. Grant heavily outnumbered the
Confederates at Fort Donelson. They were surrounded, everyone knew.
Obviously they could not withstand more siege, as demonstrated by the
federal gains on the right on February 15. Now the Confederates were
going to attack down this road again and cut their way through to
safety, perhaps to Nashville.

Hanson halted the regiment in a ravine near the scene of its success
of yesterday. He had passed a sleepless night, as usual, yet he never let
himself relax in his effort to keep the men ready for the fight. He was
earning his $195 per month colonel's pay. The regiment stood in line
for an hour, perhaps two. A. G. Montgomery of Company B was not
with it, doing some volunteer duty for Buckner. Then a message came
to Hanson. He spoke to the men, "said to us in a husky voice," one
recalled, "Go to your places, boys, and cook something to eat." Then
he added, "The war is about over for us!" There would be no attack,

no breakout, no escape. Private Montgomery had carried a flag of truce to Grant. Floyd and Pillow, with Forrest's cavalry, had escaped from the encircling enemy during the night. Buckner had refused to go with them. "For my part," he said, "I will stay with the men, and share their fate." Their fate would be captivity, for the message Private Montgomery bore to Grant was a request for terms of surrender.

Dejection overpowered the command. All of the Orphans, Hanson included, believed that they had taken an avenue of escape that would have saved most of the Army, had Pillow not called them back on the day before. Now to be told that they were prisoners, soon to be captives in some northern cell, while Floyd and Pillow had escaped to safety, was bitter news. Many would never forgive the generals for escaping. None would ever forget the loyalty and self-sacrifice shown by Buckner in remaining to stand by them.

Soon federal guards appeared and the Orphans were disarmed, and Graves relieved of his field pieces. It was a humiliating experience, yet one with ironic overtones. Men from the 7th Iowa mingled with Hanson's Kentuckians in disarming them and took particular note of the Mississippi rifles carried by some of the captives. One soldier saw an inscription on the stock of a rifle and shouted out in surprise. It indicated that this was one of the rifles with which old John Brown of Kansas armed his followers in their raid on Harpers Ferry, Virginia, in 1859. When Brown's men surrendered, their weapons went into the Virginia arsenals, and when Virginia seceded, these same weapons were given to the Confederate service. Among those thousand rifles that Governor Letcher so kindly sent Breckinridge last fall, then, were some of the very same rifles that had fired what many regarded as the first real shots of the war over two years before. Having carried these rifles for a couple of months now, it came as some surprise to the Orphans that they were using John Brown's guns to spit lead back at the abolitionists.

There was time to count the wounded and tally the dead. Reports conflict, Hanson's own being lost not long after he filed it. Of the 2d Kentucky, Hanson had a total strength of 618, and Graves's battery numbered another 113. Hanson's losses were 13 killed, among them Lieutenant Hill. Lieutenant Keene would die soon from his wound as well. Four other officers of his regiment lay wounded, among them Captain Charles Semple of Company K. Indeed, brother officers at first thought Semple killed, and led their men into the last charges yelling "Forward, men! Avenge Charlie Semple's death!" He would recover, however, as would most of the 57 wounded in the regiment. All told, Hanson lost almost 12 per cent of his regiment as casualties. Graves fared far better, with 5 wounded and none killed.

Some of the wounded actually escaped capture. Major Jim Hewitt, to whom the regiment must have been thankful for its overcoats during the cold nights at Donelson, took a painful but not serious wound in the nose early on February 15, and joined other wounded aboard a steamboat that managed to escape Dover and steam up the Cumberland to Nashville. A few other wounded were dropped at Clarksville along the way. Private Washington Taylor of Company F was wounded in the head during the last day's fighting. The next morning his sister in Harrison County, Kentucky, told their mother about the nightmare she had during the night. She saw him in her dream, she said, "coming from the yard gate to the house with the front of his coat all clotted with blood." Taylor's wound was not serious. He would recover to fight again. But on that night of February 15, thanks to his wound, the breast of his coat was covered with his own blood.[11]

The next day Hanson and the Kentuckians went aboard federal steamboats for the trip to a northern prison, Buckner among them. They were going farther from home than ever, farther from their brothers and Breckinridge, to an orphanage with sentinels and bars.

The news came to "Old Breck" when he and the other Orphans marched through Nashville. It was not a surprise. Indeed, with that extra sense of soldiers in any war, the men in the Kentucky regiments knew that something had happened at Donelson. At first they created and told stories of great battle and victory. But then reality crept into their musings. By the morning of February 16 the whispers stole through their lines, first among the officers. Donelson and every man in it surrendered, they said at first. "Rumors of the wildest nature flew from regiment to regiment," wrote Hodge. The Federals were even then on their way to Nashville, would be there within the day, there was no hope, and the like. Later in the day, as the brigade bivouacked below Nashville, confirmation of the actual siege and surrender reached Breckinridge. Bleak news, to be sure, but not so hopeless as the rumor.

To add to the Orphans' gloom, the rain poured incessantly that night. Dejected from word of Hanson's fate, the Kentuckians gave little attention to pitching their tents, with the result that the next morning they found them flooded. They huddled around smoldering fires, heaps of soaking blankets and clothing futilely expected to dry nearby, the brigade animals braying and whining, all under a sky filled with ominous clouds and dropping a steady drizzle. "All combined," said Ed Thompson, "to complete a picture of half-despondent wretchedness that cannot be described." Johnny Green, less eloquent perhaps, characterized the scene with equal description. "It was," he wrote in his diary, "the muddiest, most dismal place in the world."[12]

There came small cheer the next day when the wagonmaster of the 2d Kentucky reached Breckinridge's headquarters with fourteen empty wagons, which he had stolen away from Donelson. In view of the panic still gripping Nashville, "Old Breck" loaded them with necessary articles for his command, food, dry clothing, and medicines before all such items were either destroyed or plundered from the city. He spent hours on the northern bank of the Cumberland overseeing the movement of the cattle herd he brought from Kentucky to provide his men beef. The retreat would continue, and he would be certain that his Orphans had as much comfort as he could provide. It was a father's duty.

The march continued on February 20, and Breckinridge once again had to reprimand his Kentuckians for their behavior. Despite locating their night bivouacs near abundant forests, they persisted in vandalizing farmers' fences for firewood. Worse, they stole animals and practiced not a few other acts of petty thievery. "They are acts of naked plunder," their general told them. General Johnston himself brought it to Breckinridge's attention, "to my great mortification." Furthermore, by his own observation, not one man in eight carried his knapsack with him on the march, the rest depositing them in the wagons. All this would stop, he said in a stern order to the men. "This Brigade *at least* shall preserve the good name it has heretofore maintained." Yet, in the spirit of dejection and disappointment then abroad among the Orphans, the general faced a rugged adversary. Circumstances, the weather, and now whisky again, conspired against him.

When the brigade halted at Murfreesboro for several days while Johnston reorganized his army, several Orphans set to guard a commissary depot managed not to observe their messmates boring a hole in the bottom of a wagon. Once the gimlet passed through the floorboards, it ground its way up through the bottom of a barrel of whisky. As the liquor poured, the thirsty soldiers caught it in buckets. The next morning none of them could stand to answer roll call. The guards, protesting that they had seen nothing of what happened, found them-selves standing extra tours of duty. Johnny Green believed that "it is quite probable that they took good pains not to see any one." Captain Philip Vacaro took a few drinks himself, and then, perhaps out of guilt, stove in the head of the remaining barrel of whisky and poured it on the ground. The men of the 5th Kentucky—Hunt's 5th—did not think too highly of Vacaro's gesture. Henceforward, when he passed by men of the regiment, they would cry out in unison, "Pour it Out, Pour it Out."[13]

In Murfreesboro Breckinridge's own command underwent some reorganization. Certainly Hanson and Graves and their units were no longer a part of the 1st Kentucky Brigade. He still had the 3d, 4th, 5th, and 6th regiments, however, Byrne's and Lyon's and Cobb's bat-teries. Formally attached to him as well now were Morgan's squadron, Ben Helm's 1st Kentucky Cavalry, a battalion of Tennessee infantry under Charles C. Crews, the 4th Alabama Battalion led by Lieutenant Colonel J. M. Clifton, a company of cavalry, and another Alabama battalion of infantry. The object was to build Breckinridge's command into substantial size after the loss of his largest regiment, the 2d Ken-tucky. Johnston's intent now was for Breckinridge's command to be a "Reserve Brigade," a sort of floating support for any one of the three divisions that composed his army. Breckinridge's own military family underwent change here as well. The month before, his adjutant, George Hodge, won a seat in the Confederate Congress. Now Breck-inridge replaced him with an old friend from Kentucky, Theodore O'Hara, one of the more colorful—if erratic—Kentuckians of his time. His chief notoriety sprang from having composed a stirring poem about Kentucky's fallen men in the war with Mexico, *The Bivouac of the Dead*. Fittingly, he took his inspiration for the poem from hearing Breckinridge deliver an oration at their state funeral. Another addition to his staff was the grandson of an old friend who, thankfully, was not alive to see what his America had come to. He was young Lieutenant James B. Clay, Jr.; his grandsire—Henry Clay.[14]

Then it was on the march again. On February 28 they left Murfreesboro and withdrew farther into the Deep South. Eighty miles they trudged straight south to Huntsville, Alabama, then on toward Decatur twenty miles farther. "History records no example of a retreat conducted with such success under such adverse circumstances," wrote

Hodge, still with the Army. The rain fell without pause. The entire countryside lay flooded from swollen streams and saturated soil. The roads were "literally a river of liquid mud," Hodge found. "For miles at times the wagons would be submerged in ooze and mire up to the hubs of their wheels." Ascending a modest plateau a distance of two miles took the brigade a full day. Respite came at Huntsville, but only briefly. Ladies of the town kindly gave the 6th Kentucky a battle flag of silk, but Lewis would have been foolish to let it fly in the rain as they continued the march toward Decatur.

By March 10 Breckinridge and his Orphans stood within three miles of Decatur. Ahead of them lay the flooded Tennessee River, absolutely impassable, out of its banks for miles on both sides. Fortunately, a railroad crossing had been built with this sort of weather in mind, the rails laid atop a fifty-foot embankment that ran for two miles either side of the river. With the rails still above the flooded plain, Breckinridge could march his men across. Only seven feet wide, the passage did not admit of speed, but it was safe. Except for Johnny Green, that is, who borrowed Colonel Hunt's horse before the brigade crossed. In riding the embankment he had the ill fortune to encounter a locomotive coming in his direction. With twenty feet of water on either side, "the tussel I had to keep that horse from jumping into the river or getting under the train was indeed strenious."

On the night of March 14, just before the Orphans reached Decatur, they camped in a pasture. The sky told that there would be rain during the night, so the men pitched their tents, and secured the cattle herd nearby but out of the way. They cooked the evening meal, and some had retired when "a low sound, at first as of falling rain, then of approaching wind, arrested attention." The sound quickly grew louder and then, with a mighty blow, something akin to a hurricane, it grasped the Kentucky camp and "created such a stir as no one who was present can ever forget." Men and officers alike sprang at once to their tent poles trying vainly to hold them against the wind. Within seconds every tent in the camp lay ripped apart or blown hundreds of yards from its site. "Some thousands of men were uncovered at once to the fury of a Southern hurricane," Thompson recalled. Blankets, hats, every bit of unworn apparel, and all the camp and mess equipage of the brigade flew about the pasture in a mad carnival of tin, canvas, and denim. Now the cattle panicked. The noble beasts raised a fearful noise, then charged directly toward the huddled Orphans. "No one relished the idea of dying by the inglorious means of either a bullock's horns or his hoofs," wrote a Kentuckian. They were diverted somehow and thundered along the edge of the encampment.

As for the men, they took what shelter they could. Green and some of Hunt's regiment just squatted on the ground and held scraps of what had been their tents over them "& took the storm as best we could." Others found shelter inside and under the brigade wagons. Some of the more calm souls—Thompson thought they were really just "opposed to violent exertion"—simply stood and took it until the storm was spent, then returned to their camps, erected a modest shelter, and went to sleep.

A number took refuge in nearby "gin houses," burrowing under the bales and loose cotton as if to hide from the violently flashing lightning. They looked like snowmen the next morning, their clothing covered with tiny bits of white cotton. Others made their way into Decatur itself, where they found another sort of gin house. They straggled back to camp the next morning with stories of hospitality so fine that it would have been ungentlemanly of them to refuse it. When at last they did return in the premorning darkness, stumbling along the railroad line, they left several behind in holes and cattle culverts. It seemed they were too drunk to discover the hazards ahead except by sending a man in advance. When his comrades heard him fall in the water, they knew there was a hole. These Orphans would never miss a chance to "wet up," and this night they wetted inside and out.[15]

The Orphans won the hearts of the people of Alabama. "Waving of handkerchiefs, cheers, words of welcome and encouragement, met them from the time they entered" the state, wrote Ed Thompson. Had the men remained in Decatur long enough to become rowdy, the welcome might have waned. They did spend nearly a week in its environs, but then one night Breckinridge put the brigade aboard a train bound for Corinth, Mississippi, one hundred miles west. There Johnston was marshaling his army to move north against Grant.

The Kentuckians reached Corinth on March 19, and three days later occupied their assigned bivouac at Burnsville, about twelve miles southeast. Here, as in Johnston's other camps in the vicinity, Breckinridge rigorously drilled and trained his brigade to bring them back into trim after the depressing retreat from Kentucky. The whole Army sensed that a big battle approached. For almost all of them it would be their first. General P. G. T. Beauregard, the hero of Bull Run, arrived to join forces with Johnston in the move against the Federals. Grant himself lay camped just twenty miles north of them at Pittsburg Landing on the Tennessee. Breckinridge sent a screen of cavalry north to monitor the enemy's movements, not knowing how many old friends from better days now peopled that hostile army. The colonel of a federal Kentucky cavalry regiment out there, James Shackleford, had been a private in Major Breckinridge's regiment in the war with Mexico. On the march to Mexico City the private was so weary and broken down that Breckinridge dismounted and gave him his horse, while he walked instead. There would be less courtesy should they meet in this war.[16]

On March 29 Johnston reorganized his army once more, now into three corps led by Major Generals William J. Hardee, Leonidas Polk, and Braxton Bragg. A reserve corps, smaller than the others, he created as well, to include Breckinridge's Kentucky brigade. Command of the reserve corps Johnston assigned to George B. Crittenden, but on March 31 he was relieved of his position for alleged drunkenness. This left Breckinridge the senior brigadier in the corps and, automatically, he assumed its leadership. Johnston may have felt some hesitation in this. Breckinridge was the only corps commander not a West Point graduate with battlefield experience. Yet he had performed well so far as a soldier. Furthermore, if the Confederates could push Grant back into Kentucky and follow him, Breckinridge would be invaluable in rallying the state to the South, a vain hope that the Confederacy would never entirely abandon. And Johnston's popularity lagged badly after the loss of Henry and Donelson. Some clamored for his relief, and a few in Richmond even suggested that Breckinridge should replace him. Kentucky lobbyists in Congress were already at work trying to secure a major generalcy for Breckinridge. With Johnston losing favor, they wanted another high-ranking Kentuckian handy to fill the possible void. When advised of these machinations, however, Breckinridge refused to countenance them, deciding, "I will not move in the matter." However much he sought advancement in political life, he would never in this war politick for command or promotion.

Even before his elevation, the Kentuckian readied his Orphans for the coming battle. When he evacuated Bowling Green, the brigade wounded had been sent by rail to Atlanta. A number of others straggled or deserted, and some infantrymen had been held there under orders to act as nurses in the hospitals. Breckinridge sent Colonel Hunt to Atlanta, and Lieutenant Tom Winstead of the 4th Kentucky to Chattanooga and Atlanta, with orders to bring back all men able enough for duty. Winstead was told even to arrest those who would not come freely. As for Hunt, he was chiefly to look for deserters. Once in Atlanta he ordered all convalescents from the brigade aboard cars for Corinth, Gervis Grainger among them. Hunt found one healthy Orphan, however, who had been detailed as a nurse in a military hospital, and the doctors would not release him. Breckinridge immediately ordered a dispatch sent to Atlanta that was unusually blunt. "The Kentucky boys didnt ship for orderlies to 'Pill rollers,'" he said. Indeed, some of the Orphans even returned under lock and key. A group of thirty convalescents from Chattanooga were locked inside a boxcar by Winstead. A still-ailing Johnny Jackman sat among them. It took twenty-four hours for them to reach Corinth. "We got off the train," he wrote in his diary, "and I never again saw the Lt. He was such a 'goober' I don't believe he knew which road to take." But then, Johnny was a bit resentful at being locked up.[17]

However they came to Burnsville, whether in confinement or like the two men of the 6th Kentucky whose wives accompanied them on the train with baskets of goodies, Breckinridge rushed to prepare them. The old question of inadequate arms arose again. He found that eleven hundred of the brigade guns needed repair, and that boxes of ammunition and kegs of powder were damaged. He sent it all to Corinth for repair or replacement. Hunt requisitioned six hundred new rifles for his 5th Kentucky. Somehow their wants were satisfied for a change so that Breckinridge might look forward to a command well prepared for the coming battle. To the men he gave explicit instructions on conduct under fire. They must shoot "with deliberation at the feet of the enemy," he said, thus avoiding the tendency to overshoot. Officers were to prevent the men from firing uselessly when not actually engaged. He advised to attempt to wound enemy soldiers rather than kill them. In part this was because a wounded man took one and sometimes two of his comrades from the battle line to help him to the rear, whereas the dead were left where they fell. It may date as well from the sensitivity of Breckinridge's nature. A man of very tender sensibilities, as a lawyer he could never bring himself to act as a prosecutor. Now, even in battle, he hoped to spare life.

"It was the deliberate Sharp Shooting of our forefathers in the Revolution of 1776 and at New Orleans in 1815 which made him so for-

midable against the odds with which they engaged," he told the brigade. Now they must do the same. They must stay in ranks, and not
leave the line to assist wounded. Let the enemy do that. "To quit the
standard on the field of battle under fire under pretense of removing
or aiding the wounded will not be permitted." Violators would be shot
on the spot.[18]

Now that Breckinridge commanded a corps, leadership of the Kentucky brigade devolved upon the senior colonel, Robert P. Trabue. For
the first time Breckinridge was separated from his Kentuckians, making all the more apropos his sobriquet for them. How many more commanders would leave them orphans before this war was done?

As March became April, an undercurrent of excitement flowed
through the otherwise peaceful camps at Burnsville. On Sunday,
March 30, the Orphans "rubbed up" their brass for the usual inspection, but that evening they heard the ominous sound of cannon fire in
the distance to the north. It lasted for some time, and Jackman found
that it "made one feel 'devilish.'" As the thunder of the guns rolled
over the hills to Burnsville, curiosity coursed through the men. Hunt
ordered three of his companies to leave before dawn the next day to
determine the cause of the firing. They returned on April 1, to report
that Breckinridge's scouts had fired on a federal gunboat on the Tennessee, and the cannonade they heard was its deck guns answering.

The men were mostly idle on April 2. Johnny Jackman had time to
observe the progress of the new season, finding that nature was "tardy
in robing old earth in a mantle of green." Still, the forests looked more
verdant than before, and flowers bloomed. "These remind me of happier days," he wrote in his diary.

The next day it came. That afternoon Breckinridge received the
order to be ready to march at first light on April 4, expecting to give
battle within twenty-four hours. This same day several hundred of the
long-requested Enfield rifles reached Burnsville and found eager hands
awaiting. Through the day the Orphans received and cooked three
days' rations. Forty rounds of ammunition per man issued forth from
the quartermaster. Johnny Green found "the whole command greatly
rejoiced at the prospect of battle." That evening Hunt called his regiment to assemble in front of his tent, and he read to them General
Johnston's battle order. "I have put you in motion to offer battle to
the invaders of your country," it read. "You can but march to a deci-
sive victory . . . remember the fair, broad, abounding land, the happy

1. General Simon Bolivar Buckner who gave birth to the Kentucky State Guard and, thereby, the First Kentucky Brigade. *(Courtesy Massachusetts MOLLUS Collection)*

2. The Kentucky State Guard encampment at Louisville, August 23, 1860. In less than a year these men will flock to the South. (*Courtesy Kentucky Historical Society*)

3. Orphans to be. Several State Guard companies at the Louisville Fairgrounds in 1860. (*Courtesy Kentucky Military History Museum, Kentucky Historical Society*)

4. John Hunt Morgan's Lexington Rifles in 1860. Gay now, they faced hard years to come in the Orphan Brigade. (*Courtesy Kentucky Military History Museum, Kentucky Historical Society*)

homes, and the ties that would be desolated by your defeat." He hardly need remind the Orphans of what they fought for. Even in defeat most of the other Confederate soldiers in this army would still have homes safely behind their own lines. But a victory by Grant in this contest would only drive the Kentuckians farther from their home fires.

Reveille interrupted the Orphans' fitful sleep at 4 A.M. that morning. They arose in a pelting rain and packed the brigade baggage into wagons that would take it to Corinth. Their tents went with it. Poor John Jackman, still not fully recovered from his Bowling Green illness, felt weak and in need of a stimulant. In the rush of packing he found an unattended bottle and thinking it was whisky, decided to "wet up" for the march. It turned out to be alcohol mixed with camphor, a back-rubbing potion for rheumatism. "I thought the stuff would burn me up," he told his diary. "That taught me a lesson."

By daylight the twenty-four hundred Orphans stood in the road, ready to march to the battle they expected on the morrow. Their measured step took them through a swamp where, in places, the mud sat knee deep, and the rain continued through the morning. Already the weaker men, or those not yet recovered from their illness, fell out of line or lagged back. Jackman had to take advantage of the brigade's occasional halts in order to regain his place in line. It meant that he had no rest. Finally the sun appeared at noon, warming the day but not easing the march. When Jackman stopped at a spring to drink, he rested his Enfield against a tree. He returned to find that another Orphan had traded with him, leaving in its place a rusted old flintlock. Finally, like many others, he gave up walking and climbed onto an ordnance wagon.

The bivouac that night had no tents, and the rain fell again until dawn, dampening men and spirits, and making the roads even more difficult. Already the artillery and wagon train ran several hours late. By now the Army should have been ready to attack Grant at Pittsburg Landing on the morning. Instead it lay still a day's march from the enemy, and Johnston found no alternative but to postpone the attack until April 6.[19]

The next day's march was little better, though in the warmth of the sun, spirits renewed. The rain soaked the Orphans' rations of bread. "Notwithstanding wet bread is not very appetizing," found Johnny Green, "we ate up the three days ration in half that time & consequently we are all very hungry." When Hunt bivouacked his regiment at 5 P.M. that afternoon, his starving Orphans immediately raided a turnip patch, flushing a rabbit in the offing. For some time the creature darted about as one avenue of escape after another closed in its path. Finally it ran toward Green, who followed the rabbit, and shortly he fell headlong into a ditch filled with water. "But Brer Rabit was there too," found Johnny, "& was a poor swimmer." That night Green's mess dined on barbecued rabbit and boiled turnips and "ash cake," corn meal and water baked in ashes between cabbage leaves. "Our mess lived high that night."

Not far away, Breckinridge lay on a blanket by the roadside discussing the situation with Johnston and the other generals. Beauregard and Bragg wanted to turn back, certain that their delays and a few brushes with federal outposts had cost them the surprise they hoped to achieve. Johnston and Polk still wanted to attack. Breckinridge, feeling terrible from fever or tension, still sat upright to add his counsel that they should go ahead. Finally Johnston decided to attack and laid forth his battle plan. While Bragg and Hardee assaulted, Polk and Breckinridge would be held in reserve. Johnston said he wanted to keep the Kentuckians in reserve because, used as they were to hard marches and fast ones, they could move speedily to any threatened point in the line. It may have been, too, that Breckinridge had never before been in a battle.

That night the Orphans slept with their arms at their sides. "The night was clear, calm, and beautiful as such nights always are in the spring-time," wrote Ed Thompson. Tired as they were from the hard march, the Kentuckians slept well except for the occasional firing of scouts in their front. The morrow was the Sabbath. In their front, behind Grant's unsuspecting lines, lay Shiloh Church. With the coming of dawn these slumbering Orphans would attend the devil's service.[20]

FIVE

"Baptized in Fire
and Blood"

"THIS DAY WILL LONG BE REMEMBERED," Jackman wrote in his diary
on April 6, 1862. Indeed it would. The men roused from sleep at
3 A.M. that morning. No bugles sounded the reveille in order not to
alert any lurking Federals that an army stood poised to attack them.
Instead, orderly sergeants shook the men of their companies to awaken
them. They started fires and boiled water for their morning coffee.
Just then Breckinridge galloped along the line yelling, "Boys, fall in.
You have better work before you than eating." Minutes later they
heard the roar of cannon as the battle opened just over a mile from
their camp.

The Kentuckians formed in the road, the other brigades of the
reserve corps taking place behind them. Officers spoke quietly to the
men, calming their nerves. Others harangued their privates, trying to
excite their martial ardor. Captain D. E. McKendree of "Old Joe"
Lewis' Company D addressed his men briefly in the road. He was a
jolly sort, one used to making his rounds of a camp, visiting everyone
briefly before moving on to the next group or tent, always saying,
"Well, men, *I must let my light shine around!*" Now he shone as he
told his nervous charges: "Boys, we are about to be engaged with the
foe for the first time. It will pain me to see any man falter; and for
heaven's sake don't let it be said, by those whom we love at home, that
one member of Company D disgraced himself."

Soon the brigade stood ready to move, "Old Trib" Trabue at its head. When Breckinridge gave the order, the Orphans marched up the road at the double quick, some of them still munching the hardtack from their interrupted breakfast. They were twenty-four hundred strong, reasonably well armed, and as ready for a fight as they would ever be. This was the battle that would drive Grant out of Tennessee, out of Kentucky, and return them to their homes. Thus it was fitting that at least one member of Hanson's 2d Kentucky marched with the brigade today. John Mahon, an Irishman of Company G, took a wound at Donelson and thus left before the surrender. He was back in the ranks now for his revenge.[1]

Marching in the darkness toward the sound and flash of the big guns, the Kentuckians found their advance slowed by Polk's corps in their front. Finally, still before light, they drew close enough to the battle line that Trabue ordered them to unsling their knapsacks in a pile and leave a guard for them. Trabue called for volunteers, but no one wanted to be left behind and miss the battle. The man finally ordered to stay tried bribing another to take his place with extra pieces of hardtack, to no avail. Indeed, even men of the brigade who had been in arrest begged release long enough to take part in the fight. One of Breckinridge's teamsters, in the guardhouse for some infraction, talked the general into freeing him just for the battle.

The men seemed lighthearted. To a captain of the 4th Kentucky it seemed incongruous. "Why did we not be more serious, and shake each other by the hand and bid fond *adieus?*" For a time even, the brass band of the regiment played martial airs, until too near the battle line. Then they "melt away into thin air and are seen no more."[2]

The battlefield ahead of Breckinridge and his Orphans was already a mess. Pittsburg Landing lay on the western bank of the Tennessee River, amid a hilly, wooded terrain crisscrossed by small creeks and forest roads. The left of Grant's thirty-three-thousand-man army rested about four miles below the landing, against the river. The Federals' right extended perpendicular to the river and almost six miles from it, its right center intersected by the Corinth road. It was upon this road that Johnston's corps advanced. He hoped to press back Grant's left, past Pittsburg Landing, almost two miles to Snake Creek, thus denying the possibility of federal reinforcement by way of the river landing. To make the attack, Johnston intended to send Hardee's corps against Grant's right, while Bragg's corps would do the work of driving back the Federals along the Tennessee. Breckinridge and Polk, of course, were to assist where needed.

The plan went awry immediately. Johnston achieved a tactical surprise that sent the enemy army into absolute consternation. Yet the Unionists speedily began organizing themselves for a defense, hoping to hold out long enough for twenty-five thousand reinforcements, led by Major General Don C. Buell, to reach them from downriver. As Hardee first struck, and Bragg soon after, it became apparent that Johnston's plan would not work. The generals and their men were green, and the two corps soon became largely intermingled. Indeed, for the rest of the day officers would lead not so much their own commands as just any group of soldiers who came to hand. It would be a learning battle.

As they neared the field, Breckinridge ordered Trabue to move forward in readiness for easy deployment behind Polk, and soon thereafter he told "Old Trib" to form in line of battle. He put the 3d Kentucky on the right and the 4th Kentucky on the left, the other regiments in the center, and Byrne's and Cobb's batteries in the rear. Morgan and his squadron were already out in front, and Helm guarded the right flank. In this fashion they moved forward until sometime after 8 A.M., when Breckinridge received an order to take the two rear brigades of his corps and move to the right to assist Bragg. It meant that, in its very first battle, he had to leave his Kentucky brigade on its own, but there was no choice. He told Trabue to keep on Polk's left rear, continue advancing, and tend toward the left. Trabue would be moving almost directly toward Shiloh Church. Then Breckinridge bade him farewell, and both marched toward their fate.

The first sight the Orphans had of the effects of the fighting was a nearly demolished federal battery, "dead men, dead horses, and broken gun carriages, all lying in a mingled condition." About 9 A.M. Trabue encountered Morgan's resting men. "Cheer, boys, cheer," sang a cavalryman, and the foot soldiers responded in kind. They filed down a wooded slope and into a swampy area along the Shiloh Branch. There sat a large open field before them with enemy camps on the opposite side. The Federals stood in line in the woods near their camps, and over to his left Trabue saw two more enemy campsites occupied by bluecoats. At the same time he could see none of his own troops, being separated from Polk's left by a rise of ground. Trabue appeared to be at the very end of the Confederate line, somewhat isolated, and had discovered a substantial body of the enemy who might hit Polk's unsuspecting flank with ominous results. Trabue would have to attack.

Just before reaching this position, Trabue lost the 3d Kentucky, Byrne's battery, the 4th Alabama, and Crews's battalions, when Beauregard ordered them to the right in support of another brigade. So now his command stood reduced to less than two thousand, and already the enemy was forming to meet him. The federal artillery opened on the Kentuckians first. A shell killed two of Cobb's gunners and severed both hands of a third, who stood looking at the bleeding stumps and cried, "My Lord, that stops my fighting." Another shell passed less than two feet in front of Johnny Green and killed three men of the regiment and carved a leg from a fourth.[3]

At about this time an unidentified advance Confederate regiment in the fighting withdrew, and its line of retreat brought it straight back through Trabue's line. This, combined with the heavy fire and confusion already reigning, would have disrupted many green regiments. But as these withdrawing Rebels broke through the 4th Kentucky, Nuckols kept his men in hand. He even tried to halt and rally the other unit, but with no success. Then, when the Kentuckians' own bugler sounded the recall, so that the regiment could join in meeting the threat from the Federals to their left, the men of the 4th at first would not respond. They feared it would be thought they were retreating with that other demoralized regiment. Finally Major Tom Monroe had to give a verbal order to get the 4th to withdraw.

Trabue seemed to be everywhere steadying his men before the fight. He rode calmly along the line, speaking in low, soothing tones to the men, "apparently as free from excitement as when on review." Every regiment saw him; most of the men heard him as he casually remarked upon the course of the battle. Here, for the first time, a superior officer appeared on the field, Major General Hardee. Since fighting had taken place here well before Trabue's arrival, the ground lay littered with dead. Thus he found it difficult to form a perfectly straight line, though he compelled the Kentuckians to stand even astride the dead in the attempt. Hardee smiled, perhaps because of this, and offered his compliments to Trabue.

"General, I have a Kentucky brigade here," said the colonel. "What shall I do with it?"

"Put it in where the fight is the thickest, sir," Hardee responded, then rode away. Such was the degree of command being exercised even by professional soldiers this day.

Left to his own discretion, Trabue moved Hunt's 5th Kentucky farther to extend his own left, completed turning the brigade to face the Federals in their front, and attacked. "In a few minutes we were in the thickest of the fight," wrote Johnny Green. Several color corporals of Hunt's regiment fell dead in the first few minutes, and Green himself took a wound. When litter bearers readied to take him from the field, he told them, "There is too much work here for a man to go to the rear as long as he can shoot a gun." Fortunately, as Johnny put it, the bullet that hit him "glanced off my hard head."

Most of the 4th Kentucky carried Enfields now, and used prepared cartridges that allowed relatively rapid fire. "The ground in front of us was heaped up with dead men," wrote John Weller of the 4th, but their own men fell as well. Captain John B. Rogers saw his own brother killed on the skirmish line and soon after fell himself. John Marshall took a bullet in the breast pocket that only missed snuffing his life thanks to burying itself in a Testament given him by a woman in Kentucky.

Trabue estimated that he battered the Federals in his front for an hour and a quarter. He put the 4th Kentucky on his left, Lewis' 6th Kentucky in the center, and Hunt's 5th on the right, holding the 31st Alabama in reserve. He no longer had Cobb's battery, it having been ordered to the right shortly before. "The enemy appeared to outnumber us greatly," he reported. After a time Trabue put the Alabamians on his left to extend it, and then finding portions of two of Bragg's brigades in his rear, he put them in line, ordered bayonets fixed, and charged. He said it was a "complete success."

The regiment immediately fronting the 4th Kentucky was the 46th Ohio. As Nuckols readied his regiment to charge them, giving the order to "change front forward on 8th Company," the Ohioans, too, changed their front to meet them, maintaining a steady fire as they did so. Finally the two hostile regiments stood little more than fifty yards apart when, at the command, the Kentuckians delivered a volley that threw the Buckeye outfit into utter confusion. When Nuckols charged, the enemy did not stand at all, but withdrew without looking back. Another federal regiment tried to take its place without being able to stop the Orphans' charge. Lewis and his 6th Kentucky met with lesser resistance in his part of the assault, though an enemy bullet killed his horse under him. As for Hunt, his regiment, only eight companies strong and still under temporary organization, suffered heavy casualties. Captain Caldwell took sixty-four men into the fight in his company and lost 64 per cent of them, himself suffering a broken left arm. They, too, succeeded in their advance. When Trabue's line passed the first enemy camps in their path, some of Hunt's men found a beautiful silk banner with the goddess of liberty and the motto "We will die for our country" on one side, and "Victory or death" on the other. Considering that the owners of the banner left it without a fight, Hunt quipped that "the entire command was killed, for they surely could not have thrown away their colors after going in to win or die." The flag they would give to Breckinridge as a souvenir, while its staff they appropriated to themselves to replace their own banner's flagstaff, shot in two earlier in the day.[4]

So far the men and officers acted superbly for untested volunteer soldiers. Until now, Trabue noted, no part of the brigade faltered or fell back at any time. The 4th Kentucky engaged in assaulting a second encampment, called on Lewis and the 6th for assistance, and the regiment moved smartly to its aid. Hunt, Breckinridge would later say, "conducted himself with the utmost coolness and courage." At this point even civilians took a hand. Governor George W. Johnson, who had been acting as a volunteer aide, found his services curtailed when his horse fell dead. Without hesitation he took a musket and joined the 4th Kentucky as a foot soldier.

Byrne and Cobb had been busy too this day. Most of the artillery on the left side of Johnston's line concentrated against a division of Federals led by Brigadier General Benjamin Prentiss. In all, eleven batteries, including Cobb and Byrne, took part in the bombardment of Prentiss' position, which continued for hours during the morning and afternoon. Byrne sat on his horse giving orders, while members of Bragg's staff looked on admiringly. At one point a colonel raised a cheer for Byrne, a shout taken up by his gunners and passed on along the line. Bragg doffed his cap in salute. Furiously the artillerists worked their guns, pouring scores of shots into Prentiss' besieged position. The enthusiastic colonel, so enraptured with what he saw, dismounted and put his hand to the barrel of one of Byrne's guns, saying that he just "wanted to feel it."[5]

After his initial success, Trabue found that he had to move forward slowly due to the broken terrain. At the same time a confusion of colors slowed his advance thanks to a Louisiana unit to his left whose blue uniforms gave him pause. He sent an aide to determine their identity, but not before some of the Orphans accidentally gave them a volley. This produced speedy results, the soldiers quickly turning their blue coats inside out and raising their Confederate battle flag well into view.

Gradually, as the federal resistance in his front continued to pull back, Trabue turned his brigade to the right. The whole Union line steadily withdrew through the day, except for the stubborn Prentiss and his division. By 4 P.M. he was nearly surrounded, but still held his place in his camps, buying time for Grant to establish a better defense in the rear. Hardee shifted most of his corps to the left of the line, and Bragg and Breckinridge's two brigades faced Prentiss' front and left flank. Now Trabue found himself on Prentiss' exposed right flank, almost directly across the path he would have to take should he attempt to escape.

Just as he reached this position, Trabue saw Federals from Prentiss' camps attempting to withdraw. Wheeling the brigade slightly, Trabue sent several volleys into them and they fled back into the "hornets' nest" from which now there could be no escape. Then he advanced and, almost simultaneously, so did the rest of the Confederates encircling the federal position. Soon a man in the 31st Alabama saw a white flag arise over what he presumed to be Prentiss' headquarters. The fight at the "hornets' nest" was done, the Federals surrendered after a stand of exceptional heroism. At the same instant Trabue and the Orphans entered Prentiss' camps from the left, and Breckinridge and his staff approached from the right. "Then and there," wrote Hodge, who was present, "in the full fruition of success, the Kentucky Brigade and its General met for the first time during that bloody day since their separation in the morning, both covered with glory; both proud of and gratified with each other."[6]

It had been quite a day for Breckinridge, too. After leaving Trabue, he attempted gradually to feel his way toward the Tennessee River on the right, where Johnston wanted him to turn and press Grant's left. With no maps and no knowledge of the terrain, Breckinridge found the way difficult, and it was almost noon by the time he reached the front. The Federals on Prentiss' left had just pulled back into line with him, and now the Kentuckian took his two brigades and one lent him into a front over a mile long. Soon Johnston himself joined them as they readied their first assault.

Breckinridge waited under a large oak, where he made quite a picture in his uniform of dark-blue Kentucky "jeans." Always before clean-shaven, he was growing a dark, flowing mustache now. Johnston's adjutant, Thomas Jordan, saw him there and found that "His dark eyes seemed to illuminate his swarthy, regular features, and as he sat in his saddle he seemed to me altogether the most impressive-looking man I had ever seen." Just then a federal shell struck the oak, exploding within it, and Breckinridge dashed out in a storm of flying splinters.

His first advance occupied a federal camp without opposition, but then an enemy battery opened on them. "Never mind this, boys," he told the men, "press on!" By half past noon he had undisputed possession of the camp. Advancing another three quarters of a mile toward a second federal position, he finally met Prentiss. For the next hour he led his brigades in repeated attacks against the "hornets' nest," and then decided upon a last desperate charge. But a Tennessee regiment would not rally to take its part, and he requested help from Johnston. He told the army commander that he feared he could not get the men to make another charge. Johnston calmly said, "Oh yes, General, I think you can." He would help him.

They rode together along the line encouraging the men, then Breckinridge took a place at the right of the troublesome regiment and Johnston at its left.

The line moved with a shout. Breckinridge had not proceeded far when he saw his aide, Charlie Ivey. "We were just getting into what was afterwards called the hornets' nest," wrote Ivey, "and in my blind enthusiasm and love for Gen. B., fearing he would be struck by the rain of shot and shell, I rode around in front of him, placing myself and horse between him and the enemy." Breckinridge saw what Ivey was about and "roasted me," ordering the boy to the rear, "so mortified and completely undone" that he could not face the general for the rest of the day.

Down a slope Breckinridge led his men full into Prentiss' line. It broke, with the Confederates racing on and Breckinridge yelling, "Charge them, Tennesseeans! Charge them!" Every single member of his staff took a fall or wound here. Hawkins was hit in the face; Hodge, right next to Breckinridge, had his horse killed under him;

Cabell Breckinridge, at his father's side with "beautiful composure and serene fidelity," lost two horses. Another staff member saw his own leg torn to pieces by a federal shell. "Breckinridge," wrote General Johnston's son, "leading and towering above them all, was the only one who escaped unscathed." Then, about two-thirty, a special messenger came to the general bringing word from Colonel William Preston that General Johnston was dead. He had bled to death from an otherwise minor wound.[7]

It was more than two hours later that Breckinridge led his command into Prentiss' camps and met with Trabue and the Orphans. It was a happy reunion for both. Hardee was on the scene and he ordered Trabue to send a regiment to escort the federal prisoners to the rear. Trabue sent Crews's Tennesseeans. Then he gave the Orphans a brief rest and let them rummage through the captured camp, exchanging their old muskets for the Enfield rifles just liberated from Prentiss' men. In all, some 1,393 rifles were taken, along with 11 swords and 4 cannon, enough to greatly enhance the Orphans' armory.

The Kentuckians created a bit of a stir among the wounded enemies lying about the camp. As far back as their stay in Bowling Green, Federals believed many of the Orphans to be Indians. Some members of the brigade took the title of "Buckner's Indians" as a result, and now one of them shouted to the wounded, "Here comes yer Buckner's Indians." Bluecoats timidly peered about looking for painted faces and scalping knives. One poor fellow sat up, put his hand to his hair protectively, and said, "And you have Indians with you sure enough, haven't you? I heard that you had." Their fears were soon relieved, however, and those who had hair were allowed to take it to the rear with them.[8]

Breckinridge did not allow the men to loot the camps and brought them back into line within a few minutes after they exchanged their rifles. He reunited Trabue with his other two brigades, and led the corps forward again toward the enemy, now withdrawn with its back to Pittsburg Landing. It needed only one more push to drive Grant away from the landing, and isolate him from Buell. They halted overlooking the landing for an hour, undergoing a terrible cannonade from gunboats on the river. Breckinridge readied a charge in the gathering dusk, but just as he was ready to move he received an order from Beauregard, now commanding, that he was to retire to shelter for the night. He thought it a mistake, yet complied, moving Trabue back to the vicinity of the 46th Ohio camps, though not before a last federal shell struck the 4th Kentucky, killing three men and tearing the leg from Irish John Gillen. He refused all attentions, knowing himself dying. "There is many a better man than myself that has died here today," he told them. He died that night.[9]

It had been a tense day, and not just for the Orphans in the battle. In Corinth in the hospitals, Kentuckians like Gervis Grainger heard the boom of the cannon and musketry. "Every one stood aghast," he found; "scarcely a word was spoken for hours together." For him they were "hours of anxiety and suspense," not much relieved late in the day by the arrival of the first wagons bearing the wounded.

Closer to the fight, Johnny Jackman finally reached the rear hours after the battle began, having to borrow a horse to ride. He first encountered the wounded retiring from the line. "I felt then that I was getting in the vicinity of 'warfare.'" He could hear the wounded in the ambulances groaning and shrieking in their pain as they bounced along the rutted road. Dismounting, he found the strength to head for the front on foot, and soon met a skulker who looked at him sheepishly and asked in a heavy drawl, "Has you'ns been in the fight yet?" Johnny did not entirely understand, and asked in reply just what brigade it was that "General Youens" commanded.

Finally Jackman found the Orphan Brigade hospital. "There were heaps of wounded lying about." The doctor in charge asked him to stay and help. Jackman administered chloroform to the men before the surgeon amputated mangled arms and legs, his handkerchief so saturated with the chemical that Johnny frequently swooned himself. By nightfall, when the firing finally stopped, "I was tired, sick, and all covered with blood. But I was in far better fix than many that were there." He sat on a medicine chest in the surgeon's tent, nodded his head, and slept the night through.[10]

Some distance away Trabue tallied his losses for the day. As the rain opened again, his officers made returns that told the story of the day's fight. All told, 75 of the Orphans lay dead, and another 350 wounded filled the makeshift hospital. The 4th Kentucky took the worst casualties among the infantry, but it was Cobb's battery that was hit hardest. In effect, it no longer existed. In the fight against Prentiss it lost all its battery horses killed and 37 of its men wounded. Cobb had to draw his guns away from the field with mules.[11]

The men settled for the night, some in the 46th Ohio's camp, the

5th Kentucky in that vacated by the 6th Iowa. Hunt's Orphans found an abundance of candles among the spoils and illuminated their bivouac as they surveyed their plunder. They commandeered piles of new blankets and filled their haversacks with "rare delicacies for the palate." "Here was a chance for a feed, such as we had not had before for months," recalled Marshall of the 4th Kentucky. They found "all the comforts and luxuries of life," and Marshall concluded that the sutler of the 46th Ohio "must have catered for the Burnet or St. Charles in days gone by." There was everything to tempt their appetites, "and as it was a free lunch we stood not upon ceremony." Men put ten pounds of tea in a single kettle, enough to brew a cistern full. Whole cheeses they hoisted upon their bayonets. Tins of beef and fruits flew from one to another, and into knapsacks already bursting with booty. Beer, wine, and brandy made their appearance as well, and the men of the 4th had a good "wet." In all "it was a grand feast," said Marshall. "It was hinted, more than once, that the troops might be, to some extent, demoralized for the next day's work by reason of the night's debauch, but there was nothing in it, albeit some may have felt as I did, just a little thin about the gills."

Johnny Green and his comrades in Hunt's 5th Kentucky "had little doubts that all we would have to do next day would be to bury our dead." Consequently, they, too, reveled. For dinner they supped on hardtack, bacon, cheese, and all the tea and coffee they could drink. While some boiled water, Green went with a bucket to the Shiloh Branch for water. He stepped on what he took for a log as he bent down, then found that "my log was a dead man." He could not see that the creek brimmed with the dead, else he would not have taken the water back to camp. Before bedding for the night he told a friend, "Gos" Elston, that he thought he saw him killed earlier that day. "Greenie!" Elston replied, "you can bet your last dollar that Elston will come out safe."

Others were not so sure of themselves. Several months before, Major Tom Monroe of the 4th Kentucky confided to John Marshall a presentiment that he, Monroe, would be killed in his first battle. Tonight, as the two shared a tent, Marshall reminded him of it in good humor and laughed at him for "entertaining such old-time superstitions." Monroe did not laugh back. "The enemy will be heavily reinforced to-night," he said, "and to-morrow's fight will be more severe than to-day's by reason of the increased odds against us, and as the two-days' fight will constitute only one battle it is too early for your congratulations." Monroe finished his smoke and said, "Now as it is late and we shall need all the rest and sleep we can get, I bid you good night."[12]

As Monroe predicted, the morning found Buell and Grant together, and now the Confederates were outnumbered. The Orphans awoke, many of them with little sleep thanks to thunder during the night and an occasional shell fired from enemy gunboats. There was no surprise to lose this morning, so the brigade buglers sounded reveille and the men gleefully prepared their breakfast. Then came an abrupt order from Trabue. Discharge their muskets and reload afresh, and form. Some felt they noted a lack of that enthusiasm they saw displayed the day before. Either the men were tired or hung over, or more apprehensive when they believed that Grant was still in their front. Marshall told Monroe of his feeling, but the major just laughed and said he probably ate too much the night before. Elsewhere on the line Colonel Hunt ordered the men to discard their booty and prepare for battle. When he saw that Sergeant Henry Cowling still sported a big round of Ohio cheese at the end of his bayonet, Hunt "almost took his head off & made him throw the cheese away."

As the regiments went into line, Governor George W. Johnson looked toward a distant hill and saw it swarming with the enemy. He asked Captain Ben Monroe of the 4th Kentucky to formally swear him in as a private in his company. Monroe raised his military cap, unsheathed his sword, and asked the governor to raise his right hand. Johnson took the oath then, seeing Breckinridge on his horse nearby, spoke briefly with him, and asked that he look after his effects in case of his death.[13]

Breckinridge first heard firing on his right, as did Trabue, and shortly Beauregard ordered the Kentucky brigade sent forward, past Shiloh Church, to join Bragg. Trabue placed Byrne's battery on a rise beside the principal road from the church to the landing, and here the artillerist opened a fire that did not abate for nearly four hours. Grant's right wing lay in their front, but they held his advance, though at heavy cost. Several enemy field pieces concentrated fire on Byrne during the morning, eventually putting nearly a third of his gunners out of the action. The rest soon exhausted themselves, thanks to the recoil of their guns rolling them down a slope up which the men then had to manhandle them for each succeeding fire. "Old Joe" Lewis sat

watching the action nearby when Byrne came to him and asked for a
detail to relieve his gunners and assist in the barrage. John Slusser
of the 6th Kentucky yelled almost indignantly, "No detail! Call for
volunteers, and we are there!" Byrne made the call and the volunteers
flocked to the guns. Slusser soon fell with a severe wound, but another took his place, and Byrne's fire continued. Nearly one thousand
rounds he sent into the federal positions, Trabue noting that he
"served his guns with skill and gallantry." He silenced one enemy battery and severely damaged another. Several times the bluecoats
charged Trabue's line, but Byrne's fire and that of the infantry
defeated their intent. Morgan's squadron, now on Trabue's left,
formed and counterattacked, but had to turn back. Then Hunt led his
5th Kentucky in a charge. Before they could reach the federal battery
they sought, the enemy pulled back.[14]

As Byrne's battle waned, Trabue heard the fire increasing over on
the center and right of the Confederate line. A strengthened foe was
advancing to regain the ground lost the day before, and shortly
Trabue received orders to move the Orphans to the right to support
the new threat. He did not get far before becoming engaged with
bluecoats, and had to stop to face them. Here, without Trabue's
knowledge, Bragg removed the 4th Kentucky and the 4th Alabama
from the brigade and ordered them to assault the Union positions on
the north side of a broad field.

Until this time, the day's only casualty for the 4th Kentucky had
been a pet dog hit during Byrne's duel with the federal batteries. Now,
however, as the Orphans moved forward they once again met a storm
of enemy fire. They advanced within a hundred paces of the Union
line when they took a withering fire in front and on both flanks. Yet
here they stayed for nearly twenty minutes trading blows with the
enemy until the Yankees fell back to their reserves. The Kentuckians
prepared to charge with the bayonet, when a counterattack drove
them back. For an hour more the two lines jostled forward and backward indecisively. They were fighting fellow Kentuckians in General
William Nelson's division. Nelson himself was an old friend of
Breckinridge, and many of the men on one side of that field had
friends and even relatives on the other. Yet, as one Confederate artilleryman noted, "Wherever Kentucky met Kentucky, it was horri-
ble."

The losses mounted. Nuckols took a bullet in the ankle that lodged between two bones, causing the most excruciating pain. A surgeon extracted it on the field. Then, as Nuckols was carried to the rear, someone started singing. It was the "Kentucky Battle Song," a tune often sung at Camp Boone, though that seemed a long time ago now. "Cheer, boys, cheer, we'll march away to battle," it went. Well, they had done that now. "Cheer, boys, cheer, we'll nobly do our duty." The Orphans were doing that, and more. "And give to Kentucky our hearts, our arms, our lives!"

Giving their lives they were. The 4th Kentucky began the battle on April 6 with 431 men of all ranks. By the end of this fight they lost half of their number killed or wounded. After one repulse, Monroe brought the regiment back to the south side of the field and ordered the men to stop firing. Excited to recklessness, they ignored him, and he had to ride in front of the left wing of the regiment to enforce the order. Just then the men saw him fall back on the crupper of his horse, shot through the shoulder. They rushed forward and lifted him tenderly from his horse to carry him to the field hospital, but they could not help. He lived for two hours. His brother Ben, himself wounded, rode to the hospital to see him. "Ah! old fellow," said the dying major. "I knew you would come." He told his brother he was ready to die, gave messages of love and reassurance for his family, and then "expired quietly, consciously, and with more perfect calmness and serenity than I ever witnessed in any one before." They buried him beneath a tree and carved his name into the trunk, his prophecy fulfilled.

Another man took a mortal wound in that field. Governor George W. Johnson would never govern in Kentucky. Two bullets found him, one in the right thigh and the other in the abdomen. Thanks to the strength of his constitution, he stayed alive on the field for over twenty-four hours. The Federals found him on April 8, one of them recognizing a Masonic distress sign that he raised. His enemies treated him kindly, but he could not be saved. He died aboard a hospital ship on April 9. Some mistook him for Breckinridge and were disappointed when they discovered it was a mere rump governor. Others showed more respect. Johnson's body was entrusted to the care of one of his former political foes and received every attention.[15]

While the 4th Kentucky fought and bled, the other Orphans did not stand idle. Trabue fought them constantly for over an hour on the left side of the same field. He watched the performance of the men with pride, Lewis and his men winning his special admiration. "Old Joe" lost his second horse here and spent the rest of the battle on foot. His officers showed every heroism. Captain McKendree, so worried the day before that his company behave well, took a bad wound but refused to be carried from the field. "No, I do not wish to be carried away yet," he protested, "the boys will fight better if they know that I am near them." Generally they stood steady in the line, though John Philpot of Company F had his troubles. Calm as anyone as he fired at the enemy, he suddenly felt a bullet crease his scalp, and it momentarily drove him from his wits. Throwing down his gun, he furiously beat and scratched his head like a man being stung by bees. He regained his composure after a time and saw the grins on the faces of his companions. He put his hat on again, picked up his gun, and sheepishly went back to firing.

Elsewhere on Lewis' line Nat Crain of the same company, and the son of a Methodist minister, heard a mate who prayed so loudly as he fired into the enemy that others heard him over the din of battle. Moving to him, Crain told him, "Get up here, Will! what's the use in praying when the devil's done come?" The devil was there indeed. Two Thompsons of Company F, Elliott and Nat, engaged in a sort of duel with two bluecoats who fired from a vantage point aloft in a tree. They traded shots repeatedly without effect, when Nat told Elliott, "Let's stand out; then we can fetch 'em." They jumped to their feet, abandoned their cover, took aim, and fired in unison. At the same instant orders came to pull back. Elliott could not tell if their shots found their marks in the trees, but he did get a glance of Nat Thompson lying dead on the ground, a bullet through his forehead.[16]

Even the enemy admired the work of "Old Joe" and his 6th Kentucky. The regiment immediately facing them as the Orphans fought and then pulled back was the federal 9th Kentucky. It had organized in Adair County, just a few miles from Glasgow, where Lewis and his regiment had their homes. There were a number of Adair County men among his Orphans, and the Kentucky bluecoats earned a healthy respect for them. "They retired slowly and sullenly," said the 9th Kentucky's colonel of Lewis' withdrawal, "fighting over and disputing well every inch of ground, taking advantage of every tree, thicket, log, or other protection."

Hunt, too, won his share of admiration as Trabue strove to hold the left flank of Beauregard's hard-pressed line. He took his 5th Kentucky to the right and encountered General Beauregard, asking where he should go into the fight. "Put them in right here," said the general, pointing in his front, and Hunt ordered the charge. Here "Gos" Elston fell with a mortal wound. Hunt drove the Federals before him for a distance and through one of their camps. Johnny Green saw one Yankee hide behind a tent and take a shot at Captain Price Newman. Newman pitched headlong forward, and Green was certain he lay dead, not knowing that at the instant the Federal fired, the captain caught his foot on a tent rope and stumbled. When he arose again he shot the Federal with his pistol.

Poor Johnny thought himself gone a few moments later. He ran to a clump of bushes to reload in cover. Just as he raised his rifle to fire again he was hit in the chest, just over the heart. "I felt sure it had gone clear through me." The only thought in his mind was that he had time for one more shot before he died. He rose and fired. Then he felt his breast for the wound. What he found was a part of the bullet inside his clothes resting against his chest without breaking the skin. "I was surprised to find that I was still alive." The bullet coursed through the stock of his rifle, splitting it in two when it hit the ramrod. One piece lay next to his chest, and the other tore through his jacket and buried itself in the seemingly ever-present Testament that tended to stop bullets. More than one pierced Bible made its owner a true believer.

Hunt pressed on a bit more but then got Trabue's order to retire. The Orphans ran back at full speed under fire of an enemy battery, and just at this point Breckinridge galloped up to them and thought they were routed. He ordered them to halt, which they did in spite of the fire. "Can it be that Kentuckians are running off the field of battle?" he exclaimed. Quickly the nature of their orders was explained to the general, whereupon he allowed them to continue their retreat.[17]

Breckinridge himself twice felt the sting of spent balls striking him, while bullets tore several holes in his clothes. He had been fighting most of the day with the other brigades of the reserve in the more hotly contested center of the line. Indeed, Trabue held the Confederate left almost unassisted, and the manner in which he did it won the praise of his superiors. Bragg was frequently on the scene, particularly during Byrne's marathon shelling, often waving his hat in salute to their bravery. "For this gallant and obstinate defense of our left flank," Bragg wrote a few days later, "we are indebted to Colonel Trabue's small brigade."

By about 2 P.M. Beauregard realized that any chance for victory died when Buell reinforced Grant. With his army disorganized and exhausted, Beauregard saw no alternative now but to withdraw. The Federals were slowly extending their right in the attempt to turn Trabue's flank when Breckinridge received a message from the commanding general informing him of the planned retreat. Breckinridge and his reserve were to cover the movement and act as rear guard.

The Orphans held a position not far from Shiloh Church when the news reached Trabue. By this time both armies lay near exhaustion from the most fierce contest that had yet taken place on the continent. Still, the Kentuckians stood in line for another two hours against tired enemy attacks, while Hardee, Polk, and Bragg withdrew toward Corinth. Breckinridge brought one of his other brigades to assist Trabue. "This was a hard duty, exposed as the command had been and wasted as they were by the loss of more than half their numbers," Trabue reported, "but the general was equal to the great undertaking, and his officers and men shared his devotion to duty." Indeed, even with all his energies taxed in holding his line, Trabue could still take note of "the resolution, ability, and endurance of General Breckinridge." The Orphans were glad to have their general with them again.[18]

They bivouacked that night a mile and a half from the battlefield. "We were greatly exhausted & suffering for water," wrote Johnny Green. They slept on their arms again, in another pelting rain, the disappointment widespread that they had not won the expected victory. "My own feelings were too bruised and crushed to be talked of," said John Marshall. And this night there were no Yankee stores to plunder, no wheels of cheese and kegs of beer or sides of beef. "We were hungry, mad, tired, and in that subdued condition of mind and body when hardtack and sow-belly better suited our fallen fortunes." All through the night the wounded came into camp, and the ambulances carried those who could not walk along the slushy road toward Corinth. John Jackman spent the day at the brigade hospital and as darkness came assisted in removing the casualties. The wagons hardly moved in the dark and mud, but he and others kept them going, often by browbeating the drivers. Jackman's own wagon contained William Bell, adjutant of the 5th Kentucky, a bullet through his chest. Bell had refused to leave the line when Hunt ordered him to the rear, saying, "Col I shall follow you as long as there is breath in my body." Now he lay mortally wounded on the wagonbed and, after a few miles, an exhausted Jackman climbed inside, propped his feet up on the injured adjutant, and managed a little sleep.[19]

The next morning the command slowly retired about three miles toward Corinth, and here Breckinridge and the Orphans stayed for the next three days removing wounded, burying the dead, and sending captured property south to Beauregard. The commanding general told the Kentuckian to cover the retreat, and Breckinridge's reply had been, "Your orders shall be carried out to the letter, sir." So they were. He kept Forrest's cavalry posted in his front to discourage enemy skirmishers and scouts, while his main line sat ready for an attack should it come. The men ate damaged rations of bread and raw pork. They continued for days to straggle into the camp, the 3d Kentucky only now rejoining the brigade after being separated since the morning of the first day's fight. Even Breckinridge shared in the privation. The morning of April 8 he had only two biscuits for his breakfast. Then he saw two weary privates and gave one to them, while he shared the other with an aide.

Breckinridge feared at first that his troops were so worn that they would not stand after the first volley, but they surprised him. Finally, on April 10 Beauregard sent the order that the rear-guard action could be terminated. Breckinridge and the Orphans were to come to Corinth.[20]

The Kentuckians regained their usual jollity as they marched south. Soon began the boasting and jibing. John Slusser of the 4th, called "Devil Dick" so much that many knew him only by that name, bragged that he would tell his grandchildren one day, "I was in the great battle of Shiloh, and what I saw and what I did. They'll think of course that grand-pap was a hero, because the little things can never know how bad the old man wanted to get away from there!"

Some of the men who before were convinced that one Orphan could "whip five Yankees apiece," were forced to admit, "Over yonder last week, now—we didn't do it, did we?" Someone suggested that Grant's Army was not really "Yankee," since most of its men came from Kentucky and Ohio and Illinois. "Oh they were not Yankees; they were western men—men like we are!" That explained everything, though some found it sobering to note that from Canada to Florida, the woods were full of such western men. The Orphans' encounter with them forced some to amend their boasts. The preacher's boy Nat Crain used to yell that he was a "roaring tiger, with double rows of teeth—one for vegetation and one for Yankees." When he began the same brag now, he caught himself midway. He was still a roaring tiger with two rows of teeth, one for vegetation, "but *none* for Yankees!"

Some turned contemplative, finding irony in their designation as reserve corps. Before the battle, said an Orphan, he did not know what a reserve was. He knew now. "Yes; it means the best body of men that can be found to go in early, stay all the time, and afterward hold back the enemy for two or three days till the rest can get away with themselves and their impedimenta. It's a funny term, though—reserve."21

They were never modest, these Kentuckians, but they had just claim to pride in their performance at Shiloh. In their first battle of the war they held on two successive days a vital point on the left flank of the Confederate line, often beating back vigorous enemy assaults, and themselves taking considerable ground. They cut off Prentiss' route of escape, making sure of the surrender of the "hornets' nest," and the next day stood their ground near Shiloh Church to ensure the escape of their own army. The ferocity of their fighting told in the losses. Of a total of 2,400 ready for duty on April 5, 844 now lay dead or wounded, more than one third of the brigade. Trabue's own 4th Regiment lost half its effective number, and Cobb's battery was temporarily wiped out as a fighting force. Many good men lay in the sod around Shiloh. Johnson, Monroe, and other familiar names would not be heard again at the roll calls. The wounded included Lieutenant Colonel Bob Johnson, Cofer, McKendree, Nuckols, Ben Monroe, and Tom Thompson. On the morning of April 8, only 1,600 formed for the roll. "Breckinridges brigade suffered heavily," wrote a Kentucky officer in his diary, "but won imperishable glory." Their general, too, covered himself with plaudits. He made a lot of mistakes in the battle, but then so did all of the generals. He provided an example of undisputed calm and bravery, and in this war that counted almost as much as tactical skill. It was a learning time for him as well as for his Orphans, and he never again made the same mistakes. Hodge declared, "He had won for himself, throughout that entire army, the reputation of a skillful General, a brave and courageous captain." "I long to grasp your hand and tell you how you looked and fought at Shiloh," wrote a friend of the general's. "You have won golden opinions with the people as well as the army."22

"We went into it raw recruits," John Marshall wrote of Shiloh, "and came out of it stern and daring veterans. . . . We were literally baptized in fire and blood." Looking at his worn and dirty socks, he changed them for his fresh pair, thinking of their maker's warning not to turn their heels to the enemy. After what they had passed through, surely, he thought, she could be nothing but proud of them.

Looking back to their baptism that Sunday, an Orphan declared, "Yes, boys, it was the largest meeting that was ever held at Shiloh Church. And wasn't the music grand that day? Talk to me about pianos and organs; I never heard such a big organ as was played last Sunday."

An Irishman met Ed Thompson in Corinth a few days later, and quipped, "We went to church last Sunday week, didn't we?"

"Yes, to Shiloh Church."

"Well, I'm not going anymore," said Irish. "I don't like the sermons they preach there."[23]

SIX

"Your Gallant Band of Kentuckians"

GERVIS GRAINGER saw what "seemed to me an army of dead and wounded" coming into Corinth after the battle. They arrived for days after the action. Fortunately, the fight tired Grant's Federals as much as the Confederates, and he displayed no great anxiety to pursue. For the rest of the month the Orphan Brigade rested awhile. Johnny Jackman went fishing several days in a row. Johnny Green and his mates reveled in finally donning some new clothes they "liberated" in the enemy's camps at Shiloh. Only after wearing them did he discover that he captured more than clothing—the garments teemed with lice, and had to be boiled before they were inhabitable.

Breckinridge's first priority was to look after the comfort and health of his Kentuckians. He immediately made heavy demands on the Army's commissary, providing the Orphans rations of pork and bacon, fresh and salt beef, flour, cornmeal, peas, beans, rice, sugar, coffee, molasses, vinegar, even soap and candles. Riding through his camps he discovered that some Orphan regiments did not have "sinks," and that the "atmosphere was becoming tainted." He quickly gave them a lesson in camp sanitation, at the same time prohibiting them from stripping bark from trees for quick fires, thus ruining the forests. If they thought the aftermath of battle would provide a relaxation in discipline, they were much mistaken. There was detail work to do as well, nursing the wounded, guarding supply trains, carpentry at the hospitals, cattle droving, and protecting civilian property from soldier depredations. Yet life seemed easier by comparison. Officers of the 4th Kentucky enjoyed the luxury of hiring nine black cooks to serve their mess at a cost of only twenty dollars a month. Company C of that regiment received a "Company Fund" of sixty dollars sent from Union County, Kentucky, for the purchase of a few precious delicacies.[1]

The Army reorganized while it rested, and the Orphans could hardly remain untouched. Barely did Breckinridge reach Corinth when he notified Beauregard, "I am engaged in reorganizing my corps." "The reserve corps, was much engaged in the thickest of the fight, and did much to add fresh renown to the lustre of Kentucky arms," reported the Richmond press, but if it was to continue that renown there was much to do. The wounded were still being tallied, among them Irishman John Mahon of the 2d Kentucky, hit at Donelson and now again at Shiloh. It seemed to be a habit. There were also desertions to report and investigate, among them Sim G. Rucker of the 4th Kentucky. Courts-martial had to be formed to try those found derelict in their duty. On June 4 alone seven men faced a court. Even officers were not immune, as Lieutenant J. T. Shackleford of the 5th Kentucky would have discovered had he not resigned before his court met. And there were changes in the makeup of some of the companies. The Reverend E. P. Walton of the 4th Kentucky left on April 15 to go to Virginia and serve with another Confederate unit known by a sobriquet, the Stonewall Brigade. Lieutenant James Wilson, captured with Hanson at Donelson, escaped his northern prison and now appeared at Breckinridge's headquarters for duty. He became ordnance officer, and a personal favorite with the general. And an altogether unique character stepped forward to enlist on June 8. The Confederacy would never agree on how to spell his name. He presented himself as Kenshattentyeth or Konshattountzchette. Understandably, his fellow Orphans preferred to call him Flying Cloud. Here was a Mohawk sachem to outdo any of Buckner's Indians. A handsome man, he apparently led the life of a soldier of fortune and did rather as he pleased. He lived the white man's way most of the time, but when the mood struck him he stalked about camp with his blanket around him in Indian fashion, occasionally wearing a headband and feather. Obviously the southern people wherever the Orphans camped quickly took an interest in the red man, and Flying Cloud, for his part a bit vain, delighted in parading for the ladies especially.[2]

To re-form a brigade from the ruins of Shiloh, and the new material now in hand, Breckinridge and Trabue first faced an overabundance of officers. They consolidated companies to bring them up to strength, and the general asked permission to discharge bad officers in the process. Where there were casualties in the officer corps, he violated the rule of seniority and appointed the most efficient men, not necessarily those next in line. He even consolidated Crews's little Tennessee command with the understrength 5th Kentucky, all of Crews's officers agreeing to resign and serve under Kentuckians. Company K of the 6th Kentucky, never fully organized, now broke up and replaced the men and officers elsewhere in the regiment. Other companies elected their officers, and Lewis and Hunt's regiments, being only twelve months' volunteers, here began to reorganize for a period of three years or the war to match the enlistment of the other Kentucky regiments.[3]

Higher promotions occupied Breckinridge as well. Notified that he could nominate two of his colonels for general's stars, he easily settled on Robert P. Trabue as one of them. For his "gallant and meritorious conduct" at Shiloh Breckinridge wrote a letter that Beauregard endorsed recommending Trabue as a brigadier general. Unfortunately, nothing came of it, there being perhaps too many Kentucky generals on the rolls already. This did not stop Breckinridge. Ten days later he suggested Colonel Hunt for a promotion as well. "He is in all respects an admirable officer with a marked aptitude for command," the general wrote. This suggestion, too, came to naught, but when the general recommended Hodge for a brigadiership he got it. Some, however, declined promotion. To Captain Tom Thompson, Breckinridge offered a colonelcy and the command of an Alabama regiment in another of his brigades. Thompson turned it down, telling the general he felt he was too young, but in fact he simply did not want to leave his Kentuckians.[4]

For Breckinridge, promotion certainly loomed immediate. Less than two weeks after the battle, President Davis nominated him for a major generalcy, and the Senate confirmed it to date from April 14. When Bragg received the commission, he forwarded it to the Kentuckian with his own warm endorsement, "Nobly won upon the field, with . . . hearty congratulations." Beauregard himself declared that the Kentuckian "displayed great aptitude and sagacity, and handled his brigade with skill and judgement." Beauregard also noticed the gallantry of Breckinridge's son Cabell, and promoted him first lieutenant and aide on his father's staff.[5]

The makeup of Breckinridge's corps changed too, and it materially affected the Orphans in a way neither they nor their general ever suspected. Beauregard ordered now Brigadier General William Preston to report to Breckinridge, and soon thereafter two other new Kentucky generals, Hawes and the freshly commissioned Ben Helm, arrived as well. Here Beauregard did something inexplicable: He divided the Orphan Brigade. Perhaps it was because he wanted to portion them among more than one Kentucky brigadier. No one explained it then or later, but the result was that Trabue's 4th and Hunt's 5th Kentucky combined with the 31st Alabama, Byrne's battery, and another Alabama battalion to form a brigade for General Hawes. The 3d Kentucky and "Old Joe" Lewis' 6th joined a revitalized Cobb's battery, an Alabama unit, and the 7th Kentucky in making Preston's brigade. Helm received no Kentucky units at all in his command.

The Orphans were furious. An "ill-advised arrangement," Ed Thompson called it. It created a problem of nomenclature if nothing else. The Orphans took pride in their designation as 1st Kentucky Brigade. "It was founded upon some special fitness of things," he said. "To Kentuckians, the designation that they bore from the first . . . was as dear as that of 'Stonewall' to the brigade of Jackson." Consequently, there was widespread dissatisfaction among the Orphans. Hawes's command, officially the 1st Brigade of Breckinridge's corps, contained the 4th and 5th regiments, and they continued to call themselves the 1st Kentucky Brigade. But Preston's outfit, with three Kentucky regiments and Cobb, regarded themselves as the 1st Kentucky Brigade. On one occasion a Kentuckian from each of the two brigades passed each other, one hailing, "Hey, John!—what brigade do you belong to now?"

"First Kentucky Brigade," John replied, drawing out the words like a drillmaster.

"Ah-ha! you do!" shouted the other. "There," he said pointing to his own camps, *"there's* the First Kentucky Brigade!" And so the confusion, and discontent, prevailed for several months to come.[6]

Just how Trabue reacted, not only to being replaced as brigade commander, but also to seeing his Kentucky regiments separated, he did not say. But late in April he felt so unwell that he asked to be excused from duty. It is a certainty that another Kentuckian, Ben Helm, had other reasons for seeking leave. On May 4 he informed Breckinridge that he suffered from an "inability to perform the duties of a soldier." A statement by the Army's medical director was only slightly less delicate in saying that Helm underwent an operation on the lower bowels. But an examining surgeon called to look into Helm's application for leave, disspelled all the mystery. "I have carefully examined this officer," said Surgeon J. C. Cummings, "and find that he has Hemorrhoids, and fissure of the anus." Alas, how fleeting the glory of war.[7]

While one Kentucky general lay in his bed *hors de combat,* so to speak, his comrades tried their best to bring another one back to the fold. After his capture at Donelson, Roger Hanson went first to the prison at Camp Chase in Columbus, Ohio, and then to Fort Warren near Boston. Almost from the time of his capture, his friends and family worked for his release by exchange, whereby he would be freed in return for Confederates freeing a captured Union officer of equal rank. Foremost in the effort stood Eli M. Bruce, a Kentuckian who closed his extensive packinghouse operation in the North to go South to Chattanooga and supply the Confederacy. Many times during this war he took the interests of the Orphans as his own, and in May he inaugurated an attempt to free Hanson that nearly worked. His first step produced a letter written by Breckinridge, Preston, and others. In this, Bruce actually acted under the advice of a captured bluecoat officer who wanted to be exchanged for Hanson. Bruce told Breckinridge the case would require "your *advice* and *influence,*" and the general did what he could. "I regard Colonel Hanson a most valuable officer and his exchange most desirable," Breckinridge wrote. Not content with that, Bruce represented "Bench-leg" to the Secretary of War as "the best colonel in our service."

Problems arose, however. For one thing, the Union men in Kentucky did not want Hanson, Buckner, or any others exchanged. "They should not be exchanged or paroled while the war lasts," wrote a Kentucky congressman. Another said it was the state's "right" that these men remain prisoners. Yet the federal War Department relented and on May 23 authorized Hanson's exchange, though on condition that it be for Colonel Michael Corcoran. That same day "Old Flintlock" left Fort Warren for Fort Monroe, Virginia, the exchange point. There he hit real trouble, the bureaucratic mind. The man in charge of prisoner exchange at this point for the Confederates, Major General Benjamin

Huger, wanted not just Hanson but a group of captured privateers as well. They were sent as agreed, but somehow Huger did not feel he had been properly notified of the fact. He stalled and obfuscated for two months, Hanson all the while waiting without knowing what was happening. By July 20, having spent a good deal of time with relative freedom in Baltimore on parole, "Old Bench-leg" returned once more to Fort Warren, a victim of one of war's most deadly weapons, red tape.[8]

The Orphans could not wait for Hanson. They must wait, instead, for Henry W. Halleck, Grant's replacement in command of the federal army before them. He moved slowly toward Corinth, but move he did, and that meant a return to active campaigning. By the end of April Breckinridge again cautioned the Kentuckians to "fire with deliberation at the feet of the enemy." At Shiloh, he said, there had been "a lamentable waste of ammunition." It was mid-May when Halleck came close enough for skirmishing to begin, and finally on May 22 Johnny Green believed "a fight to the finish was at hand." There stood just under sixteen hundred Orphans ready for duty when the drums sounded the long roll that morning. The Kentuckians fell into line, two days' rations in their haversacks. A train of ambulances followed as they moved toward the battle line, hardly a comforting sign. Breckinridge, dressed in civilian clothes and wearing a broad-brimmed felt hat, rode along the regiments, Hunt's 5th Kentucky first. The men cheered him as he passed, and he stopped. "Boys," he said, "I shall try and be with you more to-day, than before." He said he felt he had not needed to be with them at Shiloh, knowing they would do well. Johnny Jackman considered this "quite a compliment," and joined in the huzza as Breckinridge rode on to be cheered by each regiment in turn. After a march of three miles the Orphans formed a line of battle and waited for the expected fight to begin, but it never did. Instead, they lounged about, then returned to camp, disappointed at not "hearing the bear growl."[9]

By the end of the month the Confederates determined that they could not meet Halleck on even terms at Corinth. Nearly besieged, they must evacuate. On May 28 Beauregard set his plan in motion, hoping to move his Army out of the fortifications without Halleck knowing it. To do so successfully he needed a reliable rear guard, and once again he turned to Breckinridge. To serve as rear guard for his own corps, "Old Breck" selected "Uncle Tom" Hunt and his 5th Kentucky, with Cobb's battery and a Mississippi regiment.

On the morning of May 28 Hunt broke his tents, sent his wagons to the rear, and marched the men into the trenches. There they sat all day, sometimes with heavy skirmishing. In the evening the Federals advanced close enough to lob a couple of artillery shells into the fortifications, but Halleck still did not appreciate what was happening. The Orphans in the trenches were not sure either. "Cannot tell whether we are going to wait for an attack, or retreat," Jackman scribbled in his diary. There they stayed the next day as well, the enemy not pressing them much. About dusk signal guns roared in the town, calling all but the rear guard to the trains that took them south toward Tupelo.

This left Hunt and the Orphans, with all the federal army before them. The next several hours passed quietly, many of the men dozing until midnight, when the whispered order to fall in passed from man to man. In absolute silence the Kentuckians padded back from the trenches. "It was so dark we could not see our file leaders." During the day the men speculated what would happen, not knowing about the evacuation. Now they would either attack or retreat. "We were in suspense—all were silent and anxious." Then, just as the column moved, someone accidentally set a tent ablaze. "The light dazzled only a moment on the aslanted guns of the gray column, as it wended through the colonnade of old oaks, then died away leaving inky darkness." They found now that the rest of the Army had gone, and when they turned left, south, they knew that they, too, were on the retreat. Still they bantered cheerfully when Hunt lifted the order for silence. "The 'orphans' are always cheerful," thought Jackman, "whether sharing the glories of victory, or in the midst of disaster."

They found Cobb and his guns and the whole of them moved south, the darkness so impenetrable that the artillery and even the men often bumped into trees lining the road. Crossing a bridge over a swamp, several Orphans fell into the mud below. By the coming of the first gray hints of dawn, the command saw Corinth to their rear, and rising from it the long black pillars of smoke that told of tons of stores set on fire to prevent capture. "All was quiet as death," Jackman noted. Nothing moved but a few broken-down horses gnawing at the grass. They were all the spoils that the Confederates left behind. That afternoon Hunt camped the Orphans at the crossing of the Tuscumbia

River after burning the bridge, effectively eliminating the best federal avenue of pursuit. For the first time in thirty-six hours the Orphans lay down to a good sleep, though Johnny Green wished he had not. When he awoke the next morning, he saw a rattlesnake coiled atop the blanket he shared with a mate. Green rolled out quick enough, and then warned his comrade, "Rattlesnake in bed with us!" The friend made speedy his exit, "but mr Rattler after poking out his tongue once or twice crawled quietly away beside a log near by & coiled up again." Jim Burba grasped the snake and waved it in the faces of several in camp before Captain John Wickliffe ordered him to kill the reptile.

Hunt marched all day and night June 1, and the next day halted at noon when he received word that federal cavalry had somehow ridden around him and now held a junction at Booneville that cut off his route to the main Army. While he allowed the men to rest and eat, Hunt consulted with the Mississippi officers and Cobb about what they should do. The Orphans could tell something was amiss. "We saw the field officers riding about looking 'blue,'" Jackman entered in his diary. Then a report came that the enemy was closing on them, and Hunt ordered the men into line.

With Tom Hunt in command of the rear guard, charge of the 5th Kentucky temporarily rested with Robert "Uncle Bob" Johnson. He missed capture with his regiment at Donelson and, Lieutenant Colonel Caldwell of the 5th being wounded at Shiloh, Johnson was filling his place. "Uncle Bob is a clever brave man," thought Johnny Jackman, "but utterly ignorant of military tactics."

The Orphans stood in line awhile as Hunt and the others tried to reach a consensus, and then several of them sat. Johnson gave a loud oath and ordered them back on their feet, saying they "didn't know the first principle of drilling." He gave the order to right face, but no one moved. "He grew purple with rage, thinking he had a little mutiny on hand."

"Why don't you move?" he shouted.

Someone reminded him that they had to have the order to shoulder arms first. He cooled slightly, mumbled something about everyone being able to make a mistake now and then, and gave the proper order. "The boys were full of laugh," said Jackman, "and knew that he would make other mistakes, and resolved to show them to him." Johnson marched them about for a bit until they halted where he wished, and gave the order to face the front. They did, but in the opposite direction. "Why in the h———l don't you turn around this way?" he shouted, but all he got in reply was a laugh from five hundred throats.

Johnson was saved further embarrassment when Hunt ended his council of war. The other commanders could not agree what to do, and finally Hunt told them to fend for themselves, that he would take his regiment straight through Booneville, enemy or no enemy. As "Uncle Bob" sheepishly moved to the rear of the 5th Kentucky, Hunt took the lead and marched south, the remainder of the rear guard deciding to follow him. Fortunately, the Federals in their front felt too weak to stop them and retired with only slight skirmishing. That night Hunt led his Orphans back into Breckinridge's lines to join their siblings. The general himself seemed overjoyed. Hearing that the enemy held Booneville, he feared that Hunt had been captured. That night, having successfully conducted yet another rear-guard action, Hunt's Kentuckians took a much-deserved rest. Johnny Jackman hardly understated when he wrote, "We were a tired set of boys."[10]

It was June 7 when the Orphans, still divided between two brigades, reached the rest of the Army at Tupelo. Here they might have thought to rest. It was oppressively hot, unaccustomed as these Kentuckians were to the rigors of summer in the Deep South. They might have hoped to spend a few weeks doing nothing more than seeking shade and trading with the farmers for food, though the latter proved something of a battle in itself. They asked outlandish prices for every kind of fowl from spring chickens to tough old ganders, and as for vegetables, Jackman declared that the enterprising tillers of the soil would charge "50 cts for peeping over the fence into the garden!"

Of course it could not last. Already it appeared that the Orphans and their general would not be allowed to rest or stand idle when there was a need for good men. Certainly the Confederacy would always be short of soldiers in this western theater, yet with notable regularity henceforth, when the call went out, the Kentuckians would be sent to answer. Now the call came from Vicksburg.[11]

Breckinridge left the command for a brief leave on June 9, Preston taking the reserve corps in his place. On June 19 the order came to proceed with the corps to Abbeville, Mississippi, to meet an anticipated move by the enemy against an important railroad bridge. Yet this was only a brief stop. Four days later, on June 23, instructions arrived to bring the brigades to Vicksburg and report to the Confederate commander there, Major General Earl Van Dorn. The Orphans found the march, and the ride from Jackson to Vicksburg by train, sobering. "Armies, whether friend or foe, desolate a country," wrote Jackman after viewing the waste of Mississippi. When he tried to buy his supper in a hotel in Canton, he had to stand in line to buy a ticket, then crammed into the dining hall with scores of other soldiers. He found too little food, too few of the young black waiters, and not nearly enough patience. Soldiers shouted for soup or beef, one threw his cornbread like a cannon ball, exploding it against a waiter's head. Someone else sent a roast potato "à la solid-shot" against the other side of the poor black's battered pate. Handfuls of onions and radishes rained like shrapnel, and soon steaming collards flew with the dispatch of grenades. Jackman pitied the waiters. "There were guests to the right of them, guests to the left of them, guests in front and rear of them." Finally the dark brigade charged under the tables for cover, only to be driven out the back door with a volley of hard crackers. The enemy routed, Jackman and the other Orphans captured the kitchen, where he finally got a piece of beef so tough his teeth "could not even make a print." He dined that night out of his own haversack.[12]

It was on June 30 that the Orphans caught their first sight of the environs of Vicksburg. They made camp under the bridge trestle of the railroad to Jackson, in a beautiful dell that unfortunately afforded no fresh water. Except when they went into the city itself, where cisterns held rain water, they relied upon stagnant pools here and there whose sweet, unpleasantly warm beverage contained a host of contaminants. No wonder that more of them feared catching yellow fever than an enemy bullet. Yet here they would stay for the next four weeks, though hardly idle.

Vicksburg, always a prize in federal strategy, controlled passage down the Mississippi to New Orleans, which the Yankees had recently captured. Should Vicksburg fall, then Lincoln's minions would enjoy unrestricted use of the Father of Waters, and thus split the Confederacy in two. To this end, a small army led by Brigadier General Thomas Williams moved toward the city from New Orleans, while a fleet of gunboats commanded by David G. Farragut steamed upriver to bombard the river fortress. To counter this threat Van Dorn needed the Kentuckians.

Breckinridge rejoined the command on July 1, the same day that the Orphans marched into the heart of the city. For many this was their first view of the Mississippi, and they found it impressive, the more so because of the enemy gunboats in plain sight below the city, and the smoke from others visible upriver. That night they went on picket duty on the riverbank, and for the next several days acted as guards for the river batteries. Here the Kentuckians encountered a real shelling for the first time, and they met it with varied reactions. "There can be no dodging of mortar shells," Jackman found. "One has to stand bolt upright, like a duck in the rain, and take the consequences." Some men dove into sink holes to escape, but ran the risk of being buried alive if the shell burst too near. They heard the deep boom of the mortars three miles away and soon saw the shells whirling high in the air before "they would come shrieking down." If one burst in the air, they first saw a little tuft of white smoke, then heard the explosion, and then a bizarre symphony as each of the jagged pieces of iron hummed on their way to the earth, "the different sized pieces making the different notes in the demoralizing music."[13]

For the next two weeks the shelling continued with little abatement, the Orphans alternating between duty on the river batteries and resting in their camp by the bridge. Finally on July 15 they received orders to move their permanent camp into the city. It came as a great relief. Already the bad water took its toll, and the sick list grew daily. In Vicksburg they would have good cistern water. The mosquitoes, too, would be less troublesome in the town. The gunners on the batteries slept under insect netting, which the Orphans did not have. "I had often heard that Mississippi mosquitoes were large enough to carry a brickbat under their wings upon which to whet their bills," Jackman wrote one night after the insects enjoyed a good feed at his expense, "but I was never so impressed with the truthfulness of the story." In the city, too, Breckinridge got better rations for his men. The beef sent them at the bridge spoiled before it arrived, but here he could requisition fresh bacon.[14]

Other changes of more importance took place. Van Dorn reorganized Breckinridge's command, making it no longer a corps but instead a division within his own Army. To this the Kentuckian readily agreed, for at first he and Van Dorn got on famously. Indeed, early in the shelling they even played together, manning one of the guns in a battery personally and firing away at an enemy gunboat "to amuse themselves." Yet it did not take long for Breckinridge to find Van Dorn's blatant egotism offensive, and thereafter their relations became very formal. The Orphans, too, resented Van Dorn's demeanor. One day one of the Kentuckians chanced to be near headquarters when the two generals appeared together. He found himself appalled. There he saw "the finest-looking man in the Confederacy, and that man a Kentuckian, subordinate to one so apparently inferior in every way." His blood seethed, and he exploded in rage when he returned to his mates in camp. "Coxcomb, dandy, fop, ball-room beau," he called Van Dorn, "and such a thing of paint, perfume, and feathers to command our Breckinridge—and us!"

While they simmered over Van Dorn, the Orphans did find encouragement in another new commander for them. Ben Hardin Helm, his illness behind him, so to speak, reported for duty on July 8, and Breckinridge assigned him to replace Hawes in command of the brigade containing the 4th and 5th Kentucky regiments. The Orphans themselves, of course, were irrepressible as usual. Tommie Conelly, Company I of the 4th, always seemed to have a dozen or so cartridge belts around his neck. He repeatedly proved unsuitable as a soldier despite all his officers' efforts, and when it came to marching in time, he was utterly useless. "Ah, Captain, I am not the height for a soldier," he said in his heavy brogue, "I'm not the height." The Irishman more than once demonstrated himself an able hand at raising a glass, however, and one night here in Vicksburg he was probably well anesthetized when "Vicksburg lamp-posts," as they called exploding federal shells, started their trip to the city. Just as Tommie passed through a railroad cut, one of the "lamp-posts" came shrieking overhead and Conelly jumped for cover. "Be jabers, boys!—faith, and why don't ye get out of the way?" he cried. "Don't you hear the locomotive coming?" Hunt's regiment, not to be outdone for the ridiculous, organized a race between two soldiers riding wild hogs. Grabbing them firmly by the ears, the Orphan riders held on for dear life as the race began and their comrades cheered. The enemy heard the cheering, however, and sent a few shells their way to dampen spirits. One burst close enough to the hogs to scatter them with dirt, hurting no one, but putting such a fright into the swine that they bolted at a frantic pace. One threw his rider, but Charley Edwards, just three months with the company, held on to his mount. The hog rushed straight for a fifty-foot bluff. Despite the efforts of those present to stop it, the animal ran off the edge with Edwards still astride. The hog survived, but the fall broke Charley's back and in a few minutes he died. "This cast a gloom over all," wrote Johnny Green. As a measure of revenge, they slaughtered and dined on the late Edwards' noble steed.[15]

Of course, the Orphans were here for action, and they saw some almost from the first. It seemed their lot to encounter the unusual in this war. Here at Vicksburg, after two weeks of suffering the intermittent bombardment, several of the men turned sailor for a time. On July 15 the Orphans heard the thunder of firing upriver and rushed to the banks to learn its cause. Soon they saw a new Confederate ironclad ram, the *Arkansas,* passing through the federal fleet unscathed to dock at a wharf below the city. Thousands cheered the feat of daring, though it came not without cost. The ship took some casualties, and now Breckinridge called on Helm for twelve Kentucky volunteers to turn webfoot. They should be experienced seamen if possible and, if not, then artillerists who could work the vessel's guns. Helm got Lieutenant R. B. Mathews and five men of Cobb's battery who volunteered, as well as Cabell Breckinridge, and several others. They reported to Captain Isaac Brown, commanding the *Arkansas,* and served a gun during that evening's fighting with Farragut's gunboats. "We worked the gun throughout the engagement to the best of our abilities," Mathews reported. That night they left the ship when the firing ceased, Captain Brown giving thanks for their services in what Mathews afterward called "our aquatic expedition." To Preston, Mathews proudly reported that his men acted "as Kentuckians have always and will continue to act before the enemy, whether on land or water." This did not end the Orphans' service with the vessel, however. Four days later Breckinridge called again for volunteers, preferably sailors or artillerists, this time adding that those who volunteered would be permanently transferred to the Navy. Several stepped forward, at least one, Caleb Allen from Lewis' 6th Kentucky, making the transfer and winning distinction in his service aboard ship. Several others, including four men from the 3d Kentucky, liked the Navy less, and deserted the ship the same day. On July 22 Breckinridge called for sixty more volunteers. By this time there was less enthusiasm. When Johnny Jackman thought he was destined to join the *Arkansas'* crew, one man in his company ran away, and he noted, "We all objected to such a fate." The ship looked like a death trap. The lieutenant in charge of the sixty-man detail said that if that was the sentiment of all the men, then he would resist the order.

When morning came, however, the lieutenant took the men to the ship just the same, having learned that they were only wanted as a work detail. That night they spent many laborious hours recoaling the ironclad. Then they were done.[16]

While the Orphans served aboard the ship, or guarded it at night from ashore, all of the Kentuckians suffered mightily from the disease incident to the climate. Almost daily John Jackman complained to his diary of feeling tired, feverish, unfit for duty. Johnny Green noted the same thing. "Sickness has been playing great havoc," he wrote. The problem was chiefly the water. That from the river was thick with mud, while well water "is almost milk white from the soapstone soil." Green himself went into hospital and became delirious. Twice he took a pan in hand and wandered away from the tent to a nonexistent spring his fevered mind could see but his feet not reach. Jackman, too, reported sick and the surgeons confined him to the hospital for several days.

The main disease was malaria, but diarrhea and dysentery took their portion from the ranks. Breckinridge tried relieving the Orphans from duty during the hottest part of the day, but it availed little. In the 4th and 5th Kentucky regiments the number on the sick list doubled by the end of July. On the 22d of that month, 628 men out of the five Kentucky regiments stood on the hospital report, and this did not include many sent away from Vicksburg for their illness. Even if the enemy could not defeat the Orphans at Vicksburg, the climate would.[17]

Thus, the timing could not have been worse for Van Dorn to send the Kentuckians on an ill-advised expedition against the Federal Williams and his command, now downriver at Baton Rouge. Yet on July 25 Van Dorn gave the order. At his own request, Breckinridge led his troops and commanded the campaign. Thanks to the illness and exhaustion among the men, it took three days before the Kentuckian put his Orphans and the rest of his division aboard the train. Always thinking of their wants, Breckinridge sent overland a herd of beef cattle and managed to coax a few new uniforms from the quartermaster. Alas, poor Jackman could not go. He was too ill. And Johnny Green, even though he arose from his cot and grabbed his rifle, telling the surgeon, "I would not stay away from my regiment when they were ordered to battle," returned to the hospital under threat of arrest. "I was mad enough then to cry." When the train bearing the soldiers left on the evening of July 27, it left a number of saddened Orphans behind.

But it left as well with the people of Vicksburg a high regard for these men of the Bluegrass who abandoned their homes to defend a country their state did not recognize. Just before leaving the city, Breckinridge received a letter from one citizen who declared, "I like your gallant band of Kentuckians, and now in exile from . . . home."[18]

The route led first to Jackson, then south to Camp Moore, Louisiana, not far from Tangipahoa, fifty miles east of Baton Rouge. Here Breckinridge joined other troops awaiting him, and bivouacked on July 28 while he organized his small Army into two divisions. Helm's brigade he placed in the 1st Division, and Preston's brigade—now led by Colonel Albert P. Thompson of the 3d Kentucky—in the 2d Division. Even before he could march, the sickness followed him to Camp Moore. "The climate and exposure are reducing regiments to companies," he complained to Van Dorn. Then there were the rattlesnakes. In Gervis Grainger's 6th Kentucky, one snake put five hundred men to rout. "Evidently we feared a rattlesnake more than the bluecoats." Breckinridge tried to delay for a day here, hoping that Van Dorn would cancel the attack, but on July 30 came a peremptory order to proceed.

That same day they started the march, fifty miles of nightmare. The heat became so intense that the men, many without shoes, could not bear to walk on the sandy road. Their thirst drove them in flocks to every stagnant pool of murky green water, ensuring more dysentery. They fell out of ranks in numbers. "Almost every farm-house on the roadside was converted into a hospital," wrote a newspaper reporter who accompanied the march. The wild razorback hogs caused them misery as well, stealing into their night bivouacs and making off with the Orphans' haversacks of cornmeal rations. Faced with all this, Breckinridge decided to cancel the attack on his own unless Van Dorn would send the *Arkansas* downriver. With the ironclad to attack Baton Rouge from the rear, the Kentuckians' reduced numbers of infantry might still have a chance against Williams' soldiers. Van Dorn agreed and dispatched the ship. It would arrive, he said, at dawn on August 5.[19]

By August 3 Breckinridge's command reached the Comite River, just ten miles from its objective. The march cost him 600 men. To cheer the Orphans now, he made a speech. "My brave, noble, ragged Kentuckians," he began. He promised to lead them personally in the coming battle, then gave them a day of rest. "We enjoyed the luxury of a plunge and a swim in the bright, beautiful water," recalled Grainger. Ordered to prepare two days' rations, the Orphans foraged —or plundered—in the countryside thereabouts. Ganders and potatoes were cooked to carry, and the men each received a portion of vinegar to add to the water in their canteens. It did not improve the water's taste, but might kill whatever lived in it. The general was still losing men to the climate. "The sickness had been appalling," he reported. He started from Camp Moore with perhaps 3,400 men. When they marched toward Baton Rouge at 11 P.M. on August 4, he had less than 2,600.[20]

"It was a rather dark starlit night," wrote Major John B. Pirtle. The men knew they marched to battle, yet some like Grainger so gave in to fatigue that they actually slept while they walked. When the column halted, they awoke only by bumping into the men in their front. Helm's brigade marched in the advance, and when he reached the vicinity of Baton Rouge halted shortly before dawn. Prior to this, some partisan rangers from the rear of the column slipped through the infantry and rode ahead of Helm. In the gathering dawn they stumbled into Williams' advance pickets, and firing ensued. Grainger heard "the ringing crack of a dozen rifles about four o'clock A.M., followed by another volley in a few seconds." He heard the evidence of a terrible accident. The partisans, surprised by the Federals they encountered, turned and raced back toward their column. But Helm did not know that the rangers were in his front. "Suddenly there came galloping down on us at full speed what, from the noise made by the horses' hoofs, seemed to be a regiment of cavalry," wrote Pirtle. At this moment Helm was sitting his horse at the front of the column. His aide, Captain Alexander Todd, brother of Helm's wife and of Mary Todd Lincoln, was just then talking with Lieutenant L. E. Payne, giving him messages to be sent home should he fall in the coming battle. Already one Todd son had died in the war.

Taking the horsemen thundering toward them for enemies, Helm's Kentuckians scattered to either side of the road and delivered the second volley heard by Grainger. "A scene of the wildest confusion ensued." Frightened artillery horses trampled men about them, two of Cobb's field pieces overturned, their caissons mangled as the teams bashed them blindly into trees. Horses fell, crushing men beneath them, and men and animals dropped on the spot from the wild bullets flying in the predawn light.

Helm soon realized what had happened and calmly rode among the troops calling on them to stop firing. Before he could succeed entirely, a bullet killed his horse beneath him, and the animal fell on Helm's thigh, so badly crushing it that he would be out of action for some time. Several enlisted men were killed, and Lieutenant Colonel John Caldwell of Hunt's 5th Kentucky narrowly averted death. One of the first bullets fired wounded his horse, and the animal bolted, running blindly toward the rear. As it approached his own regiment, Caldwell's men mistook him for a Federal and opened fire. His clothes took several balls, and his horse fell dead, in the act throwing Caldwell against the wheel of one of Cobb's caissons. Miraculously he survived and, with Helm now out of action, Hunt would take command of the brigade, and Caldwell of the 5th Kentucky. Alex Todd was not so fortunate. A stray bullet killed him instantly, his last letter to his mother still on his body.[21]

Once the Kentuckians restored order, Breckinridge arranged his battle line. The 1st Division, with Hunt and the 4th and 5th Kentucky, he placed on the right, and the 2d Division with Thompson and the 3d, 6th, and 7th Kentucky on the left. It was this latter command that first encountered the enemy as the Confederates advanced around 5 A.M. Colonel Thompson put the 3d Kentucky on his right, the 7th in his center, and the 6th Kentucky on his left. "Old Joe" Lewis was himself ill now, and Martin Cofer led the 6th. The Orphans advanced nearly a mile before they met Williams' skirmishers. The going was tough, the ground broken and covered with briars that some of the boys without shoes thought a bit "luxuriant." Then came the order to double-quick, the Orphans raised the Rebel yell, and on they charged into the edge of the federal camps and into a cemetery. Here the first Orphans fell, appropriately, some of them never to be found again. The other brigade of their division gave way on their right, leaving them isolated for a time, and the order was passed to lie down. "We promptly obeyed," said Grainger, "stretching ourselves like lizards." Some were in a pea patch, others like Grainger in a sweet-potato field. The bullets sounded like bees as they buzzed over their heads. Then they rose and advanced again. "The Third, Sixth, and Seventh Kentucky regiments were going ahead like a hurricane," wrote another newspaperman who witnessed the fight. "Nothing could stop their fearful and determined progress. The more obstinate the resistance the fiercer their onset. Overwhelming as were the odds against them, they

pressed forward, mostly at the 'charge bayonet,' yelling like madmen."
They halted briefly at a fence for cover, the men of the 6th Kentucky
taking several casualties from a Yankee hiding inside a tent until
Grainger and a half-dozen comrades sent a volley into it.

To their left they saw a battery that the Orphans nearly silenced by
their fire. Cofer believed he could have taken it, but just then he received orders to retire a few hundred yards. For the next hour Thompson's Kentuckians remained in position, firing almost constantly at the
enemy, who made only feeble attempts to counterattack.[22]

Meanwhile, Hunt and the other brigade of the 1st Division also enjoyed an initial success. They drove the Federals out of one of their
camps and back into the environs of Baton Rouge, but almost at the
first, "Uncle Tom" Hunt took a bad wound and had to leave the field.
In order to save time, Breckinridge gave command of the brigade to
Captain John A. Buckner of his staff rather than to the next senior
colonel, Buckner being immediately available. In the continuing advance a number of officers fell killed or wounded, and Buckner's brigade was considerably disorganized when it was ordered to retire so
the division's other brigade could continue the attack. Buckner
brought the men to the cover of a ravine, where he and Breckinridge
re-formed the brigade. The general drew his sword before the 4th and
5th Kentucky and gave them a look of inspiring appeal. "Come, my
brave boys, and follow me—I will lead you on to victory!" he cried.
Another witness gave his words as somewhat more terse. "My men,
charge!" Whichever it was, the Orphans rallied and followed their
general into the fight. They rushed without particular order, but drove
the Federals relentlessly from their camps and back to the river under
cover of a few gunboats. "During the whole engagement the Fourth
and Fifth Kentucky displayed the utmost gallantry," wrote a witness.
"Better men never followed a flag or faced an enemy than these two
regiments." Poor Caldwell, still hurting from his accident earlier that
day, had to leave the field from exhaustion, while thanks to injury and
illness, Trabue's old 4th Kentucky had no field officers and fought
under its senior captain, Joseph Millett. Yet "it proved a host, bearing
through the heat of the fray its tattered and bullet-riddled banner."
Millett took pride in the performance of the 4th, boasting that it "did
not abuse the confidence the commanding general has in his 'ragged
Kentuckians.' "[23]

Now with Buckner leading his brigade forward, Breckinridge ordered Thompson to charge as well. Thompson himself took a wound that put him out of action, and Colonel Ed Crossland of the 7th Kentucky assumed command. This final advance drove all of the Federals into the town and under cover of their gunboats. For an hour they battled the enemy, all the time now coming under fire from the boats on the river. The much-anticipated *Arkansas* did not show. She had been stopped by Union ironclads, disabled, and destroyed to prevent capture. Breckinridge could not know this. Now it was 10 A.M. Looking about him, he saw not more than a thousand men, all thirsty, all exhausted. He had done all he could with them, and would not expose them further to the heavy artillery fire. If the *Arkansas* should finally appear, he would renew his attack. He ordered the enemy's camps and stores set afire and, that done, retired his divisions from the field, taking them first to a creek a mile from the line. It proved dry, and so he advanced again to some cisterns in the suburbs of Baton Rouge, and here the Army remained for the rest of the day. Late that afternoon word of the *Arkansas'* fate finally reached him. Now there was nothing more that the Confederates could do with those enemy gunboats safely in the river and still bombarding them. Breckinridge gave the order to withdraw, and that night they camped once more on the Comite River.[24]

It had been, for its size, quite a battle, and the Orphans, though divided between two brigades, accounted for the bulk of the fighting. Indeed, one of the newspaper correspondents present wrote, "I speak of the Kentucky regiments more in detail . . . for the reason that they bore the brunt of the fight. But this was only in accordance with the promise of Gen. Breckinridge, who, in a brief address a few days before, told his 'brave, noble and *ragged* Kentuckians' that he would lead them wherever there was danger." So he had, and it showed in their losses. All told the Kentucky regiments lost 24 killed or mortally wounded, 82 wounded, and 4 missing and presumed dead. Poor John Mahon took another bullet, his third wound in three battles. Helm, of course, lay disabled and even now recuperating in a home nearby where he would suffer considerably until September. The Orphans had seen the last of him for a while. The cost in animals had been great, too. The good-looking, six-foot, one-inch John Wickliffe of the 5th Kentucky lost a horse valued at $350, his gray eyes teared at the death of a good friend.

The day after the battle Breckinridge issued a congratulatory ad-

dress to the men. The sickness, forgotten for the moment with the battle, returned again, and Breckinridge was warned that his little Army
might soon be destroyed by malaria and dysentery. Despite this he put
Helm's brigade on the march toward Baton Rouge once more, then
turned them to the right and occupied Port Hudson on the Mississippi, a commanding place that would become a bastion of the Confederacy's river defense for almost a year to come. Trabue was well
again now and rejoined the command, taking Helm's post. The
weather remained hot, water scarce, and the Orphans naturally re-
verted to their errant ways. Men of the 6th Kentucky, angry because
the gander they cooked before the battle had been thrown away by
its owner—"blamed if I could afford to be killed with a stolen goose
swung around my neck"—cornered a farmer's cow and forced her to
"stand and deliver." Cognac appeared miraculously, probably lifted
from a drawing room in Baton Rouge, and it made the rounds, only
serving to increase their appetites. Still, the foraging proved to be
good, and the Orphans looked forward to a period of rest at Port
Hudson. Then came more orders.[25]

Breckinridge's performance at Baton Rouge aroused the interest and
admiration of the Confederate people. Congress in Richmond voted
him and his Army its thanks, and Van Dorn even complimented the
"skill and intrepidity" shown at Baton Rouge. Others were interested
as well. Ever since the Confederates had been forced out of Kentucky
early in the year, they dreamed of going back. It was a dream that
lasted as long as the war. Beauregard was gone now, and Braxton
Bragg commanded the principal army in Tennessee. He conceived of
an invasion of Kentucky for the fall of 1862, expecting that the appearance of a southern army in the Bluegrass would act as the catalyst
needed to persuade Kentuckians to flock to his banners with their arms
and their supplies. And the state, once safely Confederate, would be a
key to successful defense of the entire South.

Obviously, Bragg would enjoy a great advantage in his campaign if
the more prominent Kentucky generals and their troops marched with
him. Breckinridge and his Orphans were first choice. Indeed, on the
very day of the fight at Baton Rouge, Kentuckians in Richmond urged
the President to send Breckinridge to Bragg. "I should regard it as a
very serious misfortune to our cause in Kenty if the army were to
reach the state and you absent," wrote a friend. The general was not
unaware of the planned movement, and had made it known that he

wished to be a part of it, but only if he could take the Orphans with him. His friend J. Stoddard Johnston reached his camps on August 14 and brought with him a letter from Bragg in which the latter claimed that his Army had promised to make him military governor of Ohio. "As they cannot do that without passing your home," Bragg wrote with a rare touch of humor, "I have thought you would like to have an escort to visit your family." Speaking seriously, Bragg went on. "Your influence in Kentucky would be equal to an extra division in my army." But he wanted the general to leave his Kentuckians and come by himself, and that Breckinridge would not do. "I would make any sacrifice to join you," he wrote Bragg on August 10, "except leaving the remnant of my command." All he could send, he said, was his heart.[26]

Bragg wanted Breckinridge badly enough that the problem was quickly solved, or so it seemed. On August 18 an order reached camp, the content of which soon spread throughout the Orphans' bivouac. At once the smoldering embers of the cooking pits blazed with bonfires. Regiment after regiment raised the cheer. The men began cooking their rations for what they hoped would be a speedy trip to join Bragg. "No body could sleep," an Orphan wrote in his diary. They sat awake all night at their fires, talking of other hearths at home that they would soon see again. Once during the excitement, all the regimental bands joined together in song. They played a Stephen Foster tune, "My Old Kentucky Home."[27]

SEVEN

"Breckinridge's Wild Kentuckians"

"I HAVE ENCOUNTERED EVERY DIFFICULTY a man could meet," complained General John C. Breckinridge. Despite Bragg's order for the Kentuckians to join him, Van Dorn did not wish to let them go. He had a campaign of his own in mind. For several weeks the situation remained fluid, Breckinridge still subject to Van Dorn's orders all the while. "I groan and obey," he lamented. Finally Bragg gave Van Dorn a peremptory directive to release the Kentuckians, but it was only an order from the Secretary of War himself that finally brought action. As a result, a full month passed after leaving Port Hudson before the Orphans finally started on their way to Knoxville and Bragg.

It was for Breckinridge perhaps the most frustrating month of the war, and the Orphans felt the tension too. On August 19 they marched gaily out of Port Hudson, the general at their head. "We moved off with a light and bouyant step," wrote John Jackman, now back with his regiment. The bands played "Get Out of the Wilderness," and the Kentuckians did their best to do just that. Even the rains did not dampen their spirits. Hunt's men felt hardy enough to raid a watermelon patch along the way. Their clothes hung from them in tatters, their feet blistered from the burning sand, and to passersby they looked altogether like something from a fantasy. Naturally, this perverse notoriety appealed to the Orphans. When civilians stopped to marvel at their thoroughly ventilated clothes, the boys often as not asked them how they liked the style of their pants, commenting that they themselves found them wondrously "light and cool," by far the latest in military dress. With pride they pointed to their banners, on which Breckinridge allowed them to inscribe "Shiloh, Vicksburg, Baton Rouge" in honor of their performance. They looked fondly to marching past their homes under those banners, but when they reached Jackson and went into camp, the mood changed. "This regular camp does not look much like going to Kentucky soon," lamented Jackman, and he was right.[1]

It was on September 19 that the Orphans finally boarded the train that took them away from Van Dorn for good, and toward home. "Going to Kentucky certain this time," Jackman told his diary. Johnny Green was back, too, and he shared the elation. "When once started our hearts beat high with the hope of once again treading our mother soil." The train took them to Jackson again, then on to Meridian. The roadbed was not of the best on this last leg, and at one point a car jumped the track. Convinced that the whole train would soon crash, "Uncle Tom" Hunt, still wounded but recovering, jumped from his car. His staff, "not questioning rank," followed. When the train stopped, Jackman looked back to see the track lined for several hundred yards with Orphans lying down, sitting up, feeling their bodies for broken bones, and generally laughing. The car was righted back on the tracks, and the train finally reached its destination. Here another train boarded them and took them back through Meridian and south to Mobile, where everyone disembarked to await a steamer that would carry them up the Alabama River to Montgomery.

With a night on their hands, the Kentuckians, officers and men alike, went into Mobile to "have a time."

"Old Trib" tried to keep the Orphans at the railroad depot, but despite his best efforts they escaped him, some by melting into the darkness, and others by claiming that they had to go into town to find their missing friends. What they all really wanted to find were some of Mobile's famous oysters. "Soon the whole brigade was scattered over the city," wrote Jackman, "all bent on having a spree." Johnny Green and some boys from the 5th Kentucky marched straight for the Battle House and gaily entered its supper room. Imagine their surprise when the first face they saw belonged to Colonel Robert P. Trabue. Not as dense as they thought he was, "Old Trib" knew just where the Orphans would go and beat them there.

"What in -H- are you doing here?" he shouted.

When told they were looking for stragglers, he retorted, "Yes, you are looking for straggling oysters. I know what you are up to. Now get your suppers quick & get back to the regiment or I'll put forty b[a]yonets through you." Green noticed that the colonel had already eaten a bit himself, and done "a little more than his share of drinking."

On September 27 the Orphans embarked aboard two steamers, the 5th Kentucky on an old cotton boat, the *Waverly,* and the 4th and 6th Kentucky on a fine passenger packet, the *R. B. Taney.* Once they cast off, it seemed that a race between the two boats was inevitable, given the competitive spirit of the Kentuckians. The *Waverly's* steam was down at the start and the other boat easily passed her, the men on the *Taney* cheering, their band playing, and the boat's caliope screaming in victory. But Company H of Hunt's regiment were almost all steamboatmen, and they would not be outdone. They took control of the *Waverly* and soon had her plowing the waves "like a thing of life." Every man in the regiment turned fireman for the race, throwing anything combustible into her fireboxes. Before long they overtook the *Taney* and passed her, despite the other boat's turning sideways in the river to try to block passage. During the excitement Sergeant Bartholomew Sullivan of Company H, 4th Kentucky, got a bit too excited, or else he was still a bit "wet" from the spree in Mobile. He was careless, fell overboard from the *Taney,* and drowned without a trace.

On September 30 they finally reached Montgomery, and without a rest boarded a train for Atlanta. Along the way the ladies of the towns they passed thronged at the depots to cheer them. By the time they reached Atlanta the cars bulged with the bouquets thrown to them along the way, but their reception now was much different. They were getting a reputation, these Orphans, and not just in the Army. "In Atlanta all the people were scared," lamented Johnny Jackman, "having heard that Breckinridge's *wild Kentuckians* were coming through." About all that greeted them at the depot were a number of refugees from Kentucky, "bright eyes" from the "promised land."

Breckinridge rode with the Orphans throughout the trip toward Knoxville, and as the train passed Dalton, Georgia, he entered Jackman's car for the remainder of the journey. Word of his coming spread before him, and at every stop on the route people gathered around the train and asked him to step out and speak to them. Invariably he declined, and finally left the car to join Hunt and others in the caboose. He had given up speaking for a better occupation, he said—

fighting. Finally he napped as the train proceeded on its way, and when the crowd called for him at the next stop, the mayor demanding "Gineril Brackanridge," someone pointed to Dr. John E. Pendleton instead. A good-looking man in his own right, the surgeon of the 5th Kentucky kept quiet, allowed the people to gaze sufficiently at him for several years' worth of stories of how they saw the great General Breckinridge, and then the train left. The same scene repeated itself at subsequent stops until they reached Knoxville late on October 2.[2]

Immediately upon arriving, Breckinridge wired Bragg that he was near. Bragg and his Army already lay deep in Kentucky. The next day, having captured Frankfort, they installed Richard Hawes as Confederate governor of the state, but advancing Federals forced them to retire immediately. The Kentucky campaign had gone sour almost from the beginning, and Bragg was a man psychologically unable to take responsibility for defeat. He must have someone on which to blame the failure of his great endeavor, and that would be the unsympathetic people of Kentucky, their self-important generals in his Army, and particularly the foremost Kentuckian of them all, John C. Breckinridge. Thus Bragg was not receptive to Breckinridge's statement that "I hope you are satisfied with my energy since I was allowed to leave." It did not matter that in just two weeks the Kentuckians had traveled over eleven hundred miles on seven different railroads and one water route, hampered all the way by official interference. Indeed, Bragg had already been hard at work for a month building his case against Breckinridge. "I had hoped General Breckinridge would be with me soon, but he is far behind my calculation," Bragg complained early in September. By September 17 he was blaming the Kentuckian for not being with him, even though he knew that Van Dorn would not allow him to leave at the time. By September 25 Bragg claimed that "the failure of Genl Breckinridge to carry out his part of my program has seriously embarrassed me, and moreover the whole campaign." Just days before the Kentuckian reached Knoxville, Bragg declared that "Breckinridge has failed." Within the recesses of his own twisted mind, Braxton Bragg made himself an enemy of the Kentuckians as deadly as any federal bullet. Soon he would strike.[3]

Immediately upon reaching Knoxville, Breckinridge organized the troops with him and those found there to take them into Kentucky. True, Bragg was retreating from Frankfort, but fresh troops and the presence of the Orphans in their native state and led by their general

TO THE PUBLIC!

I have authority from the Confederate States, to raise a regiment of infantry, and for that purpose am now, by the order of General Buckner, encamped at Cave City, Barren County, Ky.

Kentucky might have been spared the calamity of a civil war, if Union men had in good faith adhered to the policy of neutrality, for which they clamored in the beginning; for Southern rights men, all over the State, for the the sake of peace, had agreed to acquiesce in it. We might all have been united, and at one time were united in opposition to coercion; but our Representatives in Congress, false to their pledges, and untrue to their State, deliberately pledged their constituents to the support of the war. Even after troops from the North and South had respectively occupied Kentucky, we might still have been a unit upon the proposition to drive out both parties.— But the Legislature foolishly and wickedly spurned this last overture of peace, and now we behold armies in hostile array in Kentucky, and civil war inevitable—yea, actually existing. Calm and considerate men must inquire the reason for this base betrayal of the interests and peace of Kentucky by her members of Congress and Legislature. It cannot be that they sanction this war with any hope of ever subduing the South. The man who thinks nine millions of people, as brave and united as are the Southern people, can be conquered by even four times the number of their present enemies, knows little of Southern character, and cannot appreciate the spirit of men fighting for their liberties, homes and the right to govern themselves. And he is ignorant of the first principles of a free government who believes a union is worth preserving that requires the conquest and subjugation of more than one-third of the entire population for its preservation.

This day the government of the United States under the administration of Lincoln is as corrupt as the Austrian, and as despotic as the Russian monarchy. Men's property, lives and liberties, are daily paying the forfeit for disobedience to his oppression, unlawful and wicked edicts. Insidiously and secretly he has introduced into this State and placed in men's hands weapons purposely to be used against their neighbors. Kentucky's roads and rivers have been blockaded, her commerce suspended, and corrupt and insolent agents set over us in the towns, and on public highways, from whom peaceful citizens have been absolutely compelled to buy the privilege of selling the produce of their farms, the wares from their shops, and goods of their stores. Let any man if he can, tell the difference between the highwayman who demands the traveler's life or purse, and the Lincoln agent, who allows the contraband goods to pass if a fee is paid him, or confiscates it if the fee is refused.

Where is the honor of Kentucky, that her people should longer listen to, or be controlled by the corrupt base and vindictive Yankee at the head of the Louisville Journal. Shall, to the humiliation of having permitted her policy to be controlled by him, be now added the infamy of being bartered away and sold by him to Lincoln? Shall a million of people be sacrificed by civil war, to enrich a Yankee editor or to give places and positions to the families of recreant Congressmen?

The Legislature has determined that the friends and protectors of Southern Rights men shall be driven from the State; that their enemies and oppressors shall be invited to stay. The great law of self preservation requires us to repudiate our Legislators, and with our strong arms do for ourselves what they refused to do for us—protect our lives, liberties and property.

Let no Southern man flatter himself that a timid acquiescence in Lincoln's policy will save him from the vandalisms of his hirelings. If he is so deceived, he has but to know Maryland's wrongs and Missouri's woes, to read his own fate.

Already has one of Kentucky's Ex-Governors, (Hon. Chas. S. Morehead,) been carried to another State a prisoner, and others fleeing before Lincoln's army to save their lives. Even now free speech has given place to military law. I have already learned of outrages upon persons and property being perpetrated.

The only hope for Southern Rights men is to unite now and show those who would oppress and wrong us that we are able to defend ourselves. Then let every man come to the camp. Come at once. Delay is sure destruction. Union amongst ourselves, prompt action and a bold front will save us, NOTHING ELSE WILL. It is not my purpose to invade any man's private rights. I do not intend either to injure or deny protection to any peaceful citizen, merely because he is a union man. It is only those who place themselves in a hostile attitude to the South and Southern rights men, that I war on.

JOSEPH H. LEWIS.
September, 23, 1861.

5. Colonel Joseph H. Lewis' appeal to the Barren County men to join his 6th Kentucky Infantry. *(From Joseph H. Lewis Scrapbook. Courtesy Helene Lewis Gildred)*

6. The father of the Orphan Brigade, Major General John C. Breckinridge. The love of each for the other became legendary. *(From the
Author's Collection)*

7. "Old Trib." Colonel Robert P. Trabue raised the 4th Kentucky, then led the Brigade at Shiloh. He wasn't much for tactics, but the men knew he was a leader. (*From Thompson,* Orphan Brigade)

8. "Uncle Tom" Hunt, like Trabue, would have made a good general. Yet he, too, had to abandon his Orphans. (*From Thompson,* Orphan Brigade)

9. Major Thomas B. Monroe died on the field at Shiloh at the head of his 4th Kentucky. They buried him beneath a tree and put his name on the trunk. (*From Thompson,* Orphan Brigade)

10. Captain D. E. McKendree made quite a speech to his company of Orphans before Shiloh. They did not fail him, but they did lose him at Dallas. (*From Thompson,* Orphan Brigade)

11. Brigadier General William Preston commanded part of the Orphans for a time but left them to go where they would not—Kentucky. *(Courtesy Massachusetts MOLLUS Collection)*

might still retrieve the campaign. After two months of constant frustration in his efforts, Breckinridge would not give up yet, though he was tired, angry, and showing signs of an unaccustomed irritability. His frustration eased a little when he found an old friend awaiting him in Knoxville, or rather old friends. "Bench-leg" Hanson and the rowdy 2d Kentucky were back to join the Orphan Brigade.

It had not been an easy time for "Old Flintlock" and his imprisoned Orphans, though it could have been worse. At first the Federals even considered allowing his wife, Virginia, along with Mrs. Buckner and other spouses, to visit their husbands before they reached Fort Warren. This they later denied, but still Hanson could write. He begged Virginia to write to him every day, warning her that "you need not hope to see me while I am a prisoner. The rule here is inflexible." Meanwhile, he comforted her that "I have nothing to complain of." As for coming home or rejoining his brigade, he tried to put it from his mind. "When I shall get my liberty again is a question I do not discuss or think about. I shall abide patiently my fate and hope I shall have the heart to meet any emergency that may befall me." Virginia took his incarceration hard for the first months, and this pained him more than his own situation. "What is the use of being sad?" he asked her. "That does not make my imprisonment of shorter duration or more agreeable."

At first Hanson shared a room with Buckner and others, but soon the general was placed in solitary confinement. Those who remained made a comfortable lodging of their cell. "Bench-leg" took particular pleasure in the softness of his straw mattress, reminding Virginia, "You know *I like a soft bed.*" Indeed, he told her, "We live as well as I have ever lived in my life." By the beginning of May he began thinking of exchange. "I am expecting every day to hear something about *exchange*," he wrote, but what followed was the fiasco with Huger. "Just as the little boy says," he wrote Virginia, "*I want to go home.*" Indeed, he never despaired of release even after the bumbled attempt at exchange for Corcoran. "I can not believe that two Governments in this age of the World will be so cruel as to keep ten or fifteen thousand prisoners each in prison when they have the power to release them." One year hence such naïveté would bring smiles, if not laughter.

There were other means of passing the time as well. Friends and relatives from Kentucky wrote and sent small packages of delicacies. Poor Captain S. F. Chipley received letters from his father "lecturing him

upon the *glories* of the *Union*," but one example of the families of
Kentucky that this war divided. Hanson took good-natured barbs from
old friends in the Bluegrass who supported the Union. Chief among
them was a man personally beloved, yet politically despised, by a host
of Kentucky Confederates, George D. Prentice, editor of the Louisville
Journal. Shortly after Hanson took residence at Fort Warren, Prentice
sent him a demijohn of whisky and the injunction, "I hope, my old
friend, that you will take things calmly. I hope you are a philosopher,
which is the next best thing to a patriot, which is the next best thing to
a Christian. Pray be the first, for I almost despair of your ever being
either of the last." Hoping that "Heaven and the United States Government" would deal kindly with Hanson, Prentice gave his affec-
tionate regards. Hanson responded in kind, gleefully reminding Prentice that his own sons now wore the gray, and rejecting the whisky, "as
I do not drink myself." He did admit that on a couple of occasions the
two of them raised a glass together in happier times, "but upon neither
of them do I believe that you were in a condition to tell how much
anybody else drank." Since Prentice liked to refer to Hanson as a
drunkard in his editorials, "Old Flintlock" turned the same accusation
against him. "I hope you will become a sober man," he wrote, "which
is the next best thing to a truthful man, which is the next best thing to
an honest man—pray be the first as I almost despair of your being either of the two last." Noting Prentice's wish that God and the Lincoln
administration would be kind to him, Hanson closed with his own
hope that "hell and your conscience may deal as kindly with you." He
signed the letter "Your old friend." What remarkable people these
Kentuckians.[4]

Though Hanson stood his captivity in some comfort, the enlisted
men of the 2d Kentucky Infantry met a different lot in Camp Morton,
Indiana. There the frills the officers received did not abide. They did
have their regimental dog, Frank, captured with them at Donelson,
but little else. As a result, escape loomed inviting, and these Orphans
never stopped trying. John Crockett of Graves's command led one attempt to overpower a guard, while Jim Fagan of the 2d, a native of
Indiana, actually reached the outside but ran into some patriotic
farmers with squirrel rifles and soon rejoined his comrades. At one
time the Orphans rose in a mass in their determination to be free.
They overran a weak point in the stockade only to meet federal guards
outside. A small battle ensued, and the Orphans found themselves

overpowered, bloodied, and returned to their barracks. J. F. Collins actually escaped with fifty others and got a mile from the prison before the guard caught him. He surrendered, but from confusion or cruelty, they shot him. Of the few who did escape to Kentucky, most, like Lieutenant H. F. Lester of the 2d Kentucky, rejoined their commands. Others became partisans or guerrillas instead. Jerome Clark of the 4th Kentucky helped serve Graves's guns at Donelson before capture. When allowed to bathe in a river near the prison, Clark and three others overpowered their guards and fled for Kentucky, intending to find their brigade. Instead, Federals found them, and one of their company was almost murdered. Clark swore revenge. Escaping his captors, he became one of the most dread bushwhackers and guerrillas in the Bluegrass, known as "Sue Mundy." And, though none of the Orphans might care to remember the fact, there were those Kentuckians unable to escape who could no longer take captivity. They had one alternative —taking the oath of allegiance to the United States. Five of "Benchleg's" Orphans took the oath, as did one of Graves's. It was a matter not spoken of by the others.[5]

Yet exchange came at last for Hanson's men, and for him on August 5, 1862. By September he was in Chattanooga, Tennessee, organizing supplies and arms for Bragg's Kentucky expedition, and hopeful of joining in it himself. He commanded an ersatz brigade for a time, incorporating his own 2d Kentucky, but expected all the while to be reunited with the 1st Kentucky Brigade when Breckinridge brought them by on their route home. On October 3, as "Old Breck" and the Orphans reached Knoxville, Hanson was ready. Anxiously he wired Breckinridge, "Do we go with you?"[6]

Yes, Hanson would go with him, if he went at all. For Breckinridge the frustration of the last two months did not lessen upon reaching Knoxville. Rather, it increased; for here he encountered new difficulties, including the governor of Tennessee trying to appropriate his troops for other purposes. Normally a man of unusually pacific temperament, the general felt increasingly the weight of his thwarted efforts to enable his Orphans to campaign for their homes. Amid all the worry and frustration fraying his nerves, he did not need additional aggravation. The 1st Kentucky Brigade could not have chosen a more inopportune moment to mutiny.

No more independent men served the Confederacy than its Kentuckians. However wild and reckless their conduct, they were men who, like their state, guarded jealously every right, every prerogative. Considering the peculiar relationship they bore with the new nation, they felt entitled to stand on their rights. Unlike any other unit from a genuine Confederate state, they were entirely volunteers. The draft could not apply to Kentuckians. They were here because they wanted to be here. Indeed, they did not even fight for their own state. They fought and died for a nation their native soil refused to countenance. As a result, they resented being treated like soldiers from the seceded states. Not citizens of the Confederate States of America, they did not feel bound by its actions. In particular, they objected to the conscription.

The roots of the trouble dated from the time Hunt's 5th Kentucky formally organized. While most regiments for southern service were raised for three years or the duration, Buckner enlisted this regiment for one year on the condition that they provide their own arms. This they did, though soon thereafter Breckinridge tried to get the War Department to pay them for their guns, with something additional to allow for the inflation of Confederate currency. It is unclear whether these Orphans ever got the money, but if they did, it rather effectively negated their part of the enlistment contract. Thus they should have been eligible for three years' service too.

The men began to feel uneasy on this score that summer of 1862 when they saw other twelve months' volunteers automatically being continued in the service for three years or the war, with or without their consent. By early September the rumor coursed through Hunt's camps that Breckinridge intended they should be held in service after their year expired. Fearful that it might be true, the officers of the 5th Kentucky addressed a letter to their general on September 16, even as the move toward Kentucky finally commenced. They pointed to their "contract" with Buckner and declared that "in view of the fact, that at the time of the enlistment of the men, they were citizens of another nation; and also that our native state has never been under the control of the Confederacy, . . . They do not consider themselves liable to the provisions of the Conscript Act." They asked to be discharged when their year expired.

The thought of being forced to remain in the service created unrest in the 5th Kentucky, and "the existing dissatisfaction would materially impair, if not completely ruin the efficiency of the Regt. and bring disgrace upon our noble state." If discharged, they believed that most would voluntarily re-enlist or else go into Kentucky and recruit. Whichever, they would not be *forced* to stay soldiers against their will. Being impelled to do anything forcible simply outraged the honor of Kentuckians.[7]

With Hunt still absent healing from his wound, the officers prevailed upon Lieutenant Colonel Caldwell to deliver the letter to Breckinridge. The general took two days to think about it, then replied. "Nothing since I have been in the Army has given me greater pain than your declaration," he said to them. "Nothing will be wanting in me to remove any just cause of complaint on the part of . . . a Regiment which for conduct and courage is not surpassed by any in the service of the South." Yet, he reminded them that a representative assembly of Kentuckians did secede from the Union in the rump convention at Russellville, and that the state sent delegates to the Congress in Richmond. On that basis, the Orphans stood subject to Confederate laws as much as soldiers of any other state. He could only promise to send their application to Richmond for a decision. Meanwhile, he said, "I never will believe the 5th Ky capable of meditating any course that would bring grief to our friends at home and tarnish its well earned renown." When Breckinridge forwarded the matter to the War Department, he stated more emphatically his belief that Hunt's men possessed no cause for complaint, and later Richmond would agree.[8]

Events prevented any immediate act by the disgruntled Orphans, for they left for Jackson, Mississippi, "going to Kentucky certain this time," the day after the general replied. But three days later the dissatisfaction erupted in action. On September 22 Companies A and C of the 5th Kentucky stacked their arms at Meridian and declared that their time was up, they would serve no longer. Caldwell appeared on the scene shortly and arrested both companies, detailed Company B to guard them, and on the spot reduced all noncommissioned officers among the mutineers to the ranks. "Both companies had unanimously refused to do duty any longer," he told Breckinridge. "A sincere desire to heal the troubles in the regiment and save from disgrace the men who came into the service with me" prevented Caldwell from taking more harsh measures for the moment. That evening "Uncle Tom" Hunt hobbled before the mutineers on his crutches and persuaded them to take their arms and return to duty. He promised that the officials in Richmond would be consulted on the matter of conscription.[9]

The next day they left for Mobile. On the face of it, the matter rested. Yet beneath the surface, tempers continued to inflame. Before the Orphans reached Knoxville, the fever spread to Lewis' 6th Kentucky as well, they being another twelve months' regiment. Their enlistments expired on October 2 in the main, some earlier. Lewis did not miss the unrest in his regiment, nor the threat of trouble, yet for several days he remained quiet, listening much, saying little. He consulted with his officers, he took counsel with Hanson, and finally wrote a personal letter to Breckinridge. "I do not fear open resistance to authority," he told the general, "but I have not the philosophy to meet, with composure, the gradual destruction of a regiment, by a slow poison, that has hitherto conducted itself so gallantly." He wanted nothing more than to command the 6th Kentucky Infantry, he concluded, "but I wish to be spared the pain of witnessing its defection on account of unjust treatment."

Then the Orphans mutinied. On the evening of October 8, even while a desperate Breckinridge feverishly tried to clear their path to Kentucky, a number of Lewis' men refused to do duty. "We, in a body," wrote Grainger, "demanded discharge, or to be made 'mounted infantry.' " They did not answer roll call and declined to take orders of any kind. This was the second mutiny in the brigade in two weeks.

The news reached Breckinridge that night or early on October 9. It came within hours of receipt of the word that Bragg's Army had suffered a major defeat at Perryville the day before, and would be retreating toward Nashville. The Kentucky campaign might end before he and the Orphans could join it, this after all the worry and effort. Now another of his regiments rising in mutiny proved finally too much. In the closest thing to rage that he would know, he went to the camp of the Kentucky regiments and ordered them drawn up on three sides of a square. Then he took a place at the open side where everyone of them could see and hear him, took his hat from his head and held it at his side, and began to speak. "I spoke," he wrote the next day, "under a degree of mortification and excitement produced by the occurrences of the previous evening which are quite unusual with me."

Even in his ire, Breckinridge proved the master orator, knowing instinctively how to capture and mold his audience. He did it on the stump a hundred times as a politician. It was no different now. He

began by giving them "a little raking over" for their wildness and vandalism during the trip from Mississippi. The Orphans would never
change their ways in that regard, but he never stopped trying. Then he
turned to the matter of the Meridian mutiny, addressing the men of
the 5th Kentucky. "He told them he was surprised at their having
acted so," Jackman wrote in his diary. The fact that they did it to call
attention to their situation mitigated only a little. He knew his own
duty, he said, and "would perform it at all hazards." Had he been
present at Meridian, he would have sacrificed his own life "and the life
of every man under arrest in this Regt for mutiny" before he would
have released them without their promise to return to duty uncon-
ditionally. There would have been "either unconditional surrender,
or unconditional mutiny." It was passed now, and there was nothing
to be served by arresting them again. Since both he and Hunt promised an investigation, he reiterated his guarantee that they would
receive an answer from Richmond.

Then he turned to the mutineers from Lewis' regiment, and his tone
changed, or so they would claim. Johnny Green later said that the general explained the needs of the service and that the Army and the
cause could not spare them. Gervis Grainger recalled that he delivered
"a most touching and eloquent appeal," concluding by asking those
willing to follow him through weal and woe "and to die if necessary in
the last ditch" to re-enlist. There were cheers for Breckinridge and
shouts of "Let's re-enlist for thirty years or during the war." Adjutants
prepared papers for three years, "but thirty years would have been
signed for by the boys, such was their earnest devotion to the cause."
Perhaps. But Green and Grainger wrote their recollections in after
years with forgiving memories. Johnny Jackman put in his diary that
same day that "Old Breck," after saying what he would have done to
the bolters of the 5th Kentucky, even to death, "wound up by giving
the mutineers, in the 6th, fifteen minutes to return to duty, and they
all did so before the time expired." There rings a note of truth.[10]

Both regiments re-enlisted for three years or the war, ending any
further attempts at mutiny, but the anger did not die in many. Indeed,
word of the Orphans' discontent spread even to the enemy. One federal prisoner briefly held in "Old Breck's" camp reported to his superiors that "the Kentucky regiments are in a state of mutiny," and
added that many were "skedaddling." Not long afterward two men of
Hunt's regiment deserted to the enemy and gave information on Con-

federate movements. "They were twelve-months' men, whose time was out in September," a bluecoat reported, "and this is the first chance they have had to get away." It would take a long time for the echoes of the mutinies to die away. The same day of Breckinridge's speech, Caldwell wrote indignantly to the general complaining of an imagined criticism of his own conduct in handling the Meridian insurrection. Breckinridge calmed him and apologized, saying that no condemnation was intended. It was a measure of the man who led these Kentuckians that Breckinridge ordered his letter of apology read before Caldwell's regiment at dress parade, and then put it into the brigade's official records. There must be no injustice to any Kentuckian.[11]

While quelling mutiny within the ranks, Breckinridge struggled to get his Orphans into Kentucky. He found no cooking utensils for them in Knoxville, and had to order Hanson to bring them with him and his regiment from Chattanooga. When "Old Flintlock" asked if he would accompany the march into Kentucky, Breckinridge said yes and told him to hurry forward, bringing any convalescent Kentucky troops with him. Every kind of supply problem bedeviled them both. Hanson could not get tents from the quartermaster for his men. Despite an abundance of them sitting idle in warehouses, he could only obtain one tent that would sleep sixteen men. With winter coming, fully a third of his Orphans slept on the open ground. Then the doctors refused to let him take the convalescents with him, and made the matter a test of authority. Hanson, recalling perhaps his order at Bowling Green that not more than two men per day were allowed to be ill, complained that "several of my men without my knowledge got into the Hospital." They wanted release to join him, and it finally took an order from Breckinridge to get them out.

Meanwhile, Breckinridge drilled the Orphans to ready them for the hard march ahead. Three hours a day they practiced, while the general sent Joe Nuckols, Hanson's cellmate Stephen Chipley, and several others into Kentucky ahead of them to begin recruiting. Visitors from home appeared to encourage the Kentuckians. James B. Clay stopped with his old enemy and older friend, Hanson, who proudly gave him a tour of his regiment. By October 12 Hanson led his men into the camp at Knoxville, reuniting the Kentucky regiments for the first time since February. That same day Breckinridge finally cleared the remaining impediments to his advance and sent the first contingent of his division forward. The Orphans, fifteen hundred strong, he would start on October 14. They were going home at last. Just three days' march away lay Kentucky.[12]

Yet another delay followed, but finally on the morning of October 15 the Orphans broke camp and started their tramp toward Cumberland Gap. "All marched with a buoyant step," wrote Johnny Jackman. The usual stragglers stayed with the column as "our hearts beat high with hope." The weather turned seasonable; everything looked encouraging. They covered twelve miles or more that day and camped before sundown. "We are going to Kentucky in grand style," boasted Jackman.

The next day they did even better, marching fifteen miles, all the while the mountains surrounding Cumberland Gap looming before them darkly like a blue cloud. The autumn day turned beautiful. "Indian summer," an Orphan called it. They passed Maynardville and camped three miles beyond in a field of clover. Cumberland Gap, and Kentucky, lay barely twenty miles away. They could make it tomorrow if the weather held. There was no question that their spirits felt equal to the challenge.

Reveille sounded early on October 17 and the men sped through their morning meal, anxious to be on the road for home. They formed line of march in the clover field and the head of the column, Hanson and Breckinridge in the lead, stepped into the road. A little cloud of dust ahead gave the first warning that a courier approached, and before the entire brigade was yet in the road, Breckinridge ordered the column to halt. The courier handed the general a dispatch, which he opened hastily. It came from Bragg's adjutant. "The general commanding directs me to say that you will halt . . . and return to Knoxville." He was to go to middle Tennessee, as Bragg expected the Federals to move there any day. "The general commanding is now en route to follow you."

If ever the Kentuckian felt real despair during the long struggle to take his men home, surely it was now. Here, when they could see the mountains of their native state on the horizon, they must stop and go no farther. And the last sentence that Bragg would be joining him removed all lingering hope that the march might be resumed. The Confederate Army was leaving Kentucky, the great and glorious campaign ended in defeat.

The men stood in the road and the field for a time, then their officers returned them to their bivouac. For hours the rumors flew through the regiments. Some believed that they simply had to delay while Bragg sent a large train of captured supplies through Cumberland Gap. When it passed they would move again. Others said he must have been defeated. "Thus the day wore on," wrote Ed Thompson, "and a painful day it was, too." That afternoon the brigade formed on dress parade as usual, but already the real truth seemed to have taken hold of the men. The 2d Kentucky formed on the east side of the road, and the other regiments on the west. "The silence that prevailed in the ranks then was not the silence of restraint," said Thompson; "it was the silence of stern manhood bowed down by bitter disappointment." No one even whispered. Gone was the gaiety, the shoving and shambling and guying of the usual parade. They performed their manual of arms with stern efficiency, then returned in quiet to their tents. The regimental bands that night played sentimental songs, such as "My Old Kentucky Home" and "Home, Sweet Home." Thompson saw tears on many faces.

They rested in camp a day while Breckinridge awaited further orders, and now the official announcement came to the Orphans that their dream had died at Perryville. Then on October 19 they struck their tents and with "heads all lowly bending," turned their eyes toward Knoxville once more. As the march began, a spontaneous shout went up from fifteen hundred Kentucky voices. Thompson could never tell if it came from desperation or defiance, but it was their only outward expression of feeling. "With sad hearts we turned from our cherished hope," wrote Johnny Green, and on they marched "with stern determination to manfully do our duty." The straggling that day was substantial. To his diary that night, Jackman woefully confided, "Going to Kentucky 'played out.'" It was as close as they would ever get to their mother state in this war. Orphans they had been, and Orphans they would remain.[13]

Once back in Knoxville their old spirit returned, and on the trip thence to Chattanooga, down to Bridgeport, Alabama, and then back into Tennessee to Murfreesboro, the Kentuckians regained the lighthearted air that characterized them on the march. No doubt reverting to their customary depredations on farmers' property along the way helped restore their élan. In Bridgeport, what's more, the siblings were reunited after several months' official separation. Breckinridge reorganized them into one brigade again.

Many changes had taken place since Baton Rouge and Shiloh.

Byrne and his battery left the service shortly after Shiloh as a result of a dispute over promotion. Morgan and Helm's 1st Kentucky Cavalry went to other service before the Orphans appeared at Vicksburg. And of the other Kentucky regiments with them when the Orphans split between two brigades, the 3d and 7th Kentucky remained with Van Dorn and never joined the Orphans again. Indeed, though Kentuckians, they never really enjoyed a full brotherhood with Breckinridge's men.

Now on October 26, 1862, the general re-created the brigade with the 2d, 4th, and 6th regiments, and with Hunt's old 5th Kentucky finally designated by its new title as 9th Kentucky Infantry. Graves and his battery took the place of the lost Byrne, and Cobb's guns filled the artillery complement. Several new companies finally brought Hunt's 9th Kentucky up to strength. The men of Nuckols' old 4th who went to man Graves's guns returned to the infantry, as the young gunner enlisted enough men of his own. A few weeks later Breckinridge would add the 41st Alabama Infantry to augment the Orphans' strength. This done, the brigade for a time was complete.[14]

The brigade once again belonged to "Old Bench-leg." It was a command sadly depleted by the ravages of the last year. As he took them into camp at Murfreesboro they numbered just 2,563, but that included the Alabama regiment, which mustered nearly double the strength of Lewis' 6th Kentucky. Of actual sons of the Bluegrass in the brigade, 1,847 stood present for duty. In fact, more Orphans were on the rolls as sick or absent—2,418—than were present. Their number would increase slightly during the remainder of the year, but only a little. Unlike other regiments in the Confederate Army, these Kentucky units could not recruit men to replace those killed, disabled, or deserted. One had to go home for that, and they could not. And so as the war labored onward, the Orphans' numbers grew ever fewer as they were adopted by maiming bullets, the cold sod, or simply ran away from home.[15]

All of November and December the brigade remained at Murfreesboro, shortly to be joined by Bragg's retreating Army. Now for a change the Orphans rested and reveled in nearly two whole months of inactivity. Murfreesboro proved to be a beautiful little place. "There we lived like lords," recalled Gervis Grainger. Messages, letters, even clothing and edible delicacies ran the federal blockade from Kentucky to reach them here. Visitors from home came, and even many of the officers' wives joined them. Mary Breckinridge and Virginia Hanson began housekeeping in Murfreesboro, and "Old Breck's" wife later recalled the days in the quiet Tennessee town as among the happiest of her life. Theirs was a joyful reunion. "I had been separated so long," she later wrote him, "that when I did see you I was in a *transport* of joy."

For those whose wives remained in Kentucky, however, there were only dreams. Captain Tom Winstead of the 4th Kentucky, Company B, wrote frequently to his wife, Mollie, but seldom did her letters reach him. "You do not know what I would give to get a letter from you," he wrote that November; "it would almost make me wild with joy." The Confederacy's mail service could not operate in Kentucky, so written communication depended almost entirely upon letters reaching Washington in the federal mail, being transferred by flag of truce to Richmond, and then finding their way to wherever the Orphans happened to be. Small wonder that, instead, most people relied on sending their letters with friends who crossed the line. Either method was uncertain, and most letters disappeared, just as the Kentucky men who wrote them seemed lost to their families. "There is not a night I do not dream of home," Winstead wrote his wife, not knowing if she would ever read the words.[16]

There was gaiety for a change. Morgan, now a dashing general with a brigade of cavalry, married in Murfreesboro, with General Polk performing the service and Kentuckians like Breckinridge his ushers. The men pranked, the officers like Hanson and Trabue vied with each other for having the finest and most valuable horse in the brigade, and the 4th Kentucky band and all "field music" of the brigade reported to a new bandmaster and chief musician, J. E. Beatty. The discontent in the 6th and 9th regiments diminished considerably, but alas poor Trabue's only increased. The recommendations of Breckinridge and Beauregard after Shiloh came to nothing, and he was still a colonel. Worse, after being replaced prior to Baton Rouge in command of the brigade, now he found Hanson superseding him. It hurt after leading the brigade in battle and on the march. On the day Hanson assumed command, he wrote to a friend on President Davis' staff and asked that his promotion to brigadier be pushed if possible. If it could not, then he requested that he be transferred to a different command with the Army in Louisiana. "To leave a regiment I have so highly disciplined, one so devoted to me, and with which I am identified by every tie which a soldier prizes," he wrote of leaving the 4th Kentucky, "would be to me most painful, but my own interests and probably the interests of the service would be promoted" by such a transfer. Ambition thwarted always galled Kentuckians.[17]

Hanson busied the men with drilling, and once again the Orphans encountered his almost forgotten mania for discipline. "He was the best disciplinarian we ever had," Jackman recalled. "He brought down upon the 'boys' the strictest kind of discipline while here encamped." Since leaving Mississippi, the brigade's commanders alternated from Trabue to Hunt to one or two lieutenant colonels, and consequently guard, drill, and police duties looked rather lax by the time they reached Murfreesboro. "Old Flintlock" changed that soon enough.

His very first night in camp someone heard a mighty growl shortly before dawn, and the word spread in the brigade that "Bench-leg" had passed where a guard line should have been, but was not. That evening at dress parade he gave notice of how things would be henceforth. Every officer must report in full uniform, and with his coat *buttoned*. Poor Major Cripps Wickliffe of Hunt's regiment would not like that. He despised brass buttons constraining him. But it must be. Thereafter Hanson inspected the officers first even before the strains of reveille died each morning. "He went every-where," wrote Ed Thompson, himself now a disciplined lieutenant, "saw every thing, knew every body upon whom any responsibility rested." He tested the officers constantly, though the result often seemed underwhelming for they, like the men, had too much of the prankster in them. When Hanson asked Lieutenant Phil Murphy of his old 2d Kentucky, "What constitutes a good soldier?" the response was, "One who can sleep on a fence-rail and cover with a shoe-string." Not exactly what the colonel had in mind.

Once again he attacked the morning sick report, finding too many officers thereon. So far as he was concerned, they were just evading duty. "Officers are called on not to report themselves sick when they can help it," read his order. Headaches and the like would not suffice. Before going on sick report henceforth, "The illness must be such as to endanger life." Yet one lieutenant in the 2d Regiment chose not to heed the stricture, and several days running his name appeared on the sick list. Suspicious, Hanson inquired and discovered that the young officer had been drinking and gambling late into the night repeatedly. Walking one morning to the man's tent, Hanson looked in and found the culprit wrapped in his blankets. He demanded to know why the lieutenant did not report at roll call. The officer suspected he had been found out and determined to try a diversion. Feigning agony he groaned, "I'm sick this morning—really too unwell to attend roll call."

"Sick!" shouted Hanson. "Sick, sir! I've heard from you—I know you, sir! You can sit up all night to drink whisky and play cards, but you're too sick to get out and do duty!"

Trapped, the lieutenant appealed instead to Hanson's sense of humor. "Yes, General, yes—yes," he said with a sigh. "General Hanson, the other officers all say that you're mighty hard on 'em—mighty hard; they think that you're a little disposed to be tyrannical, General, but I tell 'em, sir, that *you're a mighty good man.*" That threw "Old Flint" off the attack just enough to draw a smile from him. "Come out of there, sir!" he said once more for effect, and then left the lieutenant to finish his morning nap.[18]

Good news came for Hanson here in Murfreesboro, as indicated by the malingering lieutenant's mode of addressing him. For some time the indefatigable Kentucky lobby in Richmond sought a brigadier's commission for Hanson, and in this instance his own wife played an important part in marshaling friends in the capital. "I have a ruling sense that has taken possession of me," wrote Virginia Hanson to Eli Bruce, "to have my husband promoted." She called on Bruce, "and through you to his other friends in Congress to exert yourselves on his behalf." Her entreaties won Bruce and the rest of the Kentucky delegation, and they put their influence to work. It helped that the enemy exchanged Hanson in August. He would return to the brigade before long and as senior colonel would take command. Since a brigade called for a brigadier at its head, promotion for him seemed only natural. Yet in appealing to President Davis, Bruce put more emphasis on Virginia Hanson. "Her labors and charities have been unceasing in camp, in hospital, and in prison," he wrote. "Her ambition ought to be gratified, as *she* has *won promotion.*" By November hope reached Murfreesboro that a general's wreath would soon surround the stars on Hanson's collar. "Is Col. Hanson made Brigadier?" Breckinridge asked of Bragg. Just when formal notification came is unclear, but on December 13, 1862, President Davis himself visited the Army. The first unit he reviewed was the 1st Kentucky Brigade, and as Jackman wrote in his diary, he "was well pleased with the 'orphans.'" They passed before him marching in perfect order, and before the review ended,

Davis formally promoted Roger W. Hanson to brigadier general. He never had time to sew on the wreath.[19]

Even a brigadier could not contain the wildness and insubordination of some of the Orphans. Drinking remained a problem, the men of Lewis' 6th Kentucky particularly distinguishing themselves in this regard at Murfreesboro. As late as November 28 Hanson still complained that "the roll call is a mere farce," and now he started punishments. When Lieutenant Minor Moore of the 6th Kentucky missed the roll, Hanson reprimanded him in front of the whole regiment.

More serious offenses mounted. The Orphans stole or destroyed four hundred dollars' worth of wood, flooring, flour, and meal at the Beard and Brothers Mill. Lieutenant B. F. Arnett of Company D, 9th Kentucky, went to trial for abandoning his company in the fight at Shiloh, and was cashiered. Lieutenant G. W. Jones of Lewis' 9th Regiment found himself convicted of forgery and absence without leave, and cashiered. Even small mutinies continued. On November 6 several men of the 2d Kentucky fell out without permission, and when Private Michael Morris was ordered to conduct them to the guardhouse, he replied, "I'll be damned if I go on guard. Will go in the guardhouse for one month first." He went for ten days.

As usual, Hanson's old regiment caused the most trouble. In December the 2d Kentucky listed more men absent without leave than all the other Kentucky units combined. When Moses Ricketts of Company E created a disturbance and an officer threatened to shoot him, Peter Snapps stood by Ricketts, saying that they would have to shoot him too, and Ephraim Campbell refused to assist, saying he was "as good a man as the officer" and besides "this is Tennessee soil." All three did thirty days and forfeited two months' pay. The worst incident came in Graves's battery, when Private Virginius Hutchen called on his mates to resist the guard placed on him. He denounced his officers as cowards and incompetent tyrants, and threatened to kill the officer of the day. Those who guarded him he accused of being tools of the officers, cursed them, and shook his fists at the officer in charge. He would spend three months in solitary confinement. When released, the testy Irishman went on to become one of the best soldiers in the brigade and, of all things, a poet.[20]

In December 10 per cent of the brigade's strength reported absent without leave, though most of those were not deserters, but just men

wandering about the countryside foraging, or sleeping off the revels of
the night before. Indeed, a few longtime wanderers even returned.
One irascible and pretentious young man, John H. Blanchard of Company I of the 4th Kentucky, who disappeared at Shiloh, now reappeared. Everyone believed that he had deserted while his company
suffered nearly half its strength lost in the battle, and little good was
said of him in the ensuing months. Now he told an improbable story
of taking part in the battle with another command and being captured. The first man of his company that he met was John Marshall,
who warned him that no one would believe his tale. "My faith in him
was not gone," wrote Marshall, and he took Blanchard to the tent of
Lieutenant Colonel Andrew Hynes. The officer gave Blanchard a verbal drubbing, refused to allow him in his tent, and said he was "a disgrace to an old and honorable family" and should be drummed out of
the Army. Hynes did relent to appoint a court of inquiry to examine
the boy's story first, and Marshall detailed the court. It met, but an
hour passed without the necessary witnesses for the prosecution arriving. Captain Joseph Millett then moved that, in the absence of prosecution witnesses, Blanchard be declared innocent and returned to his
company. The motion passed unanimously. Marshall conducted the
boy to his old comrades and told him frankly to change his old
haughty ways and forget the fairy tale about his capture, "to do his
duty like a man and without a murmur." When next the regiment
went into battle, he concluded, Blanchard must make his performance
in it just as conspicuous as had been his absence at Shiloh.[21]

Unfortunately, Blanchard's case was the exception. Actual desertions continued, fired now not just by the old resentments, but as well
by news that Bragg actually conscripted Kentuckians in their native
state during his recent campaign. This amounted to slavery in the
Orphans' eyes, and Breckinridge saw that it stirred discontent once
again in the 6th and 9th regiments. Added to this was the beginning of
a war-weariness in the brigade, well expressed by Winstead. "Oh, how
I wish the war would end and peace return that we might go to our
wives and friends," he lamented in a letter. The leaders on both sides,
he declared, should leave their Congress halls to "reflect upon the
sadness and desolation they are casting over one of the happiest coun-
tries that ever existed. There is a mourner in almost every house in
the south." Men seemed to have lost their reason. "The war must end
and will end, but why not end it now?" To be sure, Winstead's loyalty

never wavered. Indeed, as he looked at his men he saw that "We are in high hopes of our success . . . and when we are whipped it will be when we are exterminated, and not 'till then." Others did not see it that way. On December 5 Hanson ordered Cofer and Caldwell to pursue and capture a new group of deserters from the 6th and 9th Kentucky. They were to take as long as necessary to find and bring back the felons, among them Private Asa Lewis of Cofer's Company E. He deserted on December 4 or 5, and three weeks from now would come close to starting the Orphans into the greatest mutiny of all.[22]

While the search for Lewis and the others progressed, the Orphans finally saw their first action of the season. On December 4 Bragg issued orders to Breckinridge to have the Kentucky brigade ready to move the next day with four days' rations and its ambulances. That meant a fight. A federal garrison of twenty-one hundred men lay camped at Hartsville, forty miles north of Murfreesboro, part of the federal Army now commanded by Major General William S. Rosecrans. Positioned as they were on the Cumberland River, the Federals might be captured if sufficient surprise were achieved. Morgan conceived the plan, and received Bragg's approval and the use of Kentucky infantry to assist his mounted men in the attack.

Early on December 5 the sergeants woke the men and issued them forty rounds of ammunition each. Poor Jackman was ill again, and so could not go, but he watched. "A heavy snowstorm was passing, and soon the gray column was lost to view in the whirling snow." The Orphans marched eighteen miles to their first night's bivouac, where they slept in four inches of snow. Here Hanson remained with the 4th and 6th regiments and Graves's battery. Hunt, commanding a detachment of the 2d and 9th Kentucky, and Cobb's battery, led his men forward again shortly after noon on December 6, following Morgan's cavalry. After several miles the horse soldiers exchanged with the infantry and let them ride their mounts in order to rest. The whole command numbered less than fourteen hundred, Hunt's Orphans making barely over eight hundred. By 10 P.M. that night they reached the Cumberland River. With only two boats available to ferry them, it took seven hours for the command to reach the north side. Only constant bailing kept one of the boats afloat, and frightened cavalry horses nearly kicked the planks from the other.

Once across, Hunt's march toward Hartsville, five miles away, lay over terrible ground, often so hilly the men almost lifted Cobb's guns up the slopes. Morgan intended to surprise the Federals before dawn, but the slow advance and an accidental encounter by the cavalry destroyed his hopes. Thus, by the time the Orphans sighted the enemy camp, the Federals awaited them in line on the crest of a hill, their artillery ready to rake the Kentuckians with metal.

Morgan dismounted his cavalry to form the left of his line, and sent Hunt to hold his right, the Kentuckians taking position under an already heavy fire. The cavalry, led by Basil Duke, opened the fight with an attack that drove the federal right flank back on its center nearly half a mile. Already the enemy was in trouble. With the Cumberland at their backs and Morgan and Duke in force on their right, their only means of escape would be their left, yet at this moment Hunt sent his screaming Kentuckians forward.

The 9th Kentucky on the right, the 2d on its left, the Orphans charged up the hill before them. Duke noticed that many of the men stumbled badly, their feet frozen during the night, "but the brave boys rushed in as if they were going to a frolic." Hunt shouted, "Boys, kill a man with every shot," and on they charged. The 2d Kentucky moved first, their advance unimpeded until they reached rough ground, where Major Jim Hewitt, commanding, halted and formed the men in line under fire. It was an ill-advised move, for the enemy already seemed to be falling back before them, yet now poured a deadly fire into the exposed Orphans. Among the fallen was Sergeant Tom Maddox of Company E. With his mouth opened in a Rebel yell, he took a bullet in his arm and another in the chest. At the same instant yet a third ball entered his mouth, killing him instantly.[23]

While Hewitt and the 2d Kentucky stood the heavy fire, Captain Bob Cobb and the two field pieces he brought with him went into battery on the right of Hunt's line and supported the advance. They also drew deadly accurate fire from two enemy guns on the opposite hill. The second or third federal shell struck one of Cobb's caissons while poor Private Tom Watts sat atop it. The caisson exploded with a thundering roar, scattering men, and bits of Watts, all over the hillside. Cobb limbered his guns and moved them to support the 9th Kentucky, which would advance next.

With Hunt commanding the Kentuckians here, and Caldwell looking for deserters, command of the 9th now lay with its senior captain, James Morehead. He ordered them forward at the double-quick, then yelled, "Charge bayonets! Forward march!" While the regiment rushed forward, officers in the 2d Kentucky, among them Moss and Phil Lee, renewed the charge of that regiment as well so that shortly both Kentucky units in a line raced up the slope toward the federal lines. They got within fifty paces of the enemy, then stopped, and for ten minutes traded volleys. Then they charged again and completely overran the Yankees, driving most of them under cover of their artillery.

In pursuing the enemy, many Orphans found a bluecoat here and there hiding in a hole or behind a rock. "Surrender or I'll kill you," Jim Burba yelled at one Federal. Instead the man fired point-blank at Jim, but missed. Burba did not. Meanwhile, Morehead and Hewitt pressed their regiments through the enemy's camps to where the Federals, now completely surrounded by Hunt and Morgan, took refuge behind the brow of a hill overlooking the Cumberland. Their two field pieces sat in front of their line, and Color Sergeant John Oldham of the 2d Kentucky rushed forward and planted the colors of his regiment on the guns. Almost immediately the rest of the line passed him and pressed toward the enemy. At the same time Morgan's dismounted cavalry swept against the other side of the Federals and even got behind some of them. There was a last hot firefight, and then a white flag fluttered behind the Yankee line. A. G. Montgomery of the 2d Kentucky, the man who carried Buckner's flag of truce to Grant before the surrender at Donelson, now conducted Colonel A. B. Moore of the 106th Ohio to Hunt, where he surrendered 1,834 Federals.[24]

In fact, it was not much of a battle. The Federals behaved badly, many retiring without a fight, and Moore himself later resigned rather than be cashiered. But the Confederates did not know that now, and they reveled in their victory. The men roamed the enemy camps, looting joyously. Jasper "Jap" Anderson of Company B, 9th Kentucky, found a mule and commenced loading it with blankets, thirty pounds of coffee, and a dozen or so canteens filled with apple brandy. Johnny Green rushed into Colonel Moore's tent, donned the officer's overcoat, and was in the act of removing some flannel shirts from a valise when the colonel entered.

"My good fellow, don't take my clothes," said the mortified Moore. Green gave him the shirts but refused to hand over the coat. They would keep the colonel warm in prison, he said.

"Do give me my over coat & get the Major's in the next tent; he was killed in the fight." Johnny would not.

"You may have the Major's," he said, "I'll keep this."

The victory did not come without a cost, however. Hewitt lost sixty-five killed, wounded, or missing, most of them falling when he mistakenly halted the regiment under fire. Morehead took eighteen casualties, and Cobb ten. In all, the Orphans lost ninety-three of their number, and now the surgeon and nurses roamed the field looking for them. With other enemy garrisons within supporting distance of Moore, Morgan could not afford to wait. He would have to leave those too injured to walk or ride behind. Dr. John O. Scott, surgeon of the 2d Kentucky, stayed with them. He gathered the injured. On the field they found the mangled remains of poor gunner Watts, recognizable only by his bloody artillery cap. Nearby lay Lieutenant Charles Thomas of the 2d, blood spurting from an open wound in his chest, and dead alongside him was Lieutenant John Rogers of his same company. W. E. Etheridge, who that morning jokingly asked comrades to write to his lady fair should he die, now lay dead.

Scott commandeered a wagon belonging to some blacks and with it transported most of the wounded to the nearby house of a Mrs. Halliburton. Soon Morgan and Hunt left to return to Murfreesboro, and Scott and his wounded Orphans were on their own. It was not long before federal cavalry rode into Hartsville and took possession of the now empty battlefield. Many of the bluecoats turned out to be Kentucky cavalry, and when Scott was escorted to their commander, he saw Colonel John Harlan. "How are you, John?" one Orphan shouted as he recognized an old friend. "As soon as that social bombshell was exploded," wrote Surgeon Scott, "all soon recognized each other and there was a general shaking of hands and greeting of friends." Harlan and his men and officers visited the wounded at Mrs. Halliburton's and vied fiercely with each other in acts of kindness and cheer. "It was a grand sight to see the man in the blue in all kindness and affection," wrote Scott, "assisting his brother of the gray." Harlan himself ordered coffee and rations for the Confederate wounded. For a time they became his Orphans, too. Once they were turned over to federal surgeons, the colonel allowed Dr. Scott and his nurses to return to Murfreesboro.[25]

The next two weeks passed in relative quiet for the Army at Murfreesboro, but not for the Orphan Brigade; for now it appeared that Braxton Bragg was ready to make open warfare against the Kentuckians. Four years later Basil Duke would write of Bragg, "The

wrongs he did Kentucky and Kentuckians, the malignity with which
he bore down on his Kentucky troops, his hatred and bitter active antagonism to all prominent Kentucky officers, have made an abhorrence
of him part of a Kentuckian's creed." The seeds of Bragg's antipathy
for Kentuckians went to his failed campaign, the fact that men of the
state did not flock to his banner, nor even support him by providing
supplies. Further, the failure of Breckinridge and the Orphans to join
him enraged his already paranoid mind against all men of the Bluegrass. It did not help that the Kentuckians also enjoyed an unusual
influence in the capital, and with the Kentucky-born President Davis.
It was time they were put in their place.

He started by ordering conscript officers to treat Kentucky men in
exile in the South the same as anyone else liable to the draft. To this
Breckinridge objected strongly, and it was even rumored that "Old
Breck," Hanson, and Buckner threatened to resign in protest. That is
questionable, but certainly it made Bragg the enemy of all Kentuckians. "The Kentucky vanity is as irritable, although not as radical,
as the Virginian," Duke would say, "and sees a slight in every thing
short of a caress." Bragg hardly caressed them.

Into the middle of this situation stepped Mr. Thomas Estes, formerly a private in Helm's 1st Kentucky Cavalry. Now he spent his
time hunting deserters and returning them for a bounty. On December
8 he received ninety dollars for bringing three men from the 6th Kentucky, Company E, back to the Army. Two of them were Frank Dris-
coll and James Gillock. The third was Private Asa Lewis.

On December 20, 1862, a general court-martial sat to try Lewis and
several others in the Army on charges of desertion. The indictment
was read, violation of the Twentieth Article of War, to which Lewis
then pled not guilty. As his story unfolded, it appeared that he enlisted
originally for only twelve months, and did not feel that the reorganization of his regiment for three years or the war bound those who did
not individually re-enlist. He did not. Further, his father now lay dead
and his mother, Sallie, and three children needed him as their only
means of support. Apparently he requested a furlough to go home and
lay in a crop for them, but it was denied, and finally he told his friends
in the company that he would go anyhow, and return to his place
when he provided sufficiently for his family. Johnny Green believed
that Lewis had actually deserted for this purpose once before, being
brought back and let go with a reprimand. It would not be so now.

Despite representation by good counsel, Lewis heard the court find him guilty as charged. The sentence was death. When the court passed their findings to Bragg, he approved the sentence. "The said Asa Lewis," he said, "will be executed by shooting in the presence of the troops of the Brigade to which he belongs." Bragg set the date for December 26, between ten in the morning and two in the afternoon, and ordered that Hanson direct the proceedings.[26]

Now the Kentucky officers began a campaign to get Lewis' sentence commuted. They pled with Bragg to relent, but to no avail. Most of the Kentucky officers signed a petition that they delivered to the commanding general on Christmas, begging that he reconsider. Breckinridge personally visited Bragg, who now despised him, but the general would not move. Kentucky blood was "too feverish for the health of the Army," Bragg reportedly said. He was sick of the Kentuckians' grumbling and troublemaking. He would put a stop to it if he had to execute every Orphan in the brigade. Obviously he sought to make Asa Lewis an object lesson, a test of his strength of will over the Kentuckians whom he thought sought to bring him to ruin. Breckinridge became furious. Kentuckians were not slaves, and Bragg would not treat them as such. Shooting Lewis would be murder. Bragg stood firm.[27]

Christmas came and despite Lewis' predicament, most of the Orphans enjoyed it as they could. "Christmas day was a real Christmas," wrote Grainger. Several boxes of good things from Kentucky arrived through the lines. Johnny Green's mess obtained eggs and onions, and even a goose, buying them for a change, and Johnny himself baked a pound cake which, though it fell in the center, did not dampen their spirits. Some of the captured Hartsville brandy enlivened the holiday for them as well. Squire Helm Bush, of Company B, 6th Kentucky, saw that several men of his company "got a little funny & enjoyed themselves," many staying the night at a ball in Murfreesboro.

And the mysterious scribe of Company C, 4th Kentucky, once again took a pen to the company's clothing account book. "December the 25th 1862," he wrote. "Another Christmas has come and still we are engaged in the Bloody Struggle to be free . . . for more than two years we have been combating with the Vandal horde—to Day our army is stronger and more thoughroly [sic] equipped than ever before." He still found hope.[28]

Asa Lewis did not. On Christmas night Breckinridge visited him in the Murfreesboro jail and frankly told him that his efforts had been fruitless. Lewis took the news with composure, and then gave the general all his worldly possessions, a pocketbook and a comb, and a few letters. "Old Joe" Lewis came soon after dawn the next morning, and yet again he and Breckinridge tried to sway Bragg without success. In Kentucky it was rumored later that this morning several companies of Orphans ran to their arms threatening mutiny before they were calmed.

A general order called for the field officer of the day to select one lieutenant, one noncommissioned officer, and three men from each regiment in the brigade for the firing detail. Three rifles were loaded with blank charges. Then arose a problem. The field officer selected at least two, and perhaps three, lieutenants to command the detail, but each refused. When he ordered Lieutenant G. B. Overton of the 2d Kentucky to perform the task, Overton said, "I'll give up my sword before I'll command that detail!" Finally another officer agreed to take the distasteful task, and the brigade formed on the parade ground, making three sides of a hollow square.

At 11 A.M. a wagon bearing Lewis appeared and stopped on the open side of the square. Behind it lumbered another carrying a coffin. There followed the officer of the day, and most of the brigade commanders on horseback, Breckinridge among them. Thompson recalled of Lewis, "As the wagon passed near me I could see the pale but firm countenance; the somewhat unnatural glare of his eyes when he looked upon those fellow-Kentuckians." The detail stood Lewis facing the brigade, his back to the open side of the square, and bound his hands behind him. Thompson said he asked not to be blindfolded. Johnny Green said he asked for the mask so that he would not have to recognize the comrades who soon would kill him.

Breckinridge dismounted and walked to the condemned man. They spoke in hushed tones for a moment, then the general remounted and rode aside. Lewis addressed the Orphans, telling them not to be distressed. "I beg of you to aim to kill," he closed, "it will be merciful to me. Good-bye."

The lieutenant ordered "ready." The firing squad, just ten paces in front of Lewis, brought their rifles to their shoulders. In the pattering of a heavy rain the condemned man heard the metallic clicking of the hammers being drawn back.

"Aim." Every rifle pointed to the Orphan's heart.

"Fire."

A host of images followed, which the Kentuckians never forgot. Ed Thompson remembered how the "sudden crash reverberated over the field." Others closed their eyes and felt only the rain. Some looked toward Breckinridge who, when Lewis fell dead, pitched forward on his horse's neck "with a deathly sickness," and had to be caught by his staff before he fell to the ground.

Asa Lewis was past remembering. The detail placed him in the coffin, and buried him the same day in Murfreesboro next to a cousin who died there the year before. Then, said Johnny Green, "a gloom settled over the command." As for Breckinridge, he recovered his composure and placed Lewis' few belongings with his own things for safekeeping. He would carry them with him for the next seven years in keeping his promise to the condemned man. Finally, when he received a letter in 1869 stating, "I am the widowed mother of the unfortunate young man who was killed (or rather butchered) at Murfreesboro," the general redeemed his pledge and sent the comb, and letters, and pocketbook to Sallie Lewis.[29]

Braxton Bragg won this little battle with the Orphans, but it came at great price. "It created a profound sensation," wrote one observer, "and incensed Hanson's Kentucky brigade beyond measure." In protest, they declined to pass sentence on future Kentucky soldiers convicted of desertion. In the soldiers of the brigade, the commanding general now had hundreds of enemies, and their officers proved instrumental in the campaign to replace him in command of the Army. Breckinridge apparently never mentioned the matter to Bragg again, for other grievances would soon arise between them to supplant the death of this one poor Orphan now gone home. A federal army was on the move, and soon Bragg, Breckinridge, and the Orphan Brigade would pass through fiery hell. With the earth covering Lewis still moist, Bragg and the Kentuckians approached the watershed of their stormy career.[30]

EIGHT

"My Poor Orphans"

"I NEVER SUFFERED SO FROM COLD in any one day in all my life," Squire Bush wrote in his diary on December 30. It was not only the cold that set him shuddering that winter day. As well it could have been from the prospect of a great terrible battle that would commence at any moment, for facing Bragg's Army at Murfreesboro this day stood forty-one thousand well-equipped Federals and General William S. Rosecrans, ready to fight.[1]

Four days before, as Asa Lewis went to his grave, Rosecrans moved his army south from Nashville. Bragg's cavalry delayed his advance but still, by December 29, Federals approached Murfreesboro. Rosecrans would drive Bragg and his thirty-five thousand Confederates from Tennessee, he hoped, and he could do it here at Murfreesboro, along Stones River.

The river ran north to south in a crooked path a mile east of Murfreesboro, and was easily fordable at several points. Bragg placed the bulk of his army across the stream, while Breckinridge's division he situated on the Murfreesboro side, on a group of hills that commanded the entire field. There he could cover the town and, as well, be in a position to make a wide flank attack against the enemy should Bragg see the opportunity.

On the morning of December 29, Breckinridge sent Lewis and Hunt's regiments, with Cobb's battery and the 41st Alabama, to occupy a particularly prominent hill in his front, which overlooked the river. From this eminence his artillery commanded virtually the entire enemy line when the battle began. The rest of his division had taken their place the day before, Jackman watching the stream of glittering bayonets as they passed through Murfreesboro toward the field. "Uncle Tom" Hunt returned from a furlough just begun in order to be in the coming fight. Adjutant Henry Curd of his regiment felt an overpowering premonition of death, and left messages and effects with Jackman and others. A near-freezing rain drizzled all that day (the twenty-ninth) and into the dark, yet no fires burned that might reveal the Confederate positions. Midnight passed before the men received their rations of beef and cornmeal, cooked in the rear and carried forward still warm.

They heard cannon in the distance all day, and Jackman thought he could smell the saltpeter in the air. Then, just before dark, Bragg ordered a large brick house in their front set ablaze to deny its shelter to enemy sharpshooters. It was a "gloomy sight at such a time as this," thought Jackman. That evening the Orphans' skirmishers, Company D of Hunt's regiment, unexpectedly saw a body of Federals coming at them in the darkness, and a firefight ensued in which the Kentuckians withdrew up the slope of the hill toward Cobb's guns. The enemy pursued, overrunning some of the skirmishers, and advancing right to the muzzles of Cobb's field pieces. Jackman heard one of them yell, "Boys, here is a cannon, let us get away from here." At the same moment the 6th and 9th Kentucky advanced and fired a volley into the darkness surrounding the bluecoats. The enemy withdrew in haste.

As the Federals retired, they passed once again a few of the Orphan skirmishers whom they overran on the way up the hill. One was Irishman Mike McClarey, who struggled to help a wounded comrade hit in the leg. Finally he carried him into friendly lines again. "Sure are you trying to kill your own men," he asked as he sat his friend on the ground. Then he saw that his comrade was dead, a second bullet through his head. "I thought you said it was your leg you were shot in," said Mike. Soon the whole brigade withdrew some distance, leaving only a strong skirmish line in advance of the hill. Breckinridge did not know what might be behind the enemy, who nearly reached Cobb's guns, and would not chance a surprise attack in the night.[2]

The next day, Tuesday, December 30, the day so cold to Bush, Cobb's guns reoccupied the hill in their front, supported now by Trabue leading the 2d and 4th Kentucky. Hanson gave Trabue orders to hold the hill at all hazards, but no enemy attempt at capture came. Instead, the only real action was seen by Cobb, who the next day turned his guns to the left, to where Bragg and Rosecrans battled back and forth west of the river. All day long the Orphan gunners sent their shells into the attacking Union columns, and all day the enemy artillery replied in kind. Hanson had to move the infantry supports at least once to protect them from the enemy fire. "First a shell would tear up the ground in front of us," wrote Jackman, "then we would go a little slow; then a ball would plow up the ground in rear of us; then we would quicken our pace." When the Orphans finally huddled just behind the crest of the hill where Cobb and now two other batteries did their work, they saw enemy cannon balls strike just in front of them and jump over their heads. Twenty or thirty Kentuckians did not get the benefit of the bounce, and casualties mounted, so that Hanson moved them yet again.

Cobb himself lost eight men in the day's artillery duel. Poor Adjutant Curd was hiding behind a small thicket about sundown when a cannon ball bounded out of the brush and passed straight through him. Just a moment before he gave Jackman some tobacco and laughed at his premonitions of death. At nearly the same moment another federal ball struck Captain Jo Desha of the 9th Kentucky in the head. An ambulance rushed him to the field hospital of Dr. John Scott, now returned from Hartsville. Taking him to be dead, or nearly so, Scott prescribed only a cold compress for Desha, then went to his more promising patients. When Scott returned after an hour, Desha was gone. He recovered his senses, sat bolt upright, grabbed his sword, and stormed out of the tent, having just remembered that he had charge of the picket line that night. The men of his company stared in surprise when their captain, thought dead, appeared like an apparition in the night, his head swathed in white bandages, and took command of the picket as if nothing had happened. Desha's head was a good deal harder than Corporal J. F. Hawes's of Cobb's battery, alas. Detailed to serve with Dr. Scott, Hawes begged, "Doctor, I must go to my gun. If I get killed, tell my sweetheart that I died like a hero." Two hours later a cannon ball hit him in the head, too, and tore it from his body. Sergeant Richard Whayne of Cobb's command saw his leg shot off by an enemy ball, then died before his bleeding could be stopped. That night the gunners buried him on the spot, and called the scene of their bloody day's work Whayne's Hill.[3]

The old year, too, died that night. As if in its memory, the antagonists lay relatively quiet on January 1, 1863. "Both armies seem to be taking a 'blowing spell,'" thought Johnny Jackman. By standing idle, Bragg lost an opportunity to hand Rosecrans a signal defeat, having steadily driven the enemy before him on December 31. The problem was, he believed he already had a victory, and spent New Year's Day waiting for the Federals to retire. They did not. Instead, Rosecrans massed his artillery on the west bank of Stones River, roughly opposite a large hill in Breckinridge's front, and then crossed one of his divisions during the night to occupy the hill. Late that evening Bragg began to suspect that something other than a retreat was taking place, and he ordered Hanson to send his skirmishers across the river to see if the Yankee artillery was there. When "Bench-leg" protested that the movement could not be made in the dark, Bragg relented and withdrew the order.

That night Breckinridge sent a note into Murfreesboro to tell Mary he could not leave the front. His son Clifton brought coffee to him that she brewed, and a letter as well. "I hope God will answer my prayers," she wrote, "and I feel that he will."[4]

With the dawn of January 2, the Orphans could be thankful that they had suffered very little in the first three days of the battle. All the infantry fighting of any consequence took place west of Stones River, and they had been spared the bloody work that severely mangled the rest of Bragg's Army. Yet with the light came the realization that Rosecrans had not retreated as expected. This battle, in Bragg's eyes, was not done yet. Today would be the Orphans' turn.

That morning Breckinridge sent Captain William P. Bramlette of the 4th Kentucky to make a reconnaissance of the enemy position in his front. Bramlette found the federal division placed on the hill in their front but, more disturbing, he saw as well some fifty-seven field pieces massed on the bluff across Stones River. Bramlette believed them to be set in a trap to destroy Breckinridge's division should he advance to drive the bluecoats from his front, and so reported to the general. Another officer sent in reconnaissance brought the same intelligence. Then Breckinridge himself rode forward to see it with his own eyes. The reports were true.

Between noon and 1 P.M. that afternoon, Bragg summoned Breckinridge to him for orders. Breckinridge met him under a large sycamore near the river. The commanding general wanted artillery placed on that hill now occupied by Federals, and directed the Kentuckian to advance and take it. He told him that, since his command had been spared so far during the battle, it was natural that now he should take this hill. Others would later believe that, in fact, Bragg hoped Breckinridge and his men would be killed in the attempt. Whichever the case, the Kentuckian now argued strongly against such an attack. Sketching the relative positions on the ground with a stick, he showed how the massed enemy artillery would destroy any force trying to hold that hill. Bragg remained adamant. "Sir, my information is different. I have given the order to attack the enemy in your front and expect it to be obeyed."[5]

Infuriated, a helpless Breckinridge galloped back to his division and discussed the order with his officers. He first met Joe Nuckols, who the night before had commented that the hill they were to take would be a good artillery position. "Ah! Colonel; this is a pet measure of yours, I believe," said Breckinridge. "Do you desire as much as ever to place the Fourth there?" Nuckols now realized what they faced, and demurred. "Well," said the general, "we must take it anyhow."

The other officers received the news with less aplomb. Trabue "denounced the project as impractical madness." Breckinridge rode to General Preston, now commanding another brigade in his division, and told him, "General Preston, this attack is made against my judgment, and by the special orders of General Bragg. Of course we all must try to do our duty, and fight the best we can. If it should result in disaster, and I be among the slain, I want you to do justice to my memory, and tell the people that I believed this attack to be very unwise, and tried to prevent it." It was the only occasion of the war when Breckinridge spoke of death before a battle.

Hanson was even less restrained. Clifton Breckinridge recalled that he "denounced the order as absolutely murderous and felt so infuriated at the men being ordered to do an impossible thing that he wanted to go at once to headquarters and kill Bragg." It was hardly out of character for Hanson, but Breckinridge and Preston restrained him. "Old Flintlock" complained that it was "simply murder to carry out the order." Now he, too, felt a premonition. Minutes later he said with a sadness entirely uncharacteristic of the man, "I believe this will be my last!"[6]

Hanson formed the regiments for the assault. Hunt and the 9th Regiment would remain as a reserve on Whayne's Hill, along with

Cobb and Graves. Breckinridge had four brigades for the attack, and arranged them in two lines, one about 150 yards behind the other. The Orphans made the left half of the front rank, while to their right sat the brigade of Colonel John B. Palmer. But Palmer did not command, for at the last minute Bragg gave the brigade to one of his cronies, and a man not unknown to Hanson and the 2d Kentucky, the intrepid General Gideon J. Pillow. Breckinridge knew Pillow for a liar and coward, but could do nothing about it now.

Lewis and the 6th Kentucky held Hanson's extreme left, the other Kentucky regiments filling out the line on his right. Trabue aligned the 4th Kentucky, the men seeing on his face "a look of half-sleepy indifference." It was resignation. Yet there was one man in his regiment who looked forward to the fight with enthusiasm. Young John Blanchard of Company I, who showed the white feather at Shiloh, now begged his captain to be watchful and see if any man in the company should advance farther toward the foe than he. Blanchard had much to prove to his comrades, and to himself.[7]

The signal gun to begin the attack fired at precisely 4 P.M. "Up, my men, and charge!" shouted Breckinridge to the center of his front line. Hanson rode to Lewis and said, "Colonel, the order is to load, fix bayonets and march through this brushwood. Then charge at double-quick to within a hundred yards of the enemy, deliver fire, and go at him with the bayonet." Hanson called out to the Orphan regiments, "Attention!" other officers repeating it along the line. Then, "Forward, march!" The 1st Kentucky Brigade, part of an attack force of five thousand, moved forward. From his position with the second line, Breckinridge saw with pride the order with which his Kentuckians advanced to the fight. "Look at old Hanson!" he exclaimed to his staff. Then, looking to the right of the line, he saw Pillow cowering behind a tree while his brigade went to battle. Breckinridge personally had to order him to join his men.

The Orphans swept forward, their step unfaltering as they passed around a large pond of water, scrub, and brush in their path. As soon as they reached the forward slope of the hill they were to take, they delivered a volley and then rushed toward the crest. The Federals replied in kind but were disorganized by the weight of the Confederate fire. They could not rally beyond a single volley and withdrew. Hanson and his Kentuckians pursued them over the crest of the hill. Seeing the enemy streaming in flight toward Stones River, the Confederates did not halt with their hill won, but continued to follow the bluecoats. "Our intrepidity demoralized the enemy," said Grainger, "and they began to flee like blackbirds." But then, with the Federals gone from the hill and the Confederates exposed upon it, the massed Union artillery on the opposite bank opened fire, as Breckinridge had predicted it would. At once the Orphans began falling. Among the first of them was Brigadier General Roger W. Hanson.[8]

One of those enemy cannon on the height across the river fired a three-inch spherical case shot toward the hill. The projectile, a round cast-iron hollow sphere filled with iron balls, rocketed across the stream toward the hill now teeming with Confederates. The powder in the time-train Bormann fuse sputtered into the main charge just as the shot reached the Orphans. In the explosion, a dozen or more balls hurtled through their ranks, perhaps striking flesh, or only earth. As for the Bormann fuse, its primary work done, it now became a projectile as pieces of the shot casing flew about. On the fuse careered until it found Hanson's left knee. It tore through the skin, slashed past muscles and veins, through the main artery, and imbedded itself in the bone.

Hanson fell at once, his old cellmate Steve Chipley rushing to his side. While a staff officer raced to the rear for an ambulance, Breckinridge himself rode to the wounded man and tried with his hands to stop the flow of blood, without success. The two generals spoke briefly, and then the ambulance arrived. As it bore Hanson to the rear, he received words of encouragement from other officers along the way. He remained cheerful, and when General Leonidas Polk said he hoped the Kentuckian would recover, Hanson admitted that it was a serious wound, but that it was "glorious to die for one's country."

As soon as he reached the rear, Hanson felt Dr. Scott's kindly hands on the wound. He gave the general a stimulant. "Hanson did not utter a groan or speak a complaining word," Scott would recall. When the doctor finished, "Old Flintlock" told him to leave Chipley with him and then go and see to the other wounded. Chipley took him to a nearby home and there Virginia and Mary Breckinridge did their best to make him comfortable. Dr. David Yandell arrived and examined the wound, determining that Hanson had lost too much blood to survive an operation to remove the leg. He gave the general a faint hope of recovery and "Bench-leg" told him, "Well, do your best for me, doctor. I would like to live to see the war through. I feel that we are right, and ought to succeed."⁹

As Hanson bled, his Orphans continued their trial under the rain of fire from the federal artillery. They continued to follow the fleeing bluecoats right to the river's edge, and a number of the Orphans, particularly in Lewis' 6th Kentucky, went across after them. Gervis Grainger waded the stream and waited for the rest of the brigade to come over, not realizing—as none of the Orphans did—that they were not supposed to go beyond the crest of the hill they had taken. The artillery fire, said Grainger, "shook the earth under my feet." He could barely see through the cloud of thick white smoke that wafted down the bluff from the mass of artillery. Then looking to his right, he could see that the federal infantry had re-formed and now readied itself to counterattack. He discovered that most of his comrades who crossed with him were on their way back to the hill, and Grainger himself jumped into the river up to his armpits and flailed his way across under a patter of enemy bullets. On the other side he found a riderless horse and tried to mount it just as a cannon ball decapitated the animal. He ran toward four men carrying a fifth on a litter, in time to see another shot pass through one bearer, the wounded man on the litter, and another bearer at the other end. He joined the remaining two men and raced to the safety of their own lines.

All order and discipline disappeared in the rush to pursue the enemy off the hill, which accounts for the inability of the Kentucky officers to hold the men from crossing the river. Then the second line of the division moved too quickly and collided with the first. Add to this the fall of Hanson, and pandemonium reigned for fifteen minutes on that terrible hill. A. G. Montgomery, the man who took a prominent part in two surrenders, was killed here by a confused wretch in his own company. Captain McKendree took a bad wound in the thigh, and thought he was doomed, yet insisted on staying with his command. Captain John Rogers, who lost a brother at Shiloh, now saw his brother George fall forward with a fatal bullet in his side. Yet there was presence of mind. As Trabue rallied the Orphans on the crest of the hill, he sat calmly on his horse. Nearby he saw on the ground an enemy bugle. "There, pick that up," he told a man nearby. "We'll need that." No true Orphan could pass over booty, even in battle. Soon thereafter Trabue saw a man running for dear life from the misadventure at the river. "Halt, sir! Don't *run*. You're in just as much danger running as you would be in a walk." The Orphan stopped briefly, thought, and replied, "Oh yes, Colonel, I know *that;* but then, you see, *we get away so much quicker!"* Off he ran.[10]

Lewis tried to rally the 2d and 6th Kentucky after the disaster at the river, calling on an officer to gather the men around a regimental flag just in the rear. But in the space of a few minutes four color bearers fell dead before the men could rally to the banner. Nearby Joe Nuckols, who never learned to ride and always entered engagements on foot, brought away safely the colors of the 4th Kentucky, but only after three bearers fell before him. As the Orphans withdrew, the 2d Kentucky's dog, Frank, flushed a rabbit in the midst of the hell around him and, oblivious to the battle, chased it straight toward the advancing enemy line. Some of the men cheered Frank but then the rabbit changed course, and raced back through the Kentucky line, Frank in hot pursuit. "Run, cotton-tail, run!" shouted Tom Wilson of the 6th Kentucky. "Had I no more reputation to sustain than you, I would run too." An enterprising corporal of Lewis' regiment heard a bullet pass through his canteen. Filled as it was with hard cider, the Orphan quickly weighed the priorities before him, dropped his rifle, and drained the container dry before it ran out on the ground. And young Blanchard, the coward, stood in the forefront of the 4th Kentucky, headmost in the advance, and among the last to withdraw.[11]

It had been, Squire Bush wrote in his diary that night, "the most desperate charge that was ever made!" It was also the most senseless. Trabue stormed furiously at Nuckols. "I saw from the first that there was no use going there! I was afraid, too, that all our boys would be needlessly killed." As he said this, he finally received word of Hanson's wounding, the command of the brigade now devolving upon him. "Old Trib" at once set about re-forming the men and pulling them out of the artillery fire to the line they occupied at the beginning of the charge. Nothing remained to gain from holding that terrible hill.[12]

The Orphan Brigade began that charge with no more than 2,247 men, 395 of them in the 9th Kentucky, which took no part in the fight, though Hunt stormed about trying to get his men sent in. That left just 1,852, of whom 1,197 were Kentuckians. The charge itself lasted barely an hour, the hardest fighting and most damage requiring barely 20 minutes. When Trabue re-formed the brigade and took a hasty field report, he found something more than half the men present. When a final tally came in, Trabue reported that 431 of the brigade lay dead, wounded, or missing and probably killed, on the field. That was nearly one fourth of the command, and of the Kentuckians engaged, over 27 per cent fell. It was the highest loss of any brigade in the assault. Hanson was dying, Nuckols badly wounded, Bramlette and several other officers killed. In the 4th Kentucky 13 of its 23 officers lay dead or wounded. Hanson's rowdy old 2d Kentucky lost 108 out of 422 engaged.[13]

Shortly after Trabue re-formed the brigade, Breckinridge rode the length of his now much shorter line, surveying the damage done. His anger mounted as he saw the wreck left by Bragg's insane order. Finally he came to the Kentucky brigade. "I never, at any time, saw him more visibly moved," said Joe Nuckols. "He was raging like a wounded lion, as he passed the different commands from right to left; but tears broke from his eyes when he beheld the little remnant of his own old brigade." The loss of Hanson, Rice Graves now severely wounded after supporting Pillow's advance, the gaps in the lines of his old Kentuckians, proved too much for the general. "My poor Orphans! My poor Orphans!" he cried as he passed them. "My poor Orphan Brigade! They have cut it to pieces!"[14]

That night the Kentuckians rested, dazed from the fury of the afternoon. They wrapped themselves in blankets and huddled around their pitiful fires for warmth in the bitter cold. Those on picket had no fires, and some of them found their socks and trousers—thoroughly wetted from the crossing of Stones River—frozen on their feet. "This night of sleet & discouragement was trying," wrote Green, "but never a man faltered." The most miserable were the wounded who still lay on the field where comrades could not retrieve them. Bragg's generals met in war council sometime after 10 P.M., when they determined to stay in position the next day, Bragg still hoping that Rosecrans would retire first.

The meeting done, Breckinridge went to see Hanson. He found the general dying. "Old Flintlock" could not restrain his emotion when he saw his commander. "General," he said, "Dr. Yandell does not think I will live, nor do I; but I have this satisfaction, I shall die in a just cause, having done my duty." Virginia Hanson's own agony seemed frantic. Mary Breckinridge had cut the boot from the injured leg and torn strips of her own clothing for bandages. After a time, at Breckinridge's request, Mary left to attend to Rice Graves, while her husband took on the midnight vigil. "Old Bench-leg's" constitution was strong, and it took him a long time to die. Slowly the face that smiled so often set still in pain, the old humor, the irascibility, the nature that tried so hard to change the Kentuckians yet was so much like them, faded away. By morning, January 4, he was gone. The Kentucky Brigade was orphaned yet again.[15]

By the time Hanson breathed his last, his Kentuckians were already gone themselves. During the night of January 3–4, Bragg finally decided that his Army could not remain in Murfreesboro. The Federals were too powerful. That night he issued orders for the retreat and, in what by now seemed custom, the Kentucky brigade acted as rear guard. Breckinridge assigned Hunt's 9th Kentucky and the 41st Alabama to join Cobb in covering the withdrawal. He expected it to be a perilous duty and issued double the normal ammunition, but in fact the movement took place virtually unopposed. Bragg's Army itself marched forty miles south to Tullahoma, while Hunt's command remained ten miles in the advance at Manchester. Behind them on the battlefield at Stones River, they left all too many of their comrades. Among them, wounded severely and a prisoner of the Federals, was Ed Porter Thompson.[16]

Now the season demanded that the Army go into winter quarters, and meanwhile the high command needed to replace Hanson. Temporarily Hunt took charge of the 1st Kentucky Brigade, and this suited the Orphans very well. On January 14 twenty-five officers of the brigade, chiefly from the 6th and 9th regiments, sent a petition to President Davis requesting that "Uncle Tom" be promoted to brigadier general and given permanent command of them. "During the recent series of engagements in front of Murfreesboro he displayed the same judgment, coolness, & gallantry which has characterized him upon every battle field, and endeared him to the officers, and men of the brigade," they wrote. Hunt himself did not know about the petition, but when the Kentucky lobby in Congress learned of it, they quickly lent their voices.

While awaiting a permanent commander for the brigade, Bragg assigned Brigadier General Marcus J. Wright of Tennessee to take charge of the Orphans. He assumed the responsibility on January 17, 1863, surely realizing that he would not have it for long. Trabue was known to be continuing his quest for a promotion. Some thought of Helm, now fully recovered from his Baton Rouge operation. The Hunt petition did not long remain a secret, and now another Kentuckian entered the lists, one with the best claim of all. Simon Buckner wanted his brigade once more.[17]

While the 6th and 9th Kentuckys petitioned for Hunt, the officers of Hanson's old 2d Regiment wrote to Buckner as soon as they reached Tullahoma. They wanted to serve with him, not that they were at all dissatisfied with Breckinridge, but because so many of them had served with Buckner even before the war in the State Guard. "I know the men have formed for me no common attachment," he wrote. He also knew of their problems. "A restlessness originating in various causes, which have been the subject of several conversations between Gen. Breckinridge and myself pervades the entire Kentucky organization." He believed he could cure the problem, or at least contain it. "The fortune of war has placed them beyond my command, and I have forfeited any claim I formerly have had to command them," he noted, but it hardly lessened his fatherly concern. He believed they would yet be important to the Confederacy. "They have already shown themselves amongst the best of her soldiers." Even though he now commanded a military department in the South, he offered to take an inferior position as a mere brigade commander if they would give him the Orphans. Once he commanded Breckinridge; now he would be delighted to be commanded by him. "I would now serve under Gen. Breckinridge with the same alacrity, and with the same confidence in his abilities, that he has heretofore manifested towards me." He feared that his superiors might regard his request as "quixotic," but promised this was not the case. "Though I may appear to court a degradation of military rank, I seek only to gratify the natural feelings of a man by associating myself again . . . with those who love me as their friend and confide in me as a leader." To President Davis, Buckner spoke more strongly. "They are my children," he said, "take me from my department—put me at the . . . Brigade's head . . . I want no higher honor."[18]

The matter remained unresolved for a time. Meanwhile, the Orphans settled into their winter quarters, and one of their number made an arduous journey toward recuperation from his Stones River wound. Mary Breckinridge heeded her husband's request and had Major Rice Graves loaded into a wagon, assisted by her son Cliff and two lieutenants. The trip to Chattanooga, where she would care for him, proved long and tiresome. "I had not the remotest idea what was before me," she wrote the general. Twice she hired mules to assist the horses, and the men in the party had to whip the animals to make them pull, while another pulled the horses, and one man pushed at the wheels and chocked them every few feet as they ascended the Cumberland Mountains. "Sometimes they would not pull at all and those two gentlemen just had to whip and lead and work every way with them to get along at all." Once arrived in Chattanooga, Mary met General Helm, commanding the post there, and he found rooms for her and Graves. She also met the charming Major Throckmorton of the large-lipped horse. With his customary chivalry he refused her suggestion that he take the mules with the horses when he returned the ambulance over the mountains. She hoped he would have just as rotten a trip as she did. "I shall never laugh at his remarks again."

As for Graves, he shortly wrote to Breckinridge's adjutant that "the trip across the mountains has inflamed my wound very much and I am proportionately suffering." Yet he recovered quickly, though saddened when Mary Breckinridge left for Alabama to winter. "Mrs Breckinridge is very much missed," he wrote the general; "the establishment is not near so pleasant since her departure." Not long thereafter, Breckinridge recommended that the War Department promote Graves and give him command of a North Carolina unit in need of a colonel. "He is an excellent officer," wrote the Kentuckian, betraying a little of the fatherly feeling he had for the young artillerist.[19]

For Mary Breckinridge herself, regarded by many of the Orphans as the mother of the brigade, the winter proved hard as she spent most of it separated from the general. Always she urged him to join her. "If I only had you here after all of your dangers and hardships I would be so happy," she wrote. "I want to hear from you so much." She passed the time by tending wounded soldiers, sewing shirts for the general, making soap for the Kentuckians' hospitals, and buying delicacies like white sugar and French gelatine for the soldiers. From her wedding dress she made a beautiful battle flag, which she sent to her husband, instructing him to present it to his best regiment. Fearful of being accused of favoritism, Breckinridge did not give it to one of the Kentucky units but, instead, to the 20th Tennessee of his division. Further, thinking that if her name were mentioned in connection with the flag, the Federals might arrest her, he made no mention of the flag's maker. Mary did not like that. "I regret very much not having the flag presented in my name," she wrote him. "I thought the beauty was in coming from your wife." Furthermore, "by all means it ought to have been given to a Ky regiment." Of course, she could not stay angry for long. The general obtained a brief leave of absence in late January to spend a few days with her. When he returned to the Army, she begged him—he was never much of a letter writer—to correspond frequently. "If you knew how much pleasure they gave me," she said of his letters, "I know you would write oftener. I will be willing to take short ones and much space taken up in writing my name and yours and my place of residence &c &c." Any word at all was better than nothing.[20]

Besides, as the winter moved on from January, Breckinridge and the Kentuckians quickly found themselves embroiled in one of the most disgraceful episodes in the history of the Army of Tennessee. Braxton Bragg, with yet another strategic defeat on his hands, sought scapegoats once more. After the Perryville debacle he naturally looked first to Breckinridge, particularly since the disastrous charge at Stones River. Silently Bragg started to gather his evidence against the Kentuckian. Breckinridge's aide, Theodore O'Hara, first detected what the commanding general was about. "B.B. is evidently preparing & marshalling all his resources of shallow cunning and foolish chicanery, energized by a ranting hate, to make war upon you & wreak to the utmost his ignoble spite against you," O'Hara warned the Kentuckian. Breckinridge respected O'Hara and thought he had the "quickest eye" he had ever seen on the battlefield. O'Hara's eye proved even quicker for intrigue.

Bragg attacked Breckinridge in his report of the fight at Murfreesboro, and quickly tried to lay all the blame for its loss on him, implying chiefly that the failure of the January 2 assault was directly attributable to Breckinridge. To support his case, he falsified official reports of numbers and losses, virtually ordered a subordinate to submit a perjured report, and received some materially damaging testimony from General Pillow. The latter claimed that Breckinridge entirely mismanaged the assault, though how he would have known it from his hiding place behind a tree is a mystery. Pillow was easily persuaded to offer false witness, since he knew that at any time Breckinridge might press charges against him. Indeed, on January 3, even as he lay in pain awaiting the ambulance that would take him to Chattanooga, Rice Graves prepared charges and specifications against Pillow. "Brig. Gen. Pillow yesterday was guilty of conduct unbecoming an officer and soldier," he wrote. "The said Brigadier General Pillow during the charge yesterday afternoon did screen himself behind a tree" while his brigade advanced. Breckinridge discussed the charges with Hardee, who advised that nothing be done in the matter. "I have accordingly acted as if it was not in existence," wrote Breckinridge.

The Kentuckian himself did almost nothing in the controversy, gathering a little testimony in his behalf, but holding it until a hoped-for court of inquiry, which never came. The controversy eventually found its way to the press, but did more harm to Bragg than Breckinridge. When the latter's friends in Richmond tried to publicize his side of the matter, he restrained them. "I have written to nobody at Richmond about the affairs of the army," he said. "I have engaged no press, made no statements. In a word, *have done nothing* in conflict with strict military propriety. . . . Since I entered the service I have been simply a soldier trying to serve a cause which every true Southern man is willing every day to die for." If Bragg, a professional soldier, wished to act in this distinctly unprofessional manner, let him. "If anything is said to my discredit," wrote the Kentuckian, "I hope my friends will be silent unless it touches my honor or that of my command. When a man is right there are no remedies equal to silence and time. It is only when he is wrong that it is necessary to preoccupy the public mind by clamor." What probably galled Bragg most of all was seeing the restraint with which Breckinridge conducted himself. It showed him to be the better man, which only made Bragg hate him the more.

As for the Orphans in this controversy, their love for their general only increased as they saw him unjustly persecuted. When they saw Bragg's condemnatory report of the battle and heard of his underhanded methods, they reportedly asked Breckinridge "to resent the insult" to his honor and theirs. Supposedly they actually asked the general to resign his position and challenge Bragg to personal combat, so enraged did they become. Instead, Breckinridge calmed them by reminding them of a higher duty they all faced, and that they must endure with him this personal wrong for the sake of the greater goal. It is even claimed that the general promised that, should both he and Bragg survive the war, he might then seek a gentleman's redress. Since Breckinridge abhorred dueling, this last rings false, yet certainly he calmed the Orphans for a time. But Braxton Bragg was not done with the Kentuckians and would strike once more before their paths parted.[21]

While the controversy raged, the Kentucky brigade finally got a new commander, but it was not Buckner, and it was not Hunt. And alas, it was not Robert P. Trabue, who perhaps deserved—and certainly wanted—it most. Even General Wright favored Trabue. Just four days after assuming command of the Orphans, he wrote to his brother John in Congress in Richmond regarding the Kentuckians. "It is a fine Brigade," he said, "and one that any man should be proud to command." He believed, however, that the man commanding it should be a Kentuckian, and that Kentuckian should be Trabue.

Trabue himself put the letter in John Wright's hand, for late in January Trabue went to Richmond in person to argue his case for promotion. He took as well a recommendation from Hardee, a letter from Hunt, his own petition signed by several officers of the brigade, including Hewitt and Lewis, and yet another recommendation by Breckinridge. Once in Richmond he visited Hodge, himself now a congressman, and from him received a letter to the President. Since no more promotions to brigadier could be made for Kentuckians, they even tried to argue that Trabue was really a Louisianian, having spent twelve years there before the war. All of this, with a recapitulation of the year-long history of requests for his promotion, Trabue presented to the Kentucky lobby in the capitol. Then, one week later, he had the misfortune to die. The final impediment to his promotion, a raging fever, called "congestion of the brain" by some, struck unexpectedly and ravaged him almost overnight. He died penniless on February 12, the anniversary of the day that he and his brigade began their exile from Kentucky. The Kentucky delegates in Richmond raised the funds to send the body to Natchez for burial from their own pockets. The news struck his friends like a thunderbolt. "We are all shocked to hear it," wrote Mary Breckinridge. "In the midst of life we are in death." Two weeks after his death, the official announcement was made to the Kentucky brigade. "Let us mourn his loss and emulate his valor," it read. The author was the new commander of the Orphan Brigade, Brigadier General Ben Hardin Helm.[22]

The appointment arrived on February 14, and two days later Helm announced his staff. Following his wound at Baton Rouge, he convalesced for some time before taking command of the post at Chattanooga. Since the other Kentucky brigadiers at the moment already had commands, and Buckner was deemed too important to waste on a brigade, Helm appeared the natural choice to lead the Orphans. He was a gentle man, but if the Kentuckians thought he would treat them easy, they proved much mistaken.[23]

Indeed, it seemed as if old "Bench-leg" Hanson had never left them. Still they had to wear their uncomfortable caps on the parade ground. He chastised them for trading their ammunition to farmers for food. When Sergeant William Lawrence of Hunt's Company A left his guard post, Helm gave him a month at hard labor and reduced him to private. Never mending their loose ways with private property, the Orphans did $150 worth of damage to a house in Manchester, and later a woman signing herself "A Tennessee Mother" accused them of "depredations" even against women, children, and widows. To all Helm meted severe justice. Even the medicos in the brigade found their lessons in the proper manner of sick reports handed them, and the malingerers obtained no more solace than before. The surgeon of the 4th Kentucky, a stout, pompous young fellow, always dealt curtly with the slackers. One Orphan came to him repeatedly. "Had a fever all night," he said, "took cold, I reckon." Or "I got pains in my jints— headache fit to bust," or worse. The surgeon tired of seeing the man, growing naturally skeptical. When he saw the malingerer approach, he usually addressed him, "Well, old pine-knot; tired of drilling, hey?" At every visit he took two placebos from his right vest pocket and sent the man back to duty. One day, however, he extracted the pills from his left pocket. "Hold on, doctor," said the lazy Orphan, "that's the wrong pocket."

"Don't make any difference," said the good surgeon. "Shirking ain't fatal, but it is incurable."[24]

Yet the Orphans bore life in winter quarters with their usual spirit. Indeed, this was their second winter of the war. They were old hands at it now. Even before they reached Tullahoma the Kentuckians began those camplife adventures that so ably characterized the brigade. Jackman started it by awaking on January 6 to find a goose roosting on his head. "Late that night I waked up with something heavy on my face." It belonged as a pet to some men of his company. "I presume he saw that I had no feathers under my head, and concluded to put some on top instead of underneath. I thanked him by flinging him against a stump."

While Hunt's 9th Kentucky occupied Manchester for several weeks, they managed somehow to win the affection and respect of the townspeople. "They thought the 9th Ky. was the best regiment in the army," Jackman discovered. When other regiments came to town they slaughtered hogs, burned fence rails, and the like, but not Hunt's boys, or so they thought. "If our boys ever did do such things, which is highly probable," wrote Jackman, "all went to the credit of the other regiments." As a control over such depredations, Lewis, Nuckols, and Caldwell formed a "Council of Administration" for the brigade, a sort of internal police. Yet they could not prevent the Orphans from drinking. In Tullahoma Squire Bush and several comrades went into town one night and bought whisky. "All got a little funny," said Bush. "I was drunker than I ever was before in my life."

The music of the regimental bands provided considerable diversion as the winter progressed. On St. Patrick's Day the 4th Kentucky band serenaded Breckinridge, himself a Scots-Irishman. Even more entertainments were to be had in Manchester. Jackman found that his comrades "found enough society to keep up amusement, and all the winter were flirting with the young ladies." Some cajoled farmers' wives, hoping to be invited to dinner. Others attended balls and frolics. Manchester was particularly diverting for the 9th Kentucky before the rest of the brigade joined it there, swelling the town with soldiers. The young ladies vied with each other in flattering Hunt's ragged Orphans. They gave a party at a tavern, replete with ham sandwiches, pies, and cakes. "You were expected to go up to any girl who was there," found Johnny Green, "tell her your name & be sure of a cordial welcome." She handed over the food and gushed about the bravery of Confederate soldiers. All had a good time, and Green speculated, "I dont know for how many matches the foundation was laid this evening."

The Orphans of the 9th decided to reciprocate. Gus Moore and Phil Vacaro suggested that they stage a theatrical in a nearby paper mill. There would be some cost involved, and the boys agreed to pay it all themselves. There was no playbook at hand, but Moore believed he could write down the lines from *Bombasties Furioso* from memory. He and Vacaro acted as producers and cast the play from men of the regiment, poor Johnny Green being selected to play the young lady Distifena. While other Orphans sent invitations to the young ladies of the town, craftily removing their mothers' objections by hinting that there would be an abundance of pure coffee for refreshments, Moore began constructing the stage in the paper mill. And Johnny Green started looking for a dress.

Of course, every lady in town had a dress, but it did not seem exactly proper just to step forward and ask for one. "I picked out the finest-looking house in the neighborhood to bestow my attentions upon with the hopes of finding among its inmates a young lady whose clothes would fit me." This done, he began courting the good opinions of the family and its two daughters. He took Johnny Jackman with him on one visit to occupy one girl while he worked his charms on the other, Miss Sukey Hickerson. After a couple of visits she agreed to lend a crinoline. Moore and Vacaro, meanwhile, built scenery and rehearsed the actors. Once his dress was safely in hand, Green also undertook to obtain a barrel of oysters from his cousin in Mobile. They, with cakes and coffee, made a splendid feast after the play. The Orphans staged their theatrical on February 24. It attracted virtually every young woman of the town. "Saw a great variety of the fair sex," wrote Squire Bush of the event. In all about two hundred local people attended the broad farce, Colonel Hunt himself escorting "the Belle of the county." "It was a mirthful occasion for every body," Green decided. After the play and the refreshments, the young women danced with the Orphans while their mothers luxuriated in that free coffee.

With all the frolicking, the Kentuckians turned more spiritual as well, now that the war entered its third year. Certainly they knew they had enough sinful doings to atone. Elder Joseph D. Pickett preached to them every Sunday, their officers sometimes requiring the men to attend divine services. He spoke to them from the eighth chapter of Acts. "This is life eternal," Pickett said to them from John. And he preached from Psalms, verse ten of the forty-sixth chapter. "Be still and know that I am God," he read. "I will be exalted among the heathen. I will be exalted in the earth." One could not have asked for a more "heathen" lot for the Lord to pass among than the Orphan Brigade, nor for men more exalted and God-fearing. With all their petty sinning, their faith did not waver. Their difficult lot in this war only served to make them better Christians. That is, except for Konshattountzchette. He was a "heathen" and no mistake. Captain Tom Winstead caught the essence of that spiritual feeling. "I am not the same lighthearted man I was at home," he wrote to his wife. "I cannot lay down at night and drop off to sleep as I have done in other days. . . . There is not a night but a thousand memories crowds my brain."[25]

The generals, too, provided diversion for the Kentuckians. In addition to the routine practice, Breckinridge and Helm arranged several drill competitions and reviews. Ranking generals like Hardee and

Joseph E. Johnston viewed their evolutions, and pronounced them among the best-drilled units in the Army. In mid-May General Daniel W. Adams, commanding a Louisiana brigade in Breckinridge's division that took pride in its drilling skill, challenged the Orphans to a contest. Helm accepted. Each regiment would compete against another regiment of the other brigade, then the best-drilled regiment within each brigade would meet its opposite number, and finally the brigades as a whole would match for the championship.

The first competition occurred on May 19. Two colonels acted as judges, and Hardee umpired. It was a festive occasion. "Looked like 'fair times,'" wrote Jackman. Breckinridge, Humphrey Marshall, Adams, Helm, Hardee, and a host of lesser luminaries observed the meet, while carriages brought ladies and gentlemen from miles around. The Orphans dressed in their best military finery. Officers polished their swords and buttons and strutted for the ladies like gamecocks. The first two regiments to meet were Lewis' 6th Kentucky and the 16th Louisiana, and the judges decided in favor of the Orphans. The next day, May 20, Adams' best regiment, the 13th Louisiana, met the rowdy old-timers of Hanson's 2d Kentucky, led now by good old Bob Johnson. Surprisingly, despite Johnson's demonstrated ignorance of drill, the Orphans once again bested the Louisianians. "Both regiments drilled splendidly," wrote Jackman. The next day the 4th Kentucky ran through its evolutions under the eye of its newly commissioned colonel, Joe Nuckols, recovered from his wound. They, too, defeated their rival regiment, the 19th Louisiana. The latter's colonel was a Prussian whose broken English on the drill field set the boys laughing out loud. It remained only for Hunt's 9th Kentucky to meet Adams' 32d Alabama, a contest that would have decided a title not only for the division, but unofficially for the Army as well, since it was widely told that Adams led the best-drilled brigade in Bragg's command. Unfortunately, active operations commenced once more on the day that the Orphans and Alabamians were to meet. They never finished the drill competition, but the men of Kentucky never doubted who deserved the championship.[26]

If Jackman and his mates in the 9th Kentucky had stepped onto the drill field that day, they would have answered the commands of another new colonel, John W. Caldwell. "Uncle Tom" Hunt had resigned.

Hunt first tried to tender his resignation in January, despite the petition from his officers that he be promoted to brigadier. He did not want promotion. "I have lost my fortune," he lamented to Eli Bruce. "Worse than this I have entirely neglected my family." He would have welcomed an unsolicited promotion at one time, but now necessity compelled him to leave the service. Hardee, however, refused to allow it. "Colo. Hunt is one of the most valuable officers in my corps," he wrote to the War Department, "& his services cannot be spared." Indeed, Hunt's reputation for reliability reached the very top command of the Army. In April Bragg asked Hardee to send "Uncle Tom" with his own and Lewis' regiments toward Murfreesboro on a reconnaissance, with orders "to proceed as far as he possibly could." Both Jackman and Bush noted in their diaries the hurried preparation of rations for the march, and then the mysterious cancellation of the march after midnight of April 26. What they never knew is that, after following his duty by giving Hunt Bragg's orders, Hardee went to the commanding general and told him that it simply would not do to give Hunt and his Orphans such an order, "for they wouldn't stop this side of hell!" Bragg countermanded the order.

Hunt did oversee Wickliffe and a small detachment from the brigade saving some valuable stores in government warehouses at McMinnville a few days earlier and won compliments for the way "the troops from this Brigade did valuable service." But still Hunt wanted out of the Army. Finally on April 22 the President accepted his resignation, and on May 1 Hunt—temporarily commanding the 1st Kentucky Brigade in Helm's absence—formally turned the Orphans over to Lewis. The sadness of Hunt's leave-taking brought tears from many in his old regiment. Some of them dated back to State Guard days with kindly "Uncle Tom." "Few among them could take his hand in parting, without tears," wrote one, "and all were sad and depressed." Hunt repaired to Augusta, Georgia, to join his refugee family, and there entered business. For the rest of the war he lent aid to the Orphans when he could. After his departure from Tennessee, Helm sent to Hardee a testimonial to Hunt's "conduct, true courage, and unusual judgment as an officer." He grieved to lose him, as did the 9th Kentucky. "The resignation of so gallant a soldier and devoted a patriot is painful," yet all understood the motives that compelled Hunt's action. Fortunately they did not have long to mourn his absence. By the middle of May the Orphans were needed again.[27]

The summons came from a familiar quarter, Vicksburg. Though Williams failed in his attempt to take the fortress city the year before, another man in blue with more men and more determination laid

siege to the city just the day before the drill competitions began in
Breckinridge's division. U. S. Grant did not discourage like other men,
and now he had the Confederate Army in Vicksburg surrounded. Its
only hope lay in support from the outside. General Joseph E. Johnston
was organizing a small army to provide that support, and he called on
Bragg for assistance. This gave Bragg a much-wanted opportunity to
rid his Army of its troublemakers. He ordered Breckinridge's division
to march to Johnston's aid, and Vicksburg's.

The general received the order late on May 23, and that same night
set the Orphans to work cooking rations for the trip ahead. Early the
next morning the 1st Kentucky Brigade formed, just 2,048 strong, and
marched 12 miles to Wartrace, arriving about noon. Along the way the
men speculated among themselves about where they were going. "All
the boys suspected that the brigade was ordered to Mississippi and
were grumbling a great deal," said Jackman, "not liking to make another summer campaign in the state." Breckinridge soon dispelled any
mystery. Shortly after the Kentuckians stacked their arms, he sent orders for them to form at headquarters. He wished to speak to them, he
said. On their way to brigade headquarters a number of the men complained that if they could vote on their probable destination, they
would choose to remain in Tennessee rather than spend another miserable summer in Mississippi. When the brigade assembled, the general
stood on a stump so they all could see him, and announced that he
had orders to bring all except his Tennessee troops here to board a
train for Atlanta. Further orders would meet them there, but he had a
good idea of his ultimate destination, and supposed they did too.
Knowing how the Orphans felt about that, he had asked Bragg if he
might not leave them in Tennessee and take a Mississippi brigade with
him instead, men who would be glad to go home. Bragg left the matter to Breckinridge, however, and now he asked the Orphans their
preference: going with him to Johnston, or staying with Bragg.

"The boys felt that if they did not vote to follow their Maj. Gen'l.
outsiders would think they also condemned him as well as Bragg,"
wrote Johnny Jackman. "To stay with Bragg while others were sent
with Breckinridge," said Johnny Green, "would be taking part against
their beloved Breckinridge." Men who a few minutes before spoke of
voting for Tennessee if they had the chance, now cast unanimously to
follow their general, their father. "Whither thou goest," said Green,
"there we will go also." They raised their right hands to a man, then
followed the balloting with a round of cheering for Breckinridge. He

thanked them in a brief speech—"He is the most eloquent speaker I ever heard," Jackman decided—then left to bid farewell to his Tennessee regiments. Already moved by the Orphans' gesture, he broke down when saying good-bye to the 20th Tennessee, to whom he had given Mary's wedding-dress flag. He uttered only a few words before tears overwhelmed him. Abruptly he wheeled his mount and galloped out of sight. A month later the men of the 20th sent him a new horse "as a simple expression of the feelings cherished by soldiers for their favorite chieftain."[28]

The trip from Wartrace to Atlanta, then Montgomery, and on to Jackson, repeated in reverse their journey of the previous September, and with no fewer adventures. Once having decided to go to Mississippi, the Orphans assumed their usual demeanor. When their train left Montgomery, a bystander saw that "all seemed in the highest spirits, cheering and yelling like demons." In part they cheered in thanks for being alive, for on the very day they left Wartrace by train the 6th and 9th Kentuckys very nearly ceased to be. Their rickety engine and broken-down cars ran out of control coming down a 7-mile grade. By Jackman's timing, they covered the 7 miles in 4½ minutes. He watched the moon as it appeared from moment to moment between the crags overhead, and thought of saying good-bye to it. "We thought every moment the car would be dashed in pieces against the rocks or be pitched off some of the cliffs and be ground into dust." How much worse it must have been for those men who "bivouacked" on top of the crowded cars. The rearmost car actually flew to pieces and disappeared from the end of the train, yet not a man was killed. One poor Orphan riding atop it when it disintegrated found himself flying over the telegraph wires and into a briar bramble. Miraculously he survived, "receiving no other injury than being 'powerfully' scratched." The men from the wrecked car and from another damaged car had to bivouac beside the track and wait for the next train. The rest of the Orphans "spent the remainder of the night roaring and clattering over the rails to Chattanooga."[29]

By the evening of May 31, 1863, Breckinridge and the Kentuckians reached the end of their travels, just six miles short of Jackson. The trip that had taken two weeks in 1862 he now accomplished in one. In Jackson, however, the brigade lay idle for nearly a month while Johnston frantically tried to increase his army. For the Orphans it was a month of monotonous camp life, relieved by fishing, swimming, and bathing, and listening to the distant sound of Grant's artillery shelling

Vicksburg. The men caught fish by the hundreds using their blankets, though Squire Bush complained that "after dividing by long division there remained a very small share for each man." Johnny Green sampled eel for the first time. Late in June several of the men captured in earlier days arrived, having been exchanged. Tom Moss told the boys how, denied exchange, he and twenty-two other prisoners overpowered their guards on the exchange boat and took command, steaming it into Confederate shores. And this month came Lewis' turn for the petition ritual. Whenever the Orphans had time on their hands, they seemed always to use it recommending their officers for promotion. On June 18 Nuckols, Caldwell, and the other ranking officers of the brigade petitioned the War Department to make "Old Joe" Lewis a brigadier. Helm agreed, and Breckinridge endorsed the petition by saying, "He is surpassed by none [in the] service for courage and conduct on the field."[30]

Only on the first of July did Breckinridge receive orders to move at last toward Vicksburg. It was a hot, miserable march, some men falling dead with sunstroke. More than half of Caldwell's 9th Kentucky fell by the roadside with heat prostration. Dr. Walter Byrne, surgeon of that regiment, went on a "bender," as Jackman put it, with a barrel of whisky the two had brought from Atlanta. He kept poor Johnny awake all night "by pulling my blankets, and bothering me generally." During the march on July 2 the Orphans "foraged" as usual in the fields they passed, today making free with corn and blackberries from Briarfield plantation, which just happened to belong to President Jefferson Davis. At least they were ecumenical. The Orphans would plunder from anyone.

Here they remained for two days, making further requisitions upon President Davis' fields. On July 5 they marched toward Vicksburg again in the afternoon, noticing now that the incessant cannonade of the past several days had stopped. When they formed for the march in the road the next morning, expecting to attack Grant's rear, their orders turned them instead toward Jackson. Vicksburg had fallen two days before, and now Johnston had to get his army in its earthworks at Jackson before the victorious Federals reached them first. The Orphans marched as rapidly as possible in the heat and dust. Because of the cloud raised by thousands of tramping feet, they could not see ahead to know how far they were from their bivouac. Sergeant Jim Lee of the 6th Kentucky asked a passing farmer how far it was to Clinton. "Four miles." Some distance farther he asked another native.

12. The battered bugle of the First Kentucky Brigade, like the Orphans it called to battle, vanquished, but unbeatable. (*From Thompson,* Orphan Brigade)

13. "Old Flintlock." Brigadier General Roger W. Hanson died in the senseless charge at Stones River that made them all Orphans. (*Courtesy Jack McGuire Collection*)

14. Colonel Martin Cofer helped raise the 6th Kentucky, and led it when "old Joe" Lewis took command of the Brigade. *(From Thompson,* Orphan Brigade)

15. Colonel John W. Caldwell was not above challenging his general when his honor was impugned. *(From Thompson,* Orphan Brigade)

16. Joseph P. Nuckols took over the 4th Kentucky from Trabue. They sang him the "Kentucky Battle Song" at Shiloh and died for him at Stones River. *(From Thompson,* Orphan Brigade)

17. Major Rice E. Graves, the artillerist who became a personal favorite with everyone. "Old Breck" wept over him at Chickamauga. *(From Thompson,* Orphan Brigade)

18. The gentle general, Ben Hardin Helm. Lincoln cried of Absalom when his brother-in-law died at Chickamauga. *(Courtesy Massachusetts MOLLUS Collection)*

. "Six miles." That was too much for the poker-playing Sergeant Lee. "By me sowl, Pathrick," he said, imitating an Irish friend, "by me sowl, Pathrick, why didn't ye stand? He's raised you two!"[31]

They reached Jackson on July 7, and here for the first time Johnston officially announced the fall of Vicksburg. "The news cast a gloom over most of the troops," wrote Jackman in his diary, "but did not seem to affect the 'Orphans' much." Two days later the Federals appeared in their front. The 1st Kentucky Brigade, now 2,089 including Cobb's battery, took position on the extreme left of the Confederate line. On their right sat their old drill rival, Adams' Louisianians. The Kentucky officers sent a party into Jackson to impress blacks for work in building up their fortifications, and found "quite a crowd" of them brought back. Several were barbers who did not much fancy working with pick and shovel, but the Orphans gave them little choice. "We layed around & took it easy while the negroes used the picks, spades & axes," wrote Johnny Green. Jackman made his "headquarters" in a gentleman's grape arbor.

Skirmishing began that same day, but nothing of note took place until July 11, when the Orphans were ordered to the right of the line to assist in meeting an expected assault. Caldwell's 9th Kentucky took position immediately behind a lovely mansion belonging to an old gentleman named Withers. The old man himself shouldered a rifle to help defend his yard against the Yankees. He had previously moved all of his fine furniture into his back yard to protect it from enemy artillery fire, but this afternoon it started to rain, threatening ruin to the upholstered pieces. Jackman and several other Orphans volunteered to help Withers move the furniture into the house again and out of the downpour. They moved everything in by the back door, safe from enemy sharpshooters. But that left an enormous mahogany bedstead, which could only enter by the front. Despite the fire of Yankee marksmen, Jackman and the others moved the bed safely, no doubt giving the enemy cause to wonder just what was going on. Already they rumored among themselves that Breckinridge's Kentucky soldiers were "considered the best in Johnston's Army." But best at what: fighting or furniture moving? The next day old Withers died fighting for his home, and a few days later furniture, house, and all disappeared in flames.[32]

The next day brought the only real fighting at Jackson, when three enemy brigades made a reconnaissance in force against the center of Breckinridge's division. They engaged other brigades, but Cobb's guns were chiefly responsible for repulsing the enemy with heavy loss. Spectators of a fight for a change, the Orphans marveled at the scene. "This is the grandest site I ever saw," Squire Bush wrote that night. "The sun shone most beautifully, the fire burning the large houses, the roaring artillery and the rattle of musketry, all combined, made it the most sublime sight that my eye was ever permitted to witness."

The good Reverend Pickett watched the firing with a few other officers that day when a spent bullet struck his foot. One of them picked up the ball and handed it to Pickett, who remarked that he was glad it had hit his foot and not his head. He and the 2d Kentucky were there in support of Cobb's battery, but Pickett was the only man hit. "You see, now," he remarked, "that chaplains are not bullet-proof." Pickett was a favorite with the Orphans. "Their [sic] is not a man or officer in the Brigade who does not love him," Private A. W. Randolph wrote his parents. Pickett proved a great friend to the sick and wounded, and always appeared on the field to lend cheer and aid. "He has no fear for him self."

Thanks chiefly to fire from Cobb and another battery, the Federals fell back, leaving two hundred prisoners and two or three stands of colors. It was a puny battle, but in the aftermath of the Vicksburg loss, any little victory was prized. The Kentuckians lost only two killed and seven wounded, all from Cobb's battery, and Johnston congratulated Breckinridge and "your gallant Division." Yet it was also clear that the Confederates could not remain in Jackson much longer. With all of Grant's Army in Vicksburg and nearby, Johnston could be over-whelmed if he allowed himself to be besieged. While a route of retreat still lay open, he must take it. On July 16 he readied for the evacuation. Even before orders arrived, the Orphans could tell from the look of things that another retreat was in the offing. At midnight they fell in line and marched out of their works. As a matter of habit now, the Kentuckians acted as a rear guard for the withdrawing Army, but the Federals did not pursue. "It has covered so many retreats," Jackman wrote, "the boys know just how such things have to be done."

In all they marched about fifty miles in the next six days, first in dust and heat, then in torrential rains. Even the usually cheerful Ben Helm grew depressed. "As usual, we are on a grand retreat," he wrote his wife, Emily, "the sufferings of which, so far as I am personally con-cerned, are unparalleled in the war. We have to drink water that, in ordinary times, you wouldn't offer your horse; and I have hardly slept out of a swamp since we left Jackson."[33]

The Orphans found themselves tense and nervous on the retreat.

Tired, marching until well past dark, their perceptions were faulty. Once the mere act of an adjutant's horse coming close to stepping on a man in the dark set nearly the entire 4th Kentucky into a stampede, and some time passed before the men calmed. In the dark they suddenly took each other for the enemy, and only eased back into their place in the road after calling out their names—all except "Devil Dick" Slusser, who found the whole business a bore and laid down in the road to sleep until the confusion subsided.

Their merry nature returned as always. In the retreat Johnston somehow lost track of his orderlies and baggage for the military court. He made inquiry of Breckinridge, asking that he consult his brigade and regimental commanders to see what they knew of the missing men and records. Helm's adjutant, Fayette Hewitt, passed the inquiry to Jim Hewitt, commanding the 2d Kentucky, asking, "Has anybody found a Military Court lying around loose?" Jim Hewitt did not think so. "If this court understands herself (and she think she do), she haint seen that court," he said in passing the matter on to the 4th Kentucky. "Narry sich as that about the Fourth Regiment," came the response. And Caldwell of the 9th reported, "I hain't neither seen nor hearn of a thing like that." Johnston may not have gotten back his court, but the Orphans certainly recovered their spirit.

Johnny Green even received an invitation to General Breckinridge's headquarters. Once there Johnny found a cousin who claimed he was now an aide to the general. When Green said he knew that his cousin could be no such thing as an aide, the man replied, "The hell I cant," and produced two jugs of whisky and a basket filled with bottles of champagne. "Dont you call that aid?" he said. The man had written some time before to a friend in Union-occupied New Orleans complaining, "You no doubt are wallowing in ease & luxury with all things good to eat & drink while John Breckinridge & I & a multitude of your other friends are barely keeping alive on Bull Beef & corn bread & are actually dying for something to drink." The friend sent the liquor, and Johnny Green's cousin proudly declared now, "There is no doubt that I saved Genl Breckinridges life." In fact, Breckinridge gave the whisky to his commissary for the men.[34]

The brigade spent the next month at a spot a few miles from Morton, Mississippi, that they dubbed Camp Hurricane. Later some claimed it to be the most peaceful month they ever knew during the war. There was little duty to do, and the men spent time building arbors of branches for shade. The brigade glee club sang the strains of

"Lorena," "Neapolitan," "Come Where My Love Lies Dreaming," and "Take Me Home to the Place." Most of the songs turned on a home theme, and they became rather popular with the local citizenry. "General," a farmer would say to Breckinridge, "I wish you would send them singin' boys over to my house to-night," and off they would go, the general and staff usually attending. John Marshall played the violin and sang tenor, John Weller bass, and with guitar, banjo, flute, and even a cornet, they sang for their supper. Every performance began with "We Come Again with Songs to Greet You."

Some of the other Orphans found less pretentious ways to amuse themselves. They established a brigade market near a spring, just to the right of the 9th Kentucky's bivouac. Breckinridge authorized the place for soldiers to "speculate" in fruits and vegetables, but he also established fixed prices on all goods the men could buy from the local farmers. Peaches and apples must go for no more than fifty cents per dozen, or six dollars the bushel. Fresh pork and mutton went for fifty cents a pound, but a single watermelon might bring as much as three dollars if large enough. Jackman and Green both claimed to have paid as much as forty dollars for one! The Orphans were to buy only from citizens. Any soldier caught selling goods to another soldier would be punished. That mattered little. They had no need to profiteer on vegetables, when right next to the market the Orphans established a primitive casino. They ran poker and keno games "& a few were raking in the money of many," said Green, until Breckinridge sent his provost to visit the "sporting gentlemen" and end their enterprise.

Some were contemplative. Johnny Jackman read Dickens' *Great Expectations* in August and was "well pleased with the book." Helm obtained a leave of absence to visit his wife, who had herself recently invited Mary Breckinridge to visit her sisters with her. "That would be amusing," wrote Mrs. Breckinridge, "for me to go on a visit to Mrs. Lincolns sisters."

President Jefferson Davis declared August 21, 1863, a national day of fasting and prayer. The Orphans built a large arbor specially for the divine services that day. The occasion sobered many of them, particularly after the defeats at Vicksburg and Gettysburg. "We must have been a little too puffed up with pride & confidence in our own powers," Green decided. Yet, he said, "The boys are all of one mind. Fight on until death."[35]

In less than a month Braxton Bragg would give them a chance to do just that.

NINE

"The Greatest Thing of the War"

Poor Breckinridge applied for a leave to visit Mary on August 23. His timing was terrible. Two days later orders arrived for him to pack his division and once again make the long trip from Mississippi to Tennessee. Rosecrans had maneuvered Bragg almost out of the state, forcing him into the vicinity of Chattanooga. Now, as September approached, the federal Army threatened to attack, and Bragg needed all the troops he could muster. With Breckinridge sitting idle at Camp Hurricane, Bragg shelved his animosity for the moment and called the Kentuckian to him.

Once again the Orphans made the trip in a week. For them this was the third time in a year for this thousand-mile journey. On August 26 they set ablaze their arbors and marched to Morton to board trains. Seven days later they made camp near Tyner's Station, just under a dozen miles from Chattanooga, and the general reported to Bragg, then in the city.

During the next two weeks the Orphans largely rested and did light picket duty while Bragg awaited Rosecrans' advance. As usual the boys foraged from the local farmers, and at one point Helm had to send an officer around at breakfast to check for those eating fresh pork. He found quite a bit, requisitioned by night from civilian pens, but pronounced it "beef" and left the offenders unmolested. As usual, too, nearby fences stood in great peril with the Orphans around. A farmer, no doubt aware of the Kentuckians' reputation with unattended rails, asked Breckinridge to protect his fences, and the general issued the suitable order. But then he gave the men an order to cook two days' rations, and they considered the last order so imperative that it superseded the first. Farewell fences. When Mr. Farmer complained, Breckinridge rode to the Orphans' camps in a rage and gave them a hearty scolding, calling them, so they thought, "a lot of vagabonds and thieves." That hurt. For the next week they nursed their anger at the outrage of their general so abusing them.[1]

Once in the vicinity of Bragg's Army, the Orphans saw again for the first time a regiment of old friends, the real 5th Kentucky Infantry, Williams' regiment now led by Hiram Hawkins. It belonged to another brigade, and the Orphans guyed and bullied the men of the 5th, whose battlefield experience seemed minimal compared to theirs. They warned them not to hurt themselves with their own rifles. Since most of the men in the 5th Kentucky came from the mountain counties of the state, where ginseng root was dug and sometimes used in barter, the Orphans now dubbed their fellow Kentuckians as "sang diggers." Before the month was out they would change their attitude toward these fellow alumni of Camp Boone. And that the service of all Kentuckians in the Confederate Army might be recognized, Governor Hawes detailed Lieutenant W. D. Chipley of the 9th Regiment to collect, arrange, and perpetuate the names, rank, services, and casualties of all native-born Kentuckians then in the field. These men of the Bluegrass always had a sense of history, and more particularly of their own place in it.[2]

Their place now would be in line of battle. Rosecrans finally met Bragg's advance elements on September 18, near the meandering stream called Chickamauga Creek, ten miles south of Chattanooga and across the state line in Georgia. Breckinridge's division now formed part of a corps led by Lieutenant General D. H. Hill, and held the extreme left of Bragg's line. The 1st Kentucky Brigade itself spent the afternoon of September 18 in relative idleness at its station near Glass's Mill on the east bank of the creek. Nothing more occurred than a little skirmishing with elements of a federal corps led by Major General Thomas Crittenden, another Kentuckian well known to the Orphans, and a childhood playmate of Breckinridge.

The first real action came about 9 A.M. the next morning, when Helm took the brigade, now only 1,682 strong, across the creek. Cobb's battery supported them and sent a shot into a house several hundred yards off, which sparked an artillery duel. The Confederate field pieces silenced the enemy before long, but at a loss of 14 Orphans killed and wounded. The carnage thus begun would not end for two days.

In the afternoon Breckinridge pulled the brigade back across Chickamauga Creek and marched them north the entire length of the Confederate line, six miles to Reed's Bridge. The rest of Bragg's Army fought inconclusively that day, but as evening approached he was readying a far greater battle for the morrow. Now he ordered Breckinridge and his command to the extreme right of his line. To-morrow, in company with the division of General Patrick Cleburne, Breckinridge would deliver the main attack on the Federals' left flank.

The Orphans bivouacked in an old field and built huge bonfires to drive away the cold. Their baggage being behind the lines, many of the men did not have their blankets with them. Johnny Jackman huddled in his overcoat all night but did not sleep. Occasionally they heard the moans and screams of the wounded lying on the day's bat-tlefield, and throughout the night came the rumble of wheels as Bragg moved his artillery into place for the coming contest. Here for the first and only time in the war Johnny Green entertained a premonition of personal disaster. "I could not shake off the conviction that I would meet my death in the next days battle." He prayed silently and begged that he would die doing his duty, and that his death might serve a purpose.[3]

Breckinridge awoke the men well before daylight and moved them toward the launching place for the attack. Due to delays in the Army's high command, however, it was nine-thirty before he started the as-sault, and it did not begin well. His division and Cleburne's were to at-tack four enemy divisions under General George H. Thomas. Yet when the attack began, Cleburne still was not in position, which meant that Breckinridge moved alone against more than four times his num-bers. Worse for the Orphans, their brigade held the left of the assault-ing force, and with Cleburne late, that meant Helm's own left flank would be exposed in the attack. Yet forward they went.

Before advancing, the Orphans sat or stood in line calmly. Jackman heard them "cracking jokes as usual." Ben Hardin Helm sat against a tree in the rear of the line talking with Caldwell. Two hundred yards in front of the brigade, the skirmishers under command of Wickliffe kept up a peppery fire against the enemy. They became so hotly en-gaged that Helm sent Nuckols and the 4th Kentucky forward to their support. He led his men to the skirmish line under a hot fire and then rode along the command steadying the men and telling them they must hold here until the main attack came. When he reached the center of his regiment he dismounted to take his own place, when a bullet hit his left arm below the elbow and shattered the bones. The wound was at once intensely painful. Combined with his already frail health during the past year, it was sufficient to put him out of active service for the rest of the war. He had come so far since Camp Boone. He had seen first Monroe and then Trabue die. Now he was out of the war, too. The 4th Kentucky continued the fight under its lieutenant colonel, Thomas Thompson.

It was between nine-thirty and ten that morning that Major James Wilson galloped to the tree where Helm sat and gave him verbally the order to attack. Johnny Jackman looked on and saw that "The General got up and mounted his horse, laughing and talking as though he were going on parade." He rode along the line, as did Breckinridge, steadying the men. The brigade formed with Lewis and the 6th Kentucky on the right, Hewitt and the rowdy 2d on the left, Caldwell's 9th Kentucky next to Hewitt, and 41st Alabama on their right, and Thompson and the 4th between it and Lewis. With a yell the Orphan Brigade surged forward to meet the enemy.[4]

Soon the main line passed the skirmishers, who now took their place with their comrades in the charge. Then they came in range of the enemy's rifles, and already began suffering casualties from the fire of artillery. Yet on they went. Helm posted himself at the left of the line with Hanson's old 2d Kentucky. Lewis, next senior, advanced on the right in company with his own 6th Regiment. "Our men all went into the fight with a determination to conquor," wrote Randolph of the 6th Kentucky. Dr. J. M. Tydings of the 9th Kentucky watched the assault, perhaps even participating in it himself. A few days later he composed a poem he called *The Charge of the First Kentucky Brigade at the Battle of Chickamauga.*

> See, up yon hillside a dark line is sweeping,
>   Breasting the thick storm of grapeshot and shell,
> Shouting like demons o'er abattis leaping,
>   Sons of Kentucky, ye charge them right well!

Breckinridge's division advanced against the extreme left wing of the federal Army. In fact, the Confederate brigades to the right of

Helm actually overlapped and passed beyond the enemy flank, attacking the Union in side and rear. As for the Orphan Brigade, they encountered the actual end of the blueclad line and it split the brigade in two. Helm, with the 2d and 9th Kentucky, and three companies of the Alabamians, fought the Federals in direct frontal assaults, while Lewis with his two Kentucky regiments and the remainder of the 41st Alabama passed beyond the end of the enemy line and joined in the attack on Thomas' flank and rear. Thus the Orphans fought two separate battles this day.[5]

For Lewis the fight went well. Having passed beyond the end of the enemy breastworks, he did not have to contend with heavy defenses, "consequently fighting the foe on something like equal terms." In a single charge they drove Thomas' men before them about one hundred yards without hesitation, almost to the road leading to Chattanooga. At this point Lewis saw a section of two enemy field pieces about fifty yards the other side of the road and believed he could take them. In the same instant, however, he looked back and discovered for the first time that the left half of the brigade was no longer with him, being engaged in battling the enemy breastworks. Faced with a dilemma, Lewis decided he could neither halt and wait for Helm, nor withdraw to rejoin him. Breckinridge rode with this part of the line during the assault, but Lewis decided on his own to take the enemy artillery and continue the charge.

Forward they went. The enemy guns came straight in the line of advance of the 4th Kentucky. As usual, the irrepressible 4th's Orphans were already amid a series of seriocomic adventures, even in deadly battle. Frank Chapman of Company D, known as the "silent man" because he seldom spoke, never fired his rifle in the entire battle because he could not see an enemy clearly—his eyes were sore—and did not want to waste his ammunition. So he just walked into and out of the battle with his mates. A somewhat obese lieutenant of the same regiment, presumably an excellent target, enjoyed a reputation for enduring battle after battle without being scratched, as he did in this charge. "Devil Dick" Slusser decided that it was because before each fight the officer chalked the outline of a normal-sized man on himself, and if hit anywhere outside the line, he simply did not count it.

There were serious moments as well. John Marshall still watched his once-cowardly young friend John Blanchard. As at Stones River, Blanchard, now a changed man, ran to the forefront of his company in the assault. There a federal rifle gave him his "red badge of courage" and he was borne to the rear, taking with him the respect of his company. Not so, however, the young man in Company E of the 6th Regiment who took cover behind a tree while his regiment pressed forward. If he fired at all, he stood a good chance of hitting one of his own men as they advanced. When his sergeant remonstrated with him and dragged him from his refuge, the Orphan pointed to a passing missile and cried, "Say! Didn't you see that cannon ball? Suppose it had hit me—it would have killed me!"

"Oh suppose!" said the good sergeant as he hauled the boy to his place in line. "Suppose you were a pig, rooting in a potato patch; but you're not!"[6]

On Lewis pressed toward the enemy field pieces. "The charge of our Division is the greatest thing of the war," boasted young Randolph a few days later. One of Forrest's cavalry watching from some distance on the right saw that "the Kentuckians gave up their lives in reckless fashion." And so thought Dr. Tydings.

> Up to the cannon's mouth, on to the rampart,
>   Shoulder to shoulder they gallantly press;
> Steel into steel flashing fierce in the sunlight,
>   Pulsing out life-drops like wine from the press.

With a last rush the Orphans crossed the road, and the men of the 4th Kentucky swarmed over the two federal cannon. At once they turned the guns and began preparations to fire them at the retreating foe. Breckinridge rode to the Orphans to congratulate the captors on their prizes, when Ephraim Smith jumped atop one of the guns, waved his cap, and shouted exultantly, "Gen. Breckinridge, see what your thieves and vagabonds have stolen!" He, at least, had not forgotten that scolding over the fence rails several days before. Now, amid one of the most fiercely contested battles of the war, the general took time to explain to Smith and his comrades that they misunderstood his reference. "I didn't say it," he protested. "I said that people would *consider* you thieves and vagabonds!" Then, the momentous clarification out of the way, the Orphans returned to their battle of life and death.[7]

While Lewis and one half of the brigade enjoyed marked success, Helm and the remainder of the Orphans found hard going in their course. "A perfect shower of grape shot tore through our ranks," said Johnny Green. The rifle fire came not only from their front, but into their unprotected left flank as well, and it brought men down in fearful numbers. A bullet hit Captain John Weller just under the eye and passed out behind his ear. He thought himself killed, refused aid, and urged the men forward. Then a burst of canister from an enemy gun flew into Green's company, and Johnny went down. Hit in the groin, he spun about and fell on his back. At first he thought his leg had been severed, but soon found it in place. He could detect no blood anywhere, but did find a shot in his pocket, where it had torn through his clothes and struck the metal clasp on a pocket purse. In a few minutes he could walk again and soon rejoined his regiment battling right in front of Thomas' breastworks.

The fire was hot enough to clutch Otho Haydon's hat from his head as he bent down to help a wounded friend from the field. Tom Strother of Caldwell's Company G was seen to shake his left foot at every step, blood dropping from it as he did. A comrade asked him the problem, and he said, "O, nothing; only a minie in my shoe." When an opportunity presented, Strother took off his shoe and pulled the minie bullet from his big toe, then put the shoe on again and continued the fight. Hervey McDowell of the 2d Kentucky likened the musketry fire to the sound of a woodman's ax, and commented to an officer, "This is the biggest wood-chopping you were ever at, ain't it?" Certainly it was for John Mahon. Wounded at Donelson, Shiloh, and Baton Rouge, he took another bullet now. He might well have paraphrased the words of a much-wounded Union officer who quipped that he was not of the blood of the South—it was of *his*.

Here, too, poor Flying Cloud had his beauty spoiled. A bullet hit him in the face, removing much of his upper jaw. When the painful wound healed, it left him with a contorted and "rather hideous" expression. He swore vengeance on all Yankees.[8]

Helm advanced his line about four hundred yards and then charged toward the enemy defenses. When Green rejoined his regiment the Confederates were only thirty yards from the Federals, "giving & taking death blows which could last but a few minutes without utter annihilation." In all, Helm led three separate assaults against Thomas' breastworks, each one repulsed. Lieutenant Colonel James W. Hewitt fell dead in front of his regiment. The poor 2d Kentucky. First they lost Hanson, and now they were orphaned again. With Colonel Bob Johnson incapacitated with dysentery, Major Jim Moss took command of the regiment.

Hewitt fell in the first charge, whereupon Moss brought the regiment back seventy-five yards to form line with Caldwell's 9th. Once there he discovered that Caldwell, too, was out of the fight, his right arm badly injured by a federal bullet. John C. Wickliffe took command of the regiment, presumably now allowing himself the luxury of unbuttoning his blouse. Once Wickliffe and Moss were aligned, they discussed the whereabouts of the remainder of the brigade. Unable to determine what was happening on the right, they determined to renew the attack, and charged once more. They got within forty yards this time, but the enfilading fire from their exposed left forced them back. Major Rice Graves, now ordnance officer on Breckinridge's staff, accompanied these regiments on the left, and here he, too, fell with a desperate wound. Captain Peter V. Daniel of the 9th Kentucky fell dead on the spot.

> Hark to the answer! That shout of defiance,
>   Rings out like a knell above the fierce strife,
> 'Tis death without shrift to the dastardly foe,
>   And heaven have pity on sweetheart and wife.

Once again Moss and Wickliffe re-formed. Then a message came from Breckinridge. They must assault again, as Lewis was attacking on the right, and a united effort might dislodge the enemy. Even with the support of Cobb, who brought his battery behind the 2d Kentucky, and now gave his fire to protect their exposed left, the Orphans could not take the federal works. Yet a third time the Orphans fell back. When they did, General Ben Hardin Helm was dying.[9]

Helm and John B. Pirtle moved forward with the 2d Kentucky during the first assault. Just when he was hit is uncertain, but at some point a rifle ball entered the general's right side and he fell from his horse. At once several of his staff rushed to him, a litter came forward, and gingerly they bore him nearly a mile to the hospital in the rear. Wickliffe ordered Johnny Jackman to ride Helm's horse to the rear, and there he gave it to Pirtle, who in turn would ride the animal to Lewis and give it to him. Word was sent to Breckinridge, then some distance to the right. "He sat erect on his horse," said an onlooker, "his whole body seeming to indicate attention to the business on hand." John Castleman was struck with "the impressiveness of the scene." The message came to Breckinridge, he read it, and then with considerable emotion announced, "Helm has been killed, Colonel

Caldwell has been wounded, Colonel Lewis commands the Kentucky Brigade."

The general looked at his staff, then called his son Cabell to him. "Bear this message to Colonel Lewis," said Breckinridge. Theodore O'Hara volunteered to make the dangerous journey instead, but the general sent his own son. The boy made the ride successfully and informed Lewis of his new command. A sergeant-major of the 9th Kentucky declared, "When Lieutenant Cabell Breckinridge reported to Colonel Joseph H. Lewis and rode from the field alive, his escape seemed miraculous."[10]

> The battle is over; but where is thy chief,
>   The Bayard of battle, dauntless and brave?
> There, cold and uncoffined, lies chivalrous Helm,
>   Where glory's mailed hand hath found him a grave.

Immediately upon notification of Helm's fall, Lewis placed Cofer in command of the 6th Kentucky, then started moving toward the left of the brigade to find Helm's staff. When Pirtle gave him Helm's horse, he rode with such haste that he accidentally came within a few yards of the enemy positions. Discovering the error, he spurred the animal and dashed away amid a flurry of shots that should have cut him down, but did not. A few nights before, he and his men were speaking of presentiments of death before battle, and Lewis surprised them by saying, "Well, though I am a wicked man, when I go into action my whole dependence is upon God. I trust myself to Him, with the feeling that if I do my duty faithfully by my country and my men He will take care of me." Thus far, at least, Lewis must certainly have been doing his duty.[11]

When Lewis reached the left he immediately reunited the two halves of the divided brigade. This meant withdrawing the right somewhat, as well as pulling the left out of fire and moving it to the right. Then he formed the whole command in line of battle near the Chattanooga road. He ordered the Orphans to lie down for a time. Cleburne, at last, was coming into the battle, and now the Kentucky brigade could rest and act as a reserve. Johnny Green took several canteens from his company and walked back to a spring, only to discover several enemy field pieces trained on that very spot. "It was anything but a comfortable experience to fill those canteens," he decided, and he returned with considerable relief to his regiment.

Cleburne, too, proved unable to dislodge the Federals, and withdrew, leaving the Orphans once more to take the enemy fire. Finally General Hill ordered them retired several hundred yards, their morning's fight done.[11]

> Where Hewitt and Daniel? Where trumpet-voiced Graves?
> And where the brave men they gallantly led?
> There, voiceless forever and dreamless they lie
> On the field they have won, immortal, though dead.

The work of the Orphans and Breckinridge's other brigades was not in vain that morning. Even though they did not break Thomas' line or capture his position, yet they applied such force in their attacks that he called repeatedly for reinforcements. As Rosecrans sent them from the right and center of the Union line, communications became confused, leading to a momentary gap in the federal center. Just as the gap opened, Bragg happened to have sent a major assault toward that very spot. The effect was electric. Confederates poured through the hole, causing the right of the enemy Army to disintegrate, and sending most of the federal commanders running back to Chattanooga for safety. Already, before 1 P.M., the Battle of Chickamauga was a great victory, the most complete defeat ever suffered by a Union army. Major contributions to that defeat were the terrible, though costly, attacks made by the 1st Kentucky Brigade against more than twice their numbers.

During the lull for the Kentuckians, Breckinridge rode over the field, steadying the men and looking to his losses. Soon he came to the dying form of his young chief of artillery, Rice E. Graves. Breckinridge dismounted and bent over his beloved young friend, whispering a few hurried words of encouragement, and then ordered litter bearers to take him to the hospital. Graves's last words to him expressed the belief that if only he could be nursed by Mary Breckinridge again, he knew he would recover. Once in the hospital, Graves was placed next to a man so painfully wounded that he raved incessantly. Nurses tried to move the man away from Graves to give the major more rest, but he rebuked them for proposing to cause any more pain to the poor man by moving him.

The hospital, in fact, was nothing more than a half acre of ground, with injured Orphans scattered all about. There the doctors struggled well into the night to repair the bloody damage of the guns and cannon. Yet for many, Rice E. Graves included, they could do nothing but try to make the men comfortable as they died.[12]

Through the afternoon other Confederates did the fighting for a change, as first one then another division hurled itself against Thomas' line, only to be repulsed. Thomas was standing like granite to give the rest of his defeated and demoralized Army time to escape to Chattanooga. Finally, about 4 P.M., Breckinridge asked Hill to be allowed to take his own division forward one more time, shattered though it was from the morning's fight. Hill assented, and the Kentuckian immediately began readying his line. He rode among the Orphans, Charlie Ivey at his side. "Now Charlie," he said, "we have got them in a bad fix and must finish them this time." He sent Major Charles Semple of his staff forward to reconnoiter the enemy position, but Semple fell from his horse almost immediately. A bullet struck a Testament in his pocket, deflected from it, and knocked the hilt from Semple's sword. He had taken the book from the body of a Kentucky officer killed the day before. It did little to save that man's life, but now atoned for the omission by saving Semple. However much they sinned behind the lines, every Orphan seemed to have a Bible in his pocket in battle.[18]

This was the final charge. They knew it. The generals all rode along the Orphans' line urging them to do their best. General Frank Cheatham said, "Now boys soon you will up & at 'em & give 'em Hell," and old Polk soon followed, saying, "Boys! You are going at them again. Now when the command forward is given, go at them & give them what Cheatham said." Then Breckinridge brought the brigade to attention, ordered bayonets fixed, told them to hold fire until on top of the enemy, and yelled the charge.

"The very air soon became full of shot & shell," said Johnny Green. But the Orphans were irresistible. With Cleburne in line on their left, they carried straight over the enemy works and pressed Thomas toward the Chattanooga road. As darkness was fast descending, Lewis decided to halt the brigade at the road. They captured 2 more field pieces and a number of prisoners, 250 taken by the 2d Kentucky alone. Losses in this last charge were nothing compared to the dead and dying from the morning's assaults. The ground they covered prevented Cobb from coming up behind them in support, but his guns did good work over on the right flank. Only the advancing darkness prevented Hill from pursuing the fleeing Thomas and doing more damage.

> On, on, like a wave that engulfs, do they press
> O'er rider and horse, o'er dying and dead;
> Nor stop they till night—blessed night for the foe—
> Her mantle of peace o'er the fallen hath spread.[14]

The awful battle was done. At last, the Orphans could boast of fighting in a victory. After being forced from the field at Shiloh, Baton Rouge, Murfreesboro, and Jackson, it was a heady feeling not to be covering a retreat for a change. They did not want to stop. "We were so inspirited & elated over our victory that we wanted to press right on," wrote Green. Soon it seemed there would be glory for all. Back in 1862 the Confederate Congress authorized the presentation of medals of honor for soldiers displaying conspicuous valor in battle. Many of the Orphans would find themselves on the honor rolls for their performance at Chickamauga. Already thirty-three of them won the distinction at Stones River. Now more added their names to the list. And when Company I of the 4th Kentucky selected the man who had been most conspicuous in the battle for daring and skill, Marshall suggested that John Blanchard, the coward of Shiloh, deserved it more than any other. The vote was unanimous.[15]

There were all too many now beyond medals and distinctions, alas. The Orphan Brigade bled at Chickamauga as it never bled before. Some back in Kentucky even suspected that the high losses in the brigade only reflected Bragg's hatred of the Orphans. "Bragg's animosity to Breckinridge is well known," wrote a lady in Lexington. "He puts the Ky troops always in the most exposed positions, and seems to wish nothing better than that every Kentuckian in his army should be killed." Certainly Bragg would not have wept overmuch should Breckinridge be among the slain, but in this battle the terrible losses suffered can be laid only to the Orphans themselves. In spite of immense odds against them, they did not stop assaulting Thomas. Their contribution to the victory was enormous; the price paid was ghastly.[16]

After detailing guards, nurses, and such, the brigade actually took into battle 1,404, excluding Cobb. Of that number 1,007 were Kentuckians. The 2d Kentucky went into the battle with just 282 effectives, and lost 146, more than half the regiment. The 9th started the fight with 230 and finished with 102 killed, wounded, or missing. Testimony of the fury of the fight they waged against Thomas' breast-works is the fact that the losses in these two regiments totaled 53 per cent of the entire brigade loss, though they accounted for only one third of the brigade strength. The two regiments with Lewis on the right suffered far less, only 58 killed and wounded in Nuckols' regiment, including himself, and the losses in Lewis' own regiment were inconsequential. Yet in all, one third of the Orphans who went into battle that morning did not survive it unscathed.

The scene in the field hospital that night was bedlam, yet some, like Caldwell, managed to sleep. Around midnight he dreamed a feverish nightmare in his pain when he felt "the tender touch of a sympathetic hand" upon his forehead. It was Buckner, who had come from his own command to look after the wounded among his children of Camp Boone. Some of the most severely wounded were carried to a house near Reed's Bridge. Captain Weller took a bullet in the morning's fight, and his litter bearers set him down in the same room occupied by Helm and Graves and one other soldier of the 9th. The yard outside filled with groaning soldiers, and even the hallway of the house congested with them. Mrs. Reed passed back and forth ministering to the wounded as best she could, and frequently officers and men came to visit their friends. Breckinridge himself came late in the evening. For Helm, unconscious, he could do nothing. After he was carried from the field, Helm asked his doctor, "Is there hope?" The reply came. "My dear General, there is no hope!" For the rest of the day and into the evening Helm lay and suffered. As the sounds of battle died away, he found the strength to ask its outcome, and learned for the first time of the triumph. The last word heard to escape his lips was a whispered "victory!" Then he lay silent until midnight, when he, like Hanson and Trabue before him, left his Orphans fatherless once more. Two weeks later the officers of the brigade met to form resolutions expressing their sorrow at Helm's death, and affirming their sympathy to his widow. Breckinridge wrote to Emily Helm in October and told her, "My solicitude for the welfare of the Kentuckians is in proportion to the pride and affection I entertain for them; and no one need be told that I hold them not inferior (to say the least), in general good conduct, discipline, and valor to any troops in the service of the South. Your husband commanded them like a thorough soldier. He loved them, they loved him, and he died at their head, a patriot and hero." And far from Chickamauga, in the capital of the United

States, another Kentuckian grieved at the news of Helm's death. His brother-in-law, Abraham Lincoln, sorrowed deeply. "I feel as David of old did," he lamented, "when he was told of the death of Absalom."

After a brief look upon the still face of Helm, Breckinridge turned to his young friend Graves. "Major Graves was mortally wounded, and suffering the most intense agony," said Weller, lying nearby. Breckinridge spoke to him in tones "as tender as if he were talking to his own son." Weller received a sedative, and when he awoke the next morning, Graves, too, was dead.[17]

"The Lord has given us a great victory in this fight," wrote Private Randolph, "and we cannot be to thankful to him for it." Yet as they gave thanks, the Orphans also gave their dead to the soil. They buried them in twos and threes in shallow graves marked only by crude wooden headboards with names or even initials scratched in pencil. All that passersby would see in years to come as a remembrance of the valor and pain of these Orphan dead were a few low mounds of earth, and above them the hasty inscriptions. Some poor boys could not even be identified. Atop one mound sat an oak board with the simple words,

3 or 4
Kentuckyans
C.S.A.
are burred hear

That night in the exultation of victory, the Orphan Brigade camped along the Chickamauga. Indians said the stream's name meant "River of Death." Certainly it did for these Kentuckians far from home.

Flow on Chickamauga, in silence flow on,
    Among the dun shadows that fall on thy breast;
These comrades in battle, aweary of strife,
    Have halted them here by thy waters to rest.[18]

TEN

"We Will Go with You Anywhere"

"WE HAD GAINED a complete & glorious victory," boasted Johnny Green. They expected the morning after the battle that Bragg would send them after Rosecrans to finish the job so nobly begun. But in fact Bragg proved just as dilatory in pursuit as Rosecrans had been in his advance to the battle. Bragg spent the day in collecting wounded, and not until late in the afternoon of September 21 did he send the main body of his Army after the Federals. On September 23 the Orphans, with the rest of Breckinridge's division, reached the crest of Missionary Ridge and saw, spread like a map before them, the city of Chattanooga, and the Federals vigorously erecting their defenses.

Still the Kentuckians expected that they would be ordered forward to attack the enemy before he completed his earthworks. "We thought an assault was going to be made," Jackman scribbled in his diary, "and seeing the forts bristling with cannon, and the line of works blue with Federals, we had long faces." Yet the order did not come, and that night Jackman and Green gathered a pile of dry grass and lay down together, covered only by their overcoats.[1]

Thus began two months of almost constant inactivity during which, as Jackman put it, "Both armies seem to be taking a 'blowing spell.' " The Orphans remained in and around Missionary Ridge until October 21, when they moved seven or eight miles to the rear, to Tyner's Station. Here they remained for the next month.

There was little to break the monotony of waiting for something to happen at Chattanooga. President Davis visited the Army once more, and he and Bragg rode along the lines being cheered by every command until they reached the Kentuckians. "Our boys stood very respectfully," said Jackman, "but not a man opened his mouth." Their animosity for Bragg had not cooled in the aftermath of victory. Occasionally the Confederates shelled the enemy down in the city, and the Kentucky boys liked to take seats and watch the grand incendiary display. The rest of the time they foraged for food, and here they found meager prospects. Most of the men ate only corn "dodgers" and "blue beef," some of them even picking in the stable areas for uneaten or undigested kernels of corn. Accustomed by now to changes in command, they hardly noticed when Lewis formally received command of the brigade on October 4 and announced his staff. Nor was there any comment five days later when Lewis learned of his promotion to brigadier general. Along with his wreath, he received Helm's horse in the settlement of the dead general's estate, only to have it stolen a few weeks later. Helm's widow, Emily, received a trunk *"now empty, valuable from associations,"* and the government paid her $200.67 in back salary for the general. Lincoln himself later gave her a pass that allowed her to return to Kentucky to mourn.[2]

Other changes caught more attention. Old Bob Johnson, after suffering for more than a year with dysentery, offered his resignation on September 30, 1863. Seeing "no prospect of relief" from his malady, he chose to resign "to make way for the promotion of Gallant officers now on duty." As a result, Jim Moss took command of the old 2d Kentucky permanently, winning with it his colonelcy.[3]

But one change that every Orphan met with gladness occurred on November 3, for on that day the 41st Alabama was transferred out of the brigade and into another. In its place Bragg assigned Hiram Hawkins' 5th Kentucky. After nearly two years of separation the "sang diggers" rejoined their comrades of Camp Boone. "Our brigade is now composed entirely of Kentuckians," wrote a well-pleased Johnny Jackman. Hawkins and his Orphans had seen a much different sort of war than their fellow Kentuckians. Following organization in Tennessee, it went to the eastern part of Kentucky and joined in General Humphrey Marshall's operations there and in eastern Tennessee. It was inglorious duty, with only little battles at places like Middle Creek, Kentucky, and Princeton, Virginia. At the latter place the 5th Kentucky did play the major role in the Confederate victory, but larger events in the

East so overshadowed the affair that it was quickly forgotten. Worse so far as Hawkins was concerned was what happened when "Cerro Gordo" Williams won promotion to brigadier. Instead of moving up a grade to lieutenant colonel, Hiram Hawkins, as next in line, saw some obscure captain named Caldwell given the rank instead. That hurt. "I was among the first to raise the standard of rebellion in eastern Ky," Hawkins complained to the War Department, and he had never taken a leave. Yet now the position he should rightfully assume went to a man not even a member of the 5th Kentucky nor of the brigade to which it belonged. Indeed, no one had ever heard of him. Hawkins hoped there had been a mistake made. "But for these convictions I should have retired in disgust at the gross and unheard of injustice." He advised Richmond to take care of the situation, or it would have to do without the services of Hiram Hawkins. "I cannot and will not remain in the service under conditions so dishonorable to myself." It was, he said, simply too much to be thus "overslaughed." The War Department did err, and corrected the mistake. Lieutenant Colonel Hiram Hawkins stayed with the regiment.

The 5th Kentucky reorganized in November 1862, the twelve months' men mustering out or re-enlisting for three years or the war. Now, when they elected their officers, Hawkins was made colonel, ambition rewarded once more. Still there was no glory duty for these Orphans until July 1863, when Richmond transferred them to Knoxville and into a brigade commanded by that father figure who so often appeared momentarily to look after his Orphans, Simon Buckner. With Buckner the 5th Kentucky joined Bragg for the Battle of Chickamauga and its first reunion with the other Kentucky regiments, and now, in a move that seemed only natural, it took its place in the 1st Kentucky Brigade. Hereafter for the remainder of the war, the brigade organization would remain as it now stood at Tyner's Station: the 2d, 4th, 5th, 6th, and 9th Kentucky infantries, and Cobb's battery.[4]

A few other minor internal changes took place, and familiar faces of men once captured or wounded reappeared. One of the most welcome was that of Ed Porter Thompson. Taken prisoner after his wounding at Stones River, he spent several months in prison before being taken to City Point, Virginia, for exchange the following spring. Then, on May 23, 1863, he and thirty-five other prisoners were forced to draw lots to select eighteen who would be shot in retaliation for Confederate execution of a like number of federal prisoners. Thompson selected a fortunate straw, and joined those who went ahead with their exchange. Now, though disabled for field duty, he voluntarily rejoined his old comrades in the 6th Kentucky and took a position as captain in the Quartermaster's Department.

Of course, the Orphans resumed their sinful ways. The day after moving to Tyner's Station Lewis felt the mortification of seeing several of his men walking under guard after arrest for theft and pillaging in the neighborhood. He had to send a survey party into the country to estimate the damage done by the Orphans and find people who could identify the guilty men. To the entire brigade he declared, "The fair name of this brigade won by so much fortitude under privation, hardship and suffering, and so much bravery on the battlefield shall not be sacrificed by vandalism." That did not sit very well with a number of the boys. "He is a brave, kind man," Green wrote of Lewis, "but we feel that no one can fill our Ben Hardin Helm's place." That would change.

Indeed, some of the Orphans even unknowingly stole from themselves. Part of their duty at Tyner's Station was to act as guard over quartermaster and commissary supplies stored there. Since rations formed a large part of the material they were to oversee, the Orphans made no objection to the otherwise ignoble guard duty. What did aggravate them, however, was seeing a large number of packages arrive for some Alabama troops who shared the guard duty with them. As a result, quite a few boxes that came under the eye of a Kentuckian before it reached its intended recipient, never went any farther. One evening a man of the 41st Alabama—this prior to its removal from the brigade—approached some friends in the 4th Kentucky and told them he had found an unclaimed box and removed its address label in the dark. If they would help him carry it away, they could share in the contents. Off they went and carried the treasure chest into the woods for the division of booty. It proved rich—hams, pickles, preserves, peanuts, socks, shoes, underwear, and a complete suit of "butternut" gray. Eagerly the men grabbed their spoils, then melted into the night.

After breakfast the next morning the Alabama "Yellowhammer" looked rather down at the jowls and called together his partners in the night's foray. It seems there were letters in the box and, since it came from Alabama, he took them as part of his share, hoping for news from his home state. Not until light that morning could he read them.

Imagine his surprise to discover them addressed to him. He had led an expedition to steal his own box of goodies, and now begged the Orphans to return their gains. They politely declined, leaving one sad Yellowhammer to ponder the tricks of fortune. The story went the rounds of the brigade that that very next night the Alabamian led another raid on the station to recoup his loss, and found an even bigger box but, upon getting it to safety and opening it, found that it contained the body of a soldier being sent home for burial. The whole episode so appealed to the Orphans that in later years several versions of the midnight theft appeared, with men of the 2d and 9th Kentucky claiming it was *their* box that was looted, not the Alabamian's.[5]

The rest of their time the Orphans spent drilling for an hour twice daily, serving their details, and occasionally picketing the front to feel the enemy. A bright spot was the discovery that now at last they could write home with some assurance that letters would be received, thanks to the establishment of a more efficient North–South delivery by flag of truce. Winstead was elated. "You must not be astonished at the frequent receipt of letters from me since I have learned the source of communication," he wrote Mollie. The two Johnnies, Jackman and Green, tore down an old outhouse and began building for themselves a "house" from the boards, complete with fireplace. The work occupied several days, and when done Jackman lay contentedly by his fireside reading a volume of Robert Burns. Thomas Owens of the 4th Kentucky, Company I, had surely the most unusual experience of all, though. Sent to parlay with the Federals on some minor business, he found his own brother in the enemy Army. Sergeant Owens' brother also happened to be a sergeant. His regiment was the 4th Kentucky, Company I, United States Army![6]

The lull did not last any longer than it took the Union high command to replace Rosecrans with that old nemesis of the Orphans, U. S. Grant. He broke the blockade on supply, and by late November had the federal Army ready to begin its breakout from Chattanooga. As a result, on the evening of November 23 orders came directing the 6th Kentucky to stay at Tyner's Station, while the rest of the brigade proceeded to Missionary Ridge. They got there well after dark and went into position just to the right of Breckinridge's headquarters. D. H. Hill had been relieved of his command, and now Breckinridge led his corps, such as it was. His men occupied the left half of the Confederate line on Missionary Ridge, yet were so thinly spread that a space of five or six feet separated one man from another. Their hope and confidence lay in the ruggedly steep slope up which the Federals would have to attack.

Jackman and Green saw thousands of campfires when they crested the ridge. "A belt of fires encircled Chattanooga," said Jackman. He and Green, with no blankets, huddled on another grass bed under their overcoats and tried to sleep as a light rain turned into snow. It did not work, so they sat nodding around a fire instead. With the dawn the Orphans began fortifying their position, though their main interest came in looking to their left, to where the Federals successfully assaulted Bragg's left flank on Lookout Mountain. "The flash of the guns made a beautiful sight," said Green, "but it saddened us to see the yankees had gotten so high up the mountain side." The Orphans themselves were not engaged, but early the next morning, at 2 A.M., Bragg sent orders for them to rise and move to the far right of his line where he expected the major attack in the morning. Leaving Cobb's guns behind, they marched along the top of the ridge. "A deep silence prevailed," said Jackman, "the only noise being the tramp of the soldiers as the column moved steadily on." The moon went into total eclipse.

Dawn found them placed in reserve for Cleburne's division near Tunnel Hill. It was a clear, frosty morning, bright in the late-autumn sun. The Orphans heard hundreds of axes ringing in the crisp air as Cleburne's veterans felled trees for defenses. The Kentuckians themselves had little to do, however, except bring one panicked green regiment of Georgians back to the main line after the sound of guns frightened them. Then Cleburne brought the 9th Kentucky into his front to fill a gap. At 10 A.M. the Federals commanded by William T. Sherman attacked Cleburne. The Orphans would see more of Sherman in the days ahead, but for now they gave him a volley or two and in twenty minutes' fighting repulsed the attack. The 9th Kentucky suffered but three casualties. And that was the only fighting done by men of the Kentucky brigade in the entire day.

Elsewhere disaster befell Bragg. When the federal Army moved out of its lines and assaulted Missionary Ridge, a panic previously unknown seized the Confederates all along the line. With only brief resistance, they turned and ran in the face of this magnificent Army in blue. Breckinridge was nearly killed trying to hold his corps on the ridge, and lost his son Cabell and Major Wilson as prisoners. In the center were Cobb's guns, two of them bestowed with the pet names

"Lady Buckner" and "Lady Breckinridge." Cobb, now replacing Graves on Breckinridge's staff, put Lieutenant Frank Gracey in command of the Orphan battery. When the enemy came up the slope, Gracey battled manfully to defend his guns until nearly surrounded, then sullenly retired long after the infantry supposedly supporting him melted to the rear. The Orphans never entirely forgave those who did not die defending the Kentucky guns. "Where's our battery?" they said whenever sighting the infantry that abandoned Gracey. "What did you do with our battery?"[7]

The Orphans on the right of the line did not know what took place on Missionary Ridge. Indeed, Johnny Green said, "At our part of the line we thought the battle had all gone our way." At about 7 P.M., however, orders came for them to fall back quietly. As they did, the Kentuckians met with a straggling Confederate who told them of Bragg's disaster. Breckinridge and General William B. Bate, now commanding the Kentuckian's old division, managed to rally enough of their commands to provide a rear guard and enable the rest of the Army to withdraw. Bate, too, retired, and Cleburne took his place, the Orphan Brigade still with him. That night, as on so many nights before, the 1st Kentucky was the rearmost command of a retreating Confederate Army. They bivouacked late in the evening near Chickamauga Station with the whole demoralized Army there for them to see. Around a campfire the men of the 6th Kentucky discussed Bragg and his campaigns. One, apparently in an ill-advised attempt to bolster the general's character, averred that Bragg was at least a member of the Church. "What the devil's the use of that?" shouted Sergeant Jim Lee. "If Bragg were now safe in heaven, he'd fall back in less than three days for a better position!"

The next morning the Army had all disappeared toward Dalton, leaving the Orphans to cover the withdrawal. Breckinridge rejoined them now, and remained with them until they, too, reached Dalton, Georgia. The Federals made a show of pursuing, but not much more, only occasionally testing the Kentucky skirmishers. They nearly captured Johnny Jackman, though, when he proved too slow in retiring from a position. He escaped only "by strategy, and fast running." When he looked back over his shoulder he saw the place he had been blue with the enemy. Running hard behind him came a portly messmate, Tom Berry, burdened with a big sack of hardtack. The Federals yelled after him, "Run, you damned fat Rebel, run!" Berry shouted back to them, "I'll do it," and made his escape while the laughing enemy held their fire.

As darkness fell, the Orphans marched in silence, for they feared the enemy might be close to, and in front of them. Company H of the 9th moved as flankers on the right of the brigade during the night, and after a time came to a junction of two roads. Almost at once they found themselves in the midst of a large body of soldiers, "but in the darkness could not be positive whether friend or foe." Since no one challenged them, Lieutenant Henry Buchanan kept his company moving, and marched straight through, leaving the mystery soldiers behind. Only then did he tell the men they had just passed a regiment or so of the enemy.

They reached Ringgold late that night and, pressed by the enemy, marched on to Dalton on November 28. The 9th Kentucky nearly lost Caldwell that last day. The Orphans laid a trap for the enemy skirmishers at one point, but the firing frightened the colonel's horse. With his wounded arm he could barely manage as it was, but when the horse bolted he had his pistol in his good hand and the reins in the other. The horse raced toward the Federals in the midst of a fire directed at Caldwell. Only within a few yards of some Union skirmishers did Caldwell regain control of his mount. Then he coolly emptied his pistol into a bush concealing some of the enemy, and returned to his regiment.[8]

And so the Orphans began another war winter, their third. It would be perhaps the worst for discomfort, for much of their baggage was lost or destroyed in the rout from Missionary Ridge. Indeed, even axes for chopping firewood were in such short supply that Bate rationed them. Yet the usual spirit of the Orphans did not lag. As soon as they reached their winter quarters, Jackman and Green began building another "house." They used their tent fly—the rest of the tent long gone —and arranged it with a weatherboard wall at the back and sides, and the canvas fly for a roof. "Jack is pretty good at such work," wrote Green, "if he was not so lazy. At home he was first a carpenter, then a school teacher & now a rather lazy soldier, but a christian gentleman. I have to keep at him though to get him to do any of the dirty & hard work." Well, that is how Johnny Green told the story to his diary. "Jack" Jackman gave an entirely different version to his. He told it how he helped chop trees for logs when they enlarged their house, and how he rolled up his sleeves and daubed the outside with mud to windproof it. When done, he thought it "quite a comfortable *mansion* for two to inhabit." And it served them well that winter. On New Year's Day he and Green luxuriated in their homey comfort. With a bitter wind raging outside, whistling through the branches of the oak that overhung their house, they sat inside with "a fire kindled on the earthen hearth, its convivial glow lending a perfect air of coziness to the little tenement."[9]

Most of Dalton's residents departed when the Army came. Consequently the soldiers were left to their own ingenuity to fill the long hours and days of the winter ahead. Those who could wrote letters home now that a more efficient means of getting them to Kentucky was available. They sent words of comfort. "I have been in seven engagements, but the hand of God has protected me in them all." They expressed their homesickness. "I sigh for the comforts of bygone days and regret the day I left you." They told of their camp life, trying where possible to minimize the hardships they suffered. "I have just finished a snug cabin, 10 by 12 feet square. I am well fixed for winter. I wish you could step in and see me getting dinner. I am almost an excellent cook." They affirmed their hope that "our National difficulties will soon be settled and we will all be permitted to return to our homes," but declared they would never come home until victorious or beaten. Taking the oath of allegiance to return home was unthinkable. "I can never take an oath to support a Government that I have fought eight Battles against." And into their letters crept a lurking fear for the safety of their loved ones at home. Kentucky, under the mailed hand of federal occupation, suffered some of the most cruelly inept commanders in the Union Army. Of course, any occupation would be unthinkable, and therefore abominable, to a Kentuckian, but stories of outrages against persons and property by the Union element in the state filtered into the camps at Dalton, and more than one Orphan felt first worry, and then vengeance. "If what I have heard proves to be true when I come to Ky. he may expect trouble with me . . . I will soon settle with him . . . I have sworn by the immaculate God that gave me birth that I will avenge every wrong you have sustained in my absence, it matters not to me on whom my vengeance falls." More than one soldier promised his wife or mother or father that those who wronged them "will not live long . . . after my return to Ky." Never was the separation from home more painful for the Orphans, and now with Tennessee entirely lost to the enemy, their longing grew ever greater.

Writing became a major pastime. When Jackman filled his last journal and could not obtain another, he made himself a notebook from old quartermaster supply blanks and continued his diary. Lieutenant Jim Hancock of the 4th Kentucky amused himself by drawing crude portraits of his sweetheart Mollie in the brigade's quartermaster account book. Those who could not write clustered into the quarters of Lieutenant Colonel William L. Clarke of the 6th Kentucky. There his wife entertained the men with stories of home, while the wife of the brigade quartermaster, Captain William Phillips, wrote letters dictated by the boys who could not write themselves. Far into the night she listened to their expressions of love and hope, and set them on paper for the folks at home.

When not writing, many of the Orphans read whatever they could find. Jackman read voraciously. "John is a good forager after reading matter," Johnny Green had to admit. They read Hugo's *Les Miserables,* Dumas' *Three Musketeers,* the *Bride of Lammermoor,* and much else. Since regimental headquarters occupied the Jackman-Green house frequently, the boys shared their books with John C. Wickliffe, now a colonel and commanding the 9th Kentucky while Caldwell recuperated. With their reading supply exhausted, Wickliffe began sending his orderly on forays into the countryside looking for books. Occasionally there came a good find. An encyclopedia of geography delighted Jackman, when he discovered it to be the same edition he spent happy hours poring over as a boy. A French reader and grammar, too, gave them hours of stimulating reading, with more than one elegantly mysterious continental expression entering their vocabulary that winter. But the orderly sent to find the books, alas, could not read himself. Once, declaring that he knew a place in the country with a well-stocked library, he returned bursting with pride over his latest captures. He threw open the door of the house, strode in, and held out a volume saying he thought it "a 'purty' good book." Wickliffe had been silent all evening awaiting the orderly's return, looking forward to the feast of reason he would have. Now, upon gleefully opening the cover of the coveted prize, he read the title: *Patent Office Report, 1859, Mechanics, Vol. I.*

As Wickliffe stammered to recover from the shock, the intrepid orderly brought forth from his pocket yet another volume, though apologizing for the "damned *bad print*." "I don't know whether you can read it or not." The volume happened to be one of Cicero's works, in Latin. There was nothing wrong with the printing, but to the illiterate orderly the *amos, amases,* and *amats* looked mightily like broken type. Wickliffe did not send him on any further reading raids.[10]

Some of the Orphans organized cock fights against the Louisiana troops, often betting a considerable amount of money. Taylor McCoy of the 4th Kentucky ran the largest stable of cocks. Whenever his mates found him eating chicken soup for dinner, they knew another of his fighting birds had lost. The more cultivated Kentuckians continued their glee-club enterprise, expanding it to include both serenades in the country and an occasional musicale in camp. "We were petted by the ladies and flattered by our comrades," wrote a tenor, and their officers frequently helped carry their instruments for them in hope of sharing in the edibles that rewarded a good concert. Colonel Thompson himself lugged John Weller's violin case. "He could neither play nor sing," said Weller, "but he had a wonderful 'ear' for a square meal." The only real problem was finding the most likely homes to serenade, so far as edible reward. The Orphans knew no one around Dalton, and so one night just selected the first man they found to be their guide. He led them to an imposing mansion which, "from its surroundings of taste and elegance gave promise of any number of appreciative fair ones within." The singers chose their most classical and intricate number, feeling it appropriate to the setting, and commenced. Prelude led to baritone solo, as onlookers from the neighborhood gathered on the grounds to listen. Tydings, first tenor, reveled "as the full-voiced chorus burst out upon the tremulous air." Stanza after stanza flowed forth until the climax approached, when a window of the mansion's second floor flew open and a gaunt nightcapped head thrust out. In a shrill, nasal twang, it sang out, "Say, mister; kin you'uns sing 'Root Hog 'n' Die'?" There was no further song that night and, alas, no feasting reward.

Others were more receptive, thankfully. Winstead accompanied the glee club one evening in January. Often they never really saw their hearers, cloistered within their homes in their nightclothes. Now and then a nightcap appeared at a window. Yet the young ladies frequently threw cards of thanks or invitation to the singers. "I wish I could show you some cards thrown out to the 'Ky. Glee Club' by the fair hands of the unseen beauties," Winstead wrote home. Many of the men formed romantic attachments thanks to their service with the glee, Weller among them. "For hospitality, patriotism, virtue, and jollity," he said, "I would exchange the Georgia girls for none." Weller wrote love letters for two others in his company to one girl, then fell for her himself.[11]

The rowdy was never far below the surface, despite elevated pastimes like reading and music. By now the Orphan Brigade enjoyed a reputation throughout the Army at Dalton. Caldwell later said, "They were recognized by their fellow soldiers as the mad wags of the Army of Tennessee, and when off duty spared in their rough but good natured jests neither their own officers nor those of other commands, even up to the generals of the army." Angered that Breckinridge no longer commanded their division, and that his replacement, Bate, was not a Kentuckian, the Orphans for a time expressed their dissatisfaction. Bate complained of this to Lewis, but the Kentuckian only tactlessly replied, "General, I think I wouldn't pay any attention to that if I were you. My boys are always pestering some d———d fool!" When "Devil Dick" was bored one day, he threw his own lieutenant in a wheelbarrow and took him on a hair-raising—and dignity-destroying —ride along the color line. Dick did two weeks in the guardhouse for his prank.

While the camp rang with the strains of "Old Kentucky Home" and the glee club's repertoire, other voices shouted "Keno" and "Four Jacks here!" The gambling could never be stopped no matter how the officers tried. "It was dangerous for a stray pig or a wandering lamb to visit their vicinity," said Caldwell, and cornfields after their "calling" looked like cyclone-struck wasteland. And should the Orphans find a suppressed distillery, they came by night and put it into operation once more. How often the smell of sour mash led the provost to the Kentuckians at a still!

Indeed, here at Dalton the Orphans and their whisky-drinking ways caused more problems than anywhere else in the war. Poor Lewis, always a bit "straight" though the boys loved him for it, actually issued general orders in attempting to stem the tide of John Barleycorn. He called on all the regimental commanders to stop the evil of drunkenness "lest the cantonment of this Brigade shall ere long, assume the character of a Pot House." He should have known it was useless to try. Cofer had won promotion to provost marshal general of the Army, leaving William Clarke in command of the 6th Kentucky, and thus it was one of their own that the Orphans had to deceive in getting whisky into their camps. Cofer tried manfully to enforce the edict against liquor in the bivouacs, but without success. When he posted guards to search all entering camp and confiscate whisky, some of the boys dressed as guards themselves, confiscated the "article," and then smuggled it into camp in hollowed pumpkins. Johnny Green found one such ingenious Orphan whose "entire mess were mellow for several days after that."

Worse yet, since all whisky was reserved for medical uses under Cofer's care, some of the Orphans actually arranged for shipment of the beverage to them, yet marked to Cofer's attention. Gladly he guarded their boxes until called for, entirely unaware of his integral role in the "jug trade." And when not outwitting Cofer in the matter of drink, the Orphans did their best to rob his storehouses of food. Two men of the 4th Kentucky obtained a pass to go into Dalton and take in the sights "and any thing else which was not too hot or too heavy to be carried off by them." They wandered to the railroad depot hoping to do as they had at Tyner's Station, a little business in the "box-from-home line." There they found nothing purloinable, however, but did see a sleeping guard beside some recently arrived Army beef. They determined to step up boldly and relieve him, saying that they were his replacements. While one Orphan hid, the other performed the ruse successfully, dutifully listening as the relieved sentinel gave him his instructions. Once the dupe was out of sight, Alex Leatherwood ran from hiding and seized the largest quarter of beef he could carry and raced away. His friend waited a moment, then ran after him, leveling his gun, and pretended to arrest him. Thus they marched off, presumably to Cofer's office, in full sight of scores of soldiers. In fact, the prized beef made a two-day feast for Company I.[12]

Not because of the Orphans' errant ways, but rather in spite of them, the brigade experienced a phenomenon that swept the Army of Tennessee here in Dalton, a religious revival. The spiritual movement itself remains not entirely explicable, but that it seized the Kentuckians in large numbers there is no doubt. A bevy of eminent divines inhabited the Army's camps during the winter. Jackman heard a different one every week, it seemed. There were three Protestant churches in Dalton and one Catholic. "Of Sundays these churches are generally full to overflowing with soldiers," he wrote. Their motives were not entirely spiritual. "Many soldiers go to church just to get sight of a lady," he said, and even though Jackman himself attended several times a week, he admitted to himself that in part it was because there was no place else to go. Yet the movement was genuine. Hundreds took baptism in nearby Mill Creek. Men who ran poker games turned to prayer meetings. Wickliffe told his regiment that he wanted to take credit for having the most men of any regiment attending church, and the Orphans of the 9th Kentucky went in large numbers. What they heard varied considerably. Some preachers mixed a good deal of politics with gospel. On February 7, 1864, several Orphans met to form a "Christian and Fraternal Association" for the brigade without distinction of creed. It lasted the remainder of the war, Hiram Hawkins its president. When elected, he said, "I esteem this indorsement of my moral character and Christian deportment, quite as much, if not more honor than my military rank and title." Jackman, however, remained ever the skeptic. When one parson asserted from the pulpit that "wisdom is better than weapons of war," Jackman looked around him at the Army in Dalton and decided that "From the way things look about here, there is but little *wisdom* in this locality."[13]

Christmas that year came cold and windy, a drizzling rain dampening spirits in Dalton. Some officers of the 9th Kentucky celebrated after a fashion the night before with "pine top" whisky, a noxious liquor distilled from the tips of pine boughs. So tipsy did they become that they forgot themselves and sang a vigorous rendition of "The Star-Spangled Banner" before being silenced. The next morning, "a cold, cloudy, disagreeable day," many of the Orphans went to church both at noon and in the evening. They wrote letters home, and ate their meager holiday dinner, for Jackman bean soup and bread. "The boys are not seeing a great deal of fun," he lamented. Several were drunk. But not the phantom scribe of Company C, 4th Kentucky. Once more he took out the company's clothing account book and with pen in hand, wrote again below his entries for the two Christmases past. "Dec. 25th 1863. Yes, old Brick, and *another* Christmas has come and gone, and we are still combatting with the Vandal horde; Are likely to be doing that same this time next Christmas. What a pity."[14]

Equally pitiful was the supply situation in the brigade, as well as in the Army at large. So many Orphans were barefooted that overnight guard duty was discontinued to spare their feet from the freezing cold. Constant requisitions for shoes and uniforms, mess pans, axes, drums, and even for ink and paper flowed from the brigade quartermasters. Only a few were filled. Indeed, even the brigade's record book for quartermaster stores came, in fact, from the office of the East Tennessee & Georgia Railroad depot in Dalton, where it had been a ticket book. Brigade livestock numbered just sixty-five horses and ninety-four mules, very small for the needs of over a thousand men. The whole 6th Kentucky baggage train consisted of three wagons and one ambulance.[15]

Friends of the Kentuckians, both at home and in exile in the South, did what they could to alleviate the shortage. Eli M. Bruce donated one thousand dollars to the Kentucky Relief Society for the Orphan Brigade, and donations from other prominent men of the state enhanced the fund. The Kentucky Relief Society bought shoes for the soldiers this winter, along with blankets and socks. In January and February alone it provided enough shoes for more than a regiment. The Orphans themselves added to the fund. The glee club provided occasional vocal and instrumental concerts to benefit the Society.

The Reverend Pickett founded the Kentucky Relief Society and served as its president through the war. His efforts went beyond creature comforts, however. He and other prominent men of the Bluegrass with the Army tried to consolidate all natives of Kentucky, whatever their present units, into the 1st Kentucky Brigade. Further, to make sure that the Orphans' interests received proper attention in Richmond, he addressed the brigade on January 18, 1864, and proposed that they elect their own representative to Congress. There was some division in the ranks on this issue. "As Kentucky has never seceded," said Jackman, "electing Congressmen to represent the state in the Confederate Congress is all a humbug." Nevertheless, two days later the Kentuckians formed in an old field near camp. Lewis did not require attendance, yet most of the Orphans were there to hear aspirants for their votes speak. "The old politicians," said Jackman, "have not forgotten how to 'work the wires.'" The speakers gave a regular old-time stump debate. An Army surgeon named Johnson spoke as a candidate, as did the Orphans' old brigade quartermaster, Major George W. Triplett. A current member of Congress, Judge James W. Moore, made a campaign address, and even Cofer and a couple of men from the 4th and 9th Kentuckys spoke in their own behalf. Phil Lee of the 2d Kentucky gave one of his humorous presentations, and "The 'State' of Kentucky being present en masse, the speakers 'spread' themselves and 'the state' cheered." Someone tried to nominate the Reverend Pickett as well, but he declined. When the balloting was done, the Orphans returned Moore to his seat, and sent Major Triplett with him, probably the only military unit in either Army to have its own representatives in Congress.[16]

In fact, Cofer and others feared that many of the Orphans would not vote in the election, not that they did not like the candidates, but rather because "they are determined to do nothing that can be in any way construed into a recognition of their liability to be again conscripted by the Confederate Congress." The men were tired of the infantry service. For some time talk of serving as mounted troops instead gained popularity in the brigade, and Cofer thought they would not vote unless mounted. "It is deeply to be regretted yet it is nevertheless true in my opinion that not 200 of the Brigade will ever consent in any contingency to become infantry soldiers after the expiration of their present enlistment." Of course, the whole Army was tired, and a bit disillusioned, Cofer found, yet "our Ky boys, while they have more life & hope & are more like the Confederate soldier of two years ago than any in the army, are far below what they have been in their morale and discipline." The Orphans complained that even soldiers whose homes were still safely behind the lines would not fight. They could cite Missionary Ridge as evidence of that, complaining that if such men would not battle for their firesides, what point remained in Kentuckians doing it for them? "They intend now to fight for Ky on Ky soil," said Cofer, "and if not mounted my opinion is that they will desert en masse." He believed he could not even prevent his own regiment from disintegrating.

Fortunately, Cofer figured without the deep sense of southern patriotism that underlied all the grumbling in the brigade. True, they wanted to be mounted. Their old comrade Morgan and his cavalry had been able to ride into Kentucky several times on brief raids, and if the Orphans had horses they could do likewise. Yet, cavalry or infantry, they were not deserters. Indeed, this winter in Dalton the brigade suffered less from desertions than in previous times, and in fact the command's strength improved slightly. Cofer calculated without something else, too. He did not fully appreciate the influence and hold on the Orphans of John C. Breckinridge.

After the Army went into winter quarters in Dalton, Breckinridge went to Richmond on leave. There he was reunited with Mary, and there too he joined other men of the state in lobbying for another Kentucky campaign. Should the Army move into the state, twenty thousand would rally to its banners. And the best way to rally those people would be to send the 1st Kentucky Brigade mounted. In December the Kentucky delegation in Richmond presented a petition to Secretary of War James A. Seddon. It stressed the dissatisfaction in the command, and the probability of desertion. Also, since Kentuckians could only get out of their state on horseback, a mounted Kentucky brigade would encourage them to come. Mounted, they could raid into the state for supplies and animals, and they could swell their numbers to six thousand or more. Besides, since Kentuckians learned to ride at an early age, they would serve better as cavalry than as infantry.

Seddon did not favor the plan, but sought the advice of General Joseph E. Johnston, who replaced Bragg in command of the Army of Tennessee. Johnston decidedly opposed the measure. "The question of converting good infantry into bad cavalry" was an old one to him. "We now want infantry very much, and this Kentucky brigade, though small, is an excellent one." Indeed, he said, "I would not give up Lewis' brigade of veteran infantry for the 7,000 or 8,000 mounted men it is proposed to raise by abolishing it." Considering that the Orphans at the time numbered only 1,461, that was something of a compliment. Not satisfied, however, Breckinridge handed the President a petition signed by himself, Buckner, Morgan, and Lewis, proposing that all Kentucky troops in the service be combined and mounted.[17]

Yet there was another reason for Breckinridge being in Richmond. He came to discuss his new assignment, command of the Department of Southwestern Virginia, that area bordering Tennessee on the south, and Kentucky and West Virginia on the west and north. The department already had its own troops, meager though they were, so he would not be taking his command there with him. That meant, for the first time in the war, separation from the Orphan Brigade. It was not a happy prospect, all the more reason why he argued for mounting the brigade since, with Tennessee lost, the natural place for launching raids into Kentucky would be his new department. Should he fail in efforts to get the men mounted, still he wanted to have this brigade, as infantry, assigned to him.

The movement to mount the Orphans met with no support, even when presented to Davis. Yet the Secretary of War did approve the notion of consolidating all Kentucky troops into one command. "The infantry Brigade, tho' much reduced is among the most reliable in service," he wrote, "and for the real work before our army of more value than 3 times the number of mounted men." Putting all Kentuckians together, though, and assigning them to Breckinridge where they would be poised on their state's border, would hold the men together and discourage desertions. "The hope should be held out to them as of returning to Ky most speedily," said the Secretary of War. President Davis sought the views of Johnston. This time the general approved, asking only that he be given a brigade "equivalent in value," and still protesting against mounting the Orphans. "There is a Kentucky brigade of infantry equal to any in our service," he said, and they should be kept that way. In later years the Orphans would claim that Johnston declined sending the brigade to Breckinridge, saying "there is no equivalent for it; it is the best brigade in the Confederate army," but he did not.

Breckinridge returned to Dalton on February 5 to collect his staff and baggage. Here, too, he had final conversations with Johnston, who reaffirmed his willingness to let the Kentuckian take his Orphans with him. On February 11 Johnston sent his formal approval to Richmond, and that same day Breckinridge asked Richmond for orders for the command's movement as soon as possible. He would have to leave right away.

That night the Orphans gathered outside his headquarters at the Anderson house in Dalton. They came, said a correspondent, "to testify their esteem and devotion to their heroic leader." With great enthusiasm they raised a clamor for the general to come out and speak to them. When he appeared he met repeated cheers until silence could be enforced. "I have not words to convey the deep emotion I feel on this occasion, nor expression suitable for this manifestation of your respect," he told them. He would not make a "set speech," he said, "for I presume you have had enough of that from the numerous candidates pending the late election." When the Orphans stopped laughing, he went on to say, "I want to talk to you about some things connected with you and myself."

There was no body of men on earth for whom he felt such love and attachment as these Kentuckians. He recounted the years of peril and hardship they endured together. Now he was being ordered to another theater of the war, and he declared that he had done everything in his power to have them ordered to accompany him. At this the men

cheered, and one Orphan shouted, "We will go with you anywhere—
go to-night—yes, and without rations!" When the general continued,
he expressed hope that he would yet succeed in bringing them to
Virginia, but he did not tell them that Johnston already approved the
plan, pending finding a replacement brigade. Theirs would not be a
comfortable lot in his new department. Someone shouted, "It can't be
worse than we have seen." When he resumed, Breckinridge reminded
them that they would be nearer their homes, and pointed out to them
how tempting it would be to those who had wives and families in the
state to desert and join them. And desertion, or taking the oath of
allegiance, would be the only way short of defeat for them to go home
now. Thus the temptation would be hard, "but not so hard as to be
deprived of their personal liberties and to lose all the honor and fame
won by their heroic bravery by returning and throwing their leprous
bodies into the arms of women who might love, but could not respect
them for such unworthy conduct. The shades of martyred heroes
would rise and pour out maledictions on all such."

Clearly Breckinridge tailored his impromptu address to counter the
dissatisfied element in the brigade that spoke of desertion. When he
concluded, he declared once more his belief that Kentucky was with
them in spirit, and that a just God would eventually grant the Confederacy its independence. While he may really have believed in the former, he still had no private confidence in the latter, but that the men
must not know.

Breckinridge went back inside his headquarters to the accompa-
niment of thunderous cheering from the Orphans, and immediately his
speech took the desired effect. "The boys are anxious to go with him,"
said Jackman, "so as to be nearest home." The way to insure that was
to re-enlist. That same night, months before the expiration of their
terms of service, Company A of the 9th Kentucky sent Lewis a resolution re-enlisting the whole company for the remainder of the war.
They wished to "renew our devotion to our country, and if need be,
complete the sacrifice hereafter, as our comrades, before us, have done,
whose bones lie buried in almost every state of the Confederacy." They
called on the rest of the brigade to do the same, and from brigade
headquarters came the question, "Who stands next on the roll of
honor?" By his speech and his example, Breckinridge quelled once
more the incipient disaffection among his Orphans. It was to be his
last gift to them. Despite all his efforts, the brigade never followed him

to Virginia. The men would come to believe that somehow the hand of Bragg was responsible, their old enemy now being an adviser to the President. More probable, however, was Johnston's inability to replace it with an "equivalent" brigade. Whichever the case, now at last the unthinkable had happened. Breckinridge and Lewis continued trying to have the Orphans ordered to Virginia, but without success. Left fatherless so many times—Hanson, Trabue, Helm, Nuckols, Hunt—the Kentuckians simply never entertained the thought that their most beloved parent of all might be taken from them. They would meet yet once again in this war, but that was a year and more in the future, and now as winter warmed into spring a new campaign loomed for the armies north of Atlanta. The boys would do their part, but they felt now more orphaned than ever before.[18]

ELEVEN

"Hell Has Broke Loose in Georgia"

JOSEPH E. JOHNSTON relieved Braxton Bragg of his command on December 27, 1863, and from that moment on the men of the Army of Tennessee expected a great campaign for the coming spring. Johnston was a fighter, the hero of Manassas, and he would lead them to victory. The men of the 1st Kentucky Brigade shared this confidence in the new general for, after all, they had served with him at Jackson. From the date of Johnston's arrival, the reorganization and retraining of the army commenced, and now for the first time all of the Orphans had an opportunity to assess their new brigade leader, Joseph H. Lewis.

His discipline proved stern, and he dispensed it to men and officers alike under his solid red headquarters flag. More officers sat under arrest in his administration than even in the days of the hard-driving "Bench-leg" Hanson. His own chief quartermaster, Major John R. Viley—Breckinridge's brother-in-law—he placed under arrest. A captain from his own 6th Kentucky repeatedly languished in his quarters for minor infractions, as did the captain of Company D of the same regiment. And one of his own captains he cashiered. Even regimental commanders did not find themselves immune to "Old Joe's" guardhouse. Lieutenant Colonel John C. Wickliffe of the 9th Kentucky must have left his coat unbuttoned again, or showed a spark of his razor wit when it was not wanted. On March 29, 1864, Lewis ordered him confined to his quarters under arrest "for persistent disrespect to his commanding officer." He sent Captain Winstead into Dalton repeatedly to arrest officers and men absent without leave, as well as to search houses suspected of selling whisky. Any Orphans caught brawling or quarreling took quick trips to the guardhouse.

Yet the Orphans respected Lewis, and in time came to love him as they did all their commanders. Indeed, here in Dalton Ed Porter Thompson tried to write a sketch of Lewis for publication in the *Southern Illustrated News*, but the general would not allow him to publish it. "No, no! Don't do that," said Lewis, "I am not entitled to that particular consideration."

"But," said Thompson, "the devotion and heroism of . . ."

"Old Joe" interrupted. "Oh, yes, I know about heroism, and all that, but every man in the Kentucky Brigade is a *hero!*"

Perhaps that is why they came to love him. However frequently the Orphans forgot themselves and their reputation, Lewis never did, and he guarded it jealously.[1]

As weather permitted there followed a hard regimen of drill and training to ready the brigade for the coming campaign. Grant had been sent East, and the federal general they would face now was Sherman. They must be prepared for him. Target practice began. Johnston and Hardee repeatedly reviewed the Army, and even "sham battles" complete with blank loads in their rifles pitted Cleburne's and Bate's divisions against two others in their corps. Surrounded by hundreds of spectators from the countryside, the Orphans formed hollow squares to meet a cavalry attack and broke it up by shooting cloth and paper wads at "the spurred gentlemen." One or two they wounded rather badly.

Even in their fun, the Kentuckians and the rest of the Army played at war games. When the Orphans awoke on March 22, they found almost four inches of snow on the ground, and more falling. During the morning the men of the 4th Kentucky snowballed each other, and then hurled their mushy missiles at the Tennessee brigade in their division. Before long the remaining Kentucky regiments went to the 4th's rescue. Soon the two brigades stood lined up against each other, their field officers mounted and directing their fire as though in real battle. Of course, the officers became the chief targets of the snowballs, and even the mascot dog Frank of the 2d Kentucky joined in the fray, engaging a Tennessee mongrel who left him *hors de combat* with a bite in the foot.

After a while, the Kentuckians and Tennesseeans made peace, and then set forth to attack the Florida brigade in their division. They charged their camp and drove them out, then settled amicably with them, too, and marched off to do battle with A. P. Stewart's division. Sending skirmishers in advance, the main body launched an assault that easily took Stewart's camps. "Not having seen near sport enough," said Jackman, they fell back and allowed Stewart's people to prepare a defense. General Marcellus Stovall appeared in person to command his brigade of Stewart's division, only to find himself taken prisoner along with his colors when the Orphans charged again. Jackman himself captured the flag, and bore the prize back to his camp for lunch. "I got several bruises," he noted. Indeed, some of the men began putting rocks in the centers of their snowballs, but they were soon reprimanded for violating the rules of "civilized warfare."

That afternoon a courier came to the Orphans' camps with news that Stewart's division was renewing the conflict and even then advancing against Bate's brigades. At once the Kentuckians marched to the field, formed line, and sent out skirmishers. Soon they saw the red battle flags of the advancing host against the white background. The quartermaster of the 9th Kentucky made a stirring speech to screw the Orphans' courage for the fight. Then came the first enemy volley, Stewart's men having filled their haversacks with ten rounds of snowballs per man. In the face of such a fire, the Kentuckians fell back. Stewart drove them through the camps of the Tennessee and Florida troops, who then deserted the Orphans. Yet, as they fell back, Lewis' men turned to fire from time to time, and managed to send a party by the flank that captured General Stewart himself. The 2d and 4th Kentucky lost their colors to the enemy, but the Orphans checked their advance when they reached their own camps. Then, at last, peace was made, prisoners exchanged, and much—but certainly not all—of the property captured from abandoned camps was returned. Poor Jackman, hit in the eye, felt terribly sore. Yet, he wrote in his diary that night, "We have seen more fun to-day than at any one time during the war."[2]

By late April Lewis could tell that active operations were imminent. The training and equipping of the men increased, and now he formed a new adjunct to the brigade, a corps of sharpshooters. Sometime before, an English admirer gave Breckinridge a dozen Kerr rifles, a prized muzzle-loader reputedly capable of deadly accuracy at nearly a mile. Breckinridge, in turn, donated the rifles to the brigade, and on April 24 Lewis formed a company comprising the two best marksmen from each regiment, under command of Lieutenant George H. Burton of Company F, 4th Kentucky. "I believe this officer took more pleasure in a fight than any other man I ever saw," wrote one of Burton's sharpshooters. In the campaign to come, when one of the company fell and a new man took his place, Burton personally tested the recruit's grit by conducting him to a heavy artillery fire and standing in it with him. Lewis instructed the company never to approach within four hundred yards of the enemy, but rather to keep their distance and use their superior rifles to bring down federal artillerists and officers. They were to work their way close to the enemy at night, spot his artillery positions, and then silence the batteries after dawn if possible. Probably no more elite band of marksmen served anywhere else in the Confederate Army. So prized did membership in this band become that when one of Burton's men was killed—as many were—there were numbers anxious to take his place.[3]

Finally came May. Johnston reviewed his Army once more before the anticipated commencement of the campaign. Lewis being absent, Caldwell commanded the brigade for the day. He led the Orphans with their polished bayonets and tattered flags past the reviewing stand, and heard a hum of comment among the officers around Johnston. Johnston's face supposedly lit with enthusiasm as he watched the Orphans pass. Turning to General Thomas Hindman, he said, "There goes the finest brigade I ever saw." Hindman, too, noticed their distinctive bearing and in a congratulatory order to the Army, mentioned "the Kentucky Brigade as especially entitled to commendation for soldierly appearance, steadiness of marching, and an almost perfect accuracy in every detail." Johnston would reiterate his sentiments several times in the years ahead. "Yes," he would say, "the Kentucky Brigade was the finest body of soldiers I ever saw."

Certainly the Orphans were exceptional soldiers, all 1,512 of them. And as May 1864 dawned, they faced exceptional times ahead. "We are again on the 'war-path,'" Jackman wrote on May 7. "I think I shall now have something more stirring to put in my Journal than church goings."[4]

The campaign for Atlanta about to begin would last for 117 days. Johnston, outnumbered three to two by his opponent, Sherman, would consistently find his left flank turned by the Federals. Time after time

Johnston would have to fall back, ever closer to the prize he sought to protect, Atlanta. It would be the most grueling overland campaign of the war. It would carve the Confederacy in twain. It would lay waste to Georgia. And it would destroy the Orphan Brigade as an effective body of infantry.

The same day that Jackman wrote both in hope and dread that "something more stirring" seemed in the offing, Sherman advanced against the Confederates. For the next five days Johnston kept the Kentuckians hopping about from one hilltop to another skirmishing and sharpshooting, but the enemy did not yet seem disposed to assault them. Indeed, at night the federal bands played serenades for the men in blue, and when some of the Orphans yelled out for "Dixie," the Union musicians obliged, though always ending with a refrain of "Yankee Doodle." Only on the evening of May 12 did Johnston withdraw the brigade to the vicinity of Resaca, Georgia, sixty miles northwest of Atlanta. Here the general chose his first defensive position of any strength, hoping to stall the federal tide. The Orphans marched all through the night until they reached their position about dawn. After only a brief halt, they fell back farther, and immediately began digging earthworks. There was literally no rest for them all day.

Morning of May 14 found the brigade on its way to the left of the Confederate line, where the men occupied works of logs and fence rails thrown together by some Tennesseeans during the night. That morning, too, expecting a fight, Lewis issued a small ration of whisky to the men, though some apparently received more than others, for Jackman saw Orphans so "top-heavy" they could not walk without help. Yet by 10 A.M. they finished their breastworks, and not before time. At once skirmishing commenced the whole length of the Confederate line, and in front of Lewis' brigade two seemingly endless lines of enemy soldiers emerged from the woods that covered them.

The Kentuckians held an angle in the line which faced the 5th, 6th, and 9th regiments to the west, and the 4th and 2d north. The first three regiments, forming the left part of the angle, received only one major charge, and held their fire until the enemy came within a few yards of their works. Then they gave them a volley that sent the bluecoats back to cover without much fight. On the right of the brigade, however, the 2d and 4th Kentucky regiments saw quite a time. The Federals attacked repeatedly. "Column after column came down in full view, and moved right toward us," wrote an Orphan. Some of the enemy got within seventy-five yards of their line before the 2d and 4th opened on them. "It was harvest time with the Orphan Brigade," said one, "and every available contrivance was used for reaping the field before us." The fighting became so intense that, when John Gordon of Company D, 4th Kentucky, fell dead, his comrades spent the rest of the day stepping over him in the melee. Only with nightfall could someone find time to take him from his place in the line.

While the 4th Kentucky held its own on the extreme right of the brigade, the 2d Regiment sat on its left, and the new corps of sharpshooters operated between the two and somewhat in advance. "Their terrible rifles soon attracted the fury of the Federal artillerymen," wrote an Orphan of the 4th. Before the day was out, half of the elite marksmen lay dead or wounded. Jim Guilliam only abandoned his place with his fellow sharpshooters when a fragment of enemy shell left his right arm dangling from his shoulder only by a thin bit of skin and flesh. He walked unaided to the surgeon and underwent the remainder of the amputation without benefit of anesthetic.

Captain David C. Walker of the 6th Kentucky also saw his right arm shot away. Known to his comrades as the "swearing Kentuckian," he had a good deal to curse this day. Yet others, in the midst of this terrible holocaust, found time to admire pityingly a little kitten caught between the battle lines and crying in its terror. Finally, one of Cobb's gunners jumped the earthworks and ran forward to grasp the cat and return it safely. Thereafter the tortoise tabby was a familiar sight perched on his friend the gunner's shoulder or astride a caisson. In honor of the occasion the Orphans named it "Resaca."

The fight took a heavy draught of Kentucky blood, even among the three regiments on the left of the brigade, for the Federals gave them a shelling during the morning and afternoon. It became so hot that the Kentucky artillery stood much of the fight without its gunners, who hid in the rear, waited for a brief lull, then ran forward to load and fire before the enemy guns caught them in the open. The worst of the shelling took Company A of Caldwell's 9th Kentucky that evening. One shell severed the leg of Lieutenant Tom McLean. Immediately he called for litter bearers, then turned to his company and urged the men to "be steady." Before the litter reached him, another shot almost cut him in two, then exploded and killed two others. Johnny Green stood in awe of McLean's bravery. "In all my experience I dont believe I ever knew an instance of more heroic courage," he said of the lieutenant's final words of encouragement to the men. Gervis Grainger saw his cousin killed at his side, downed by the same missile that then struck him in the knee and put him out of the campaign for a month.

Jackman looked toward the left of his regiment as Company A took the federal shelling. "I saw the men tossed about like chaff." Only nightfall brought respite from the heavy fire, and then it was to renew the digging. After their experience of the day, some of the Orphans acquired a new love for the spade, and used it with a will. They piled several feet of Georgia clay in front of them that night, intending to be ready for the renewal of the fight at dawn. Thankfully, it did not come. While Sherman's infantry attacked farther on the right of Johnston's line, the only real action for the Orphans on May 15 was skirmishing and an almost continual bombardment.[5]

By dawn the next morning Johnston had withdrawn the brigade to Calhoun, seven miles south, and for the next two days the Confederates fell back before the enemy, Bate detaching the 5th Kentucky from the brigade to help in the much-accustomed role of rear guard. By May 19 the Army was around Cassville, over forty miles from Dalton, and here Johnston decided the ground offered his first opportunity to stand and offer serious battle. At noon that day he ordered read to the Army a battle order announcing that this was the time for a fight. The Orphans met the order with loud cheers, Jackman thinking it Napoleonic in composition and spirit. "They seem anxious to fight," he wrote of his fellow Kentuckians.

That evening the Orphans moved to form a reserve for Cleburne's division, puffing and panting in the now oppressive spring heat. Yet they still cheered Johnston when he rode past, and gave old "Pat" Cleburne a huzza as well. That night Jackman closed his diary, saying, "I shall now try for some sleep, as there will be no rest for the weary, to-morrow. All looking for a big fight."

Yet the morrow only brought disappointment. Johnston's generals, so the rumor spread, did not believe they could hold their positions in the planned battle and, faced with their lack of support, Johnston decided to continue his retreat. For the Kentuckians it was a bitter decision. Every day that they withdrew toward Atlanta put them that much farther from home and from any prospect of returning to the Bluegrass.

For the next week the Orphan Brigade moved with the Army as it slowly retreated toward Dallas, with little other than constant skirmishing to occupy them. The brigade's "Christian Association" met to make proper eulogy over their dead, and the list mounted. In the campaign thus far, from May 7 to May 20, seven Orphans were killed and fifty-four wounded. Now, near the bivouac of Lewis' old 6th Kentucky, several of the Orphans, in the manner of Kentuckians of all times, met to honor those of their number now sleeping in Theodore O'Hara's "bivouac of the dead."

The night of May 25, 1864, the Orphan Brigade bivouacked less than two miles from Dallas, at the left of a Confederate line that ran from Dallas through New Hope Church and on to Kennesaw Mountain. Jackman and Johnny Green shared their tent "fly" that night, sheltering from the rain. Out in the wasted fields between the armies, the Kentucky sharpshooters kept their posts, occasionally felling one of the enemy. For most of them it was a workmanlike job, but not for all. Taylor McCoy came back from his time in front in a depressed mood, and uncommunicative. When asked the matter, he just said, "I did not want to kill the fellow." A Federal had been shooting at him and, seeing his chance, McCoy put a bullet into the man. "I struck him, and he screamed. It was the cry of a boy! I don't like to think of having killed a boy!" At other places between the lines this night, the scene was less hostile. Try as they might to prevent fraternization between the armies, the officers of both sides could not stop the private soldiers from meeting occasionally to exchange newspapers and gossip, or maybe trade tobacco for coffee or whisky. The Orphans were no different. When Hervey McDowell went on the picket line to relieve a detail, he found the Kentucky pickets joined with some Yankee soldiers in a game of cards. The Orphans knew they had trouble, and the Federals were even more apprehensive at being thus discovered. But McDowell, ever-chivalrous, simply took out his pocket watch and gave them two minutes to scamper back to their own lines before he would open fire.[6]

With the morning of May 26, the Orphans fortified positions along a ridge south of Dallas. By sundown the skirmishing in their front became heavy, and a federal battery unlimbered in their front to shell them. Lewis ordered Caldwell and the 9th Kentucky to take the guns, though the boys were not entirely enthusiastic. "We did not think we stood in any great need of the battery," wrote Jackman, yet the regiment deployed for the attack, only to have Lewis cancel it at the last minute. Still the brigade took casualties. Lieutenant Horace Watts of the 4th Kentucky was calmly lighting his pipe at a fire in rear of the earthworks when a sharpshooter's bullet killed him. A corporal in the same regiment never knew what hit him, a bullet finding him in his sleep some distance behind the lines. Jim Cunningham of Company D, 4th Kentucky, felt a bullet almost completely sever the middle finger of his right hand. Despite the pain, he conceived the novel idea of having the surgeon reset the finger backward, with the nail facing the palm instead of away from it. Apparently the digit "took" and healed in that position. He called it his "finger of scorn" and, as comrades noted, "took a savage delight in exhibiting it."

The next day saw the main fight take place in and around New Hope Church. For the Orphans at Dallas there was relative quiet except for an order from Bate to take a hill in front of their position from the enemy. The Kentuckians expected a tough fight but, instead, the Federals withdrew with little resistance. The brigade captured a few prisoners. Of far more immediate interest was a freshly butched bullock carcass that the fleeing bluecoats abandoned. That night the 9th Kentucky dined on fresh beef for the first time in weeks. Generally now their meat rations came to them green with mold, edible only when boiled and mixed with cornmeal.

May 28 brought tragedy, though it started on a bright enough note. New clothing was issued to many of the Kentuckians, and through the morning and early afternoon they had little to do except sporadic skirmishing. Some of the men found old muskets abandoned by the Federals and vied with each other to see who could fire the largest load out of the old-fashioned guns. "They roared like young cannon," wrote Jackman, but thankfully none of the Orphans hurt themselves in the foolish contest. Jackman spent his time reading a new novel and listening to a captured Federal who confessed that the Kentucky sharpshooters were excellent, but added that their artillery was "not worth a damn."

That afternoon, thinking that the Federals in Bate's front had withdrawn, Johnston ordered the general to advance his division to feel for the enemy. Bate himself spoke with Lewis and his other brigade commanders expounding upon Johnston's order, and admonishing them not to assault if they found the enemy still in strength. A brigade on the division's left would initiate the reconnaissance in force. If it met with success, then a signal would be given for Lewis and the others to advance.

It was Brigadier General Frank C. Armstrong's brigade that launched the movement. He was initially successful, entering the enemy works only to discover them still there in force. Faced with a heavy counterattack, Armstrong withdrew and Bate sent orders canceling the signal for the other brigades to move. It was too late.

At 4 P.M. Lewis ordered the Kentuckians to their places in line and ready to scale their own works and advance. Soon they heard the din of Armstrong's fight to the left. Since the noise was too great to distinguish the signal guns from the rest of the firing, Lewis just assumed that the attack was now general and ordered all of the brigade except the 9th Kentucky forward. Caldwell's regiment was to join shortly but never got the chance. What Lewis found when he emerged from the undergrowth in his front and advanced toward the enemy line was the entire federal XV Corps in position. The brigade on Lewis' right did not advance at all, and that on his left got the order to return before he did. As a result, the Orphans moved virtually alone against the enemy, both of their flanks exposed to a deadly fire. "As soon as we came in sight of them," said Weller, "we knew we had met them in vain." Still, Lewis took the first line of federal works and silenced a battery, aided by good fire from Cobb and Gracey. But then "a literal storm of shot and shell" tore into their ranks with devastating impact. Within fifty yards of the Yankee line the brigade stood its ground, then took cover behind logs and abandoned equipment, and even their own dead.

"Their line was a sheet of flame," said an Orphan, "and death was feasting in our midst." James Cleveland of the 5th Kentucky took a bullet in his left arm. He arose and continued to fight, taking another bullet in the chest. Still he fought until another ball passed through his bowels. Then he took a hit that mashed the elbow of his good arm, and another bullet "contused" his face. Only with five bullets in him did he sink to the ground for good. That night he crawled back to his own lines to linger for a week before dying. Lieutenant Colonel William Clarke, just recently relieved of command of the 6th Kentucky by the return of Cofer, felt a minie ball crush his right arm below the elbow. He managed to save it from amputation, but it put him out of the war for good. Poor Captain David McKendree, who made a speech to his men before Shiloh and then recovered from a seemingly mortal wound at Stones River, fell limp when a bullet hit his neck and severed the spinal column. He, too, lingered for a week.

19. "Old Joe." Brigadier General Joseph H. Lewis, stern, demanding, yet fiercely protective of his Orphans. He, at least, survived. (*From Thompson*, Orphan Brigade)

20. Philip Lightfoot Lee would stand by "his side of the street" in the last extremity as well as he stood by the 2nd Kentucky. (*From Thompson*, Orphan Brigade)

21. Colonel Jim Moss left his sickbed to stand beside the Orphans, and die beside them at Jonesboro. (*From Thompson*, Orphan Brigade)

22. Hiram Hawkins of the 5th Kentucky just would not be "overslaughed." He got his way and led his Orphans bravely at Atlanta. (*From Thompson*, Orphan Brigade)

23. "Cripps," Lieutenant Colonel John C. Wickliffe, always felt imprisoned in his uniform. Unbuttoned, he laughed louder. (*From Thompson*, Orphan Brigade)

24. Captain Ed Porter Thompson, who conceived the idea that the Orphans had "a kind of title of nobility." *(From* Confederate Veteran, *July 1898)*

25. Captain Fayette Hewitt did as much as any to preserve the Orphans' story when he saved their records for posterity. *(From Thompson,* Orphan Brigade)

26. Captain John H. Weller, like many of the Kentuckians, wrote widely after the war, so that the Orphans' story would not be forgotten. *(From Thompson,* Orphan Brigade)

27. The governor who became a soldier, George W. Johnson. An exile like the Orphans, he died with them at Shiloh. *(From Thompson,* Orphan Brigade)

28. Leader in postwar reunions of the Orphan Brigade for nearly forty years, "Old Joe" Lewis wept at their surrender. *(Courtesy Tulane University)*

"I know that very soon I shall die," he told his surgeons. He settled his business affairs through them, gave one his Bible, and then asked that they tell his men that "I never had one of them punished in any way without feeling sorry that duty compelled me to do it, and that I love them all." When men of his company came to visit their dying captain, he told them, "Boys, I want you to fight the Yankees as long as there is one of you left to fire a gun."

Even the little corps of sharpshooters joined in the charge up that hill, leaving one of their number dead on the field and losing the valuable Kerr rifle. Of all the Kentucky regiments, the poor 4th took the worst casualties, being on the exposed left flank. Finally Bate's order to retire reached the brigade, and the regiments began their retreat, all except for Hiram Hawkins and his 5th Kentucky. They were within twenty yards of the enemy works and did not seem inclined to back out now. Finally Hawkins had to seize the colors himself to turn his men from their assault.

The men in Caldwell's 9th Kentucky knew something had gone awry when a silence settled over the field, and then the enemy sent a cheer into the air. Soon word of the debacle filtered to them, and it was not long before Jackman and others surveyed the damage done their comrades. "The Brigade is terribly cut up," he wrote that night. The men in the ranks did not know of Johnston's order, and believed the fight had been the idea of "Old Grits" Bate. As a result, they spoke harshly of him in the bivouac that night. " 'Grits' 'catches it' from all sides and quarters," said Johnny Jackman. Only some time later did the Orphans learn the truth, and forgive their grievance toward Bate. "This is the game of war," said Green, "& we had to pay the price in blood." It was a heavy bill, with 20 killed and 177 wounded. Dallas would always be a bad memory to the Orphans, but in this campaign for Atlanta, it would only be one of many. Already the month of May 1864 put over one sixth of the brigade out of action, and still the Kentuckians had not seen a real battle.[7]

The next day the armies lay rather quiet in the Orphans' sector, but that night the Federals several times opened a heavy fire and shelling on the Kentuckians for no apparent reason. Some of the Union skirmishers even became disoriented in the flashing bedlam and approached the Confederate lines mistaking them for their own. In front of the 2d Kentucky one bluecoat topped the works and called into the darkness, "Colonel, the Rebs are making it so hot out yonder,

I can't hold my 'posish.'" His position immediately thereafter was prisoner of war. Jackman had been sleeping until the bombardment began. He sat up rubbing his eyes and asked a comrade what was happening. "Hell has broke loose in Georgia," came the response. The next morning, after the ground in the Orphans' front had been fought and skirmished over for several days, they found that "the bullets are lying around on the ground now, thick as hail stones." Jackman postulated that a few more days of this would make "a good lead mine" in the valley before them.

They did not stay long enough to salt that mine. By June 5, after several days of idleness, the Orphans once again took the road as Johnston moved his lines back yet again. Lewis and his brigade made a miserable march toward Pine Mountain in the night and a heavy rain. The distance was only about four miles, but it took hours, "the muddiest and most disagreeable march" many of the Kentuckians had made. The country seemed to be a continual swamp, and in the dark many made a great splash as they lost their footing and fell in the mire. More fortunate comrades yelled, "Get up out of that mud," and tried to identify their recently baptized friend by his manner of swearing.

On June 6 they took a final position on the crest of Pine Mountain, a detached eminence two miles west of Kennesaw Mountain. Later they moved to the eastern slope of the mountain, and here remained for the next several days, watching Sherman's advancing minions forming their own earthworks in the valley below. Once again the skirmishing began, and on June 10 the Federals sent a line of skirmishers forward against Lewis, but without success. Slowly the bluecoats advanced their works toward the base of the mountain, yet for several days more a relative calm settled over the field as Sherman gathered his breath for the next major assault.

Clouds obscured the sun on the morning of June 14, but soon they dispelled and the Orphans readied themselves for another day. Before long Generals Johnston, Hardee, and Polk rode along the Kentucky lines inspecting their positions. They did so in full view of the Federals, yet seemed oblivious to the danger. Major John B. Pirtle rode with them. Shortly the enemy spotted the cluster of high brass and sent a shell in their direction. The Confederate commanders had been warned by one of the Orphan officers of the danger, and now this enemy missile brought that danger home to them when it killed

Pirtle's horse under him. Fortunately the major arose unhurt, but the generals only shifted their position slightly. Before long another enemy shell rocketed across the intervening ground. It struck Polk full in the chest, passing through him, leaving the bishop general dead on the crest of Pine Mountain with the generals and the Orphans standing over him in shock.

Johnny Jackman did not see Polk's demise, for he sat beside Caldwell's morning fire talking with Captain John Gillum of Company A. Since the enemy artillery had been silent for the past two days, Jackman heard with surprise that first shot that killed Pirtle's horse. He offered the observation that "some general and his staff, no doubt, had ridden up the crest of the hill, and the federal batteries were throwing shells at them." Gillum agreed. "Yes," he said in a like vein, "and I hope some of them will get shot. A general can't ride around the lines without a regiment of staff at his heels." Just then they heard the second shot fired. From the sound of impact, Jackman thought it harmlessly buried itself in the mountainside. Of course, it hit Polk instead, not one hundred yards from Jackman, yet he and Gillum could not see the general because of trees in their front. Minutes later they learned what had happened, and then an order arrived for a report to be sent to Lewis' headquarters. Long disabled for active field service due to his frail health, Jackman served as regimental clerk, though from time to time he shouldered his musket when his colonel would allow.

Now Jackman armed himself with a pen and made out the report. Several federal batteries sent shells into Pine Mountain, but Jackman and Gillum, joined by Johnny Green, Caldwell, and one or two other Orphans, felt safe where they sat. The report done, Jackman raised his head to ask Caldwell if he should sign his name for him. The colonel assented, and Jackman bent over again to affix the signature.

"We were sitting around with shells bursting over us," said Johnny Green, "when it was evident from the sound that one piece of a shell was coming close to us." Some held their breath; others, immune to the sound of the guns, ignored the eerie music of the whining shell fragment. Then it struck. "Suddenly every thing got dark, and I became unconscious." The fragment hit John Jackman on the top of the head, cracked the skull and depressed it somewhat, then bounded onward, struck a rock, and finally plummeted against Caldwell's leg. The men sitting around scattered immediately but quickly came back to the prostrate Jackman, Caldwell being only bruised. The impact had turned the clerk in a complete somersault, and Green said, "We thought he was killed." But in a few moments Jackman awoke to find Gillum and Dr. B. L. Hester lifting him from the ground. Jackman stood of his own accord. There was no pain and for a moment he could not imagine what had happened. The first thought in his mind was that his head was gone, and he put his hand up to feel if there was still anything above his shoulders. Hester bandaged the wound after Green poured some water on it, and then Jackman declared that he felt so little pain that he saw no point in going to the hospital. "Jack was so bright by this time," said Green, "that we had a hearty laugh at the way he had flopped over, just like a chicken when his head is cut off." Hester insisted that he go to the field hospital nevertheless, and predicted that the wound would be more serious than Jackman supposed. That night it began hurting severely, and a week later it became inflamed and gangrene set in. The surgeons sent Jackman to the hospital in Atlanta on the same train that bore the remains of General Leonidas Polk.[8]

For the Orphans left behind on Pine Mountain, the long campaign wore on. By June 20 they were on Kennesaw Mountain, with a large detail from several regiments acting as skirmishers. That evening Sherman sent three light assaults against the Kentucky line, which each time repulsed the enemy. But a fourth attempt dislodged the Confederates, and Lewis had to send Major John B. Rogers of the 4th Kentucky to regain the lost ground. The skirmishing had been hard that day, and as men died on the line, others often volunteered to take their places. Sergeant Tom Cox, though not on the duty list, asked to take a comrade's place as a replacement, only to fall to a sharpshooter's bullet. When an orderly arrived to ask another man to come to the skirmish line, Virginius Hutchen—the same man who so cursed his officers two years before that he was arrested for inciting mutiny—stepped forward calmly. "My time has nearly come," he said with resignation, then went to the line. He saw several of his fellow Orphans, each with a bullet hole in the center of the forehead, testament to the deadly skill of the enemy sharpshooters. He asked where the dead men had been in the line, and was shown a pile of stones beside a tree. He decided to shift things a bit and took his ground several feet away from the barricade. Shortly he crawled to the rocks, put his hat atop a stick, and held it above the breastwork. Instantly a bullet perforated his head-

gear. Three more times he repeated the charade until he spotted a tuft
of smoke that betrayed the enemy marksman's position. At that moment Taylor McCoy of the brigade sharpshooters approached, and
Hutchen borrowed his Kerr rifle. One shot brought down the enemy
picket and Hutchen felt well satisfied in having, however slightly,
evened the score for his departed comrades.

Now Rogers formed his detail to retake the rifle pits. Some of the
Orphans who had lost the works to the enemy urged them, saying,
"Go in, Kaintuck! We'll yell!" Go in Rogers did, and he regained
much of the lost ground, but now it turned dark, and in the gloom
Rogers himself mistook an enemy position for one of his own. Just
what happened is unknown. Federal prisoners told of a Confederate
officer approaching them and mistaking their identity, saying they
must hold their position to the last man. Others believed Rogers killed.
In any case, the gallant major was never heard from again. Dead or
captured, he simply disappeared in the night. His men held their place
until midnight, when Lewis ordered them to retire. Some did not receive the order, and only much later did they creep through the darkness to safety, though not before Bill Hill had cocked his rifle and was
about to shoot into a dark shape approaching, only to discover it was
his friend Henry Harned.[9]

Johnston kept his Army along the Kennesaw line until July 2, 1864,
a time of constant skirmishing for the Orphans. Late that night he ordered the brigade to retire to the Chattahoochee River, and there they
took a new position on the Fourth of July. The Orphans had seen two
months of campaigning in Georgia so far, and the toll showed in their
ever-thinning ranks. On May 7, a total of 1,512 Kentuckians answered
the roll. Three days after reaching the Chattahoochee, the morning report found 974 fit for duty. More than one third of the brigade lay
dead on the road to Dalton, or else wounded in the hospitals of
Atlanta. That the grueling, depressing nature of this endless campaign
told on the Kentuckians who escaped the bullets is undeniable. In this
last month, 30 men went on the rolls as deserters, 19 of them from
Hanson's always troublesome 2d Kentucky.

Yet the spirit of most of the Kentuckians stood the test as it always
did. Good "Old Joe" Lewis finally forgave Cripps Wickliffe his
disrespect—or else could not bring him to court-martial—and returned
the popular officer to the 9th Kentucky, his buttons presumably fas-
tened. Mike Whalen of the 4th Kentucky always kept his good cheer,

and amazed his officers by somehow producing a cross-cut saw, a maul, and two wedges from his kit whenever needed. He also had a four-gallon jug of water on the march, and the regimental adjutant believed Mike could probably find a hammer and anvil if he looked deep enough into his knapsack. Even some of the wounded kept their good humor. Tom Strother, who took a bullet in the toe at Chickamauga, saw a three-inch shell nearly sever his left forearm. He used his right hand to help carry wounded on a litter, and thereafter walked several miles carrying his left hand in his right until the surgeons could tend to him. He refused chloroform, and said instead, "Give me a glass of whisky." Tom never took his eyes from the medicos at their work, then arose from the table and walked to a nearby poker game and sat in, experimenting to see if he could shuffle the cards with one hand. Thereafter he remained with his mess, though unfit for fighting, to chop their firewood. Samuel Mains of the 5th Kentucky had been crippled by "white swelling" early in life, yet joined the command in 1861 and stayed with it in every march. He could not perform the manual of arms so badly was one arm deformed, and marching was painful and difficult for his misshapen legs, yet he stayed with his regiment throughout this long, hard campaign until finally he could march no more. Instead of leaving the brigade, however, he stayed on as a cook for his messmates. And poor Konshattountzchette, his beauty spoiled forever, remained ever active once he returned to duty. He seemed particularly to desire being entrusted with captured Federals, though for what purpose his fellow Orphans could only speculate. Some hinted darkly that the Mohawk wanted to wreak a terrible tribal revenge on all Yankees for the loss of his good looks. Finally Caldwell deemed it wise not to leave the Indian alone with prisoners. As for the wounded like Captain Winstead, they too kept their spirit for the most part, and the old dream of regaining their homeland never died. "Our army is in the finest plight you ever saw," he wrote his wife, "and determined yet to come to Kentucky."[10]

By July 17 Sherman had crossed the Chattahoochee and forced Johnston to withdraw toward Peach Tree Creek, barely four miles north of Atlanta. Davis and the War Office in Richmond were by now exasperated with Johnston's constant retreats. Davis despised Johnston personally as well, and on this day relieved the general by his personal emissary, the ever-accommodating Braxton Bragg. The Orphans, by now convinced that every evil visited upon the Confederacy was in some way the work of their old enemy Bragg, were first furious, then moody. It helped only a little that the man Bragg put in Johnston's place, General John B. Hood, was a Kentuckian, for they felt little confidence in his generalship, a hesitation Davis and Bragg might wisely have shared. "The removal," said Johnny Green, "has cast a gloom over the army."[11]

Hood shortly pulled his Army into the defenses encircling Atlanta, and Bate's division he soon ordered to move west of the city a few miles toward Decatur, hoping to strike the federal left flank. Bate reached his position in the early dark hours of July 22, and placed Lewis and the Orphan Brigade nearby a little stream called Intrenchment Creek. The Kentuckians numbered 1,002 now, many of their wounded having returned to duty, as they almost always did on this campaign. Some confusion occurred in the orders for other commands to support Bate, however, so that when he ordered Lewis to advance the attack was not yet fully organized, and no reconnaissance of the ground had been conducted. Yet forward marched the Orphans. Bate's orders from Hardee were to move without letup, regardless of obstacles, yet the ground the Kentuckians crossed was so congested with brush and woods, and even a mill pond, their alignment became seriously disrupted. Then the enemy artillery opened on them. Bate and Lewis charged on, believing that the bluecoats were not covered by defenses.

When finally the Orphans caught sight of the enemy, however, they found them behind good breastworks on the crest of a hill protected as well by several batteries. Still the brigade pushed onward, though many bogged in the mill pond, caught in its mud while the federal sharpshooters shot them down. Now the lack of those supports on Lewis' left flank allowed the enemy to hit the brigade there as well. Before long the heavy underbrush on the right of the Orphans' line forced them to bunch toward the left, giving the bluecoats a tightly packed mass of Kentucky flesh to take their fire. Only the timely arrival of Fayette Hewitt, who rode through the entire length of the brigade front to reach the left, got the Orphans realigned somewhat for the final push toward the enemy works.

Johnny Green managed to get his canteen caught in crossing a fence, with the unhappy result that the strap held him pinned to the front of the fence, a perfect target for the enemy. He did his best to dodge the bullets that splintered the rails all about him until a merciful ball cut the canteen strap itself and freed him to continue the charge. Another man of the 9th Kentucky, Sol Wiel, a Dutch Jew believed to be from Amsterdam, coolly calmed his mates in the advance. When they tried to dodge the bullets whizzing past, he sang out, "Hey, Dock! Vats te use to todge tem pulletts? Tey'll hit you shust as vell vere you is as vere you ain't."

Shortly Hewitt's horse fell dead beneath him, and the men passing by thought they saw the adjutant trying to save his saddle, a peculiar bit of parsimony under the heavy fire. In fact, thriftier yet, Hewitt was attempting to dislodge a blanket he had seen an Orphan discard that morning. He knew the man would need it again that night.

Finally the brigade reached the enemy works and began driving the Federals from them. Soon the bluecoats sent forward reinforcements, however, and the Orphans were too few to hold what they had gained at such cost. Bate ordered Lewis to fall back. The whole attack had been a bungled affair by Bate and Hardee, and the other brigades who were to have supported the Kentuckians. Better now to end it. The trouble was, though, that falling back under the federal fire was even more dangerous than the advance. Many fell before they re-entered their own lines. And somewhere out there in that embattled landscape, Frank the soldier dog of the 2d Kentucky disappeared for good.

The cost had been terrible. A total of 135 Orphans lay dead or wounded, among them John and Dan Hays of the 5th Kentucky, devoted brothers, both now joined in death. The brigade lost at least 25 killed, and at the July 27 muster numbered only 809 fit for duty. Ten days before they had been over 1,000. That night Hewitt overheard two men of the 9th Kentucky talking about the day's fight, one saying he wished he could act with courage "like that man Hewitt." To himself Fayette Hewitt thought, "My friend, if you only knew how badly Hewitt was scared you *wouldn't* like it!" Yet Hewitt had done his duty. Bullets might destroy the Orphan Brigade, but never fear.[12]

There remained but one act more in the tragedy that this fight for Atlanta visited upon the 1st Kentucky Brigade, and it waited forty days after Intrenchment Creek for the curtain. They were forty days of siege life, nothing new to these veterans of Corinth, Vicksburg, and Chattanooga. The day after the disaster of July 22, Hardee's corps, including Bate and the Orphans, withdrew into the defensive works surrounding Atlanta. "The boys enjoyed a freedom, rest and relief from the severe tension," said Gervis Grainger, "such as they had not experienced since May." There was light duty for them in Atlanta, the occasional skirmish, and only one real minor engagement, in which the Orphans helped repulse a halfhearted federal attack on their front. Still, any victory, no matter how small, was important now, and their corps commander published a complimentary order lauding Lewis and his men. The day before that little fight came the best news of all, though. Lewis received an order from Army headquarters to ready his men to go to Griffin, Georgia. There they would prepare to become mounted infantry. After almost two years, the dream at last was to be realized. Once on horseback, the Orphans might somehow yet find Kentucky within their reach.[13]

But they must fight one more battle as infantry first. As part of his gradual encirclement of Atlanta, Sherman sent the bulk of his Army around Hood's left toward Jonesboro, about ten miles south of Atlanta. There the Federals might cut the Macon Railroad, Hood's last line of communication with the outside. Hood at once sent Bate's division south, placing the Orphans themselves at Jonesboro, while the rest of Hardee's corps followed. An Arkansas brigade joined the Kentuckians, Lewis taking the overall command while Caldwell assumed temporary charge of the Orphan Brigade. On August 29 they began building hasty earthworks, and late the next day the forward elements of the enemy drove the Confederate outposts into the little town. That night Hardee finally arrived along with another corps. There could be no doubt that a major battle would be fought with the coming dawn. Johnny Green wrote, "We certainly have cause for anxiety."

Lewis did not like his position, but there was no time to alter it now. Hardee, despite being outnumbered, determined that a bold attack would be his only hope of stopping the enemy from cutting the railroad. Not until 3 P.M. did he order the charge, however, and then it proved entirely an unwise move. The enemy had found time to fortify their positions with breastworks and emplace their artillery. Further, the Confederates had to advance over an open field devoid of cover to reach the enemy, and then just in front of the Yankee works they would encounter rough ground to stall them under the heaviest fire. Still Hardee ordered them forward.

The Orphans numbered about 833 that afternoon, several recently returned wounded having added to their strength. One man with them today was Colonel Jim Moss. The entire month of August he sat abed on sick leave, severely fevered. The Reverend Pickett seems to have despaired of the colonel's recovery, but not Moss. Upon learning of the impending movement to Jonesboro, Moss announced, "I am going up to the front." Pickett tried to persuade him otherwise, but to no avail. "Yes, yes; I must go up," said Moss. Hardly a well man, still he now stood at the head of his gallant old 2d Kentucky. John Mahon was with the regiment again, recovered from his Chickamauga wound, ready to offer more of his blood, if need be, in defense of the South.

Forward went the brigade. "We started at full run," said Grainger. "Their batteries opened on us by the dozen, with grape and canister shot and shell. The face of the earth was literally torn to pieces, and how any of us escaped is yet a mystery." Still the Kentuckians fired a volley and then started their final rush toward the enemy works when they discovered for the first time a gully perhaps ten feet wide and as many feet deep. Under the terrible fire, many of the men jumped into it for cover. "Jump into the ditch," someone shouted, and for those in it all thought of continuing the assault died. They would remain here until they could somehow return to their own lines.

Others meanwhile avoided the ditch and continued the charge, at least one of them under a considerable embarrassment. Poor Bill Robb of Hawkins' 5th Kentucky, a careless sort, had only one button at his trouser top to hold them up, and in the advance a contrary bullet shot the button away. Down went his pants. He picked them up again and tried to continue the advance, but could not do much holding his rifle in one hand and his last link with modesty in the other. Faced with a choice amid all that shot and shell, he finally let go the trousers and finished his part of the battle with more than his steel bare.

The heathen old 4th Kentucky, who discouraged so many parsons in this war, had another one with them in their advance. He joined recently, and was known only as Father Blemill. This man of God the Orphans respected, for he went into the fight with them, and though a Catholic, he made no distinction in his ministrations with the largely Protestant Kentuckians. He took his place just in the rear of the advancing 4th during this charge.

Finally those not stopped by the gully or the enemy bullets reached the federal line, and there for a few brief seconds the Orphans battled with the bluecoats of Brigadier General Charles Walcutt's brigade. Walcutt himself was a graduate of Kentucky Military Institute, alma mater to more than one of the Orphan officers now facing him. Lewis could not stand the fire and found the attempt hopeless. After only brief fighting, he ordered his now disorganized brigade to retire. As the Kentucky regiments fell back, they left many of their own behind. Walcutt captured three officers and twenty-five men almost at once, and in addition to them he took a mortally wounded Colonel Moss. Now, for the fifth time, the 2d Kentucky was orphaned once more. And, almost as predictable as the dawn, John Mahon was hit again. "As good a soldier as ever shouldered a musket," his captain said of him. "Was hit with a bullet in every battle."

As Lewis rode to the rear observing his broken lines, he saw Father Blemill bending over a wounded man. He lifted his hands in prayer for the dying soldier, and at once an enemy cannon ball carried away the priest's head. The poor 4th Kentucky just could not keep a preacher. "He was with us such a short time," said Captain John Weller, "that I never knew his name."

By the time the bulk of the brigade reached the relative safety of their own lines, many Orphans remained in that gully some distance in advance. The color bearer of the 6th Kentucky buried the regimental flag in the dirt for the remainder of the day, only resurrecting it after dark when he and Grainger and others silently groped their way to their comrades in the rear. Green, too, returned in safety to his regiment, carrying a wounded man of his regiment with him. All that afternoon and evening after the charge the Federals kept up their shelling of the Confederate line. In the ground between the opposing forces lay all too many wounded and dying Kentuckians, many of them screaming for help in their agony. Finally the sound became too much for some of the Orphans. Johnny Green, John Slusser of the 6th Kentucky, and Tom Young of the 9th leaped over their own works and rushed unarmed onto the field, each running to a wounded man. "The minnie balls were singing in our ears," said Green, "& raising a cloud of dust about our feet." Each reached his man and, picking him up, started back for their breastworks. As soon as the Federals saw what the Orphans were about, they stopped firing and raised a cheer, followed by a volley in the air as a salute. The three men made several trips more until all the wounded they could find were in the hospital, the chivalrous bluecoats withholding their fire all the time, and substituting for it their applause.

That night those who could visited the hospitals to look for wounded friends. Among the dying lay Robert Lindsay, color bearer of Thompson's 4th Kentucky, a great hole shot in his right chest. In his delirium he whispered to a friend, "We are to be mounted and Captain John [Weller] has promised to get me a horse. If he forgets, won't you attend to it?" His friend listened in sadness. "I would have promised him a continent." This night, too, the faithful members of Father Blemill's little congregation laid him to rest in a shallow grave.[14]

The next morning Hardee realized that he could not prevent the enemy from taking the railroad, and began pulling his corps out of Jonesboro while sending the other corps with him back to Atlanta to aid Hood in the evacuation. Hardee ordered Lewis to put the Kentucky brigade aboard cars at the Macon depot, but the Orphans waited there most of the day without further instructions. Then in the afternoon, Bate sent them to the extreme right of the now thin Confederate line and ordered them to dig in and prepare to receive an attack. They must hold on for one more day to give Hood the time he needed for a successful evacuation of Atlanta. Lewis found so much ground to guard that he was forced to place his men in a single line, with each soldier three feet from his neighbor. Not since Missionary Ridge had Confederates been spread so thin. It was a weak position, as Hewitt and others soon discovered and revealed to Hardee. Yet when the general asked if the Orphans could hold their position, Hewitt said they could, though the place was perilous. Hardee gave him two field pieces for support, and some Orphans began intrenching as best they could with a broken ax, an old shovel, and several frying pans.

They barely started the work when the federal artillery sent its first shells toward them. As the Orphans scurried into their rifle pits, occasional shells rolled in after them. William Steenberger took a bad wound at Dallas and could not use his arms to load a gun, so two comrades loaded for him. And when a shell hopped into his pit, he still managed to pick it up and calmly shove it out again. Another shell, its fuse sputtering as it approached the charge inside, fell beside Johnny Green in his rifle pit. Walker Nash of his regiment had just joined him after filling his canteen, and now coolly poured the water over the fuse until it smothered.

As the barrage continued, the Federals massed their infantry for the assault, and then came charging out of the woods toward the Kentuckians. The Orphans met them with a sure and steady fire that halted the advance before it reached their rifle pits, but soon the enemy re-formed for another attempt. This proved more successful,

and before long the Federals captured most of the brigade on Lewis'
left, though his own men once more repulsed the bluecoats in their
front. But now the Yankees came at the Orphans from front and
flank, and their third assault could not be stopped. Caldwell wanted to
withdraw, but just then came word that reinforcements were on the
way and he must hold the works at all hazard.

The fire was furious, and Kentuckians fell all along the line. Flashes
of drama sped before the Orphans' eyes, forming a montage in their
memories even as they fought for their lives. Bill Fourqueran of the
9th Kentucky trying to pull a bullet from his forehead . . . an enemy
rifle poking through the breastwork and firing a shot that killed both
Sam Butcher and Jim Adams . . . a Yankee lying just the other side
of the earthwork shouting "Surrender, you dam Rebels" . . . Booker
Reed on the opposite side replying "The H————l you say" as he shot
the bluecoat . . . Johnny Green arising to look straight into an enemy
gun barrel that fired in his face . . . a mildly injured Green placing
his own rifle's muzzle against his antagonist's side and blowing "a hole
through him big enough to have run my fist through" . . . the enemy
turning the 9th Kentucky's left flank and ordering its surrender . . .
half of the regiment giving up while Leander Applegate coolly walked
away with the unit's colors . . . several of the 6th Kentucky falling
prisoner to the Federals surrounding them . . . Gervis Grainger being
hurried to the rear by his captors . . . the colors of the 6th Kentucky
captured and the men of the 2d hurriedly tearing theirs to shreds to
prevent that humiliation . . . a shell taking the arm off Ed Hagan and
spurting blood over his comrades . . . and finally the remnant of the
brigade jumping from their pits and dashing for safety to the rear.
The Battle of Jonesboro was over, and so was the infantry service of
the 1st Kentucky Brigade.

Even their enemies admitted to the fury with which the Orphans
contested their ground. "The troops met were confessedly among the
best of the rebel army," wrote the commander of one federal brigade
that assaulted Lewis. "They fought with the greatest desperation." A
Yankee officer said a few days later that these Kentuckians were "the
most infernal set of devils that the Army of the Cumberland had ever
caught or ever encountered." General Jefferson C. Davis, commanding
the division that fought the Orphans for two days at Jonesboro, com-
mended their bravery and personally took an interest in the welfare of
the Kentucky wounded and prisoners in his care.

Most eloquent of all were the losses. They told the story not only of Jonesboro, but also of the tragedy of the whole campaign. The brigade lost 320 out of its 833 engaged in the battle. Since the campaign began back in May, Lewis' losses totaled 999, his strength reduced by constant fighting from 1,512 to a mere 513 by September 6. On this day the entire complement of the 2d Kentucky numbered 69! Cofer's 6th Kentucky reported 74 present for duty. With a mere 156 men, Thompson's 4th was the largest regiment in the brigade. Three years before, the 2d Kentucky numbered 833. Its remnant now would not have made enough for a company by 1861 standards. The whole number of Kentuckians answering roll call on September 6, 1864, were half what the War Department would have required to form a *regiment* three years before.

Yet, in the 120 days since the Orphans marched out of Dalton 1,512 strong, their hospitals recorded 1,860 cases of death or wounds, 23 per cent more than there were men in the command. Fewer than 50 men were reported as having passed through the entire campaign unblooded. Yet as quickly as they recovered from their wounds—and often before—the Kentuckians rejoined their fellow Orphans at the front, often only to be wounded again. In years ahead several Social Darwinists in America, seeking examples to establish the natural superiority of American blood, settled upon the performance of the 1st Kentucky Brigade in the Atlanta campaign to prove their claims. "A search into the history of warlike exploits," wrote one, "has failed to show me any endurance to the worst trials of war surpassing this." The record of the Orphans, said another, "has never been surpassed."[15]

TWELVE

"The Blackest Day
of Our Lives"

WILLIAM J. "POLK" STONE of Company H, 4th Kentucky, did not believe that finally the Kentuckians were to be mounted. "Boys," he said, "I'll bet the war don't last three weeks; it is certain to stop now the Orphan Brigade has got a good thing."[1]

There were those in the brigade who thought him right. When the order to proceed to Griffin for mounting was repeated on September 4, many of the men stood first incredulous, then jubilant. "There was great rejoicing when this fact became known," said Weller. "The trench-stained veterans were wild with delight." Three days later they left Bate for the last time and tramped down the road to Griffin, then on to Barnesville, where their first lot of horses awaited. "Hopes of seeing home again once more abided on the bronzed features, and the few hearts swelled with unspeakable joy." Some felt sad to leave their comrades in the other brigades of the Army, and many a veteran lamented seeing the Orphans leave. "Men, I am sorry to part with you," Hardee told them. "I hate to give you up."[2]

But part with them he did. Even as the Orphans marched, Lewis went immediately to work trying to find them saddles and equipments. He had agents scour the countryside for horses abandoned by Sherman's cavalry during their frequent raids, and soon put a detail of men from the brigade itself to work making saddles. What he found when the Orphans reached Barnesville was hardly encouraging. Only 200 horses stood ready, "and such horses," said Weller. He be-

lieved they had been abandoned as useless first by Confederate cavalry, then the same by the Federals, used for a while to pull plows, and
finally given back to the Army. A fair number of mules mingled with
them as well, and many of the men actually preferred these, as they
were in better condition than most of the horses.

Here for over a month Lewis worked to rebuild his shattered brigade and get them horsed. In the month of October 216 saddles were
supplied to the brigade, many of them manufactured by the detail of
saddlers led by Captain Christian Bosche. "It was remarkable what
good texas saddles he turned out," said a Kentuckian. Bosche even
made some fancy saddles for the officers, using saplings and pine
planking for the frame, and pigskin for the covering. Yet for all the
saddles they supplied, Lewis could get only 88 saddle blankets, and 97
bridles. This insufficiency plagued him for the rest of the war. Many of
the Orphans rode bareback.

Putting the men on the horses was another matter. Some of the tall
soldiers drew short horses, their feet almost dragging the ground.
Others who never learned to ride, could not, and remained dismounted. Thanks to a special exchange effected with Sherman, many
of the prisoners taken at Jonesboro—Johnny Green among them—
rejoined Lewis in mid-September. A phenomenon also occurred as
soon as word of the brigade's mounting spread. Slowly men who in
some cases had been missing and presumed captured since Shiloh
walked into camp and asked for a horse. Many who before deserted
the infantry service, decided now that a horse's back offered the best
opportunity of returning to Kentucky. More than once a haggard,
seedy soldier walked into camp only to hear old comrades exclaim that
they were sure they buried him back in Corinth.

The poor corps of sharpshooters traded their coveted Kerr rifles now
for Enfields, and did so grudgingly, but the prospect of mounted service eased the loss. "It was almost like commencing the war over to
start at it on 'critter back,' " said Weller. "As for myself, I felt very uncertain and uncomfortable, perched on a horse." Training the men to
care for their horses proved something of a problem. Johnny Green
claimed, "Our boys were so glad to get horses, even poor as these were,
that they treated them like they were frail & tender brothers." In fact,
Lewis and the other officers had to warn the men against misusing
their animals for fun, and issued an order that any man who abused or

neglected his animal would have it taken from him and given to an unmounted soldier.[3]

Thanks to the exchange and the numbers of returning wounded and those mysterious dead who now seemingly came back to life, the Orphan Brigade rapidly regained a measure of its strength. By the middle of September it numbered 634, by October 1 it totaled 880, and on the first day of November 1864, Lewis counted 945, this despite the loss of 25 deserters in the past two months, probably men who despaired of ever getting a horse. That problem plagued Lewis to the end. His best efforts to the contrary, he never got horses for about 200 of his brigade. As a result, for much of the remainder of the war there would be in effect two commands, the mounted men led by Lewis, and the dismounted contingent, largely doing guard duty under Wickliffe.[4]

Once Lewis had a respectable number of the men on horseback, he took them toward the Chattahoochee for picket duty to the south and west of federal-held Atlanta. Then, under orders from Brigadier General Alfred Iverson, commanding the cavalry division to which the Orphans now belonged, Lewis repaired to Stockbridge, eighteen miles south of Atlanta. Iverson was establishing a picket line on all the routes leading south from the city, and at Stockbridge Lewis was to guard an important bridge against federal advance. He sent Weller and a detachment of the 4th Kentucky several miles in advance, and gave Hawkins orders to take a detail east of Atlanta to harass foraging parties believed to be operating there. On November 15, Sherman began his advance toward the Atlantic, and at once Hawkins found himself cut off from Stockbridge. In attempting to rejoin his command he spent several days in the federal rear grabbing stragglers and gathering information. His own little force increased continually, and when finally he did rejoin Lewis late in September, Iverson ordered him to take the entire 5th Kentucky and picket along a line about twenty miles west of Savannah. Weller, too, was cut off by Sherman's advance, as well as perhaps by his own inclination to indulge himself. He established his detachment in comfortable quarters and promptly began enjoying the company of a lovely young lady in the vicinity. He visited her every morning at 10 A.M., and found her singing and conversation so enchanting that he frequently did not do his duty of inspecting his vedettes until well after lunch. "Our pleasures were only too brief," he lamented. One morning while talking with her, Weller received news of Sherman's advance. He left at once, finding his horse so unmanageable that it nearly took him right into Sherman's advancing columns until he checked the animal. Shortly Thompson arrived from Stockbridge with the balance of the 4th Kentucky, and after a brief defense the Orphans withdrew only to find more Federals in their rear. Like Hawkins, Thompson and Weller had to follow a circuitous route to rejoin Lewis.[5]

By this time, Lewis, too, was in trouble. It was late on November 15 when the Federals approached Stockbridge and he sent his skirmishers forward. Greatly outnumbered, he could only pull back, burning the bridge behind him. The enemy was not so impressed with the Orphans this time, though they overestimated Lewis' numbers by double. "He yielded it after a very feeble show of resistance," said the federal general commanding the XV Corps, noting that Lewis kept his troops "at a very discreet distance." It was a neat bit of bravado for a general who faced less than five hundred Confederate cavalry with three full divisions of Federals.

"It was now our duty to hang on the flank of the enemy & annoy him all we could," said Johnny Green. Lewis fell back to Griffin, then beyond to the Oconee River near Milladgeville. Here "Old Joe" sent Thompson and the 4th Kentucky to guard a railroad bridge over the river not far from Ball's Ferry. There they met Major General Henry C. Wayne of the Georgia Militia. "He was arrayed in a brilliant uniform, and had his staff about him in fine style," said Weller. But all the soldiers he had were some boy cadets and convicts from a penitentiary. For two days Thompson helped Wayne hold the bridge before the federal pressure became too forceful for them. Elsewhere on the Oconee Lewis, too, was pressed by the enemy, and he too had to fall back, but not before the gallant Virginius Hutchen, after taking a wound and being billeted in a nearby house, evaded capture for several days in a row when the Federals visited that very house. He finally escaped to rejoin the brigade. Surely there could be no question that this Orphan more than redeemed himself for his little personal mutiny so long before.[6]

By early December Lewis and his brigade headquartered near Waynesborough, ninety miles north of Savannah, still picketing roads and bridges along Sherman's route of advance. "I think, with my brigade in its present disposition, that I can hold the enemy in check for some time," he reported to Major General Joseph Wheeler, commanding Confederate cavalry in Georgia. But, of course, the enemy was too strong. It was the same story everywhere in Georgia now. Lewis numbered only 590 effectives mounted, and that included a small Georgia regiment briefly operating with him. Then on December 15, 165 of his brigade were called into the defenses of Savannah to help prepare it against Sherman. Even in its depleted condition this almost legendary brigade figured in high Confederate planning. Hood was moving into Tennessee again, toward Nashville, and hoping as always to push into Kentucky to rally that state's mythical support for the Confederacy. But to do so, he said, "It is very important that the two Kentucky brigades, of Lewis and Williams, should be sent to this army." They were not sent, of course, and rightly so, yet the southern people—like Hood —somehow believed that their presence would have made a difference. When Hood suffered disastrous defeat in battles at Franklin and Nashville, the Confederate press emphasized that the Orphans had not been in the battle. "Had the Kentucky Brigade been there," said a Mobile paper, "all would have been safe."[7]

Savannah was the most beautiful city in Georgia, but now a frightened, panicked place. Yet Hardee commanded here. "We have seen a great deal of service with him & the men all admire him," said Johnny Green. No man could save Savannah or the South from Sherman, however, though the citizens of the city were glad to see the Orphans. By December 22 there was nothing more Hardee and his few defenders could do against the advancing host. Already Lewis had sent the Kentuckians' horses across the Savannah River into South Carolina for safety, and that night the Orphans joined the rest of the little Army in abandoning the city as they, too, crossed over the river. The next day they reached their horses at Hardeeville. And Sherman had reached the sea.

Two days later came Christmas. "Peace on Earth, Good will to men should prevail," wrote Green. "We certainly would preserve the peace if they would go home & let us alone." Glad tidings came that day just the same, for the brigade commissary for the first time in several weeks issued soap to the men. Despite the cold water, the Orphans swam and bathed in the Savannah River, then did what they could for a holiday dinner. It was not much. Rice for everyone, a few sweet potatoes for some, and pork for a few. It rained all evening. And something sad happened, or more to the point, did not happen. For the first time in the war, the phantom scribe of Company C, 4th Kentucky Infantry, failed to make his Christmas entry in the company clothing book. The conclusion is inescapable that somewhere between this holiday and the last he gave his blood and body to the soil of Georgia.[8]

Around Christmas Hiram Hawkins and his band finally rejoined Lewis after more than a month of dangerous independent duty. Back on September 22, while the brigade was mounting, Hawkins found romance out of war and married a young Alabama girl. There was precious little honeymoon, though, and now the colonel and his 5th Kentucky had more on their minds than wives and sweethearts. In attempting to rejoin the brigade, Hawkins brought his command within five miles of Savannah, only to find no way through the besieging Federals. Instead, he led his men over forty miles south of the city, through Hinesville, to the Attamaha River. Hawkins spread his few men at several points along the way to intercept and harass enemy foragers. Sherman's "bummers" were acquiring a terrible reputation for destruction and looting of private property, a reputation more imaginary than true thanks to southern exaggerations, but Hawkins set out to protect the people from the less gentlemanly Federals where possible. Orphan justice could be swift. When the Kentuckians encountered an old man and his two daughters, much distressed after a squad of the enemy reportedly attempted to assault the girls, the Confederates tore down the road after them. The Orphans caught two of the would-be offenders before long and promptly hanged them.

Sometimes, too, these Kentuckians in their chivalrous bluster challenged Federals to a sort of individual combat. Booker Reed, riding along a rail line, found a bluecoat firing at him from behind a tree. "Finally Booker got tired and mad and challenged him to come out on the railroad track for a square duel." As they took their positions, about thirty yards apart, the Yankee sent three bullets at Reed before he was ready to start. Up he threw his Enfield and with one shot laid the enemy to rest. He later reported finding five thousand dollars' worth of diamonds on the dead Federal, proceeds of a raid on a nearby mansion.

Often as not Hawkins' men spent their nights in swamps lying in wait for their enemy. The men found it unpleasant duty, hearing the sullen plops of amphibians and reptiles dropping into the water around them, and the owls hooting overhead. "More than once a thrill of terror nearly chilled my blood as a wild, weird scream reached my ears from a perch almost within reach of my gun-barrel," wrote Tom

Owens. He thought the sound of enemy shells and bullets music compared to the noises of these birds of ill omen. One night Owens was ready to panic from the macabre sounds of the night. Then he heard a step at the other end of the bridge he guarded. "The blood stood still in my veins, the hair on my head lifted the little military cap I wore from his resting place." Then he heard the step again and fought back the urge to turn and run. He pointed his rifle and shouted, "Who comes there?" Out of the darkness "in the familiar lingo of the southern darkey" came the reply, "Nigger Jim, sir, nigger Jim." Owens had to laugh at himself over his fears and "the midnight phantoms my imagination had conjured." Thereafter he rather enjoyed the hooting of the owls.

These Georgians loved Hawkins and the other Orphans for their services. Some tried to protect them. When the Kentuckians passed through a little town and a mysterious man came shortly afterward, wearing a suspicious blue coat, the civilians eyed him warily. He asked one old son of Ireland if the Kentucky brigade had passed. The elder puffed his pipe, looked at the blue coat, and finally his wife spoke. "Yis, sir," came her brogue, "they have jist been afther marching through, and there was *twinty thousand* o' them if there was a single mon!" The man in blue thanked her and tipped his hat before continuing on his way. Then the old Irishman, thinking the deception incomplete, yelled after him, "Yis, sir, that's ivery word the truth, it is. *And they were domned big min at that!*" As for some of the more genteel ladies of the area, "the coming of Colonel Hawkins," wrote one, "was like that of an angel of mercy and peace." Two months later friends would recommend Hawkins for promotion to brigadier but, like most of the Kentucky colonels, he did not win the coveted rank.[9]

Late in December Wheeler ordered Lewis to recross the Savannah River and report to Iverson once more. Inevitably Sherman would start to move north from Savannah into the Carolinas, and it would be their task to badger his rear as he marched. Another army was already ahead of him, the remnant of Hood's command, now once more led by Joseph E. Johnston. Somehow they must stop Sherman from linking with Grant, now besieging Lee in Petersburg. To that end, the cavalrymen under Iverson needed a little time to refit and reorganize.

Lewis still had only about two thirds of his Orphans mounted. It took from September 1864 until late January 1865 to get horses for most of the 9th Kentucky, and even at that about 200 Kentuckians still constituted the "dismounted" detachment. In cases where officers or men owned their own mounts, they were not issued a government animal, and of course those who could not ride horses were not given them. Iverson did what he could to find additional mounts, and at the same time temporarily combined Lewis' brigade with the Kentucky cavalry command of Colonel W. C. P. Breckinridge. These were men who had ridden with Morgan in the glory days, and Breckinridge's brigade distinguished itself in the Atlanta campaign. But now it, too, like Lewis, was so depleted that it could hardly be called an effective fighting force. Lewis commanded the new organization, aggregating 1,066 men ready for duty on February 10, but the Orphans never really considered Breckinridge's cavalrymen truly a part of the 1st Kentucky Brigade. It was simply too rarefied a fraternity for easy admission.

Discipline among the Kentuckians now was perhaps the worst in its history. Lewis, despite his stern start when he replaced Helm, could not or would not enforce it as in the old days. After Chickamauga he never wrote a battle report as he should have, and even showed an indifference in his personal dress that would have been uncharacteristic in earlier days. Only when prominent officers or pretty ladies visited did he wear his uniform coat, and on at least one occasion he entertained some Georgia belles for two hours before realizing he had forgotten to put it on. Much more serious was the state of the brigade. When the War Department sent an inspector to examine the cavalry in Georgia, he was appalled at what he found. "The Kentucky troops," he reported, "have been neglected since mounted." Almost all of the staff departments worked indifferently, or not at all. Proper reports and descriptive lists of the brigade animals did not exist. General orders from Army headquarters were frequently not promulgated among the regiments. "Their appearance, mounted and dismounted, is indifferent. Discipline is lax." The men looked military in bearing but paid little attention at parade, and needed much practice at cavalry tactics. The once-champion drill regiments of the Army of Tennessee now showed no enthusiasm and little skill at their evolutions. The war had taken the glitter from their buttons, the glory from the march, and almost worn them out. Yet the inspector could still report an unusually high élan for this late twilight of the war. "It is gratifying to report that there are but few absentees without leave from this brigade," he said. However the Orphans might let their deportment relax, their spirit never seemed to falter. On February 11, 1865, they gathered to form and approve resolutions condemning all who spoke of submission and defeat, all who withheld from the Confederacy any scrap of aid or comfort. They sent their resolutions to the local and Virginia papers for publication. "Our services, our sacrifices," they said, "give us the right to speak; we accept no excuse for relaxing effort to conquer a peace and establish independence; we are exiles from our homes and those who are nearest and dearest to us, but we are not willing to return upon terms now proposed; we believe the minie-rifle is our best peace commissioner; we suggest that disloyal editors be placed beside true men in the ranks, where they can be taught, with Enfields in their hands, how a Government should be supported; we reassert our devotion."[10]

They also never faltered in the hope of redeeming Kentucky. Now that most of the Orphans were mounted, Lewis began sending them singly and in pairs along the long road through Augusta, into western North Carolina, and through Cumberland Gap to recruit in their homeland. These were the first Orphans to return home since they left Bowling Green so many years before. Few of them returned to the brigade. Several were captured, the end of the war caught more before they could return, and some the Federals and Home Guard murdered. Lieutenant Jerry Smith of Hawkins' 5th Kentucky ran into some bluecoats, took a wound, and recuperated at a home in Kentucky only to have a party of Home Guards find him out and shoot him in his sickbed. Captain William Lashbrook of Company I, 4th Kentucky, was within a day's ride of his home when Unionists ambushed him on the road. A gallant captain who had survived every battle of his brigade, he fell to the guns of his own fellow Kentuckians.[11]

Yet the Orphans could still refer to themselves, as Virginius Hutchen now did, as the "Cheerful Brigade." Some thought it was because they were mostly young men. Some said it was because they were unmarried. But Ed Thompson knew it was simply because "they were *Kentuckians.*" They still sang their songs, played their games and pranks, bedeviled the Georgia Militia and those commands who seemed to lose heart, told tall stories, and generally "made gawkish youth and credulous old men believe that nothing else in earth or atmosphere or sea was like things up in Kentucky." They read everything in sight. Pat Fitzgerald of the 2d Kentucky carried a small library in his knapsack, as did Johnny Jackman. On picket duty, the former was often seen putting his astronomical reading to the test by setting sticks in the ground to measure time by the sun's shadow, since he had no watch. Still they made joke of death. A soldier always took off his good shirt and replaced it with a tattered one before going to the front. "I'm not going to let the Yankees shoot my new shirt!" he declared.

Lieutenant Colonel Andy Hynes kept an old black named Jacob as his cook and barber, and the slave cut hair for all the men of the 4th Kentucky. Talkative in the manner of barbers in all times, he always finished his tonsorial performance by relating the bad fortune that invariably befell those who did not pay for their haircuts promptly. Almost without exception they died in their very next battle, but his cash customers always survived. Good old Jacob encountered very little difficulty with bad debts. And while he cut hair, the glee club commenced once more its tuneful ministrations to the brigade. They found more receptive civilian audiences here than ever before. "How we dined and supped with the good people," exclaimed second bass John Weller. The merry wags of the 4th Kentucky, "Wild Bill" and "Devil Dick" and "Nondescript" and all of the others by real name or sobriquet, kept their spirit intact.

It helped that while Lewis and the Orphans camped for refitting near Mill Haven, Georgia, many old friends returned to their ranks. Indomitable John Mahon, wounded in every battle, came back to finish the war with his brigade. He could not know it yet, but happily he had bled his last for the cause. Here, too, Lewis brought in the dismounted detachment. Just as the sun set on February 1, 1865, they came into camp, a recovered Johnny Jackman among them. "Was glad to see the boys," he wrote in his diary. It had been 7½ months since his wound at Pine Mountain. "They like the cavalry very much," he discovered. That night, in honor of the prodigals' return, the Orphans made another attack on the poor Georgia Militia. Throwing blazing pine cones before them, they drove the "milish" out of their camps and sacked their belongings. "The battle lasted for some time, and presented a beautiful sight. At times the air would be full of the blazing missiles."

Camp life was a specialty of the Kentucky brigade; they always made the best of it. When their commissary issued molasses, the Orphan organized taffy-pulling parties, as if at home with their children and sweethearts. The concerts continued, and so did the parties given the Orphans by the neighboring civilians. The more loquacious of the brigade made speeches around the campfires. Booker Reed sang "Kitty Wells" and "The Vacant Chair" after supper of an evening. The men acted the tourist, seeing local landmarks, and often places like county courthouses visited by Sherman before them. Jackman read. Green foraged and cooked with his usual flair. And Ed Porter Thompson began the collection of sources for his history of these nobles of the Orphan Brigade.[12]

The war interrupted Thompson's work. Following Sherman's move up the coast through South Carolina, Wheeler ordered General P. M. B. Young to take command of Iverson's division and follow the advancing Union Army. Sherman had taken and sacked Columbia, South Carolina, on February 17, and four days later Young ordered Lewis to ride toward the ruined city. The movement began in tragedy when Conrad Bills of the 2d Kentucky fell from his horse while crossing the Savannah and drowned. T. H. Ellis of the 9th Kentucky led a detail of his regiment in advance of the brigade some days before. After several days' ride they finally came within a few miles of Columbia, and could see the columns of smoke still rising from the burned city. When they crossed the Congaree River and entered the ruined streets, Ellis and his little band of Orphans saw for the first time the sort of desolation that this war could inflict. Ellis looked about and gathered what information he could about Sherman and his movements, then recrossed the river to look for food. He had heard that some of the blacks were hiding beans under their bedding. One of the men with him happened to be Flying Cloud, "who was eyed and shunned by the negroes." He told the sachem to approach a black in his fiercest aspect, give several war whoops, and yell "Beans!" The women and children scattered in fear, and the men rolled over their beds and brought forth the bags of beans. "Here, here, boss," they said. Flying Cloud, or "Cloud," as the Orphans called him, reassured the slaves. "Me no hurt you," he said. "Cook beans quick."[13]

That worked fine for Ellis' little band, but Young found the area too devastated to support forage for his horses and men. Shortly the Kentucky brigade retraced its steps, crossed the Savannah yet again, and made camp a few miles north of Augusta. Here the main body of the brigade remained for several weeks, anticipating an enemy raid that never came. While here some of the Kentuckians went into Augusta for the little society that remained, and Jackman at least found a lady friend, though he maintained a proper discretion in telling his diary just how the romance progressed. Indeed, here on March 19 he finally filled the last page of his old journal made of damaged quartermaster blanks, and then his diary ceased.

While most of the Orphans remained in their camps, and while Fayette Hewitt's friends teased him that he might be serving on some general's staff rather than serving with this ragged cavalry, to which he replied, "I would rather be a captain among these men, sir, than to be general of any other brigade in the army," Caldwell's turn for an expedition arose. General Young wanted Lewis to send a regiment to Sumter, South Carolina, one hundred miles east, to determine if Sherman's hordes were moving inland toward the valuable rail stock there. "Old Joe" sent Caldwell and the 9th Kentucky on March 29. The colonel, knowing he would find nothing to sustain men and horses, carried all the regiment's edible necessities with him. The whole sortie was a great trial. The ferry boats at the Santee had been sunk by the enemy, and it took Caldwell two days to raise and repair them. Once across he found intelligence that federal Brigadier General Edward Potter was even then en route to Sumter to destroy the rolling stock that Caldwell was to protect. Caldwell force-marched his regiment forty miles in order to reach the objective first.

What he found in Sumter were two hundred militia and two old iron cannon. Caldwell placed the militia in front of the city and behind a flooded bottom land, while he sent the 9th Kentucky to ride around Potter's flank with the intent of destroying the enemy's baggage train. Hopefully this would cause Potter to divide his force. At about 3 P.M. on April 8, Potter appeared in the Confederate front and three times attempted to advance on the flooded bottom-land road. Each time Caldwell repulsed him. Then the bluecoats opened with their artillery, soon silencing the two Confederate guns and driving the untrained militia into near panic. This left Caldwell no choice but to withdraw into the city, send off all the rolling stock he could save, and then take his regiment north on the road to Camden to try to slow Potter's advance toward that place.

Caldwell continued to skirmish with Potter for several days, meanwhile dispatching word of the Federals' presence to Lewis. The intrepid colonel faced perhaps 4,000 Federals with less than 200 Kentuckians, but still slowed his advance sufficiently for Lewis to reach Camden first. He brought the brigade by way of Columbia, and shortly afterward the dismounted contingent followed. "Did the mounted Kentuckians pass through here?" asked a horseless Orphan. "Yes," said a citizen, and another added, "They were the only *gentlemen* who have passed through here since the war began." The citizens showed a high regard for the Kentucky brigade and its general, asserting to passersby that at Camden it was Lewis and his men "who are doing the fighting, and they'll stick to it as long as they can find a foe to shoot at!"[14]

Lewis found about 300 militia manning works a few miles south of Camden, and at once assumed command, putting his Kentuckians into line with them. It was April 14, 1865. Scouts reported that Potter was retiring in their front, and so Lewis took his mounted men forward. That afternoon he met the federal rear guard and skirmished with it until nightfall. That evening Caldwell finally rejoined the brigade. There had been few casualties that day, the worst probably being poor Eli Lonaker of the 6th Kentucky, who accidentally killed himself with his own rifle. The Orphans could not know that another Kentuckian was dying that night hundreds of miles north of them. Abraham Lincoln had been to the theater. He never saw the end of the play.

The next morning Potter turned and advanced against Lewis. The Confederates were too few, their line too short, and steadily the enemy pushed them back toward Camden. Lewis sent Phil Lee and the 2d Kentucky on a raid to stop a flank march by some enemy cavalry, and in this the ever-ebullient Lee proved successful. He set a perfect ambush for the bluecoated horsemen, killing several and driving back the remainder. It put him in a good humor for the return to the brigade. On the way back, he passed through a hamlet and saw an old black man whom he asked, "Say, uncle, are there any Huguenots about here?"

"Well, I declare, where be you ones from?" asked the black.

"From way up in old Kentucky."

"Well, I thought so," said the old slave. "Why, in Tennessee they call 'em peanuts, in Georgia they goes by the name of goobers, in Alabama they is penders, here in South Carolina we call 'em ground peas, now you fellows way off dar in Kentucky call 'em hugonuts. Well I do declare."

Lewis did his best to fortify Camden and protect the railroad cars stored there, as well as locomotives and some considerable government supplies. He sent the militia to do the work while he tried to retard Potter's progress, but by April 18 "Old Joe" and his Orphans were driven into the town's defenses. And when he saw that Potter intended to envelop his flanks instead of attacking, Lewis knew he had no alternative but to destroy whatever he could not take with him and abandon the city. The skirmishing continued while the work of arson commenced, and here in South Carolina, so far from home, the last Orphan died in battle. A scout of ten men felt Potter's movements and rode accidentally into a squad or more of Federals. Pius Pulliam of the 2d Kentucky was in the lead, and almost at once he took a severe wound. A. T. Pullen of the same regiment felt thirteen bullets tear at his clothes, but not one touched him. He wheeled his horse and raced for the rear, but at once saw John Miller of his regiment standing on the ground beside his horse. Asked if he was hurt, Miller said not, but seemed disoriented. Pullen helped him to mount, put the reins in his hand, and then turned to continue the retreat. When he looked back, however, he saw Miller riding straight toward the enemy. Upon later reflection, Pullen believed that Miller had already taken a death wound and, almost unconscious, had no idea what he was about. Yet perhaps, just perhaps, Miller, in his delirium, knew what he was doing. Nothing could be more appropriate than that John Miller of the 2d Kentucky Infantry, the last Orphan to die in battle, should do so facing the enemy.

Lewis, too, faced the enemy for the next two days, joined now by Young. On April 21 Young formed Lewis and another brigade for an attack on Potter. Behind the line as they formed, the Orphans saw grave diggers at their work preparing a hole for a recently fallen South Carolinian. Ahead of them they heard Potter's axes felling trees for breastworks. Young rode along the line ordering out the skirmishers, and promising, "Boys, bring in the prisoners, and I will give you the furloughs." They cheered him, but Emory Speer of Hawkins' Company K saw that "the veterans around me seemed hopeless." The men in the ranks realized, he thought, that by now the Confederacy had lost everything, and that their continuing resistance was only a charade. Yet, when Young gave the order to advance, forward they went with all the old verve. It was the last charge of the Orphan Brigade.

After a few yards the enemy artillery sent solid shot toward the Kentucky line. Speer saw one cannon ball bounce along the ground like a child's toy straight toward his company. It struck a man on his right, but not killing him. Soon thereafter the brigade skirmishers accidentally fired on another of Young's brigades, and there was "much angry and some profane expostulation on their part." This last advance was not well managed. The Orphans and other Confederates knew how heavily the enemy outnumbered them. Already there were rumors of the collapse of other southern armies. Everyone seemed confused.

Yet on the Orphans moved. Suddenly there came an order to halt. Johnny Green believed that a bugle sounded retreat. Some said they saw a white truce flag pass from Potter's lines to Young. Whatever happened, General Young soon rode to Lewis and handed him a dispatch from Joseph E. Johnston. In it "Old Joe" read that General Robert E. Lee had surrendered the Army of Northern Virginia to the Orphans' old foe, U. S. Grant, at Appomattox on April 9. Further, on April 18 another old enemy, Sherman, finally compelled Johnston to sign an armistice. All troops under Johnston's command, including Young's division, were to be surrendered. The war was over. Lewis' eyes filled with tears as he finished reading the order. In a voice quavering with emotion, he cried, *"All is lost!"* Then he turned to order his brigade to retire. They had fought their last.[15]

"The saddest hours that ever fell on human hearts were the first few of that evening," said John Weller. Some could not believe it. Many who did wanted to get drunk. "I would like to go out in the woods & die drunk," said Bill Fox of the 9th, "& bury all my sorrows." For Johnny Green "This was the blackest day of our lives." He saw gloom on every face. "All was lost & there seemed to be no hope for the future."

Young informed Potter of the armistice—for the Federals did not know of it—and then withdrew his command to Augusta once more. There, on May 2, he issued a final address to the men and officers of the 1st Kentucky Brigade. Johnston had surrendered them, he said, "the last hope of success has vanished." He advised them to accept the result, to take Sherman's generous terms of parole, to go home and accept the laws of the United States once more and abide by them. "Let me thank you, my brave men," he concluded, "for your suffering and your fortitude in the camp and your gallantry on the field of battle."

Orders called for the Orphans to proceed to Washington, Georgia, to surrender their arms and take their paroles. It was not far, just fifty miles northwest of Augusta, and Lewis sent notification that he would have the brigade there by May 6 to Major General James Wilson, commanding Sherman's cavalry. Lewis asked that Wilson have an officer there on that date to receive his arms and parole the men. By doing so, Lewis almost unwittingly betrayed the Orphan Brigade's oldest and dearest friend.[16]

There were a number of Kentuckians in Washington already, men of the unmounted detachment. When Young ordered the men without horses to join him in South Carolina in April, Johnny Jackman and another man of the 9th Kentucky were too unwell to make the march. Instead, Fayette Hewitt detailed the two to take charge of all the brigade archives, over twenty volumes of record books, morning reports, letter-copy books, and the like, as well as thousands of individual orders and reports. They were to conduct the archives to Washington and there await further orders. Jackman and his friend carefully boxed the mass of documents and on April 17 boarded a train to make the circuitous journey to Washington. Along the way they traveled briefly with General Hood. "He must have known of Lee's surrender," thought Jackman, "for he looked very 'blue.' "

On the afternoon of April 19 they reached their destination, and went at once to the building where Captain Bosche and his detail were still making saddles for the brigade. There they stored their precious cargo, and Jackman, perhaps sensing the importance now of historic documents, took time to revise and recopy his old journal. Shortly Lee's paroled men started passing through the town on their way home, and Jackman knew that the worst had happened. Then came word of Johnston's surrender. "We knew then," he told his diary, "that we had 'gone up.' " Soon Johnston's men, too, marched through, many of them rampaging and looting the quartermaster supplies stored in Washington's warehouses.

On May 3 Jackman saw President Jefferson Davis pass through Washington, escorted by some old friends, Basil Duke, and part of the 2d Kentucky Cavalry. Davis and his Cabinet, following the fall of Richmond the month before, fled South, taking the government with them. Now, with his two major armies surrendered, Davis hoped to reach the Trans-Mississippi Department and the last small Confederate armies under E. Kirby Smith and Richard Taylor. He wore a broad-brimmed felt hat, black crepe encircling the crown, and a plain gray military-style coat. He looked to Jackman a sad figure, symbolic of the collapse of the South. In a week Jefferson Davis would be a federal prisoner.

The next day another familiar face appeared, this one a visage that any Orphan associated with ill omen and bad news. Braxton Bragg arrived in the morning to join the President, and together they rode out of town. Here Davis separated from his Cabinet, leaving them to go their separate ways. The government had dissolved, most of his ministers losing heart, realizing as Davis could not that all was truly lost.

Yet this afternoon there was one, and only one, member of the Confederate Government still functioning, and when he rode into Washington, Georgia, the war came full circle for Jackman and the other Kentuckians there to greet him. Here was the Confederate Secretary of War, the man who oversaw the evacuation of Richmond, who guided the flight of the Cabinet, who strove constantly to persuade Davis to accept an honorable surrender rather than ignoble dissolution into guerrilla warfare, and who advised Johnston in his surrender negotiations with Sherman: Major General John C. Breckinridge.

It had been a full war for Breckinridge after he left the Orphan Brigade at Dalton more than a year before. The department he commanded in southwestern Virginia was no plum. Understrength and overextended, his forces had to contend with one federal raid after another, yet did so successfully on every occasion but one. When a federal army threatened the Shenandoah Valley and the vulnerable left flank of Lee, then facing Grant at Spotsylvania, Breckinridge marched his scratch force to New Market and defeated a numerically stronger foe in a set-piece battle that captured the hearts and imagination of the South. It would remain for years the best-known engagement of its size in the war. Then he joined Lee in his operations for a time, repulsing his old foe Grant's terrible attacks at Cold Harbor in June, and being himself injured when his horse was killed under him. Yet, when another enemy threat appeared in the Shenandoah, he went on his sick litter to organize the defense of Lynchburg, then took command of a corps in General Jubal Early's Army in its raid on Washington, D.C. There, in July, Breckinridge came within sight of the capitol dome where once he sat as Vice President.

There followed the engagements in the Shenandoah where Early tried to stop the ravages of Philip Sheridan to no avail, and then Breckinridge returned to his old department. In February 1865, in response to widespread dissatisfaction with war policy, President Davis made two important changes: He appointed Lee general-in-chief of all Confederate armies, and he offered Breckinridge the portfolio as

Secretary of War. Despite the calumnies of Bragg, the Kentuckian was one of the most popular generals in the South, and he had political and executive qualifications exceeding even those of Davis himself. The move met with universal approval, and some in the Confederacy took heart. "Breckenridge has been made Sec of War," wrote a North Carolinian. "He has always been successful & *'prestige'* is a great element in military affairs. Napoleon believed in *Luck* & Breckenridge is not only able but *lucky.*"

But Breckinridge knew that luck would not be enough in his new post. Indeed, what he saw when he assessed War Department affairs in his first week in office only confirmed what he predicted nearly four years before. The Confederacy was doomed. Consequently, almost from the date of taking office, he made his goal a peaceful and honorable end for the dying nation. It was a great task, for Davis no longer thought with reason in the matter, wishing to fight to the last extremity. Slowly and diplomatically the secretary persuaded the President, but it was only the day before Davis reached Washington that he finally gave in to Breckinridge's arguments. And while he worked to see the Confederacy to a fitting end, the secretary also kept his beloved Kentuckians at the front of his mind. Shortly before the evacuation of Richmond, he called together congressmen from Missouri and Kentucky to discuss the welfare of soldiers from those states when the South fell. If the armies simply disbanded without formal surrender, soldiers from the cotton states would be able to go to their homes and remain probably unmolested. But Missourians and Kentuckians, whose home states were well within federal lines, would be denied that opportunity. They would be orphaned yet again, and if they did manage to get home without a surrender and formal parole, the reception awaiting them in their states might be hostile.

"Our first duty, gentlemen, is to the soldiers who have been influenced by our arguments and example," he concluded. "What I propose . . . is this: That the Confederacy should not be captured in fragments, that we should not disband like banditti, but that we should surrender as a government, and we will thus maintain the dignity of our cause, and secure the respect of our enemies." He concluded by exclaiming, "This has been a magnificent epic. In God's name let it not terminate in a farce."

That it did not end in farce is largely due to Breckinridge's efforts, and with Johnston formally surrendering and paroling his men, the

Orphans included, the Kentuckians would be able to return to their homes without fear of prosecution or proscription. Now Breckenridge, too, hoped to reach the Trans-Mississippi, not, like Davis, wishing to continue the struggle there, but rather to guide Kirby Smith in obtaining for his forces an honorable surrender. Some of the Orphans here in Washington took heart when they saw their old father. They believed he would lead them to the west to continue the fight. But Breckinridge came only to oversee their surrender, and try to aid in Davis' escape from the enemy.

Here, on May 4, 1865, Breckinridge formally disbanded the War Department. Fittingly, the majority of the troops here to witness the demise of the Confederacy were his old Kentuckians, men never formally citizens of that dying nation, who yet gave their all for it. The Confederate States of America never really adopted the Orphan Brigade. They adopted it. And in that irony so dearly beloved of history, Breckinridge's last act—the last formal act of the Confederate Government—was to accept the resignation of Second Lieutenant James B. Clay, Jr., a Kentuckian, an unofficial Orphan, and the grandson of that great Kentuckian who strove so long and hard to avert the calamity now entering its last act, Henry Clay.

Breckinridge, too, had to flee, and here is where his old comrade and subordinate Joseph H. Lewis nearly betrayed him. Having been Vice President of the United States before the war, Breckinridge was regarded as the most heinous traitor of all in the North. He and Davis and a handful of others stood under indictment in the Union, and could expect imprisonment at least if captured, and perhaps even execution. This is why he wanted to see Davis safely out of the country and why, after assisting Kirby Smith, he expected to go into foreign exile himself. Yet the Federals followed closely at the fleeing government's heels, and now Lewis' dispatch to Wilson asking for someone to parole him at Washington on May 6 coincidentally brought Breckinridge's would-be captors right to him. He escaped by only a few hours, leaving on the morning of May 5, with an escort of Kentuckians including old Orphans James Wilson and "Cub" Howard, and his own son Cabell. That same afternoon a squadron of federal cavalry rode into Washington. The next day, as Lewis led the rest of the brigade into town, Breckinridge and his escort were only seven miles south, having just encountered another federal patrol. While Colonel Breckinridge and his cavalry faced the enemy and parleyed, the general and a few followers melted into the forest to begin their bid for escape. But out of the woods the Kentuckian sent a last message to his cousin, to Duke, and to all the others it might reach. It was folly to risk the lives of the men any longer, he said. Go home. Go home to Kentucky, to their homes and families. They could do no more for the Confederacy and, much as they wished to, they could do no more for him. "I will not have one of these young men to encounter one hazard more for my sake," he said, then rode off toward oblivion.

It was quite a sight for Jackman and the others when Lewis led the 1st Kentucky Brigade into Washington, Georgia. The Orphans marched down the streets in closed column, flags flying in their tatters, arms at the parade position. The townspeople came to the boardwalks to watch them as if on review. "Steadily they marched," wrote Jackman, "the very horses seeming to vie with the riders in keeping up the military to the last. The Spring breezes gently waved the banners—banners that bore the marks of the contest, and that had the names of many fields written upon their folds—and the evening's sunlight, on the eve of fading from the hills, danced and quivered upon the long trusty Enfields, thus smiling pleasantly upon one of the last scenes of Southern pageantry."

As the Orphans marched through town to their bivouac, the federal 13th Tennessee Cavalry entered from the opposite direction. "It looked strange not to see them commence shooting at each other," said Jackman. Instead, Lewis camped the brigade for the night in a pleasant grove of beech and oak trees. As on any day before in the past four years, the bugles called out for details and duty, and at dark the campfires licked with their flames into the night, the light climbing the tree trunks to glisten among the leaves. The horses munched at their fodder while the men themselves spread out on the ground to talk in low murmurs, smoke their pipes, and walk among the campfires saying farewells to the friends of four years and a hundred fields. Lewis had spoken to the men a few days before, advising them to submit to the Union, though he said that in laying aside the gray uniform, he never expected that he would wear the blue. That was more reconciliation than he could handle. By now the irrepressible spirit of the Orphans had returned, and Phil Lee wandered the camp declaring, "The General speaks of not wearing the *Yankee* uniform. Now, as for Phil Lee, *my* opinion is that henceforth he'll wear *no* uniforms of *any* sort!"

That evening details carried the brigade's arms to Lewis' headquarters, piling them in a heap. Jackman prepared the papers for paroling the 9th Kentucky, and it was done the next morning at 2 A.M. The remainder of the brigade took parole later that morning, May 7. "We 'broke up housekeeping,'" said Jackman, "every fellow being free to wander off, as his inclinations led him, with his horse, saddle, and bridle." Their inclinations led them first to Lewis' tent. There the Orphans bid "Old Joe," their final adopted father, the long farewell. They shook his hand and said their good-byes, tears streaking every bronzed face. They would see each other again in happier times, to be sure, but never again as they had known each other for four years, never again as comrades of the "Old Brigade," the "Cheerful Brigade," the 1st Kentucky Brigade. They were going back to their homes, and the Orphan Brigade would be no more.[17]

THIRTEEN

"A Kind of Title
of Nobility"

FOR MANY the journey home seemed as long as their wanderings of the war, and for some it proved longer than they might ever have imagined. The Federals gave them their horses, and before Breckinridge left Washington he disbursed the remainder of the Confederate Treasury to the men there, about $2.50 per man. It was not much for the journey, but their former enemies did make things easier by offering free rail transportation to Kentucky for those who took the oath of allegiance. Lewis himself went immediately to Nashville and gave his oath, yet encountered over a month's delay before his pleas to be allowed to go home to Kentucky and his family met reward.

Johnny Jackman went to Augusta two days after parole, and there the bulk of the old 9th Kentucky gathered a few days later. At first they thought of going down the Savannah River to Savannah, and there taking a steamer to New Orleans and up the Mississippi and Ohio to Louisville. But that proved too ambitious. Instead they boarded a train for Atlanta. Jackman fell ill again and had to separate from his friends to spend several days recuperating with a friend near Greensburg. He fished and walked and rested until able to join three other passing Orphans late in May. They went on to Atlanta, found the railroad from there to Chattanooga out of operation, and bargained with a federal wagonmaster to take them to Chattanooga. They left the wagon when they reached Dalton, and there, where the old brigade passed that long winter of 1864, Jackman camped out on the ground for the last time. The next morning they boarded a train and reached Chattanooga. They stayed the night at a boardinghouse where "Yank" and "Confed" ate from the same platter and cracked jokes at each other, "as though they had never met in many a mortal combat." Two days later, May 29, found them in Nashville, and that evening the federal provost notified them that they could not proceed farther without taking the oath. "We were 'galvanized,'" as Jackman put it, and then boarded a train for Louisville. At 7 P.M. that night he got off at Bardstown Junction and, rather than wait for a train home the next morning, immediately started walking toward Bardstown. At 10 A.M. the next morning, May 30, 1865, John S. Jackman walked up the steps of his home for the first time in three years, eight months, and four days. Another Orphan was home.

And slowly they all came home. Johnny Green, momentarily bitter that the war ended before he could become a commissioned officer, threw away his sergeant major's sword and then rode toward Alabama with a couple of friends. All along the way he met with kindness and hospitality from the people of the defunct Confederacy. What little they had they shared with the brave men who so long had battled for their independence. Whenever he offered to pay for food or lodging, his benefactors declined. "This is all we can do for them & they certainly are welcome to it." Finally Green reached friends in Florence, Alabama, just in time to help them defend their property against the bands of renegade Federals and Confederates who preyed upon the rural South for months after the surrender, looting and robbing.

After some weeks, Green finally took himself to Nashville, too, and there learned that he would be denied passage to Kentucky unless he gave his oath. That he would not do. He found a steamboat captain who would hide him aboard his vessel. "Pay your passage & keep your mouth shut & you can travel on my boat without taking the oath," said he. This Johnny Green did, and the next day he left the boat at Henderson, Kentucky, and rejoined his father, an Orphan no more.[1]

By midsummer 1865 most of the Kentuckians were home again, or at least those who wished to be. What they found in their beloved old Kentucky seemed fully to justify the anguish they had felt for the state during all those years in exile, for the Bluegrass suffered as few other places in the country during its occupation by federal forces. Trade and industry were much retarded. Agriculture suffered terribly. The Emancipation Proclamation enraged slaveholding Kentuckians, and the passage of the Thirteenth Amendment that coming December would free over 200,000 slaves, wiping out a capital investment of at least $115,000,000. Kentuckians, though never formally in rebellion, were treated by occupying authorities with a rigid military rule. As always, they felt different from other Americans and entitled to different treatment. Instead the Lincoln administration dealt with them as felons. Add to this the unhappy fact that the Union command frequently assigned its most brutal and incompetent officers to serve in the commonwealth, and a high degree of civil unrest became inevitable. Guerrillas and irregulars roamed the mountains preying upon people of both Union and southern sentiment. Free elections were inhibited, and group and individual violence plagued the state for years. It would be said later that Kentucky waited until after the war to secede, and there is some truth in the statement. The bitterness engendered by the war in this state, where friends and families divided against each other, did not dim until long after many of the actual Confederate states had returned to relative tranquillity.

The returning Orphans coped with the change in their homeland in varying ways. Gervis Grainger, released from prison, took the direct route to vengeance by attempting to assassinate General Stephen G. Burbridge, perhaps the most hated Federal of all in the state. Friends prevented him from succeeding in his design, but Burbridge later left the state for his own safety. Others took more lawful means of reconstructing themselves and their state. That December the legislature removed all indictments against Kentuckians who served the South, and quickly the men of the Orphan Brigade became the *crème* of state society and government. Indeed, Kentucky very quickly passed into the hands of ex-Confederates, and remained there for years even while some of the actual Confederate states were ruled by transplanted Yankees. In time, the 1st Kentucky Brigade's ranks provided the state with a governor, three Cabinet members, six militia leaders, two Supreme Court justices, superintendents of public instruction, United States district attorneys, auditors, Treasury officials, four congressmen, two foreign consuls, five circuit judges, untold county legal officials and judges, three commonwealth's attorneys, a mayor for Louisville and several lesser municipalities, many state legislators, county, district, and municipal officers beyond counting, and one nominee for Vice President of the United States. Nowhere else in the reunited nation did the veterans of a single military body of men so virtually control the destiny of a state in the years after Appomattox.[2]

The individual Orphans themselves met varying fates. "Old Joe" Lewis returned to his law practice in Glasgow, then spent a term in the state legislature and three terms in Congress. In 1880 he took a seat on the Kentucky Court of Appeals, and the next year succeeded Martin Cofer as chief justice. There he served for eighteen years before retiring. To the last of his days, on July 6, 1904, he remained ever loyal to the men and memory of his old brigade, an active supporter and participant in veteran affairs.

Simon B. Buckner, too, retained a devotion to the Orphans' memory that only died with his own passing. He took the editorship of the Louisville *Courier* for a time after the war, then entered politics. In 1887 he won the governorship, and in 1896 a faction of the Democratic Party nominated him for Vice President. Ironically his running mate, John M. Palmer, was also a Kentuckian, a one-time federal general who commanded a division that besieged the Orphans at Corinth and battled them in the great charge at Murfreesboro. They ran a poor third in the ballot, but achieved a grand gesture of reconciliation. Buckner himself lived on until January 8, 1914, when he had outlived every other Confederate general of his rank.

Of the regimental commanders from the old brigade who survived the war, all were lionized in the years following the conflict. Lighthearted Phil Lee of the 2d Kentucky returned to the law, married, and won a position as commonwealth's attorney for Louisville in 1868, but his untimely death at age forty-two cut short his promising career. Tom Thompson, last commander of the 4th Kentucky, fared little better. He, too, won political office, clerk of the chancery court when he, like Lee, died early, at the same age. Hiram Hawkins broke the pattern, fortunately. He settled in Alabama with his new wife, became a college president, served two terms in the legislature, and for ten years thereafter acted as executive officer of the National Grange organization. Cofer of the 6th Kentucky went back to the law as well, took a judgeship on the circuit court at Elizabethtown, Kentucky, and died in 1881 while chief justice of the Court of Appeals. And Colonel John Caldwell of the 9th Kentucky also became a judge, of the Logan County Court, then won a seat in Congress. Twice his constituents returned him to Washington, and then he retired to Russellville, where on Independence Day, 1903, he joined in death those comrades he led on the battlefields of the South.

Jolly Cripps Wickliffe, like Jackman, returned to Bardstown and eventually assumed a circuit judgeship. In 1885 President Grover Cleveland appointed him United States attorney for the District of Kentucky, and eight years later he became brigadier general and adjutant of the state militia. Fayette Hewitt took the quartermaster generalship of the militia in 1867 and at once entered the tender business of recovering from the United States Government the money it owed to the state for Kentucky's expenses in arming and equipping her *Union* soldiers. He held the post successfully for nine years, later served as state auditor, and finally retired as president of the National Bank of Frankfort.

John Weller followed the lead of so many other Orphans by filling an office in the state civil service, but in 1893 the governor appointed him a commissioner to locate the positions occupied by the Kentucky brigade at Chickamauga, preparatory to the dedication of a national park on the site. Later he sat in the state senate, and devoted his declining years to writings historical and poetic. He composed a song, "Oh! Lay Me Away with the Boys in Gray," which became a funeral elegy for countless Orphans as they journeyed to join that final Father. George B. Hodge returned to Newport, Kentucky, at war's end, practiced law, and served in the state legislature, but later removed to Florida, where he died in 1892. Captain Bob Cobb and Frank Gracey both went into business after the war, and General William Preston, after a time in exile in England and Canada, returned to Lexington to finish his days in Democratic politics and die at his home in 1887.

The men in the ranks of the old brigade did not all achieve the positions their officers enjoyed, but they basked nevertheless in the glory of having been members of that unique organization. "I teach my children to honor the men of the Orphan Brigade above all others," said Lycurgus Reid of the 9th Kentucky. "I point them out as we meet them as men on whom the country can depend in time of need." Squire Helm Bush, brother-in-law of Martin Cofer, tried his hand at the law, but suffered to the end of his life with pain from his Chickamauga wound. He lived on until August 13, 1925, sixty-three years after he made the long trip from Louisiana to Murfreesboro. Gervis Grainger spent more than forty years after the war, first in Kentucky, then in Gallatin, Tennessee, a few bare miles from Hartsville on the east, and the now overgrown site of Camp Boone on the west. He stayed bitter against his enemies to the end of his life. John Jackman became a lawyer at the Louisville bar and dabbled at publishing, but he never recovered entirely the health that the war damaged. Elder Joseph D. Pickett took a professorship at the University of Kentucky in Lexington and became superintendent of public instruction in the state before he retired to Illinois.

Another holder of the latter office was Ed Porter Thompson. He wrote widely after the war, young people's texts and mathematics books. He served as state librarian, private secretary to Governor Buckner, and president of the Frankfort Board of Education. His mourners were legion when he died on March 5, 1903. "He could dream," said his eulogists. And the mourners were equally saddened at the loss of Johnny Green of the 9th Kentucky. He became a banker in Louisville, and a successful one, then went into a brokerage firm, staying in that business until 1920. That spring arthritis vengefully attacked his body, and neuritis brought an agony of pain to his head. For two weeks he stood the most intense pain. Then on Sunday morning, June 13, 1920, the telephone in the hall outside his room rang and his wife answered it. While she was out of the room, Johnny rose from his bed, pulled a pistol from a drawer, and put a bullet through his brain. He died two hours later without regaining consciousness.[3]

Ironically, the last of the veterans of the Orphan Brigade to return to Kentucky was the first man to step across the state line in the retreat from Bowling Green. For John C. Breckinridge, his adventures had only begun when he left Washington, Georgia, on May 5, 1865. For the next month he and a small band of followers, including James Wilson, endured a harrowing escape that paled the best Victorian romance by comparison. They rode through Georgia into Florida, sailed and rowed the Indian River on the Atlantic Coast, lived from turtle eggs and inedible slop bartered from local Indians, turned pirate by taking at gunpoint a larger boat from some federal renegades, engaged in a running gun battle between their boat and that of another party of guerrillas intent on robbery and murder, played fox and hounds with enemy patrol boats, and finally made the passage from Florida to Cuba in an eighteen-foot open boat during the worst storm at sea in several years.

After some weeks in Cuba, where he issued a final plea for all Confederates to surrender and accept the clemency of the United States, he journeyed to England, and then on to Canada to join Mary and his family, who awaited him. He lived in Toronto for a time, still concerned with the affairs of the defunct Confederacy, including paying off its legitimate debts and obtaining a good defense for Jefferson Davis in his coming treason trial. In the spring of 1866 he moved his family to Niagara on Lake Ontario. It was a pleasant place, and here he could look across the narrow waters of the Niagara River to New York, Fort Niagara, and flying over it, the Stars and Stripes. It was a comfort to him "with its flag flying to refresh our patriotism." He never wanted to leave that flag. All he wanted now was to return to it, and to Kentucky.

A considerable movement arose, first in the Bluegrass, and then nationwide, to pardon Breckinridge, or at least grant him leave to return home unmolested by the treason indictments. Even old political enemies like the irascible George Prentice called for his pardon, and Horace Greeley began an interest in the general's case. The animosities were still too strong in 1866, however, and that summer Breckinridge took his family to Europe for a year and a half to tour, to recuperate their health, and to wait for time to heal the wounds that kept him from home.

He enjoyed himself abroad, in company with a host of other exiled Confederates, many of them, too, under indictments at home. In time Breckinridge came to be a symbol for all the exiles. As a result, even though friends assured him that they could get him a special dispensation to return, he refused to consider coming home until *all* Confederates were free to return. His became the test case, and the matter finally reached the White House and the Kentuckian's old friend President Andrew Johnson of Tennessee. On Christmas 1868, Johnson finally issued a universal proclamation of amnesty. All Confederates could come home free of fear. Breckinridge had won.

He lost no time in returning. By early February he was back in Niagara, and a few days later crossed the river into New York. He went to New York City, where Greeley and other influential northern men met with and congratulated him. Then to Washington, then to Lexington, Virginia, for a last visit with Robert E. Lee. The two formed a close bond in those last months of the war. Lee regarded the Kentuckian as the best of the Confederacy's War Secretaries, "a lofty, pure strong man," he said—"a great man." Breckinridge went on to Cincinnati for a few days with friends. So many Kentuckians wanted to see their old leader that railroad stations along the routes from Cincinnati to Lexington, Kentucky, thronged with onlookers. Wishing to avoid any demonstrations, Breckinridge gave a false departure time to mislead the well-wishers, and then at dawn of March 9, 1869, he and Mary boarded the train that took them to Lexington. As they passed station after station, some people still knew he was aboard this train, and at several stops they called him out to the rear of his car. He spoke once or twice, quietly, asking their patience. "I am glad to get to my home once more," he told them. "It is nearly eight years since I was here."

It was nighttime when the train finally approached Lexington. Rain threatened. The general sat quiet for several hours watching the familiar old places pass by his window, a thousand memories stirring. A passenger behind him heard Breckinridge repeating softly to himself, "nearly eight years ago, nearly eight years ago." Then he was silent.

Breckinridge might have had any political office the state could give him if he wished. He stood easily the most popular Kentuckian of the era. Yet he was tired. The war he had not wanted had exhausted him, broken his health, and perhaps left him somewhat skeptical of the profession of politics, which had brought on the war. He wished only to practice law and do what he could to rebuild Kentucky and the South. He took the vice presidency of the Elizabethtown, Lexington, and Big Sandy Railroad, overseeing its construction and financial affairs until the Panic of 1873 ceased its operations. He accepted the presidency of the Piedmont and Arlington Life Insurance Company. At every opportunity he counseled patience, moderation, reconciliation. He publicly denounced the Ku Klux Klan as "idiots or banditti." He supported freedmen's rights, including the acceptance of the testimony of blacks in courts. As the Democratic Party in Kentucky split into conservative and liberal wings, he became identified with the latter, more progressive faction. Some believed his opposition was the single greatest factor in putting down the Ku Klux Klan during his lifetime. And no matter how the Republican administrations seemed to ride over the South, he did not lose heart. He and his old foe Grant became friends, Grant even hoping that he might, as President, enable Breckinridge to take a governorship. When friends denounced the party of Lincoln, Breckinridge's reply was, "Let the Republican Party do the worst it can; let the Republicans do fifty times worse than they are doing, and then we shall have the best government any people in the world ever had." Like the Orphans he led over so many fields, he never lost his hope or his faith in his country. It was the very essence of a Kentuckian, and he its quintessential.

The war killed John C. Breckinridge. He never recovered his health after the years of exposure and privation, and the mental anguish of seeing his country sundered and at war with itself. He lasted barely six years after returning to his beloved Lexington. His injury at Cold Harbor brought on a cirrhosis of the liver, and that, aggravated by his exertions in the war, damaged other organs. Death came quietly on May 17, 1875.[4]

No one mourned the general's passing more than the Orphans. Indeed, in the after years they took a great interest in all the brigade dead. Shortly after the war Charles Herbst of the 2d Kentucky visited the Chickamauga battlefield and erected headboards over the fallen Kentuckians. He later proceeded to most of the places in the South where Orphans lay buried, either marking the graves, or helping friends and family to arrange reinterment in Kentucky. For twenty years he continued the work, and in 1885 the veterans created a formal fund for the purpose. They managed to bring Helm's body back to Elizabethtown in 1884. Hanson's they already had in Lexington's cemetery, just a few yards from the grave of Breckinridge. Annually these Orphan graves saw pilgrimage as the survivors came in silence to garland the sod and damp it with tears of remembrance.[5]

Yet their duty to their fallen comrades seemed undone. Kentuckians, these in particular, felt a unique sense of their place in history. Posterity required more than tombs and monuments for the dead. It demanded living memorials. There was life in the word that could outlast the flesh, and in after years the Orphans took their pens and engrafted their epic upon the record of human memory. Theirs was a story worth remembering, worth repeating. Their example must be preserved for their future Kentuckians. The saga of the trials and drama of their service, their sacrifice, their triumph over physical adversity and emotional anguish, must not be forgotten.

The echoes of war barely died before the Orphans began. John Jackman took the first small steps, now totally forgotten. In 1866 he worked and expanded most of his wartime journal into a series of articles called "Army Reminiscences" for the Louisville *Courier*. There once more came to life the host of characters of the indomitable 9th Kentucky, the aide who proudly stole the patent report, Private Gibbon lighting his pipe on guard duty, Leander Applegate shouting "Borodino" for all to hear. There too he retold of "Uncle Bob" Johnson's attempt at drill, of the incredible food battle in the Canton hotel, the snowball fight at Dalton, the skirmishes with the firebrands and the Georgia Militia.

Ed Porter Thompson never abandoned his intentions, postponed by the demands of the war, and in 1868 his dream finally came to life. That year he published his *History of the First Kentucky Brigade*. It was one of the very first histories of a Confederate organization to appear following the war, and remains one of the very best. Breckinridge, still in exile, gazed from its frontispiece. The dedication offered the work "to the memory of Kentuckians who fell in defense of the South." His goal, he declared, was to do "more for the private soldier than was ever before the case in military annals." That he was able to do so was thanks largely to the Orphans' sense of history even before the war closed. Jackman had taken the brigade archives to Washington, Georgia, prior to the surrender. There Lewis detailed W. W. Badger to take charge of the books and papers, and after the parole Fayette Hewitt brought them home to Kentucky with him. When Thompson announced his intent to renew his work on a brigade history, Hewitt turned over the entire collection to him. In addition, Thompson corresponded widely with his former comrades. He even printed special envelopes for his correspondence, with an announcement of his project printed on the address side in case it might jog the memory of some Orphan turned postman. "It has devolved upon the present chronicler," he said, "before time shall have dimmed the remembrance of them, to gather from a thousand living sources the multitude of facts relating to these men, and preserve them for posterity."

He gave barely a fourth of the 931 pages to a narrative history of the brigade, and devoted the rest to capsule sketches of virtually every officer and man associated with the command. It was an enormous undertaking. To be sure, Thompson's bitterness toward the Federals evidenced itself, but there was a measure of forgiveness, too. Those who deserted he did not include, or else he simply did not mention their moment of weakness. Even poor Asa Lewis' demise he described simply as "killed at Stone River."

After Thompson's landmark book, George B. Hodge published his *Sketch of the First Kentucky Brigade* in 1874, chiefly a memoir of his own brief service with the Orphans. It, like Jackman's articles, was soon forgotten, but the next printed efforts enjoyed far more success and, like the Orphans themselves, were entirely unique.

In 1882 John S. Jackman, Captain John Weller, and John L. Marshall joined with two men who fought from other states to found a new monthly magazine. "This journal will be made up of reminiscences of the late war and incidents in any way connected with it," they announced. They called it the *Southern Bivouac*. It was one of the very first veterans' magazines following the war, and the only one devoted chiefly to the record of a single unit, the 1st Kentucky Brigade. The founders took no thought of profit. They hoped only to realize enough income from the venture to meet expenses, and thus guarantee the *Bivouac*'s future. After a year, though, they turned it over to professional publishers and they, despite hard times, made it successful enough that two years later the magazine was purchased by a large firm, and another Kentuckian and erstwhile Orphan, Basil W. Duke, assumed the editorship. Thus the *Southern Bivouac* endured for another two years, until sold again to the nationally acclaimed *Century* company.

For all its career, but particularly during the first three years, the *Bivouac* was a splendid publication. Each month's issue brought more stories and reminiscences from the pens of Jackman, Marshall, Weller, John Pirtle, Tom Owens, Dr. Tydings, and others. In the *Bivouac,* as nowhere else in the literature, the soul of the Orphan Brigade truly abides.

Yet Ed Thompson remained to be heard from once again. His efforts did not end with his first book. For thirty years after its publication, he continued his search for information to complete his roster of the Orphans, and to expand his history by the inclusion of anecdotal material that might illustrate, as his narrative did not, the real character of the Kentuckians in gray. Finally, in 1898, appeared his *History of the Orphan Brigade,* 1,104 pages of loving tribute to the heroism, devotion, and sometime rascality of his comrades in arms. It stood, and stands, unsurpassed.[6]

Coincidental with the appearance of the first issue of the *Southern Bivouac,* the Orphans met in reunion on September 5, 1882, at Blue Lick Springs. They did so every succeeding September well into the next century. Buckner, Lewis, Preston, Withers, Pickett, and in ever-decreasing numbers the men in the ranks gathered at Lexington, Elizabethtown, Glasgow, Frankfort, and elsewhere. The generals and officers spoke and reminisced, the men supped and drank together, the inevitable committees and rules and commissions formed, the pictures of Breckinridge and Hanson and Helm adorned their meeting walls, and the final flower-laden march to the cemeteries brought the old veterans together in silent contemplation and remembrance. "I like these reunions," Weller wrote in the *Bivouac.* "It is said with truth that war will bring out the character of a man quicker than any thing else. We were fortunate in finding so many good true men as we had with us. No wonder we love them and feel bound to them as if with ties of blood." At the third reunion the Orphans formally adopted Ben Helm's old 1st Kentucky Cavalry, and in that and later meetings they welcomed federal veterans to their fellowship as well.[7]

And gradually over these years the parentless old soldiers performed an adoption of their own. With no formal action, but rather by gradual acceptance, they came to call and regard themselves as the "Orphan" Brigade. Few, if any, knew how they came by the name, though a number thought back to Breckinridge's anguished cry at Murfreesboro. Thompson did not use the sobriquet in his 1868 volume, though in passing mentioning "Old Breck's" reference to "orphans" at Stones River. Hodge did not use it at all in 1874. Yet by the time the *Southern Bivouac* commenced in 1882 the nickname had taken a firm hold. Immediately after the war the veterans liked to call their outfit "the old brigade." They showed a predilection for pet names with their commanders even during the fighting, so it is natural that they settled upon one for themselves. Breckinridge first gave it utterance, and the tragic fittingness of it captured the imaginations of the Kentuckians as they looked back upon their war years. In all, over 4,000 of them had marched and fought with the old brigade at one time or another during the war. Not more than 600 were left to take parole at Washington, Georgia. They fought, bled, and died all across the Confederacy. For over 3 years they lived in exile from their native soil, yet their spirit and courage, their devotion to their duty and patriotism to their cause gave an example that other Confederates might emulate, yet few equaled. They took their distinctive civilization as Kentuckians with them wherever they went. The rowdiness, the penchant for organization and committee, the glee club and concert societies, the religious and social groups, their exaggerated individuality, and even their frequent self-importance were all to them matters of pride. Not war, nor death, nor even the anguish of orphanhood could rob them of their own sense of destiny, of who they were. That the rest of the world might know and applaud their record stood of little moment. What they knew themselves to be was what bound them together through war and on to posterity. They were Kentuckians, Americans.

They were the Orphan Brigade, and no one knew better than they that theirs was, truly, "a kind of title of nobility."

Documentation by Chapter

INTRODUCTION

1. E. Porter Thompson, *History of the First Kentucky Brigade* (Cincinnati, O., 1868), pp. 13–17; E. Porter Thompson, *History of the Orphan Brigade* (Louisville, 1898), pp. 21–22.

ONE

1. "For His Own Side," *Southern Bivouac*, II (Feb. 1884), p. 277.
2. E. Merton Coulter, *The Civil War and Readjustment in Kentucky* (Chapel Hill, N.C., 1926), pp. 1–3.
3. Ibid., p. 4; William C. Davis, *Breckinridge: Statesman, Soldier, Symbol* (Baton Rouge, La., 1974), pp. 6–7.
4. Coulter, *Civil War and Readjustment*, pp. 8–14.
5. Ibid., pp. 5–8.
6. Ibid., pp. 18–20; Davis, *Breckinridge*, pp. 51–52; Thomas W. Riley to John J. Crittenden (Feb. 8, 1860), John J. Crittenden Papers, Library of Congress, Washington, D.C.
7. Richard G. Stone, *A Brittle Sword: The Kentucky Militia, 1776–1912* (Lexington, 1977), pp. 61–62; Coulter, *Civil War and Readjustment*, pp. 82–83.
8. Thompson, *Orphan Brigade*, pp. 353–54; Stone, *Brittle Sword*, p. 62.
9. Stone, *Brittle Sword*, pp. 63–64; Coulter, *Civil War and Readjustment*, pp. 82–83; Thompson, *Orphan Brigade*, pp. 408, 424, 429.
10. Basil W. Duke, *A History of Morgan's Cavalry* (Bloomington, Ind., 1960), pp. 36–37.

11. Coulter, *Civil War and Readjustment,* pp. 83–84; Duke, *Morgan's Cavalry,* p. 41.

12. Thompson, *Orphan Brigade,* p. 408.

13. Coulter, *Civil War and Readjustment,* pp. 86–87; Thompson, *Orphan Brigade,* pp. 42–43; Frankfort, *Commonwealth* (May 11, 1861).

14. Frankfort, *Commonwealth* (July 15, 1861); Coulter, *Civil War and Readjustment,* pp. 88–91.

15. U. S. War Department, *War of the Rebellion: Official Records of the Union and Confederate Armies* (Washington, 1880–1901), Series I, Vol. 52, Part 2, pp. 106–7 (hereinafter cited as *O.R.*).

TWO

1. Thompson, *Orphan Brigade,* pp. 43–44.

2. *O.R.,* I, 4, pp. 367, 374.

3. Philip L. Lee, Compiled Service Record, Record Group 109, National Archives, Washington, D.C. (hereinafter cited as RG 109, NA); James W. Moss, Compiled Service Record, RG 109, NA; Thompson, *Orphan Brigade,* pp. 396–97, 400.

4. Coulter, *Civil War and Readjustment,* pp. 119–20; Basil W. Duke, *Reminiscences of General Basil W. Duke, C.S.A.* (Garden City, N.Y., 1911), pp. 84–86.

5. James M. Hawes, Compiled Service Record, RG 109, NA; Thompson, *Orphan Brigade,* pp. 396–97, 400, 594.

6. Henry George, *History of the 3d, 7th, 8th and 12th Kentucky, C.S.A.* (Louisville, Ky., 1911), p. 19.

7. John L. Marshall, "A Biographical Sketch of the Military Life of the Late Col. T. W. Thompson," *Southern Bivouac,* I (Sept. 1882), p. 12; Thompson, *Orphan Brigade,* pp. 485–86, 488–89.

8. "Nondescript" [John L. Marshall], "Heel and Toe," *Southern Bivouac,* I (Feb. 1883), pp. 255–56; Thompson, *Orphan Brigade,* pp. 408–9, 485, 488–89; "Orphan Brigade Items," *Southern Bivouac,* III (March 1885), p. 322; John H. Weller, "The Fourth Kentucky," *Southern Bivouac,* I (May–June, 1883), pp. 346–47; Marshall, "Thompson," p. 12.

9. Robert A. Johnson to Leonidas Polk (Aug. 4, 1861); Robert A. Johnson, Compiled Service Record, RG 109, NA; Thompson, *Orphan Brigade,* pp. 857–58.

10. Thompson, *Orphan Brigade,* p. 858.

11. Chapter VI, Volume 663, Medical Department. Register of Patients of 2d Kentucky Infantry Hospital and of Hospital at Tunnel Hill, Georgia, and Miscellaneous Data Pertaining to Other Hospitals, 1863–65 (Aug. 9, 10, 11, 13, 16, 23, 31), RG 109, NA; Rice E. Graves, Compiled Service Record, RG 109, NA.

12. Johnson to Polk (Aug. 4, 1861), Johnson Service Record; *O.R.*, I, 4, pp. 370–71, 373–74, 376, 377, 378, 379–80, 389.

13. Johnson to Polk (Aug. 4, 1861), Johnson Service Record; Thompson, *Orphan Brigade*, p. 400.

14. Fred Joyce, "Chaplains of the Fourth Kentucky," *Southern Bivouac*, I (Nov. 1882), pp. 116–17.

15. *O.R.*, I, 4, pp. 255, 405, 407; Frank Moore, comp., *Rebellion Record: A Diary of American Events* (New York, 1862), III, documents, p. 129.

16. *O.R.*, I, 4, pp. 193–94, 407, I, 52, Part 2, pp. 148–49.

17. "Taps," *Southern Bivouac*, I (Dec. 1882), pp. 179–80; "Major Thomas H. Hays," *Southern Bivouac*, III (Mar. 1885), p. 333.

18. Thompson, *Orphan Brigade*, p. 51; *O.R.*, I, 4, p. 414, I, 52, Part 2, pp. 150–51; Simon B. Buckner, "To the People of Kentucky" (Sept. 17, 1861), University of Kentucky Library, Lexington.

THREE

1. John S. Jackman Diary (Sept. 26–Oct. 5, 1861), and undated clippings in the Jackman Diary, Library of Congress.

2. *O.R.*, I, 4, pp. 415–16, I, 52, Part 2, pp. 152–53, 154; John B. Castleman, *Active Service* (Louisville, 1917), p. 73; Special Orders 171 (Nov. 5, 1861), Chap. II, Vol. 306, Orders and Circulars Received by 1st Kentucky Brigade (Nov. 1862–May 1863), RG 109, NA.

3. Mrs. George Marckmann Diary (Sept. 27, 1861), in possession of W. Maury Darst, Galveston, Tex.

4. Unnumbered special order (Nov. 7, 1861), Chap. II, Vol. 306, RG 109, NA; William C. Davis, *Breckinridge: Statesman, Soldier, Symbol* (Baton Rouge, La., 1974), pp. 280–81; Basil W. Duke, *A History of Morgan's Cavalry* (Cincinnati, O., 1867), pp. 88–96; George B. Hodge, *Sketch of the First Kentucky Brigade* (Frankfort, Ky., 1874), p. 6.

5. "Coffee-boiler Rangers," *Southern Bivouac*, I (July 1883), pp. 442–43.

6. Thompson, *Orphan Brigade*, pp. 876–77; "Sketch of Gen. B. H. Helm," *Land We Love*, III (June 1867), pp. 163–65; Beriah Magoffin to Jefferson Davis (May 9, 1861), Ben Hardin Helm to Leroy P. Walker (May 16, 1861), Ben Hardin Helm, Combined Service Record, RG 109, NA.

7. Thompson, *Orphan Brigade*, pp. 430–31, 448; Jackman Diary (Oct. 5–6, 1861); Albert D. Kirwan, ed., *Johnny Green of the Orphan Brigade* (Lexington, Ky., 1956), pp. 10–11.

8. Kirwan, *Johnny Green*, p. 12; Jackman Diary (Nov. 1861); Thompson, *Orphan Brigade*, pp. 47, 431.

9. George B. Hodge to John R. Chambliss (Jan. 2, 1862), Chap. II, Vol. 311, Letters, Telegrams Received and Sent by General Breckinridge's Command (Dec. 1861–Nov. 1863), RG 109, NA; Thompson, *Orphan Brigade*,

pp. 420–21, 703, 712, 728–29; Hiram Hawkins to Samuel Cooper (June 18, 1862), Hiram Hawkins Compiled Service Record, RG 109, NA.

10. Thompson, *Orphan Brigade*, pp. 45, 444, 481, 804; Joseph H. Lewis, "To the People" (Sept. 23, 1861), Joseph H. Lewis Scrapbook in possession of Mrs. Helene Lewis Gildred, San Diego, Calif.; Joseph H. Lewis, Compiled Service Record, Martin Cofer to Alex Cassaday (Nov. 27, 1861), Martin Cofer, Compiled Service Record, RG 109, NA.

11. Thompson, *Orphan Brigade*, pp. 457, 630, 860, 862; unnumbered special order (Nov. 1, 1861), Chap. II, Vol. 306, Inventory (Nov. 11, 1861), Robert Cobb, Compiled Service Record, RG 109, NA.

12. Thompson, *Orphan Brigade*, pp. 46, 457, 860; Special Orders 1, 2, 3, 4, 5 (Nov. 16, 1861), Special Order 13 (Dec. 3, 1861), Chap. II, Vol. 316, Military Departments, Special Orders Received, 1st Kentucky Brigade (Nov. 1861–Oct. 1862), RG 109, NA; Fred Joyce, "Why Sue Mundy Became a Guerrilla and Some Facts Concerning His Early Life," *Southern Bivouac*, II (Nov. 1883), pp. 125–26.

13. Hawes Service Record, Roger W. Hanson, Compiled Service Record, RG 109, NA; J. Winston Coleman, Jr., *Famous Kentucky Duels* (Lexington, 1969), pp. 89–95; Thompson, *Orphan Brigade*, pp. 375–77; Lexington, *Sunday Leader* (June 13, 1897); Duke, *Reminiscences*, pp. 138–40; Thompson, *First Kentucky Brigade*, p. 332.

14. *O.R.*, I, 4, pp. 484; Simon B. Buckner to Joseph E. Johnston (Feb. 6, 1863), Simon B. Buckner Papers, Huntington Library, San Marino, Calif.

15. See Davis, *Breckinridge*, pp. 268–96 passim; Jackman Diary, undated clipping; Louisville *Journal* (Oct. 14, 1861); L. B. Ulmer, "A Glimpse of Johnstone Through the Smoke of Shiloh" (1901), Choctaw County Public Library, Butler, Ala.; "Address of John C. Breckinridge" (Oct. 8, 1861), Moore, *Rebellion Record*, III, documents, pp. 254–59.

16. *O.R.*, I, 4, p. 445; Richmond *Daily Dispatch* (Oct. 22, Nov. 7, 1861); John B. Jones, *A Rebel War Clerk's Diary at the Confederate States Capital* (Philadelphia, Pa., 1866), I, p. 95.

17. H. E. Horde, "Recollections of Gen. J. C. Breckinridge," *Confederate Veteran*, XVII (Dec. 1909), p. 594.

18. Special Order No. 8 (Nov. 17, 1861), Chap. II, Vol. 316, General Orders Nos. 1, 2 (Nov. 16, 1861), Chap. II, Vol. 307, Military Departments, Orders and Circulars Received, 1st Kentucky Brigade (Nov. 1861–Apr. 1864), Morning Reports Nov. 5, 6, Dec. 25, 1861), Chap. II, Vol. 317, Military Departments, Morning Reports, 1st Kentucky Brigade (Nov. 1861–Feb. 1862), RG 109, NA.

19. General Order No. 2 (Nov. 16, 1861), Chap. II, Vol. 307, George B. Hodge to Buckner (Jan. 2, 1862), Chap. II, Vol. 311, Robert P. Trabue to Breckinridge (Jan. 17, 1862), Trabue, Compiled Service Record, "Quarter-

master Stores Delivered to Ed Porter Thompson" (Feb. 2, 1862), Thompson, Compiled Service Record, RG 109, NA; Thompson, *Orphan Brigade,* p. 439; Thomas H. Hunt to Hodge (Jan. 1862), Hunt, Compiled Service Record, RG 109, NA.

20. Johnson to Buckner (Oct. 29, 1861), Johnson Compiled Service Record, RG 109, NA; Thompson, *Orphan Brigade,* pp. 48–49.

21. Breckinridge to Charles Dimmock (Nov. 31, 1861), in "Governor Letcher's Official Correspondence," *Southern Historical Society Papers,* I (June 1876), p. 461; unnumbered special order (Oct. 30, 1861), Chap. II, Vol. 306, Hodge to George Cosby (Dec. 5, 1861), Breckinridge to ? (Dec. 11, 1861), Hodge to Chambliss (Jan. 2, 1862), Hodge to Cosby (Jan. 2, 1862), Chap. II, Vol. 311, Hodge to Allen (Dec. 19, 1861), Chap. II, Vol. 316, RG 109, NA.

22. H. E. Ferguson to "Dear Sister" (Jan. 26, 1862), in possession of Mrs. Howard Jones, Glasgow, Ky. Thompson, *Orphan Brigade,* pp. 50, 57–58; Weller, "The Fourth Kentucky," pp. 349–50; Hodge to Cosby (Dec. 6, 1861), Chap. II, Vol. 311, Special Order No. 17 (Dec. 6, 1861), No. 21 (Dec. 11, 1861), Chap. II, Vol. 316, entry (Sept. 17, 1861), Chap. VI, Vol. 663, RG 109, NA.

23. Special Order No. 18 (Dec. 8, 1861), No. 26 (Dec. 15, 1861), No. 30 (Dec. 19, 1861), Chap. II, Vol. 316, unnumbered special orders (Oct. 30, 31, Nov. 3, 4, 10, 1861), Chap. II, Vol. 306, General Order No. 3 (Nov. 30, 1861), No. 8 (Dec. 27, 1861), Chap. II, Vol. 307, Military Departments, Orders and Circulars Received, 1st Kentucky Brigade (Nov. 1861–Apr. 1864), RG 109, NA; Lexington *Morning Herald* (Nov. 1, 1897).

24. Weller, "The Fourth Kentucky," p. 348; "Orphan Brigade Items," *Southern Bivouac,* III (Mar. 1885), p. 322; "Taps," *Southern Bivouac,* II (Nov. 1883), p. 139; Ferguson to "Dear Sister" (Jan. 26, 1862), Ferguson Letters; "Taps," *Southern Bivouac, I* (Feb. 1883), pp. 271–72.

25. Undated clipping, Jackman Diary; General Order No. 7 (Dec. 25, 1861), Chap. II, Vol. 307, RG 109, NA; "H.C.S.," *Southern Bivouac,* I (Dec. 1882), p. 147; "Youth's Department," *Southern Bivouac,* II (June 1884), p. 468.

26. Duke, *Morgan's Cavalry,* p. 93; Duke, *Reminiscences,* pp. 95–99, 142; Thompson, *First Kentucky Brigade,* pp. 335–36.

27. Duke, *Morgan's Cavalry,* pp. 208–9; Thompson, *Orphan Brigade,* p. 59; Hodge to Morgan (Dec. 16, 1861), Chap. II, Vol. 311, Special Order No. 242 (Dec. 1, 1861), Chap. II, Vol. 316, Report (Sept. 29, 1861), Chap. VI, Vol. 663, Morning Reports (Nov. 5–Dec. 10, 1861), Chap. II, Vol. 317, RG 109, NA; Duke, *Reminiscences,* p. 142.

28. Hunt to Hodge (Dec. 11, 1861), Hunt, Compiled Service Record, Breckinridge to colonels of the 3d, 4th, 5th, and 6th Kentuckys (Jan. 27, 1862), Hodge to Andrew Hynes (Feb. 6, 1862), Hodge to Chambliss (Jan. 2,

1862), Chap. II, Vol. 311, General Order No. 10 (Feb. 1, 1862), Chap. II, Vol. 307, RG 109, NA; Duke, *Reminiscences,* pp. 134–36; Ferguson to "Dear Sister" (Nov. 12, 1861), Ferguson Letters; United States Congress, *Congressional Record* (Washington, D.C., 1921), LXI, Part 7, 67th Cong., 1st sess., p. 7,393; A. E. Young to "Dear Brother" (Dec. 16, 1861), A. E. Young Letters in possession of Mrs. Howard Jones.

29. Reuben Davis, *Recollections of Mississippi and Mississippians* (University, Miss., 1972), pp. 422–24; Kirwan, *Johnny Green,* pp. 14–15; Thompson, *Orphan Brigade,* pp. 518, 603.

30. *Confederate Veteran,* XXVIII (Feb. 1920), pp. 61–62; Kirwan, *Johnny Green,* pp. 14–15; LeGrand J. Wilson, *The Confederate Soldier* (Memphis, Tenn., 1973), pp. 42–43; A. E. Young to "Dear Brother" (Dec. 16, 1861), A. E. Young Letters; Chap. VIII, Vol. 69, Clothing Account Book, Co. C., 4th Ky. Vols., 1862–64, p. 222, RG 109, NA.

FOUR

1. Thompson, *Orphan Brigade,* pp. 52–54; Frankfort, *Kentucky Yeoman* (Nov. 29, 1861); *O.R.,* I, 4, pp. 539–40, 551–52, Vol. 52, Part 2, pp. 195–96, Vol. 7, pp. 447, 698, 707–8; Hunt to R. Morgan (Jan. 7, 1861), Hunt, Compiled Service Record, RG 109, NA.

2. Thompson, *Orphan Brigade,* pp. 55–56, 431; *O.R.,* I, 7, pp. 781–82; Breckinridge to William J. Hardee (Dec. 21, 1861), Chap. II, Vol. 311; Gervis D. Grainger, *Four Years with the Boys in Gray* (Franklin, Ky., 1902), p. 6; Jackman Diary (Dec. 23, 1861), and clipping on p. 197; Hardee to Breckinridge (Dec. 22, 1861), John C. Breckinridge Papers, Chicago Historical Society; Ferguson to "Dear Sister" (Jan. 26, 1862), Ferguson Letters.

3. *O.R.,* I, 7, pp. 840–41, 864, 865; Thompson, *Orphan Brigade,* p. 62.

4. *O.R.,* I, 7, pp. 418–19, 861–62; Thompson, *Orphan Brigade,* pp. 76–79; Chap. VI, Vol. 663, p. 1, General Order No. 17 (Feb. 12, 1862), No. 18 (Feb. 13, 1862), Chap. II, Vol. 307, Morning Report (Feb. 11, 1862), Chap. II, Vol. 317, RG 109, NA; Kirwan, *Johnny Green,* p. 16.

5. Thompson, *Orphan Brigade,* p. 78; Hodge, *First Kentucky Brigade,* pp. 10–11.

6. Thompson, *Orphan Brigade,* pp. 78–79; "Nondescript," "Heel and Toe," pp. 256–57.

7. Undated clippings in Jackman Diary. For a discussion of the origins of the name Orphan Brigade, see the author's Introduction to the 1973 edition of Thompson's *Orphan Brigade,* pp. vii–ix. The earliest usage in print is in Thompson, *First Kentucky Brigade,* p. 386, in 1868. Jackman uses it once in his diary but, since this was transcribed in 1865–66, it could be a postwar addition. Still, if it is referred to this soon after the war, it was almost certainly coined—though not much used—during the war.

8. *O.R.,* I, 7, pp. 342–43; Thompson, *Orphan Brigade,* pp. 62–63; Roger

W. Hanson to Virginia Hanson (Mar. 23, 1862), Roger W. Hanson Papers, Library of Congress.

9. Thompson, *Orphan Brigade*, pp. 63–65, 75, 598.

10. *O.R.*, I, 7, pp. 343–44, 348; Thompson, *Orphan Brigade*, pp. 65–67, 73; John A. Wyeth, *That Devil Forrest* (New York, 1959), pp. 46–47; Thomas Jordan and J. P. Pryor, *The Campaigns of Lieut.-Gen. N. B. Forrest, and of Forrest's Cavalry* (Dayton, O., 1973), pp. 81–84.

11. *O.R.*, I, 7, pp. 294, 333, 337, 340, 344–45; Thompson, *Orphan Brigade*, pp. 66–69, 73, 74, 355, 560; pay voucher, Hanson, Compiled Service Record, RG 109, NA; Frank Funk, "Fort Donelson," *Southern Bivouac*, I (May–June 1883), pp. 345–46; "Taps," *Southern Bivouac*, II (Oct. 1883), p. 88; James Hewitt to R. G. T. Beauregard (Apr. 14, 1862), James Hewitt, Compiled Service Record, RG 109, NA; S. M. H. Byers, *Iowa in War Times* (Des Moines, Ia., 1888), p. 105; Bromfield L. Ridley, *Battles and Sketches of the Army of Tennessee* (Dayton, O., 1978), p. 67.

12. Thompson, *Orphan Brigade*, pp. 69–71, 79–80; Hodge, *First Kentucky Brigade*, pp. 11–12; Kirwan, *Johnny Green*, p. 17.

13. Hodge, *First Kentucky Brigade*, pp. 15–18; General Order No. 19 (Feb. 18, 1862), No. 23 (Feb. 23, 1862), No. 26 (Mar. 4, 1862), Chap. II, Vol. 307, RG 109, NA; Kirwan, *Johnny Green*, pp. 17–18.

14. *O.R.*, I, 7, p. 905; Hodge to Hardee (Jan. 5, 1862), Chap. II, Vol. 311, RG 109, NA; James B. Clay to James B. Clay, Jr. (Jan. 26, 1862), Thomas J. Clay Papers, Library of Congress.

15. Hodge, *First Kentucky Brigade*, pp. 17–18; Kirwan, *Johnny Green*, pp. 18–19; Thompson, *Orphan Brigade*, pp. 80, 98–99.

16. Thompson, *Orphan Brigade*, pp. 80, 98; *O.R.*, I, 7, p. 261; Davis, *Breckinridge*, pp. 301–2.

17. Davis, *Breckinridge*, p. 301; Trabue to Thomas H. Winstead (Mar. 20, 1862), Thomas H. Winstead Papers in possession of Mr. Thomas D. Winstead, Elizabethtown, Ky.; Grainger, *Boys in Gray*, p. 7; Hunt to Hodge (Mar. 26, 1862), Hunt Compiled Service Record, RG 109, NA; Jackman Diary.

18. Breckinridge to Major Brewster (Mar. 27, 1862), Hodge to Statham (Mar. 31, 1862), Chap. II, Vol. 311, General Order No. 4 (Mar. 14, 1862), Chap. II, Vol. 307, Hunt to Major Brewster (Mar. 24, 1862), Hunt Compiled Service Record, RG 109, NA.

19. Jackman Diary (Mar. 30–Apr. 4, 1862); Kirwan, *Johnny Green*, p. 19; *O.R.*, I, 10, Part 2, p. 389; Breckinridge to Thomas Jordan (Apr. 21, 1862), Chap. II, Vol. 311, RG 109, NA.

20. Kirwan, *Johnny Green*, pp. 19–20; Thompson, *Orphan Brigade*, pp. 81–82; Davis, *Breckinridge*, pp. 303–4.

1. Jackman Diary (Apr. 6, 1862); Kirwan, *Johnny Green,* pp. 25–26; Thompson, *Orphan Brigade,* pp. 501, 597; Thompson, *First Kentucky Brigade,* p. 501; Trabue to Brewster (Mar. 23, 1862), Trabue Compiled Service Record, RG 109, NA.

2. Kirwan, *Johnny Green,* pp. 25–26; John H. Weller, "History of the Fourth Kentucky Infantry," *Southern Historical Society Papers,* IX (Mar. 1881), pp. 112–13; "Nondescript," "Heel and Toe," p. 257.

3. *O.R.,* I, 10, Part 1, pp. 386, 614–15; Jackman Diary, undated newspaper clipping, p. 198; Kirwan, *Johnny Green,* pp. 26–27; Weller, "The Fourth Kentucky," *Southern Bivouac,* p. 351.

4. Thompson, *Orphan Brigade,* pp. 100, 103, 405, 469; Weller, "Fourth Kentucky," p. 351; Kirwan, *Johnny Green,* pp. 26–27; *O.R.,* I, 10, Part 1, pp. 615–16; Jackman Diary, p. 198; Joseph H. Lewis Scrapbook, undated clipping; Thompson, *First Kentucky Brigade,* pp. 421, 425.

5. Breckinridge to Jordan (Apr. 24, 1862), Chap. II, Vol. 311, RG 109, NA; *O.R.,* I, 10, Part 1, p. 472; Thompson, *Orphan Brigade,* pp. 103–4.

6. Thompson, *Orphan Brigade,* p. 100; *O.R.,* I, 10, Part 1, p. 616; W. B. Beeson, "The Forty-ninth Alabama," Samuel D. Buck Papers, Duke University Library, Durham, N.C.; Hodge, *First Kentucky Brigade,* p. 24.

7. Davis, *Breckinridge,* pp. 304–10; Breckinridge to Jordan (Apr. 15, 1862), Chap. II, Vol. 311, RG 109, NA; Hodge, *First Kentucky Brigade,* p. 23.

8. *O.R.,* I, 10, Part 1, pp. 613, 616; Jackman Diary, p. 198.

9. Davis, *Breckinridge,* pp. 310–11; Fred Joyce, "The Irishmen of Company D, Fourth Kentucky Infantry," *Southern Bivouac,* II (Feb. 1884), pp. 268–69.

10. Grainger, *Boys in Gray,* p. 7; Jackman Diary (Apr. 6, 1862).

11. *O.R.,* I, 10, Part 1, pp. 616–17.

12. Jackman Diary, p. 198; "Nondescript," "Heel and Toe," pp. 258–59; Kirwan, *Johnny Green,* pp. 28–29.

13. "Nondescript," "Heel and Toe," p. 259; Kirwan, *Johnny Green,* pp. 29–30; Thompson, *Orphan Brigade,* p. 103; J. Stoddard Johnston Scrapbook, Vol. II, Filson Club, Louisville, Ky.

14. *O.R.,* I, 10, Part 1, p. 617; Kirwan, *Johnny Green,* pp. 29–30; Hodge, *First Kentucky Brigade,* pp. 26–27.

15. *O.R.,* I, 10, Part 1, pp. 617–18; Fred Joyce, "Two Dogs," *Southern Bivouac,* I (Oct. 1882), pp. 72–73; Barnes F. Lathrop, "A Confederate Artilleryman at Shiloh," *Civil War History,* VIII (Dec. 1962), p. 378; Thompson, *Orphan Brigade,* pp. 105, 410, 464, 519–20; John L. Marshall, "Heel and Toe, II," *Southern Bivouac,* I (Mar. 1883), pp. 301–2; Weller, "Fourth

Kentucky," *Southern Bivouac,* p. 352; Lot D. Young, *Reminiscences of a Soldier of the Orphan Brigade* (Louisville, 1912), pp. 24–25.

16. Lewis Scrapbook; Thompson, *Orphan Brigade,* pp. 102, 103, 104, 501.

17. *O.R.,* I, 10, Part 1, pp. 359–60; Kirwan, *Johnny Green,* pp. 30–37.

18. *O.R.,* I, 10, Part 1, pp. 467, 500, 618–19, 620.

19. Kirwan, *Johnny Green,* pp. 32–34; Jackman Diary (Apr. 7, 1862), p. 198; Marshall, "Heel and Toe, II," p. 303.

20. Jackman Diary (Apr. 8–13, 1862), p. 198; *O.R.,* I, 10, Part 1, pp. 619–20; Hodge, *First Kentucky Brigade,* p. 29; Davis, *Breckinridge,* p. 315.

21. Thompson, *Orphan Brigade,* pp. 105–6.

22. *O.R.,* I, 10, Part 1, p. 621; Breckinridge to Jordan (Apr. 21, 1862), Chap. II, Vol. 311, RG 109, NA; J. Stoddard Johnston Diary (July 13, 1862), J. Stoddard Johnston Papers, Filson Club; Hodge, *First Kentucky Brigade,* p. 29; D. M. Haydon to Breckinridge (Sept. 8, 1862), Breckinridge Family Papers, Library of Congress.

23. Marshall, "Heel and Toe, II," pp. 303–5; "Taps," *Southern Bivouac,* I (Mar. 1883), pp. 316–17; Thompson, *Orphan Brigade,* p. 106.

SIX

1. Grainger, *Boys in Gray,* p. 7; Jackman Diary (Apr. 13–17, 1862); Kirwan, *Johnny Green,* p. 40; Hodge to Shaw (Apr. 24, 1862), Chap. II, Vol. 311, General Orders No. 30 (Apr. 30, 1862), No. 72 (June 14, 1862), Special Order No. 24 (June 3, 1862), Chap. II, Vol. 305, Military Departments, Orders Received by the 1st Kentucky Brigade (Apr.–Oct. 1862), Special Order No. 55 (Apr. 14), No. 57 (Apr. 15), No. 80 (Apr. 17), No. 83 (Apr. 18), No. 96 (Apr. 23), No. 124 (Apr. 28, 1862), Chap. II, Vol. 315, Military Departments, Special Orders Received and Record of Details, Discharges, Furloughs, and Transfers, 1st Kentucky Brigade, 1862–63, Special Order No. 80 (Apr. 17, 1862), Chap. II, Vol. 316, entry (May 8, 1862), Chap. VIII, Vol. 71, Miscellaneous Quartermaster Accounts, 4th Kentucky Volunteers, Chap. VIII, Vol. 69, pp. 99–100, RG 109, NA.

2. Breckinridge to Jordan (Apr. 15, 1862), Breckinridge Compiled Service Record, RG 109, NA; Richmond *Enquirer* (Apr. 25, 1862); Chap. VIII, Vol. 69, p. 2, Chap. II, Vol. 315 (June 4, 1862), General Order No. 27 (June 15, 1862), Chap. II, Vol. 307, Special Order No. 86 (Apr. 20, 1862), Chap. II, Vol. 316, Kenshattentycthe Compiled Service Record, RG 109, NA; Thompson, *Orphan Brigade,* pp. 225, 623.

3. Jordan to Breckinridge (Apr. 15, 1862), Special Order No. 46 (Apr. 30, 1862), General Order No. 39 (May 6, 1862), Chap. II, Vol. 305, Breckinridge to Jordan (Apr. 15, 1862), Chap. II, Vol. 311, Special Order (Apr. 15, 1862), Chap. II, Vol. 315, Chap. VIII, Vol. 69, pp. 108–9, RG 109, NA; Thompson, *Orphan Brigade,* pp. 804, 806.

4. Breckinridge to Jordan (Apr. 13, 1862, Apr. 24, 1862), Chap. II, Vol. 311, Edward Sparrow to the Confederate Senate (Jan. 28, 1863), Trabue Compiled Service Record, RG 109, NA; Thompson, *Orphan Brigade,* pp. 405, 415, 431–32; Marshall, "Thompson," p. 13.

5. Davis, *Breckinridge,* p. 315; Richmond *Enquirer* (Apr. 22, 1862); Thompson, *Orphan Brigade,* p. 555.

6. Thompson, *First Kentucky Brigade,* pp. 13–16; *O.R.,* I, 10, Part 2, pp. 426, 550, 642.

7. Trabue to Breckinridge (Apr. 23, 1862), Trabue Compiled Service Record, Helm to Breckinridge (May 4, 17, 1862), D. W. Yandell statement (May 4, 1862), J. C. Cummings statement (May 4, 1862), Helm Compiled Service Record, RG 109, NA.

8. George Neff to Eli M. Bruce (May 3, 1862), Bruce to Breckinridge and Preston (May 10, 1862), Hanson Compiled Service Record, RG 109, NA; *O.R.,* II, 3, pp. 578, 600, 650–51, 866, 893, Vol. 4, p. 14.

9. Circular (Apr. 20, 29, 1862), General Order No. 5 (May 12, 1862), Chap. II, Vol. 305, RG 109, NA; Jackman Diary (May 22, 1862), p. 199; Kirwan, *Johnny Green,* pp. 40–41.

10. Thompson, *Orphan Brigade,* pp. 112–13; Jackman Diary (May 29–June 2, 1862), p. 199; Kirwan, *Johnny Green,* pp. 41–42.

11. Jackman Diary (June 11, 1862).

12. William Preston, Memoranda of A. S. Johnston's Death, Battle of Shiloh &c (June 9–10, 1862), Box 2, Special File, Item 16, RG 94, Special Order 16 (June 23, 1862), Chap. II, Vol. 305, RG 109, NA; Jackman Diary (June 25–29, 1862).

13. John Q. Anderson, ed., *Brokenburn: The Journal of Kate Stone* (Baton Rouge, La.: 1955), p. 126; Special Order No. 243 (July 3, 1862), Chap. II, Vol. 316, Special Order No. 10 (July 4, 1862), Chap. II, Vol. 305, RG 109, NA; John S. Jackman, "Vicksburg in 1862," *Southern Bivouac,* III (Sept. 1884), pp. 4–5; Jackman Diary (July 1–3, 1862).

14. General Order No. 3 (July 12, 1862), Special Order No. 8 (July 15, 1862), Chap. II, Vol. 312, Military Departments, Orders and Circulars Received, 1st Kentucky Brigade, 1862–63, RG 109, NA; Jackman Diary (July 21, 1862).

15. Thompson, *Orphan Brigade,* pp. 117–18; Robert G. Hartje, *Van Dorn: The Life and Times of a Confederate General* (Nashville, Tenn., 1967), pp. 200–1, 216, 240, 325; General Order No. 1 (July 8, 1862), Helm Compiled Service Record, RG 109, NA; Thompson, *First Kentucky Brigade,* pp. 541–42; Kirwan, *Johnny Green,* p. 44.

16. *O.R.,* I, 15, pp. 1,122–24; Jackman Diary (July 15, 24–25, 1862); Thompson, *Orphan Brigade,* pp. 116, 767; Breckinridge to Helm (July 15, 1862), Isaac M. Brown to M. S. Smith (July 19, 1862), Breckinridge to

Van Dorn (July 22, 1862), Chap. II, Vol. 311, Special Order No. 21 (July 19, 1862), No. 16 (July 23, 1862), Chap. II, Vol. 312, Special Order No. 17 (July 24, 1862), Chap. II, Vol. 316, RG 109, NA.

17. B. W. Avent to Breckinridge (July 22, 1862), B. F. Marshall to Avent (July 22, 1862), Chap. II, Vol. 311, RG 109, NA; Jackman Diary (July 27, 1862); Kirwan, *Johnny Green,* pp. 44–45.

18. Van Dorn to Breckinridge (July 25, 1862), Breckinridge to Van Dorn (July 26, 1862), Chap. II, Vol. 311, RG 109, NA; General Order No. 2 (July 29, 1862), G. T. Shaw to John A. Buckner (July 31, 1862), William Yerger Papers, Mississippi Department of Archives and History, Jackson; Kirwan, *Johnny Green,* p. 45; John D. Martin to Breckinridge (July 25, 1862), Breckinridge Family Papers.

19. Davis, *Breckinridge,* pp. 318–19; Grainger, *Boys in Gray,* pp. 8–9; Moore, *Rebellion Record,* V, p. 309; *O.R.,* I, 15, pp. 76–77.

20. Grainger, *Boys in Gray,* p. 9; *O.R.,* I, 15, p. 77; Special Order No. 24 (Aug. 3, 1862), Chap. II, Vol. 316, RG 109, NA; "Taps," *Southern Bivouac,* I (Sept. 1882), p. 39.

21. Moore, *Rebellion Record,* V, p. 310; "Sketch of General B. H. Helm," p. 165; Grainger, *Boys in Gray,* p. 9; John B. Pirtle, "Defense of Vicksburg in 1862—The Battle of Baton Rouge," *Southern Historical Society Papers,* VIII (June–July 1880), p. 329; Thompson, *Orphan Brigade,* p. 435.

22. *O.R.,* I, 15, pp. 77–78, 97–99; Grainger, *Boys in Gray,* pp. 9–10; Moore, *Rebellion Record,* V, p. 310; Sadie M. Wade to author (n.d., 1978).

23. *O.R.,* I, 15, pp. 83–87; Pirtle, "Baton Rouge," p. 330; Moore, *Rebellion Record,* V, p. 311; "Personne" [Felix G. De Fontaine], *Marginalia; or Gleanings from an Army Note-Book* (Columbia, S.C., 1864), p. 34.

24. *O.R.,* I, 15, pp. 78–79.

25. *O.R.,* I, 15, pp. 82, 93; Thompson, *Orphan Brigade,* p. 597; Claim 7,485 (Aug. 11, 1863), John C. Wickliffe Compiled Service Record, RG 109, NA; Moore, *Rebellion Record,* V, p. 308; Davis, *Breckinridge,* p. 323; Grainger, *Boys in Gray,* pp. 11–12.

26. *Journal of the Congress of the Confederate States of America* (Washington, D.C., 1905), II, pp. 236, 443; *O.R.,* I, 15, pp. 12, 16, Part 2, p. 995, 52, Part 2, p. 340; H. C. Burnett to Breckinridge (Aug. 5, 22, 1862), Jilson Johnson to Breckinridge (Aug. 29, 1862), Breckinridge Family Papers; J. Stoddard Johnston Diary (Aug 14, 1862).

27. Jackman Diary (Aug. 18, 1862).

SEVEN

1. Davis, *Breckinridge,* pp. 326–27; Jackman Diary (Aug. 19–24, 1862); Address (Aug. 22, 1862), Chap. II, Vol. 307, RG 109, NA.

2. Jackman Diary (Sept. 19–Oct. 3, 1862), p. 195; Kirwan, *Johnny Green,* pp. 48–49; Thompson, *Orphan Brigade,* p. 674.

3. *O.R.,* I, 16, Part 2, pp. 815, 892, 996; Braxton Bragg Papers, United States Military Academy, West Point, N.Y.

4. Hanson to Virginia Hanson (Mar. 23, Apr. 8, May 1, 8, 22, July 7, 1862), Hanson Papers; George D. Prentice to Hanson (Mar. 25, 1862), Hanson to Prentice (Apr. 6, 1862), Lexington *Sunday Leader* (June 13, 1897).

5. Thompson, *Orphan Brigade,* pp. 72–73, 617, 632, 633; Thompson, *First Kentucky Brigade,* pp. 585–86; Memorandum (Apr. 2, 1862), Chap. II, Vol. 316, RG 109, NA; Joyce, "Sue Mundy," pp. 126–28; *O.R.,* II, 3, pp. 388–89.

6. Hanson, Compiled Service Record, Special Order 14 (Sept. 17, 1862), Chap. II, Vol. 308, Military Departments, Orders Received and Orders Issued by the 1st Kentucky Brigade, 1862–63, RG 109, NA; Hanson to Breckinridge (Oct. 3, 1862), Breckinridge Papers, Chicago.

7. Hodge to Chambliss (Jan. 2, 1862), Chap. II, Vol. 311, General Order No. 97 (July 11, 1862), Chap. II, Vol. 312, General Order No. 5 (July 18, 1862), Chap. II, Vol. 317, RG 109, NA; Thomas Stith to Breckinridge (Sept. 9, 1862), Breckinridge Family Papers; Officers of the 5th Kentucky to Breckinridge (Sept. 16, 1862), Buckner Papers.

8. Breckinridge to Officers of the 5th Kentucky (Sept. 18, 1862), Breckinridge to Samuel Cooper (Oct. 3, 1862), Chap. II, Vol. 311, RG 109, NA.

9. Jackman Diary (Sept. 22, 1862); John C. Caldwell to Breckinridge (Oct. 9, 1862), Caldwell Compiled Service Record, RG 109, NA.

10. Thompson, *Orphan Brigade,* pp. 393–94; Grainger, *Boys in Gray,* pp. 12–13; Jackman Diary (Oct. 3, 1862); Caldwell to Breckinridge (Oct. 9, 1862), Caldwell Compiled Service Record, Breckinridge to Caldwell (Oct. 10, 1862), Chap. II, Vol. 311, RG 109, NA; Kirwan, *Johnny Green,* pp. 49–50.

11. *O.R.,* I, 17, Part 2, p. 326, 20, Part 2, p. 26; Breckinridge to Caldwell (Oct. 10, 1862), Chap. II, Vol. 311, RG 109, NA.

12. Hanson to Breckinridge (Oct. 3, 1862), Breckinridge to Hanson (Oct. 4, 1862), Buckner to Hanson (Oct. 8, 1862), Chap. II, Vol. 311, Special Order No. 36 (Oct. 10, 1862), No. 38 (Oct. 12, 1862), Chap. II, Vol. 316, RG 109, NA; Hanson to Breckinridge (Oct. 3, 4, 5, 1862), Cooper to Breckinridge (Oct. 12, 1862), Breckinridge Papers, Chicago; "Tribute in a Diary," undated clipping in Thomas J. Clay Papers, Library of Congress; Breckinridge to Bragg (Oct. 12, 1862), Frederick M. Dearborn Collection, Houghton Library, Harvard University, Cambridge, Mass.; Thompson, *Orphan Brigade,* p. 580.

13. Jackman Diary (Oct. 15–19, 1862); Kirwan, *Johnny Green,* p. 50; Thompson, *Orphan Brigade,* pp. 148–50; *O.R.,* I, 16, Part 2, p. 1,000.

14. Thompson, *Orphan Brigade,* pp. 492, 630, 806; Special Order (Dec.

19, 1862), Chap. II, Vol. 306, General Order No. 1 (Oct. 26, 1862), Special Order No. 4 (Oct. 30, 1862), Chap. II, Vol. 308, RG 109, NA; *O.R.*, I, 16, Part 2, p. 1,003.

15. Reports (Nov. 1, 1862), Military Departments, Orders Received, Orders Issued, and Morning Reports, 1st Kentucky Brigade (Aug. 1862–Oct. 1864), Chap. II, Vol. 310, RG 109, NA.

16. Grainger, *Boys in Gray,* p. 13; Mary Breckinridge to Breckinridge (Nov. 9, 1862, Feb. 8, 1863), Mary Breckinridge Letters, Breckinridge Compiled Service Record, RG 109, NA; Thomas Winstead to Mollie Winstead (Nov. 11, 30, 1862), Thomas Winstead Papers in possession of Mr. Thomas D. Winstead, Elizabethtown, Ky.

17. Special Order No. 1 (Nov. 1, 1862), No. 41 (Dec. 14, 1862), Chap. II, Vol. 308, Trabue to William P. Johnston (Oct. 31, Nov. 1, 1862), Trabue Compiled Service Record, RG 109, NA.

18. Jackman Diary, p. 62; John S. Jackman, "Battle of Murfreesboro," *Southern Bivouac,* III (Mar. 1885), p. 295; Thompson, *First Kentucky Brigade,* pp. 333–36.

19. Virginia Hanson to Bruce (Aug. 20, 1862), Bruce to Davis (Sept. 14, 1862), Hanson Compiled Service Record, Breckinridge to Bragg (Nov. 3, 1862), Chap. II, Vol. 311, RG 109, NA; Jackman Diary (Dec. 13, 1862).

20. General Order No. 19 (Dec. 19, 1862), Chap. II, Vol. 306, General Order No. 9 (Nov. 26, 1862), No. 10 (Dec. 2, 1862), Chap. II, Vol. 307, General Order No. 15 (Nov. 28, 1862), Special Order No. 40 (Dec. 10, 1862), Chap. II, Vol. 308, Special Order Nos. 40, 41 (Oct. 14, 1862), Chap. II, Vol. 316, RG 109, NA.

21. John L. Marshall, "Unrecorded Deeds of Daring," *Southern Bivouac,* I (Aug. 1883), pp. 471–73.

22. Winstead to Mollie Winstead (Nov. 11, 1862), Winstead Papers; Breckinridge to Bragg (Nov. 19, 1862), Chap. II, Vol. 311, Special Order No. 38 (Dec. 5, 1862), Chap. II, Vol. 308, Asa Lewis Compiled Service Record, RG 109, NA.

23. Special Order No. 8 (Dec. 4, 1862), Chap. II, Vol. 306, RG 109, NA; Thompson, *Orphan Brigade,* pp. 159–60, 166; Duke, *Morgan's Cavalry,* p. 313; Kirwan, *Johnny Green,* pp. 54–59; Jackman Diary (Dec. 5–7, 1862).

24. Thompson, *Orphan Brigade,* pp. 160–63, 164, 560; Kirwan, *Johnny Green,* pp. 56–57; Basil Duke, "The Battle of Hartsville," *Southern Bivouac,* I (Oct. 1882), pp. 50–51.

25. Kirwan, *Johnny Green,* pp. 57–58; Thompson, *Orphan Brigade,* pp. 164–65; John O. Scott, "After Hartsville," *Southern Bivouac,* I (Nov. 1882), pp. 107–10.

26. Duke, *Morgan's Cavalry,* pp. 262, 321; *O.R.*, I, 20, Part 2, p. 179; Voucher 4, Thomas Estes (Dec. 8, 1862), Manuscript No. 1526, General

Order No. 22 (Dec. 20, 1862), Chap. II, Vol. 306, RG 109, NA; Thompson, *Orphan Brigade,* p. 201; Kirwan, *Johnny Green,* pp. 59–60.

27. Frankfort, *Commonwealth* (Feb. 11, 1862); Thompson, *Orphan Brigade,* p. 201.

28. Grainger, *Boys in Gray,* p. 13; Kirwan, *Johnny Green,* p. 59; Squire Helm Bush Diary (Dec. 24–25, 1862), Hardin County Historical Society, Elizabethtown, Ky.; Chap. VIII, Vol. 69, p. 223, RG 109, NA.

29. Thompson, *Orphan Brigade,* pp. 201–2; Kirwan, *Johnny Green,* pp. 60–61; Frankfort, *Commonwealth* (Feb. 11, 1862); General Order No. 17 (Dec. 25, 1862), Chap. II, Vol. 308, RG 109, NA; Sallie Lewis to Breckinridge (Sept. 21, 1869), John C. Breckinridge Papers in possession of Colonel James C. Breckinridge.

30. B. L. Ridley, "Camp Scenes Around Dalton," *Confederate Veteran,* X (Feb. 1902), p. 68; General Order No. 29 (Dec. 23, 1862), Chap. II, Vol. 306.

EIGHT

1. Bush Diary (Dec. 30, 1862).

2. *O.R.,* I, 20, Part 1, p. 825; Theodore O'Hara to Breckinridge (Jan. 16, 1863), John C. Breckinridge Papers, New-York Historical Society; Jackman Diary (Dec. 28–29, 1862); Kirwan, *Johnny Green,* pp. 65–66.

3. Jackman Diary (Dec. 31, 1862); Jackman, "Murfreesboro," pp. 297–98; Thompson, *Orphan Brigade,* pp. 199–200, 869.

4. Jackman Diary (Jan. 1, 1863); Breckinridge to "Colonel" (Jan. 1, 1863), Breckinridge Papers, Chicago; Thompson, *Orphan Brigade,* pp. 176–77, 452; Mary Breckinridge to Breckinridge (Jan. 1, 1863), Mary Breckinridge Letters.

5. Young, *Reminiscences,* pp. 46–48; Alexander F. Stevenson, *The Battle of Stones River, Near Murfreesboro, Tenn.* (Boston, 1884), p. 131.

6. Thompson, *Orphan Brigade,* pp. 406, 411, 452; Stevenson, *Stones River,* p. 132; "Conversational Remarks by C. R. Breckinridge" (Sept. 27, 1932), Breckinridge Papers in possession of Colonel James C. Breckinridge.

7. Thompson, *Orphan Brigade,* p. 406; Davis, *Breckinridge,* p. 342; Marshall, "Deeds of Daring," p. 473.

8. Richmond, *Examiner* (Feb. 25, 1863); Davis, *Breckinridge,* p. 343; Grainger, *Boys in Gray,* p. 14; Thompson, *Orphan Brigade,* p. 179.

9. J. Stoddard Johnston Diary (Jan. 2, 1863); Thompson, *Orphan Brigade,* pp. 199–200, 306, 378, 580; J. Stoddard Johnston, *Kentucky* (New York, 1962; Vol. IX of *Confederate Military History*), pp. 166–67.

10. Grainger, *Boys in Blue,* pp. 14–16; Thompson, *Orphan Brigade,* pp. 203, 470, 501–2, 560.

11. Thompson, *Orphan Brigade,* pp. 200, 664; Grainger, *Boys in Gray,* p.

16; "Taps," *Southern Bivouac*, I (Aug. 1883), p. 488; Marshall, "Deeds of Daring," p. 473.

12. Bush Diary (Jan. 2, 1863); Thompson, *Orphan Brigade*, pp. 196, 406.

13. Morning Report (Dec. 26, 1862), Chap. II, Vol. 310, RG 109, NA; Tabular Statement of Breckinridge's Division (Dec. 31, Jan. 2, 1863), James W. Eldridge Collection, Huntington; Thomas, *Orphan Brigade*, pp. 196–97.

14. Young, *Reminiscences*, p. 51; "E. P. Thompson," *Confederate Veteran*, IV (Nov. 1896), p. 368; Thompson, *Orphan Brigade*, p. 183; Thompson, *First Kentucky Brigade*, p. 386; "Editor's Table," *Southern Bivouac*, New Series, I (Sept. 1885), p. 255; "Query Box," *Southern Bivouac*, I (Apr. 1883), p. 362.

15. Grainger, *Boys in Gray*, p. 16; Kirwan, *Johnny Green*, p. 69; Thompson, *Orphan Brigade*, p. 379; Davis, *Breckinridge*, p. 363.

16. Unnumbered special order (Jan. 3, 1863), Eldridge Collection.

17. Officers to Davis (Jan. 14, 1863), W. E. Simms and others to Davis (Jan. 30, 1863), Hunt Compiled Service Record, unnumbered special order (Jan. 17, 1863), Chap. II, Vol. 308, RG 109, NA.

18. Buckner to Joseph E. Johnston (Feb. 6, 1863), Buckner Papers; Jackman Diary (unidentified 1895 clipping).

19. Mary Breckinridge to Breckinridge (Jan. 8, 1863), Mary Breckinridge Letters; Graves to Buckner (Jan. 8, 1863), Graves to Breckinridge (Jan. 24, 1863), Breckinridge to Cooper (Mar. 29, 1863), Preston to Cooper (Apr. 1, 1863), Graves Compiled Service Record, RG 109, NA.

20. Mary Breckinridge to Breckinridge (Jan. 8, Feb. 4, 8, 14, 15, 1863), Mary Breckinridge Letters.

21. O'Hara to Breckinridge (Jan. 23, 1863), Breckinridge to Thomas Watts (Feb. 15, 1864), Thomas O'Hara Compiled Service Record, Graves to Buckner (Jan. 3, 1863), Graves Compiled Service Record, Breckinridge to Hodge (Mar. 9, 1863), Breckinridge Compiled Service Record, RG 109, NA; Rice E. Graves, Charges and Specifications of Charges Against Brig. Gen. G. J. Pillow (n.d.), Breckinridge Papers, Chicago; John B. Gordon, *Reminiscences of the Civil War* (New York, 1904), pp. 192–93.

22. Marcus J. Wright to John V. Wright (Jan. 21, 1863), John V. Wright to the Congress (Feb. 1, 1863), Hardee to "General" (Jan. 13, 1863), Hunt to Breckinridge (Jan. 11, 1863), Officers to Breckinridge (Jan. 8, 1863), Hodge to Jefferson Davis (Feb. 1, 1863), Hodge to Breckinridge (Feb. 13, 1863), Edward Sparrow to the Senate (Feb. 17, 1863), Trabue Compiled Service Record, RG 109, NA; Mary Breckinridge to Breckinridge (Feb. 14, 1863), Mary Breckinridge Letters; General Order No. 7 (Feb. 28, 1863), Chap. II, Vol. 308, RG 109, NA.

23. Special Order No. 4 (Feb. 14, 1863), pay voucher (Feb. 3, 1863),

Helm Compiled Service Record, General Order No. 1 (Feb. 16, 1863), Chap. II, Vol. 308, RG 109, NA.

24. General Orders No. 25 (Feb. 13, 1863), No. 18 (Mar. 10, 1863), No. 13 (Apr. 2, 1863), No. 18 (Apr. 20, 1863), No. 27 (May 18, 1863), Chap. II, Vol. 308, General Order No. 2 (Mar. 1, 1863), Chap. II, Vol. 306, RG 109, NA; J. F. Heustis to Walter J. Byrne (Feb. 25, 1863), Kentucky Library, Western Kentucky University, Bowling Green; "Skirmish Line," *Southern Bivouac*, III (Nov. 1884), p. 133.

25. Jackman Diary (Jan. 6–May 22, 1863); Kirwan, *Johnny Green*, pp. 70–72; Bush Diary (Jan. 27, Feb. 8, 10, 24, Mar. 1, 22, 1863); Special Order No. 49 (May 5, 1863), Chap. II, Vol. 308, G. W. McCawley to Cobb (Mar. 26, 1863), Chap. II, Vol. 314 Military Departments, Orders and Circulars Received, 1st Kentucky Brigade (Aug. 1863–Jan. 1865), Nuckols to Breckinridge (Mar. 17, 1863), Nuckols Compiled Service Record, RG 109, NA; "Orphan Brigade Items," *Southern Bivouac*, III (Feb. 1885), p. 273; Winstead to Mollie Winstead (Feb. 17, 1863), Winstead Papers.

26. Jackman Diary, p. 71; Bush Diary (May 19–20, 1863); Thompson, *Orphan Brigade*, pp. 205, 223; Special Order No. 52 (May 10, 1863), Chap. II, Vol. 314, RG 109, NA.

27. Hunt to Bruce (Jan. 31, 1863), Hunt to Cooper (Mar. 6, 1863), Hunt Compiled Service Record, Special Order No. 78 (Apr. 22, 1863), General Order No. 6 (Apr. 30, 1863), General Order No. 1 (May 1, 1863), Chap. II, Vol. 308, RG 109, NA; Thompson, *First Kentucky Brigade*, p. 423; Thompson, *Orphan Brigade*, pp. 432–33, 448–49.

28. Morning Report (June 2, 1863), Chap. II, Vol. 310, RG 109, NA; Jackman Diary (May 23–24, 1863); Kirwan *Johnny Green*, pp. 77–78; Davis, *Breckinridge*, p. 365.

29. Walter Lord, ed., *The Fremantle Diary* (Boston, 1954), p. 107; Jackman Diary (May 25, 1863); John S. Jackman, "A Railroad Adventure," *Southern Bivouac*, I (Nov. 1882), pp. 109–12.

30. Jackman Diary, p. 78; Thompson, *Orphan Brigade*, pp. 507–8; Petition of Officers to Cooper (June 18, 1863), Lewis Compiled Service Record, RG 109, NA. Bush Diary (June 5, 8, 1863).

31. Jackman Diary (July 1–5, 1863); Thompson, *Orphan Brigade*, pp. 223–24.

32. Morning Report (July 8, 1863), Chap. II, Vol. 310, RG 109, NA; *O.R.*, I, 24, Part 2, p. 540; Jackman Diary (July 7–11, 1863).

33. Bush Diary (July 12, 1863); Thompson, *Orphan Brigade*, pp. 209, 532; A. W. Randolph to his parents (Sept. 27, 1863), Kentucky Library, Western Kentucky University; Richmond *Dispatch* (July 25, 1863); *O.R.*, I, 24, Part 2, p. 654; Johnston to Breckinridge (July 12, 1863), Chap. II, Vol. 313, Military Departments, Orders and Circulars Received, 1st Kentucky Brigade (1862–63), RG 109, NA; Jackman Diary (July 12–21, 1863).

34. Fred Joyce, "Infantry Stampede," *Southern Bivouac*, II (Jan. 1884), pp. 224–25; Thompson, *Orphan Brigade*, pp. 224–25; Kirwan, *Johnny Green*, pp. 83–84. James Wilson to brigade commanders (July 31, 1863), Chap. II, Vol. 311, RG 109, NA.

35. Fred Joyce, "Orphan Brigade Glee Club," *Southern Bivouac*, II (May 1884), pp. 414–15; General Order No. 35 (Aug. 17, 1863), Chap. II, Vol. 308, RG 109, NA; Jackman Diary, p. 85; Kirwan, *Johnny Green*, pp. 84–85; Mary Breckinridge to Breckinridge (June 26, 1863), Mary Breckinridge Letters.

NINE

1. Kirwan, *Johnny Green*, pp. 90–91; Jackman Diary (Sept. 2–17, 1863); Thompson, *Orphan Brigade*, p. 226.

2. Thompson, *Orphan Brigade*, pp. 226, 807.

3. Ibid., pp. 216–17; Morning Report (Sept. 16, 1863), Chap. II, Vol. 310, RG 109, NA; Jackman Diary (Sept. 19, 1863); Kirwan, *Johnny Green*, pp. 92–93.

4. Thompson, *Orphan Brigade*, pp. 217, 413; Jackman Diary (Sept. 20, 1863); Joyce, "Chickamauga," pp. 30–32.

5. J. M. Tydings, "The Charge of the First Kentucky Brigade at the Battle of Chickamauga," *Southern Bivouac*, I (Oct. 1882), p. 62; Randolph to his parents (Sept. 27, 1863); Thompson, *Orphan Brigade*, p. 217.

6. Thompson, *Orphan Brigade*, pp. 217, 225; Fred Joyce, "The Silent Man of Company 'D' Fourth Kentucky," *Southern Bivouac*, II (Oct. 1883), pp. 76–77; "Taps," *Southern Bivouac*, I (Oct. 1882), p. 82.

7. Randolph to his parents (Sept. 27, 1863); Wyeth, *That Devil Forrest*, p. 229; Tydings, "Charge of the First Kentucky," p. 63; Thompson, *Orphan Brigade*, p. 226.

8. Kirwan, *Johnny Green*, pp. 94–95; Otho Haydon Recollections, in possession of Ruby T. Rabey, Franklin, Ky.; "Taps," *Southern Bivouac*, I (Feb. 1883), p. 269; Thompson, *Orphan Brigade*, pp. 225, 597.

9. Kirwan, *Johnny Green*, pp. 95–96; *O.R.*, I, 30, Part 2, pp. 209, 213; Tydings, "Charge of the First Kentucky," p. 63.

10. Jackman Diary (Sept. 20, 1863); "Sketch of Gen. B. H. Helm," pp. 166–67; Thompson, *Orphan Brigade*, p. 506; Joyce, "Orphan Brigade at Chickamauga," p. 32; Castleman, *Active Service*, pp. 45–46.

11. Thompson, *First Kentucky Brigade*, pp. 357–58; Thompson, *Orphan Brigade*, p. 391.

12. Davis, *Breckinridge*, p. 377; Thompson, *Orphan Brigade*, p. 459; Jackman Diary (Sept. 20, 1863).

13. Lexington *Morning Herald* (Nov. 1, 1897); Thompson, *Orphan Brigade*, p. 452.

14. Kirwan, *Johnny Green,* pp. 97–99; *O.R.,* I, 30, Part 2, pp. 205, 209, 210, 212, 214, 216.

15. Kirwan, *Johnny Green,* p. 99; *O.R.,* I, 20, Part 1, pp. 972, 975; Marshall, "Deeds of Daring," p. 474.

16. John David Smith and William Cooper, Jr., eds., *Window on the War: Frances Dallam Peter's Lexington Civil War Diary* (Lexington, Ky., 1976), p. 37.

17. *O.R.,* I, 30, Part 2, pp. 205, 206, 208, 209, 210, 214, 216; Jackman Diary (undated clipping); Thompson, *Orphan Brigade,* pp. 385–86; William H. Townsend, *Lincoln and the Bluegrass* (Lexington, Ky., 1955), pp. 312–13; Davis, *Breckinridge,* pp. 378–79; Fred Joyce, "The Mother and Two Sons," *Southern Bivouac,* II (Mar. 1884), pp. 314–15.

18. Randolph to his parents (Sept. 27, 1863); "The Confederate Dead at Chickamauga," *Southern Bivouac,* II (Dec. 1883), p. 192; unidentified newspaper clipping in author's possession; Tydings, "Charge of the First Kentucky," p. 63.

TEN

1. Kirwan, *Johnny Green,* pp. 99–100, 104; Jackman Diary (Sept. 23, 1863).

2. Jackman Diary (Sept. 27, Oct. 10, 16, 1863); General Order No. 1 (Oct. 4, 1863), Chap. II, Vol. 310, Lewis to Cooper (Oct. 9, 1863), Lewis to Breckinridge (Oct. 22, 1863), Lewis Compiled Service Record, Emily Helm to William S. Rosecrans (Mar. 15, 1864), estate settlement (Nov. 9, 1863), Lincoln to "Whom It May Concern" (Dec. 14, 1863), Helm Compiled Service Record, RG 109, NA.

3. Johnson to Cooper (Sept. 30, 1863), Johnson Compiled Service Record, Special Order No. 248 (Oct. 19, 1863), Chap. II, Vol. 310, RG 109, NA.

4. Jackman Diary (Nov. 5 1863); Thompson, *Orphan Brigade,* pp. 226, 228–30; Special Order No. 285 (Nov. 3, 1863), Chap. II, Vol. 310, Hawkins to Cooper (June 18, 1862), Hawkins Compiled Service Record, RG 109, NA.

5. Thompson, *Orphan Brigade,* p. 780; General Order No. 2 (Oct. 22, 1863), Chap. II, Vol. 314, General Order No. 2 (Oct. 23, 1863), Special Order No. 17 (Nov. 2, 1863), Chap. II, Vol. 310, RG 109, NA; Kirwan, *Johnny Green,* pp. 105–7; "Nondescript" [John L. Marshall], "A Fair Divide," *Southern Bivouac,* I (Jan. 1883), pp. 215–16. "Captain John McGrath," *Southern Bivouac,* III (Dec. 1884), p. 180.

6. Winstead to Mollie Winstead (Nov. 23, 1863), Winstead Papers; Jackman Diary (Nov. 11–21, 1863); Thompson, *Orphan Brigade,* p. 232; General Order No. 8 (Oct. 26, 1863), Chap. II, Vol. 309, Orders Received, Morning

Reports and Returns, 1st Kentucky Brigade (Jan. 1863–May 1864), RG 109, NA.

7. Jackman Diary (Nov. 23–26, 1863); Kirwan, *Johnny Green,* pp. 109–11; S. R. Watkins and John S. Jackman, "The Battle of Missionary Ridge," *Southern Bivouac,* II (Jan. 1884), pp. 53–54; Thompson, *Orphan Brigade,* p. 231.

8. Kirwan, *Johnny Green,* pp. 111–14; Watkins and Jackman, "Missionary Ridge," pp. 54–58; Thompson, *Orphan Brigade,* pp. 231–32.

9. General Order No. 6 (Dec. 19, 1863), Chap. II, Vol. 310, RG 109, NA; Kirwan, *Johnny Green,* pp. 117–18; Jackman Diary (Nov. 30, Dec. 15, 22, 1863, Jan. 1, 1864).

10. Winstead to Mollie Winstead (Dec. 5, 12, 1863, Jan. 23, Feb. 29, 1864), Winstead Papers; Jackman Diary (Dec. 13, 17, 1863, Apr. 1, 1864), p. 193; Kirwan, *Johnny Green,* p. 118; Thompson, *First Kentucky Brigade,* p. 558; drawings in Chap. VIII, Vol. 67, Misc. Q.M. Accounts 2, 4, 5, 6, and 9th Ky. Regts., RG 109, NA.

11. Fred Joyce, "Dalton During the Winter 1863–64," *Southern Bivouac,* II (June 1884), pp. 464–65; Joyce, "Orphan Brigade Glee Club," p. 413; "Taps," *Southern Bivouac,* I (Feb. 1883), pp. 270–71; Winstead to Mollie Winstead (Jan. 23, 1864), Winstead Papers; Fred Joyce, "Georgia Girls," *Southern Bivouac,* III (Dec. 1884), pp. 159–60.

12. Unidentified clipping in Jackman Diary; Thompson, *Orphan Brigade,* pp. 234–36, 237–38; "Taps," *Southern Bivouac,* I (Oct. 1882), p. 83; General Order No. 9 (Jan. 22, 1864), Chap. II, Vol. 314, RG 109, NA; Kirwan, *Johnny Green,* pp. 119–20; "Nondescript" [John L. Marshall], "Beef Seekers," *Southern Bivouac,* I (Oct. 1882), pp. 69–72.

13. Jackman Diary (Jan. 17, 21, 24, Feb. 5, 7, Mar. 6, 8, 9, 13, Apr. 4, 1864); Thompson, *First Kentucky Brigade,* p. 407; Joyce, "Dalton," p. 464.

14. Jackman Diary (Dec. 24–25, 1863); Chap. VIII, Vol. 69, p. 223, RG 109, NA.

15. Circular (Feb. 12, 1864), Chap. II, Vol. 314, Jan. 27, Feb. 8, 1864, entries, Chap. VIII, Vol. 67, Chap. VIII, Vol. 72, Misc. Record of QM Stores Issued to the 4th, 5th, 6th, and 9th Kys. Vols., 1864–65, Voucher No. 25 (Dec. 7, 1863), No. 28 (Mar. 31, 1864), Requisition No. 26 (Feb. 29, 1864), Monthly Report of Transportation (Mar. 1864), Thompson Compiled Service Record, RG 109, NA.

16. Entries for Jan. 31, Feb. 21, 1864, Chap. VIII, Vol. 72, Circular, Mar. 19, 1864, Chap. II, Vol. 314, RG 109, NA; Winstead to Mollie Winstead (Jan. 23, 1864), Winstead Papers; Jackman Diary (Jan. 18, 25, 1864); Thompson, *Orphan Brigade,* p. 532.

17. Cofer to Bruce, (Dec. 29, 1863), Cofer Compiled Service Record, Morning Report (Jan. 1, 1864), Chap. II, Vol. 310, RG 109, NA; *O.R.,* I, 31, Part 3, pp. 877–78, 32, Part 2, pp. 520–21.

18. Breckinridge, Buckner, Morgan, and Lewis to Davis (Jan. 15, 1864), Jefferson Davis Collection, Tulane University Library, New Orleans; *O.R.,* I, 32, Part 2, pp. 621, 714, 727; Jackman Diary (Feb. 11, 1864), 1892 newspaper clipping; New York *Times* (Feb. 28, 1864); General Order No. 10 (Feb. 11, 1864), Chap. II, Vol. 310, RG 109, NA; Young, *Reminiscences,* p. 90.

ELEVEN

1. Special Order No. 28 (Nov. 30, 1863), No. 36 (Mar. 29, 1864), Chap. II, Vol. 310, Special Order (Feb. 4, 8, Mar. 14, 16, 1864), General Order No. 25 (Feb. 19, 1864), Chap. II, Vol. 314, RG 109, NA; unnumbered special order (Jan. 28, 1864), Winstead Papers; Thompson, *Orphan Brigade,* p. 394.

2. Circular (Feb. 4, 10, 1864), Chap. II, Vol. 314, RG 109, NA; Jackman Diary (Mar. 22, 23, Apr. 7, 1864); Thompson, *Orphan Brigade,* p. 239; Kirwan, *Johnny Green,* pp. 121–22.

3. Circular (Apr. 24, 1864), Chap. II, Vol. 314, RG 109, NA; Thompson, *Orphan Brigade,* pp. 240–42, 268, 269.

4. Undated clippings (May 7, 1864), Jackman Diary; Thompson, *Orphan Brigade,* pp. 23–24; Morning Report (May 1, 1864), Chap. II, Vol. 310, RG 109, NA.

5. Jackman Diary (May 7–14, 1864); John S. Jackman, "From Dalton to Atlanta," *Southern Bivouac,* I (May–June 1883), pp. 319–24; Fred Joyce, "A Hot May-Day at Resaca," *Southern Bivouac,* II (Nov. 1884), pp. 500–1; obituaries of David C. Walker furnished by Grace E. Drake, Franklin, Ky.; Fred Joyce, "A Kitten in Battle," *Southern Bivouac,* II (July 1884), pp. 522–23; Kirwan, *Johnny Green,* pp. 128–29.

6. Jackman Diary (May 16–25, 1864); *O.R.,* I, 38, Part 3, p. 686; Thompson, *Orphan Brigade,* pp. 251–52.

7. Jackman Diary (May 26–29, 1864); John S. Jackman, "From Dalton to Atlanta, II," *Southern Bivouac,* I (July 1883), pp. 415–19; Fred Joyce, "Scenes at Dallas," *Southern Bivouac,* II (May 1884), pp. 376–78; Kirwan, *Johnny Green,* pp. 132–33; Thompson, *Orphan Brigade,* pp. 268, 445, 502–3, 573, 607, 730; *O.R.,* I, 38, Part 3, p. 687.

8. Jackman Diary, May 29–June 14, 1864; Kirwan, *Johnny Green,* pp. 135–36; John S. Jackman, "From Dalton to Atlanta, III," *Southern Bivouac,* I (Aug. 1883), pp. 456–58.

9. Thompson, *Orphan Brigade,* pp. 260, 270–72, 470.

10. Morning Reports (May 7, June 8, 26, July 7, 1864), Chap. II, Vol. 310, J. B. Eustis to Lewis (June 21, 1864), Wickliffe Compiled Service Record, RG 109, NA; "Taps," *Southern Bivouac,* I (Feb. 1883), p. 270; "Taps,"

Southern Bivouac, II (Nov. 1883), p. 139; Thompson, *Orphan Brigade,* pp. 226, 735; Winstead to Mollie Winstead (June 28, 1864), Winstead Papers.

11. Kirwan, *Johnny Green,* p. 142; Thompson, *Orphan Brigade,* pp. 260–61.

12. Thompson, *Orphan Brigade,* pp. 261–62, 272–73, 476–77; Kirwan, *Johnny Green,* pp. 147–50; "Taps," *Southern Bivouac,* I (Jan. 1883), p. 223; Morning Report (July 27, 1864), Chap. II, Vol. 310, RG 109, NA.

13. Grainger, *Boys in Gray,* pp. 19–21; *O.R.,* I, 52, Part 2, p. 718.

14. Morning Report (Aug. 7, 1864), Chap. II, Vol. 310, RG 109, NA; Thompson, *Orphan Brigade,* pp. 265–66, 273, 274, 398, 436; *O.R.,* I, 38, Part 3, p. 321, Vol. 52, Part 2, pp. 726–27; H.H., "Color-Bearer of the Fourth Kentucky Infantry," *Southern Bivouac,* III (Feb. 1885), p. 255; Joyce, "Chaplains of the Fourth Kentucky," p. 118; Kirwan, *Johnny Green,* pp. 154–57; Grainger, *Boys in Gray,* pp. 19–20.

15. Thompson, *Orphan Brigade,* pp. 29, 266–68, 273, 780, 848; *O.R.,* I, 38, Part 1, pp. 171, 645, 655, 674, 811, Part 3, p. 696; Thompson, *First Kentucky Brigade,* p. 470; Grainger, *Boys in Gray,* pp. 20–21; Kirwan, *Johnny Green,* pp. 157–61; Morning Reports (May 7, Aug. 7, Sept. 6, 1864), Chap. II, Vol. 310, RG 109, NA; N. S. Shaler, "Nature and Man in America, Third Paper," *Scribner's Magazine,* VIII (Nov. 1890), p. 654.

TWELVE

1. Fred Joyce, "From Infantry to Cavalry," *Southern Bivouac,* III (Dec. 1884), p. 161.

2. Ibid., p. 161; Special Field Order No. 96 (Sept. 4, 1864), Chap. II, Vol. 310, RG 109, NA; Thompson, *Orphan Brigade,* p. 269.

3. Joyce, "Infantry to Cavalry," pp. 161–62; statements (Oct. 1–31, 1864), Chap. VIII, Vol. 67, Circular (Oct. 27, 1864), Chap. II, Vol. 314, RG 109, NA; Joyce, "Silent Man," p. 77; Marshall, "Heel and Toe, II," p. 304; Thompson, *Orphan Brigade,* pp. 270, 281; Kirwan, *Johnny Green,* p. 171.

4. Morning Reports (Sept. 15, Oct. 1, Nov. 1, 1864), Chap. II, Vol. 310, RG 109, NA; Thompson, *Orphan Brigade,* pp. 283, 392.

5. Thompson, *First Kentucky Brigade,* p. 404; Thompson, *Orphan Brigade,* pp. 281–82; Fred Joyce, "From Infantry to Cavalry, No. III," *Southern Bivouac,* III (Feb. 1885), pp. 252–54.

6. *O.R.,* I, 44, pp. 81, 382, 881, 888, 907, Vol. 53, pp. 33–34; Fred Joyce, "From Infantry to Cavalry, No. IV," *Southern Bivouac,* III (Mar. 1885), pp. 299–300; Thompson, *Orphan Brigade,* p. 635.

7. *O.R.,* I, 44, pp. 922–23, 961, 965, Vol. 45, Part 2, p. 669; Thompson, *Orphan Brigade,* p. 24.

8. Kirwan, *Johnny Green,* pp. 179–80; Jackman Diary (Dec. 25, 1864); Joyce, "Infantry to Cavalry," p. 301.

9. Thompson, *First Kentucky Brigade,* pp. 404–5, 407; "Swift Justice," *Southern Bivouac,* III (Jan. 1885), p. 214; undated clipping in Jackman Diary; Thomas Owens, "Standing Picket in a Georgia Swamp," *Southern Bivouac,* I (Apr. 1883), pp. 330–32; "Taps," *Southern Bivouac,* I (Oct. 1882), p. 85; Marshall to Breckinridge (Feb. 23, 1865), Hawkins Compiled Service Record, RG 109, NA.

10. Thompson, *Orphan Brigade,* pp. 25–26, 392, 664; Special Order No. 110 (Dec. 29, 1864), Lewis Compiled Service Record, General Order (Jan. 17, 1865), Chap. II, Vol. 314, unnumbered, undated entry in Chap. VIII, Vol. 72, RG 109, NA; Thompson, *First Kentucky Brigade,* p. 359; *O.R.,* I, 47, Part 2, pp. 1,072, 1,149–50.

11. Thompson, *Orphan Brigade,* pp. 660, 666, 694, 701; John L. Marshall, "Captain William Lashbrook," *Southern Bivouac,* I (Feb. 1883), pp. 247–48.

12. Thompson, *Orphan Brigade,* pp. 291–93; "Taps," *Southern Bivouac,* I (Oct. 1882), p. 83; Joyce, "Orphan Brigade Glee Club," pp. 414–15; Fred Joyce, "From Infantry to Cavalry, No. II," *Southern Bivouac,* III (Jan. 1885), p. 222; Jackman Diary (Dec. 11, 23, 1864, Jan. 1, 10, 13, Feb. 1, 1865); Kirwan, *Johnny Green,* p. 188.

13. Thompson, *Orphan Brigade,* pp. 283, 602; T. H. Ellis, "Columbia—As Seen by a Rebel Scouting Party the Day After Sherman's Evacuation," *Southern Bivouac,* I (Oct. 1882), pp. 74–78.

14. Thompson, *Orphan Brigade,* pp. 24, 283, 436–37, 477; Thompson, *First Kentucky Brigade,* p. 470; *O.R.,* I, 47, Part 3, p. 716; Kirwan, *Johnny Green,* pp. 192–93.

15. Thompson, *Orphan Brigade,* pp. 285, 290, 394, 789; Joyce, "Silent Man," p. 77; obituary in Joseph H. Lewis Scrapbook; Louisville *Post* (Jan. 30, 1908); Kirwan, *Johnny Green,* p. 194.

16. Joyce, "From Infantry to Cavalry, No. IV," p. 301; Kirwan, *Johnny Green,* pp. 195–96; P. M. B. Young to Lewis (May 2, 1865), Joseph H. Lewis Scrapbook; *O.R.,* I, 49, Part 2, pp. 603–4.

17. Jackman Diary, pp. 177–81, 193–94; Beth G. Crabtree and James W. Patton, eds., *"Journal of a Secesh Lady": The Diary of Catherine Ann Devereux Edmondston, 1860–1866* (Raleigh, N.C., 1979), p. 672; Kirwan, *Johnny Green,* p. 196; Davis, *Breckinridge,* pp. 497–98, 522–24; Thompson, *Orphan Brigade,* pp. 395, 842; Thompson, *First Kentucky Brigade,* pp. 370–71.

THIRTEEN

1. Lewis to G. Whipple (June 27, 1865), Lewis Compiled Service Record, RG 109, NA; Jackman Diary, pp. 181–83; Kirwan, *Johnny Green,* pp. 197–207.

2. Grainger, *Boys in Gray*, pp. 42–43; Thompson, *Orphan Brigade*, pp. 1,048–49.

3. Thompson, *Orphan Brigade*, pp. 450, 477–79, 490–91, 532, 829, 1,048–54; Louisville *Courier-Journal* (June 14, 1920); Louisville *Times* (June 14, 1920).

4. Davis, *Breckinridge*, pp. 590–92, 613–14.

5. John H. Weller, "The Confederate Dead at Chickamauga," *Southern Bivouac*, II (Dec. 1883), p. 192; Thompson, *Orphan Brigade*, pp. 325–26.

6. Thompson, *Orphan Brigade*, p. 840; undated cards in Jackman Diary; "The Southern Bivouac," *Southern Bivouac*, III (May 1885), pp. 424–26.

7. Clippings in Jackman Diary; "Letter from Fred Joyce, Company D, Fourth Kentucky Infantry," *Southern Bivouac*, II (Sept. 1883), p. 31; "Third Reunion of the Kentucky Brigade," *Southern Bivouac*, III (Nov. 1884), pp. 120–21.

A Note on the Sources

It is quite surprising when dealing with an organization as large and as literate as the Orphan Brigade to discover a relative dearth of source materials. Only two bona fide diaries and one small collection of soldier letters are known to exist. Surely more are lurking somewhere, but an extensive search of Kentucky has failed to reveal them. How unusual this is when compared to the fact that more than four thousand Kentuckians served with the brigade, and that so many of them were writers and prominent individuals both before and after the war. The lack of letters, however, is probably explained by the fact that the Confederate postal service could not operate in Kentucky, and letters home had to go through Union lines and the federal post via flag of truce and a very circuitous route. Most probably never reached their destinations and were lost in transit.

How fortunate we are, then, that the sources that are available on the organization are of such uniformly superior quality. With only a few exceptions, the materials for studying the 1st Kentucky Brigade are of a character decidedly better and more reliable than those extant for any other similar unit in the Confederate Army. What follows are comments designed to illuminate the particular features of the more important sources, after which appears an accounting of all sources used in writing this book.

By far the most valuable single source for the Orphan Brigade is the collection of its official papers that Fayette Hewitt gave to the United States War Department in 1887 when that agency was compiling its mammoth *Official Records*. It is unique among the records of Confederate commands. The collection consists of twenty bound volumes of morning reports, orders and circulars, telegrams, copies of letters sent and received at brigade headquarters, records of details and furloughs, hospital reports, and quartermaster and clothing accounts. They now reside in the National Archives in Washington, D.C., designated as Chapter II, Volumes 305–17, Chapter VI, Volume 663, and Chapter VIII, Volumes 67–72, in Record Group 109. In addition to the bound volumes, Hewitt turned over thousands of pieces of individual correspondence, reports, courts-martial statements, and the like. Much of this material is now filed in the individual compiled service records of the generals, staff, officers, and men of the brigade, also in Record Group 109. The cumulative picture that this mass of official records presents is invaluable to understanding not only the formal service of the Orphans, but also their human element.

Unfortunately, the yield is not so bountiful when one seeks the personal papers of the Orphans. Simon Buckner's Papers at the Huntington Library provide little. Numerous collections of John C. Breckinridge Papers, particularly those at the Chicago Historical Society, the Huntington Library, and the New-York Historical Society add a little more, as do the Breckinridge Family Papers at the Library of Congress. Unfortunately, the bulk of Breckinridge's war papers burned in a house fire in Lexington in the early 1870s. We are fortunate in a splendid collection of Roger W. Hanson Letters at the Library of Congress, almost all relating to his term as a prisoner of war. Yet within them is much of "Old Bench-leg's" spirit, and some good comment on his 2d Kentucky. Joseph H. Lewis' papers, too, went up in flames, but a scrapbook of his does survive in the possession of his granddaughter, Helene Lewis Gildred of San Diego. The one set of letters mentioned previously are the Thomas Winstead Papers in the possession of Mr. Thomas D. Winstead of Elizabethtown, Kentucky. Though they contain relatively little about the doings of the brigade, still their very rarity makes them invaluable, particularly for their picture of the anguish one Kentuckian suffered over his defenseless family at home.

Next in importance are the unit histories, a field dominated, of course, by Ed Porter Thompson's *History of the First Kentucky Brigade* and *History of the Orphan Brigade*. Both are monumental works, and in the main far more accurate than most Civil War unit histories, thanks to a thorough grounding in the brigade's official papers. Their actual narrative portions are somewhat lackluster, being frequently long verbatim extracts from official reports. What sets them apart, however, are the rich wealth of anecdote and story scattered throughout. In the later volume, these are gathered at the ends of the appropriate chapters, but still one must glean the individual soldier sketches that make up the bulk of the book, for Thompson buried much there as well. Also, though the 1898 work is chiefly an expansion of the 1868 volume, there is still some excellent material in the earlier book that he omitted in its successor. Both must be used in tandem.

George B. Hodge's 1874 *Sketch of the First Kentucky Brigade* is largely a revision of a series of articles he published in *Land We Love* in 1867–68. No attempt is made at official history. Rather, it is a largely personal memoir that ends at Shiloh. It devotes considerable space to Breckinridge and Morgan, and gives an excellent account of the retreat from Bowling Green. Unfortunately, the same cannot be said of Henry George's *History of the 3d, 7th, 8th, and 12th Kentucky, C.S.A.*, published in 1911. The portion of it that recounts the brief service of the 3d and 7th Kentucky infantries with the Orphans is chiefly plagiarized from Hodge and Thompson. Much better is Basil W. Duke's *A History of Morgan's Cavalry*, published in 1867. This provides excellent material on the background of Confederate Kentuckians, Camp Boone, Hanson, and Breckinridge, and particularly of the Orphans' part at Hartsville.

Biographies of the leaders of the Orphan Brigade are few and of varying usefulness. Arndt M. Stickles' *Simon Bolivar Buckner, Borderland Knight* is an excellent biography that offers much on the State Guard, but little on the Orphans. William C. Davis' *Breckinridge: Statesman, Soldier, Symbol,* published in 1974, is the fullest biography of that colorful figure. In 1943 R. Gerald McMurtry published his brief *Ben Hardin Helm,* which, though the best source available on this gentle man, sheds no light on the story of his brigade.

Of soldier reminiscences there are several, but their quality varies greatly. Unquestionably the finest is John S. Jackman's Journal in the Library of Congress, a source rivaling the official papers and Thompson's books in importance. This is a copy Jackman began in the summer of 1865, working from and often expanding his actual wartime notes from the 9th Kentucky. The work was finished sometime prior to 1868, for he loaned it to Thompson when the latter was writing his first book. Jackman's journal captured the human element of the Orphans better than any other single source, and as well provides vital illumination on several subjects—notably the mutinies in the 6th and 9th Kentucky regiments—for which the official records are too brief, and Thompson altogether silent. Additionally, Jackman includes two wartime letters he wrote to southern editors for publication, and the last portion of the journal is a scrapbook of his postwar articles, clippings describing reunions, copies of speeches, and other material of great interest. It is fortunate that Jackman's ill health prevented his performing greater service in the field, for it saved him to the larger work of leaving this outstanding record of his command.

The only completely contemporaneous soldier account we have is from the 6th Kentucky, the Squire Helm Bush Diary at the Hardin County Historical Society. It covers only the period October 1, 1862, to December 1, 1863, and is more often than not frustratingly brief, but still it provides occasional glimpses of the Orphans' life and attitudes.

Of a completely different character are the reminiscences written in later years. Gervis Grainger's *Four Years with the Boys in Gray* was not published until 1902, and is almost worthless. His dates and accounts of battles are invariably wrong, and much of the major action of the brigade he missed due to illness or imprisonment. His book is useful only for occasional anecdotal material, and for his admitted part in the mutiny of the 6th Kentucky. Much the same is the case with Lot Young's 1912 edition of *Reminiscences of a Soldier of the Orphan Brigade,* his record of service with the 4th Kentucky.

A special case is Albert D. Kirwan's edition of *Johnny Green of the Orphan Brigade,* published in 1956. Regarded since its appearance as an important work on the Kentucky Brigade, it too is highly unreliable. Kirwan states that Green wrote it chiefly from memory and some wartime notes, starting around 1890. As with most memoirs written years after the fact, it is often wrong in its chronology. More than this, however, Johnny Green incorporated into his work as his own, accounts of events that he actually borrowed from others. It is clear that he drew much from Jackman's 1866 articles and his later publications in the *Southern Bivouac,* his accounts sometimes matching Jackman's almost word for word. Indeed, it is clear that Green was an avid reader of the *Bivouac,* for several anecdotal episodes described therein he appropriated into his own narrative, in the process making himself the protagonist. As a result, while Green's memoir is useful only for its colorful incidents and episodes of the 9th Kentucky, one must be careful even with them, not knowing whether they really happened to Johnny or he just borrowed them from someone else.

The first three volumes of the *Southern Bivouac* are in a class of their own. Intended to memorialize all Kentuckians in the Confederacy, its articles reflect chiefly a preoccupation with the 4th Kentucky, not surprising since two of its editors came from that unit. Articles by Jackman, John Marshall, Pirtle, Owens, Tydings, and others give an outstanding picture of the spirit of these men, and do more to add flesh to an account of their camp and field life than any other source. A special note must be made of the contributions of "Fred Joyce" to the *Bivouac.* They make up nearly half of the total Orphan Brigade articles published during those three years. Yet no man of that name served in the brigade! The name does not appear in Thompson's rosters, nor among the service records in the National Archives, but the writing rings too true to be fabricated. Clearly, Fred Joyce was a *nom de plume,* but a study of his articles gives enough clues to identify the real author. He served in Company D, 4th Kentucky. He was a member of the glee club. He was wounded at Chickamauga, recuperated at Dalton and Atlanta, and served in the mounted engagements as a captain. Happily there is one, and only one, Orphan who fits these criteria, Captain John Weller. And he happened to be one of the editors of the *Bivouac,* which explains the use of a sobriquet. Clearly it did not look good for an editor to contribute too often to his own journal, yet frequently Weller and Marshall had to write their own recollections in order to fill out an issue. Marshall used a pen name, "Nondescript," so there was no reason for Weller not to do likewise. How and why he chose Fred Joyce, however, was and is a mystery.

In light of all of the foregoing, and the general high quality of it, how unfortunate it is that no comparable sources exist for either the 2d or 5th Kentucky infantries. Aside from only one or two very brief articles in the *Bivouac,* the veterans of those units remained silent. And we have nothing from the men of Byrne, Cobb, or Graves.

For general background on Kentucky during the war, the best single source is E. Merton Coulter, *Civil War and Readjustment in Kentucky.* Also useful is J. Stoddard Johnston's *Kentucky,* Volume IX in the *Confederate Military History.* And for the story of the State Guard, the best recent work is Richard G. Stone's *A Brittle Sword.* And, of course, for any book on any aspect of the Civil War, the U. S. War Department's *War of the Rebellion: Official Records of the Union and Confederate Armies* is indispensable. It is particularly full for the early years of the Kentucky brigade's service.

Bibliography

MANUSCRIPTS

Breckinridge Family Papers, Library of Congress.
Breckinridge, John C. Papers, in possession of Mrs. J. C. Breckinridge, Summit Point, W.Va.
———. Chicago Historical Society.
———. Henry E. Huntington Library, San Marino, Calif.
———. New-York Historical Society, New York, N.Y.
———. Western Reserve Historical Society, Cleveland, O.
Breckinridge, Mary C. Letters, in John C. Breckinridge Compiled Service Record, Record Group 109, National Archives.
Buck, Samuel D. Papers, William Perkins Library, Duke University, Durham, N.C.
Buckner, Simon B. Papers, Henry E. Huntington Library.
———. "To the People of Kentucky," University of Kentucky Library, Lexington.
Bush, Squire Helm. Diary, 1862–63, Hardin County Historical Society, Elizabethtown, Ky.
Chap. II, Vol. 305, Military Departments. Orders Received by the 1st Kentucky Brigade, Apr.–Oct. 1862, Record Group 109, National Archives.
———. Vol. 306, Orders and Circulars Received by 1st Kentucky Brigade, Nov. 1862–May 1863.
———. Vol. 307, Military Departments. Orders and Circulars Received by 1st Kentucky Brigade, Nov. 1861–Apr. 1864.

————. Vol. 308, Military Departments. Orders Received and Orders Issued by 1st Kentucky Brigade, 1862–63.

————. Vol. 309, Orders Received, Morning Reports and Returns, 1st Kentucky Brigade, Jan. 1863–May 1864.

————. Vol. 310, Military Departments. Orders Received, Orders Issued, and Morning Reports, 1st Kentucky Brigade, Aug. 1862–Oct. 1864.

————. Vol. 311, Letters, Telegrams Received and Sent by Gen. Breckinridge's Command, Dec. 1861–Nov. 1863.

————. Vol. 312, Military Departments. Orders and Circulars Received, 1st Kentucky Brigade, 1862–63.

————. Vol. 313, Military Departments. Orders and Circulars Received, 1st Kentucky Brigade, 1862–63.

————. Vol. 314, Military Departments. Orders and Circulars Received, 1st Kentucky Brigade, Aug. 1863–Jan. 1865.

————. Vol. 315, Military Departments. Special Orders Received and Record of Details, Discharges, Furloughs, and Transfers, 1st Kentucky Brigade, 1862–63.

————. Vol. 316, Military Departments. Special Orders Received, 1st Kentucky Brigade, Nov. 1861–Oct. 1862.

————. Vol. 317, Military Departments. Morning Reports, 1st Kentucky Brigade, Nov. 1861–Feb. 1862.

Chap. VI, Vol. 663, Medical Department Register of Patients of 2d Kentucky Infantry Hospital and of Hospitals at Tunnel Hill, Ga., and Miscellaneous Data Pertaining to Other Hospitals, 1863–65, Record Group 109, National Archives.

Chap. VIII, Vol. 67, Miscellaneous Quartermaster Accounts, 2d, 4th, 5th, 6th, and 9th Kentucky regiments, undated. Record Group 109, National Archives.

————. Vol. 68, Miscellaneous Quartermaster Accounts, 2d, 4th, 5th, 6th, and 9th Kentucky regiments.

————. Vol. 69, Clothing Account Book, Company C, 4th Kentucky Volunteers, 1862–64.

————. Vol. 70, Miscellaneous Quartermaster Accounts, 4th Kentucky Volunteers.

————. Vol. 71, Miscellaneous Quartermaster Accounts, 4th Kentucky Volunteers.

————. Vol. 72, Miscellaneous Record of Quartermaster Stores Issued to the 4th, 5th, 6th, and 9th Kentucky Volunteers, 1864–65.

Chap. IX, Vol. 26, Secretary of War. Register of Letters Received Sept. 1862–Apr. 1863, A–L, Record Group 109, National Archives.

Clay, Thomas J. Papers. Library of Congress.

Compiled Service Records, Record Group 109, National Archives, for the following:

Breckinridge, John C.
Breckinridge, Joseph Cabell
Buckner, Simon B.
Caldwell, John W.
Cobb, Robert
Cofer, Martin H.
Graves, Rice E.
Hanson, Roger W.
Hawes, Joseph M.
Hawkins, Hiram
Helm, Ben Hardin
Hewitt, James W.
Hunt, Thomas H.
Johnson, Robert A.
Kenshattentyeth (Flying Cloud)
Lee, Philip Lightfoot
Lewis, Asa
Lewis, Joseph H.
Moss, James W.
Nuckols, Joseph P.
O'Hara, Theodore H.
Thompson, Ed Porter
Trabue, Robert P.
Wickliffe, John C.

Crittenden, John J. Papers, Library of Congress.
Davis, Jefferson. Collection, Tulane University, New Orleans, La.
Dearborn, Frederick M. Collection, Houghton Library, Harvard University, Cambridge, Mass.
Eldridge, James W. Collection, Henry E. Huntington Library.
Ferguson, H. E. Letters, in possession of Mrs. Howard Jones, Glasgow, Ky.
Flagg, Samuel G. Collection, Yale University Library, New Haven, Conn.
General Order No. 22, Dec. 10, 1862, Record Group 109, National Archives.
Hanson, Roger W. Papers, Library of Congress.
Haydon, Otho. Recollections, in possession of Ruby T. Rabey, Franklin, Ky.
Heustis, J. F. Letter, Kentucky Library, Western Kentucky University, Bowling Green, Ky.
Jackman, John S. Journal, Library of Congress.
Johnston, J. Stoddard. Papers, Filson Club, Louisville, Ky.

Lewis, Joseph H. Scrapbook, in possession of Helene Lewis Gildred, San Diego, Calif.

Marckmann, Mrs. George. Diary, in possession of W. Maury Darst, Galveston, Tex.

Polk, Leonidas. Papers, Southern Historical Collection, University of North Carolina, Chapel Hill, N.C.

Preston, William. "Memoranda of A. S. Johnston's Death, Battle of Shiloh &c.," Record Group 94, Box 2, Special File, Item 16, National Archives.

Randolph, A. W. Letters, Kentucky Library, Western Kentucky University, Bowling Green, Ky.

Reed, Grace E. Papers, Franklin, Ky.

Ulmer L. B. "A Glimpse of Johnstone Through the Smoke of Shiloh," Choctaw County Public Library, Butler, Ala., 1901.

Voucher 4, Dec. 8, 1862, Manuscript 1,526, Record Group 109, National Archives.

Wade, Sadie M. Letter to author.

Winstead, Thomas. Papers, in possession of Mr. Thomas D. Winstead, Elizabethtown, Ky.

Yerger, William. Papers, Mississippi Department of Archives and History, Jackson, Miss.

Young, A. E. Letters, in possession of Mrs. Howard Jones, Glasgow, Ky.

NEWSPAPERS

Baltimore *American*
Frankfort *Weekly Kentucky Yeoman*
Lexington, Ky., *Morning Herald*
Lexington *Sunday Leader*
Louisville *Courier-Journal*
Louisville *Times*
New York *Turf, Field & Farm*
Richmond *Daily Dispatch*
Richmond *Enquirer*

BOOKS

Anderson, John Q., ed. *Brokenburn: The Journal of Kate Stone*. Baton Rouge, La., 1955.

Baird, Nancy D. *David Wendel Yandell, Physician of Old Louisville*. Lexington, Ky., 1978.

Byers, S. M. H. *Iowa in War Times*. Des Moines, Ia., 1888.

Castleman, John B. *Active Service*. Louisville, Ky., 1917.

Coleman, J. Winston, Jr. *Famous Kentucky Duels*. Lexington, Ky., 1969.

Coulter, E. Merton. *Civil War and Readjustment in Kentucky*. Chapel Hill, N.C., 1926.

Crabtree, Beth Gilbert, and Patton, James W., eds. *"Journal of a Secesh Lady": The Diary of Catherine Ann Devereux Edmondston, 1860–1866*. Raleigh, N.C., 1979.

Davis, Reuben. *Recollections of Mississippi and Mississippians*. University, Miss., 1972.

Davis, William C. *Breckinridge: Statesman, Soldier, Symbol*. Baton Rouge, La., 1974.

De Fontaine, Felix G. *Marginalia, or Gleanings from an Army Note-Book*. Columbia, S.C., 1864.

Duke, Basil W. *A History of Morgan's Cavalry*. Cincinnati, O., 1867.

———. *Reminiscences of General Basil W. Duke, C.S.A.* New York, 1911.

George, Henry. *History of the 3d, 7th, 8th, and 12th Kentucky, C.S.A.* Louisville, Ky., 1911.

Gordon, John B. *Reminiscences of the Civil War*. New York, 1904.

Grainger, Gervis D. *Four Years with the Boys in Gray*. Franklin, Ky., 1902.

Hartje, Robert G. *Van Dorn: The Life and Times of a Confederate General*. Nashville, Tenn., 1967.

Hodge, George B. *Sketch of the First Kentucky Brigade*. Frankfort, Ky., 1874.

Hundley, David R. *Prison Echoes of the Great Rebellion*. New York, 1874.

Johnston, J. Stoddard. *Kentucky*. Volume IX of Clement A. Evans, ed., *Confederate Military History*. New York, 1962.

Johnston, William P. *The Life of Gen. Albert Sidney Johnston*. New York, 1879.

Jones, John B. *A Rebel War Clerk's Diary at the Confederate States Capital*, 2 vols. Philadelphia, Pa., 1866.

Jordan, Thomas, and Pryor, J. P. *The Campaigns of Lieut.-Gen. N. B. Forrest, and of Forrest's Cavalry*. Dayton, O., 1973.

Journals of the Congress of the Confederate States of America, 7 vols. Washington, D.C., 1904–5.

Kirwan, Albert D., ed. *Johnny Green of the Orphan Brigade*. Lexington, Ky., 1956.

Lindsley, John B., ed. *The Military Annals of Tennessee (Confederate)*. Nashville, Tenn., 1886.

Lord, Walter, ed. *The Fremantle Diary*. Boston, Mass., 1954.

McMurtry, R. Gerald. *Ben Hardin Helm*. Chicago, Ill., 1943.

Mathias, Frank F., ed. *Incidents & Experiences in the Life of Thomas W. Parsons from 1826 to 1900*. Lexington, Ky., 1975.

Moore, Frank, comp. *Rebellion Record*, 11 vols. New York, 1862–68.

Murray, W. J. *History of the Twentieth Tennessee Regiment Volunteer Infantry, C.S.A.* Nashville, Tenn., 1904.

Polk, William M. *Leonidas Polk, Bishop and General,* 2 vols. New York, 1915.

Resolution of the [Confederate] Congress [in Kentucky]. Lyndon, Ky., 1970.

Ridley, Bromfield L. *Battles and Sketches of the Army of Tennessee.* Dayton, O., 1978.

Roman, Alfred. *The Military Operations of General Beauregard in the War Between the States,* 2 vols. New York, 1884.

Smith, John David and Cooper, William, Jr., eds. *Window on the War: Frances Dallam Peter's Lexington Civil War Diary.* Lexington, Ky., 1976.

Stevenson, Alexander F. *The Battle of Stones River near Murfreesboro, Tenn.* Boston, Mass., 1884.

Stevenson, William G. *Thirteen Months in the Rebel Army.* New York, 1864.

Stickles, Arndt M. *Simon Bolivar Buckner, Borderland Knight.* Chapel Hill, N.C., 1940.

Stone, Richard G. *A Brittle Sword: The Kentucky Militia, 1776–1912.* Lexington, Ky., 1978.

Thomas, Edison H. *John Hunt Morgan and His Raiders.* Lexington, Ky., 1975.

Thompson, Ed Porter. *History of the First Kentucky Brigade.* Cincinnati, O., 1868.

———. *History of the Orphan Brigade.* Louisville, Ky., 1898.

Townsend, William H. *Lincoln and the Bluegrass.* Lexington, Ky., 1955.

U. S. Congress. *Congressional Record.* 67th Cong., 1st sess., Vol. 61, Part 7. Washington, D.C., 1921.

U. S. War Department. *War of the Rebellion. Official Records of the Union and Confederate Armies,* 128 vols. Washington, D.C., 1880–1901.

Wilson, LeGrand J. *The Confederate Soldier.* Memphis, Tenn., 1973.

Wyeth, John A. *That Devil Forrest.* New York, 1959.

Young, Lot D. *Reminiscences of a Soldier of the Orphan Brigade.* Louisville, 1912.

ARTICLES

"A.B." "The Eighth Kentucky at Pearl River," *Southern Bivouac,* I, New Series, Oct. 1885, p. 313.

"A Certain Captain," *Southern Bivouac,* II, June 1884, p. 468.

Avery, B. F. "The Southern Bivouac," *Southern Bivouac,* III, May 1885, pp. 424–26.

"Captain John McGrath," *Southern Bivouac,* III, Dec. 1884, p. 180.

Casseday, Morton M. "The Surrender of Fort Donelson," *Southern Bivouac,* II, New Series, Apr. 1887, pp. 694–97.

Chalaron, J. A. "Vivid Experiences at Chickamauga," *Confederate Veteran,* III, Sept. 1895, pp. 278–79.

———. "The Washington Artillery in the Army of Tennessee," *Southern Historical Society Papers,* X, Apr.–May 1883, pp. 217–22.

Champ, Bruce. "Dear Bivouac," *Southern Bivouac,* II, May 1884, p. 379.

"Coffee-boiler Rangers," *Southern Bivouac,* I, July 1883, pp. 442–43.

Duke, Basil W. "Address of General Duke," *Southern Bivouac,* II, Nov. 1883, pp. 105–11.

———. "The Battle of Hartsville," *Southern Bivouac,* I, Oct. 1882, pp. 41–51.

"E. P. Thompson," *Confederate Veteran,* IV, Nov. 1896, p. 368.

"Editorial," *Southern Bivouac,* I, Sept. 1883, p. 45.

"Editor's Table," *Southern Bivouac,* I, New Series, Sept. 1885, p. 255.

Ellis, T. H. "Columbia—As Seen by a Rebel Scouting Party the Day After Sherman's Evacuation," *Southern Bivouac,* I, Oct. 1882, pp. 74–78.

"For His Own Side," *Southern Bivouac,* II, Feb. 1884, p. 277.

Funk, Frank. "Fort Donelson," *Southern Bivouac,* I, May–June 1883, pp. 344–46.

"Governor Letcher's Official Correspondence," *Southern Historical Society Papers,* I, June 1876, pp. 455–62.

"H.C.S.," *Southern Bivouac,* I, Dec. 1882, p. 147.

H.H. "Color-bearer of the Fourth Kentucky Infantry," *Southern Bivouac,* III, Feb. 1885, p. 255.

Horde, H. E. "Recollections of Gen. J. C. Breckinridge," *Confederate Veteran,* XVII, Dec. 1909, p. 594.

Jackman, John S. "A Railroad Adventure," *Southern Bivouac,* I, Nov. 1882, pp. 109–12.

———. "Battle of Murfreesboro," *Southern Bivouac,* III, Mar. 1885, pp. 295–99.

———. "Foraging for Literature," *Southern Bivouac,* II, June 1884, pp. 457–58.

———. "From Dalton to Atlanta," *Southern Bivouac,* I, May–June 1883, pp. 319–28; July 1883, pp. 414–20; Aug. 1883, pp. 451–59.

———. "Vicksburg in 1862," *Southern Bivouac,* III, Sept. 1884, pp. 1–8.

Johnson, E. Polk. "Some Generals I Have Known," *Southern Bivouac,* I, New Series, July 1885, pp. 120–22.

Johnston, J. Stoddard. "Sam Laurence," *Confederate Veteran,* X, May 1902, pp. 200–1.

Jordan, Thomas. "Notes of a Confederate Staff Officer" in R. Johnson and C. C. Buel, *Battles and Leaders of the Civil War,* New York, 1887–88, I, pp. 594–603.

Joyce, Fred [John H. Weller]. "A Hot May-Day at Resaca," *Southern Bivouac,* II, July 1884, pp. 499–501.
———. "A Kitten in Battle," *Southern Bivouac,* II, July 1884, pp. 522–23.
———. "Chaplains of the Fourth Kentucky," *Southern Bivouac,* I, Nov. 1882, pp. 116–18.
———. "Dalton During the Winter 1863–64," *Southern Bivouac,* II, June 1884, pp. 463–65.
———. "From Infantry to Cavalry," *Southern Bivouac,* III, Part 1, Dec. 1884, pp. 161–62; Part 2, Jan. 1885, pp. 221–22, Part 3, Feb. 1885, pp. 252–55; Part 4, Mar. 1885, pp. 299–301.
———. "Georgia Girls," *Southern Bivouac,* III, Dec. 1884, pp. 159–60.
———. "Infantry Stampede," *Southern Bivouac,* II, Jan. 1884, pp. 223–25.
———. "The Irishmen of Company D, Fourth Kentucky Infantry," *Southern Bivouac,* II, Feb. 1884, pp. 268–69.
———. "Letter," *Southern Bivouac,* II, Sept. 1883, pp. 30–31.
———. "The Mother and Two Sons," *Southern Bivouac,* II, Mar. 1884, pp. 314–15.
———. "Orphan Brigade at Chickamauga," *Southern Bivouac,* III, Sept. 1884, pp. 29–32.
———. "Orphan Brigade Glee Club," *Southern Bivouac,* II, May 1884, pp. 413–15.
———. "Scenes at Dallas," *Southern Bivouac,* II, May 1884, pp. 376–78.
———. "The Silent Man of Company D, Fourth Kentucky," *Southern Bivouac,* II, Oct. 1883, pp. 76–77.
———. "Taps," *Southern Bivouac,* I, Mar. 1883, pp. 316–18.
———. "Two Dogs," *Southern Bivouac,* I, Oct. 1882, pp. 72–74.
———. "Why Sue Mundy Became a Guerrilla and Some Facts Concerning His Early Life," *Southern Bivouac,* II, Nov. 1883, pp. 124–28.
"Major Thomas H. Hays," *Southern Bivouac,* III, Mar. 1885, pp. 333–34.
Marriner, W. N. "The Battle of Missionary Ridge," *Southern Bivouac,* II, Jan. 1884, pp. 193–201.
———. "How Brandy Saved Two Lives," *Southern Bivouac,* III, Dec. 1884, pp. 164–66.
———. "Sketch of Lieutenant-General N. B. Forrest, Part 1," *Southern Bivouac,* II, Mar. 1884, pp. 289–98.
Marshall, John L. "A Biographical Sketch of the Military Life of the Late Col. T. W. Thompson," *Southern Bivouac,* I, Sept. 1882, pp. 11–14.
———. "Captain William Lashbrooke," *Southern Bivouac,* I, Feb. 1883, pp. 247–48.
———. "Heel and Toe," *Southern Bivouac,* I, Mar. 1883, pp. 301–5.
"Nondescript" [John L. Marshall]. "Beef Seekers," *Southern Bivouac,* I, Oct. 1882, pp. 69–72.

————. "A Fair Divide," *Southern Bivouac*, I, Jan. 1883, pp. 214–16.

————. "Heel and Toe," *Southern Bivouac*, I, Feb. 1882, pp. 255–59.

————. "Unrecorded Deeds of Daring," *Southern Bivouac*, I, Aug. 1883, pp. 471–74.

"Orphan Brigade Items," *Southern Bivouac*, III, Feb. 1885, p. 273.

"Orphan Brigade Items," *Southern Bivouac*, III, Mar. 1885, p. 322.

Owens, Thomas. "Standing Picket in a Georgia Swamp," *Southern Bivouac*, I, Apr. 1883, pp. 330–32.

Pirtle, John B. "Defense of Vicksburg in 1862—The Battle of Baton Rouge," *Southern Historical Society Papers*, VIII, June–July 1880, pp. 324–32.

"Query Box," *Southern Bivouac*, I, Apr. 1883, p. 362.

Ridley, B. L. "Camp Scenes Around Dalton," *Confederate Veteran*, X, Feb. 1902, pp. 66–68.

"Roll of the First Kentucky Brigade Reunion at Lexington, Kentucky, September 5, 1883," *Southern Bivouac*, II, Sept. 1883, pp. 16–17.

Scott, J. O. "After Hartsville," *Southern Bivouac*, I, Nov. 1882, pp. 107–9.

Shaler, N. S. "Nature and Man in America, Third Paper," *Scribner's Magazine*, VIII, Nov. 1890, pp. 650–54.

Shoup, F. A. "How We Went to Shiloh," *Confederate Veteran*, II, May 1894, pp. 137–40.

"Sketch of General B. H. Helm," *Land We Love*, III, June 1867, pp. 163–67.

"The Skirmish Line," *Southern Bivouac*, II, Jan. 1884, pp. 236–37.

"Skirmish Line," *Southern Bivouac*, III, Nov. 1884, p. 133.

"Swift Justice," *Southern Bivouac*, III, Jan. 1885, p. 214.

"Taps," *Southern Bivouac*, I, Sept. 1882, pp. 36–40; Oct. 1882, pp. 82–85; Dec. 1882, pp. 178–80; Jan. 1883, pp. 222–24; Feb. 1883, pp. 268–72; II, Nov. 1883, pp. 138–39; Dec. 1883, p. 188.

"Third Reunion of the Kentucky Brigade," *Southern Bivouac*, III, Nov. 1884, pp. 116–21.

Tydings, J. M. "The Charge of the First Kentucky Brigade at the Battle of Chickamauga," *Southern Bivouac*, I, Oct. 1882, pp. 62–63.

Watkins, Samuel R., and Jackman, John S. "Battle of Missionary Ridge," *Southern Bivouac*, II, Oct. 1883, pp. 49–58.

Weller, John H. "The Confederate Dead at Chickamauga," *Southern Bivouac*, II, Dec. 1883, p. 192.

————. "The Fourth Kentucky," *Southern Bivouac*, I, May–June 1882, pp. 346–54.

————. "History of the Fourth Kentucky Infantry," *Southern Historical Society Papers*, IX, Mar. 1881, pp. 108–15.

Index